READINGS IN JUDAISM, CHRISTIANITY, AND ISLAM

JOHN CORRIGAN
Arizona State University

FREDERICK M. DENNY
University of Colorado, Boulder

CARLOS M.N. EIRE
Yale University

MARTIN S. JAFFEE
University of Washington

Prentice Hall, Upper Saddle River, New Jersey 07458

Library of Congress Cataloging-in-Publication Data

Readings in Judaism, Christianity, and Islam / [edited by] John
  Corrigan . . . [et al.].
        p.   cm.
    ISBN 0-02-325098-4
    1. Judaism.   2. Christianity.   3. Islam.   4. Monotheism.
  5. Religion and state.   6. Religion and politics.   I. Corrigan,
John, (date)
  BM561.R43   1998
  291—dc21   97-29976
                                                      CIP

Editorial Director: Charlyce Jones Owens
Acquisition Editor: Angela Stone/Karita France
Director of Production and Manufacturing: Barbara Kittle
Managing Editor: Jan Stephan
Production Liaison: Fran Russello
Project Manager: Linda B. Pawelchak
Manufacturing Manager: Nick Sklitsis
Prepress and Manufacturing Buyer: Robert Anderson
Cover Director: Jayne Conte
Cover Design: Bruce Kenselaar

This book was set in 10/12 Palatino by Stratford Publishing Services, Inc.
and was printed and bound by Courier Companies, Inc.
The cover was printed by Phoenix Color Corp.

 © 1998 by Prentice-Hall, Inc.
Simon & Schuster/A Viacom Company
Upper Saddle River, New Jersey 07458

Printed in the United States of America
10   9   8   7   6   5   4   3   2   1

ISBN 0-02-325098-4

Prentice-Hall International (UK) Limited, *London*
Prentice-Hall of Australia Pty. Limited, *Sydney*
Prentice-Hall Canada Inc., *Toronto*
Prentice-Hall Hispanoamericana, S.A., *Mexico*
Prentice-Hall of India Private Limited, *New Delhi*
Prentice-Hall of Japan, Inc., *Tokyo*
Simon & Schuster Asia Pte. Ltd., *Singapore*
Editora Prentice-Hall do Brasil, Ltda., *Rio de Janeiro*

CONTENTS

PART III
AUTHORITY AND COMMUNITY

Chapter 7
In Judaism 157

Chapter 8
In Christianity   170

Chapter 9
In Islam   187

Part IV
Worship and Ritual

Chapter 10
In Judaism   203

Chapter 11
In Christianity   217

Chapter 14
In Christianity   266

Chapter 15
In Islam   286

PREFACE

The writings included in this collection are organized according to six themes: Scripture and Tradition, Monotheism, Authority and Community, Worship and Ritual, Ethics, and Religion and the Political Order. Judaism, Christianity, and Islam are not mere aggregates of the subject matter represented in six themes, however. Each of these religions is enormously complex and understandable only as a vibrant and fluid tradition. Judaism, Christianity, and Islam all sustain an ancient heritage while at the same time reinventing themselves in shifting cultural, geographical, and historical settings. Within each tradition, scripture, ethics, ritual, and all of the other components are comprehended together, all inextricably joined to constitute a living religion.

Readers consequently will discover that in some cases a selection that supports one theme within a tradition is relevant to one or more other themes with regard to that tradition. A document that represents Muslim thinking about authority, for example, might shed light on Islam and the political order; or an excerpt from a Christian writing on worship might help illustrate Christian thinking about ethics. In some cases, readings in one tradition can enlarge understanding of other traditions; this is especially evident in the case of Judaism, which profoundly influenced both the genesis and development of Christianity and Islam.

In many places, the materials within each chapter are organized chronologically. This enables the reader to follow the development of a certain aspect of a tradition as it is shaped in various ways over time. Such an approach is useful in demonstrating the manner in which monotheistic theologies have developed within Judaism, Christianity, and Islam. It also illustrates the process of the emergence of interpretation of scripture as an enterprise fundamental to all three traditions.

This reader is organized in such a way as to supplement *Jews, Christians, Muslims: A Comparative Introduction to Monotheistic Religions.* Readings in each chapter are matched to the themes and issues addressed in corresponding chapters of the textbook. The reader may be adopted for use independently of the textbook, however. The brief introduction to each selection situates it in time and place and comments on its significance.

John Corrigan

PART I
SCRIPTURE AND TRADITION

CHAPTER 1

IN JUDAISM

1.1 ISRAEL'S HISTORY IN THE BIBLICAL NARRATIVE TRADITION

The following selection of writings from the Hebrew Bible highlights crucial moments in the Bible's depiction of Israelite history. This history is covenantal in that all that happens to Israel is interpreted as an indication of where Israel stands in its covenantal relationship with God.

The Hebrew Bible introduces its history of Israel with a history of humanity from the creation of the world. The theme of human rebellion, established in the first chapters of Genesis, is crucial for all that follows. All translations are from the new *HarperCollins Study Bible,* slightly adapted for use here.

1.1A GENESIS 1:1–15; 1:26–2:9; 2:15–3:24

In the beginning when God created the heavens and the earth, the earth was a formless void and darkness covered the face of the deep, while a wind from God swept over the face of the waters. Then God said, "Let there be light"; and there was light. And God saw that the light was good; and God separated the light from the darkness. God called the light Day, and the darkness he called Night. And there was evening and there was morning, the first day.

[The narrative continues through the next five days of creation, in which all the heavenly bodies and the earth and its various life forms are created. On the sixth day . . .]

Then God said, "Let us make humankind in our image, according to our likeness; and let them have dominion over the fish of the sea, and over the birds of the air, and over the cattle, and over all the wild animals of the earth, and over every creeping thing that creeps upon the earth." So God created humankind in his image, in the image of God he created them; male and female he created them. God blessed them, and God said to them, "Be fruitful and multiply, and fill the earth and subdue it; and have dominion over the fish of the sea and over the birds of the air and over every living thing that moves upon the earth." God said, "See, I have given you every plant yielding seed that is upon the face of all the earth, and every tree with seed in its fruit; you shall have them for food. And to every beast of the earth, and to every bird of the air, and to everything that has the breath of life, I have given every green plant for food." And it was so. God saw everything that he had made, and indeed, it was very good. And there was evening and there was morning, the sixth day.

Thus the heavens and the earth were finished, and all their multitude. And on the seventh day God finished the work that he had done, and he rested on the seventh day from all the work that he had done. So God blessed the seventh day and hallowed it, because on it God rested from all the work that he had done in creation.

These are the generations of the heavens and the earth when they were created.

In the day that the LORD God made the earth and the heavens, when no plant of the field was yet in the earth and no herb of the field had yet sprung up—for the LORD God had not caused it to rain upon the earth, and there was no one to till the ground; but a stream would rise from the earth, and water the whole face of the ground—then the LORD God formed man from the dust of the ground, and breathed into his nostrils the breath of life; and the man became a living being. And the LORD God planted a garden in Eden, in the east; and there he put the man whom he had formed. Out of the ground the LORD God made to grow every tree that is pleasant to the sight and good for food, the tree of life also in the midst of the garden, and the tree of the knowledge of good and evil. . . .

The LORD God took the man and put him in the garden of Eden to till it and keep it. And the LORD God commanded the man, "You may freely eat of every tree of the garden; but of the tree of the knowledge of good and evil you shall not eat, for in the day that you eat of it you shall die."

Then the LORD God said, "it is not good that the man should be alone; I will make him a helper as his partner." So out of the ground the LORD God formed every animal of the field and every bird of the air, and brought them to the man to see what he would call them; and whatever the man called every living creature, that was its name. The man gave names to all cattle, and to the birds of the air, and to every animal of the field; but for the man there was not found a helper as his partner. So the LORD God caused a deep sleep to fall upon the man, and he slept; then he took one of his ribs and closed up its place with flesh. And the rib that the LORD God had taken from the man he made into a woman and brought her to the man. Then the man said, "This at last is bone of my bones and flesh of my flesh; this one shall be called Woman, for out of Man this one was taken." Therefore a man leaves his father and his mother and clings to his wife, and they become one flesh. And the man and his wife were both naked, and were not ashamed.

Now the serpent was more crafty than any other wild animal that the LORD God had made. He said to the woman, "Did God say, 'You shall not eat from any tree in the garden'?" The woman said to the serpent, "We may eat of the fruit of the trees in the garden; but God said, 'You shall not eat of the fruit of the tree that is in the middle of the garden, nor shall you touch it, or you shall die.' " But the serpent said to the woman, "You will not die; for God knows that when you eat of it your eyes will be opened, and you will be like God, knowing good and evil." So when the woman saw that the tree was good for food, and that it was a delight to the eyes, and that the tree was to be desired to make one wise, she took of its fruit and ate; and she also gave some to her husband, who was with her, and he ate. Then the eyes of both were opened, and they knew that they were naked; and they sewed fig leaves together and made loin-cloths for themselves.

They heard the sound of the LORD God walking in the garden at the time of the evening breeze, and the man and his wife hid themselves from the presence of the LORD God among the trees of the garden. But the LORD God called to the man, and said to him, "Where are you?" He said, "I heard the sound of you in the garden, and I was afraid, because I was naked; and I hid myself." He said, "Who told you that you were naked? Have you eaten from the tree of which I commanded you not to eat?" The man said, "the woman whom you gave to be with me, she gave me fruit from the tree, and I ate." Then the LORD God said to the woman, "What is this that you have done?" The woman said, "The serpent tricked me, and I ate." The LORD God said to the serpent, "Because you have done this, cursed are you among all animals and among all wild creatures; upon your belly you shall go, and dust you shall eat all the days of your life. I will put enmity between you and the woman, and between your offspring and hers; he will strike your head, and you will strike his heel."

To the woman he said, "I will greatly increase your pangs in childbearing; in pain you shall bring forth children, yet your desire shall be for your husband, and he shall rule over you."

And to the man he said, "Because you have listened to the voice of your wife, and have eaten of the tree about which I commanded you, 'You shall not eat of it,' cursed is the ground because of you; in toil you shall eat of it all the days of your life; thorns and thistles it shall bring forth for you; and you shall eat the plants of the field. By the sweat of your face you shall eat bread until you return to the ground, for out of it you were taken; you are dust, and to dust you shall return."

The man named his wife Eve, because she was the mother of all living. And the LORD God made garments of skins for the man and for his wife, and clothed them.

Then the LORD God said, "See, the man has become like one of us, knowing good and evil; and now, he might reach out his hand and take also from the tree of life, and eat, and live forever"—therefore the LORD God sent him forth from the garden of Eden, to till the ground from which he was taken. He drove out the man; and at the east of the garden of Eden he placed the cherubim, and a sword flaming and turning to guard the way to the tree of life.

The remainder of the first eleven chapters of Genesis documents the early history of humanity, portrayed as a series of violations of divinely imposed limitations: Cain's murder of his brother, Abel; the violence of humanity in Noah's generation; the pride of the generation that built the tower of Babel. These stories set the stage for a new act of God in which he attempts to bring a particular human family close to him. Thus begins the history of Israel from the Torah's perspective.

1.1B GENESIS 11:27–12:9

Now these are the descendants of Terah. Terah was the father of Abram, Nahor, and Haran; and Haran was the father of Lot. Haran died before his father Terah in the land of his birth, in Ur of the Chaldeans. Abram and Nahor took wives; the name of Abram's wife was Sarai, and the name of Nahor's wife was Milcah. She was the daughter of Haran the father of Milcah and Iscah. Now Sarai was barren; she had no child.

Terah took his son Abram and his grandson Lot son of Haran, and his daughter-in-law Sarai, his son Abram's wife, and they went out together from Ur of the Chaldeans to go into the land of Canaan; but when they came to Haran, they settled there. The days of Terah were two hundred five years; and Terah died in Haran.

Now the LORD said to Abram, "Go from your country and your kindred and your father's house to the land that I will show you. I will make of you a great nation, and I will bless you, and make your name great, so that you will be a blessing. I will bless those who bless you, and the one who curses you I will curse; and in you all the families of the earth shall be blessed."

So Abram went, as the LORD had told him; and Lot went with him. Abram was seventy-five years old when he departed from Haran. Abram took his wife Sarai and his brother's son Lot, and all the possessions that they had gathered, and the persons whom they had acquired in Haran; and they set forth to go to the land of Canaan. Abram passed through the land to the place at Shechem, to the oak of Moreh. At that time the Canaanites were in the land. Then the LORD appeared to Abram, and said, "To your offspring I will give this land." So he built there an altar to the LORD, who had appeared to him. From there he moved on to the hill country on the east of Bethel, and pitched his tent, with Bethel on the west and Ai on the east; and there he built an altar to the LORD and invoked the name of the LORD. And Abram journeyed on by stages toward the Negeb.

nantal line is passed on to the younger brother. By the end of Genesis, the eleventh of Jacob's twelve sons, Joseph, has become an important adviser to the Egyptian Pharoah. In a time of famine in Canaan, Joseph arranges for his father and brothers to seek refuge in Egypt. There the descendants of Jacob become numerous.

The book of Exodus opens in the setting of Egypt. A later Pharoah, perceiving in Israel a threat to his security, enslaves the Israelites and imposes hard labor upon them. In an effort to eradicate them, he imposes a death sentence upon all male children. One of these children is set adrift in the Nile by his mother in order to spare him. He is plucked from the river by a daughter of Pharoah and raised as a native Egyptian. His name is Moses. According to the Torah, Moses knew of his Israelite birth. One day, enraged at the sight of an Egyptian master beating his Israelite slave, Moses kills the Egyptian. When the incident becomes known, Moses escapes from Egypt to the desert of Midian. There he marries and takes up the life of a shepherd. One day, while caring for his father-in-law's flock, a profound experience changes Moses' life and the course of history. On Mt. Horeb, also known as Sinai, Moses encounters the God of Israel, who discloses to Moses the meaning of the past and a promise for the future.

1.1ᴇ EXODUS 2:23–3:20

After a long time the king of Egypt died. The Israelites groaned under their slavery, and cried out. Out of the slavery their cry for help rose up to God. God heard their groaning, and God remembered his covenant with Abraham, Isaac, and Jacob. God looked upon the Israelites, and God took notice of them.

Moses was keeping the flock of his father-in-law Jethro, the priest of Midian; he led his flock beyond the wilderness, and came to Horeb, the mountain of God. There the angel of the LORD appeared to him in a flame of fire out of a bush; he looked, and the bush was blazing, yet it was not consumed. Then Moses said, "I must turn aside and look at this great sight, and see why the bush is not burned up." When the LORD saw that he had turned aside to see, God called out to him out of the bush, "Moses, Moses!" And he said, "Here I am." Then he said, "Come no closer! Remove the sandals from your feet, for the place on which you are standing is holy ground." He said further, "I am the God of your father, the God of Abraham, the God of Isaac, and the God of Jacob." And Moses hid his face, for he was afraid to look at God.

Then the LORD said, "I have observed the misery of my people who are in Egypt; I have heard their cry on account of their taskmasters. Indeed I know of their sufferings, and I have come down to deliver them from the Egyptians, and to bring them up out of that land to a good and broad land, a land flowing with milk and honey, to the country of the Canaanites, the Hittites, the Amorites, the Perizzites, the Hivites, and the Jebusites. The cry of the Israelites has now come to me; I have also seen how the Egyptians oppress them. So come, I will send you to Pharoah to bring my people, the Israelites, out of Egypt." But Moses said to God, "Who am I that I should go to Pharoah, and bring the Israelites out of Egypt?" He said, "I will be with you; and this shall be the sign for you that it is I who sent you: when you have brought the people out of Egypt, you shall worship God on this mountain."

But Moses said to God, "If I come to the Israelites and say to them, 'The God of your ancestors has sent me to you,' and they ask me 'What is his name?' what shall I say to them?" God said to Moses, "I AM WHO I AM." He said further, "Thus shall you say to the Israelites, 'I AM has sent me to you.' " God also said to Moses, "Thus you shall say to the Israelites, 'The LORD, the God of your ancestors, the God of Abraham, the God of Isaac, and the God of Jacob, has sent me to you': This is my name forever, and this is my title for all generations. Go and assemble the elders of Israel, and say to them, 'The LORD, the God you your ancestors, the God of Abraham, of Isaac, and of Jacob, has appeared to me, saying: I have given heed to you and to what has been done to you in Egypt. I declare that I will bring you up out of misery of Egypt, to the land of the Canaanites, the Hittites, the Amorites, the Perizzites, the Hivites, and the Jebusites, a land flowing with milk and honey.' They will listen to your voice; and you and the elders of Israel shall go to the king of Egypt and say to him, 'The LORD, the God of the Hebrews, has met with us; let us now go a three days' journey into the wilderness, so that we may sacrifice to the LORD our God.' I know, however, that the king of Egypt will not let you go unless compelled by a mighty hand. So I will stretch out my hand and strike Egypt with all my wonders that I will perform in it; after that he will let you go. . . ."

Acting upon his commission, Moses returns to Egypt. There, with his brother, Aaron, he engages in a struggle with Pharoah to gain Israel's release from bondage. Finally, after God sends ten plagues upon Egypt, the Israelites are released. This sets the stage for the central moment in the Torah—the public revelation of God to all of Israel on Sinai. Here the covenantal relationship begun with Abraham is formally sealed with the entire people, and its terms are spelled out. Most of the latter portion of Exodus, all of Leviticus, and much of Numbers detail the covenant obligations. The covenant law includes concern for ethical behavior, criminal and civil statutes, ritual rules, and all manner of other matters relevant to the smooth functioning of a society. We cite here representative material from Exodus. The scene opens on the third day of Israel's encampment before the mountain of God.

1.1F EXODUS 19:16–21, 20:1–21; 21:1–6; 21:12–14; 21:22–26; 22:21–24; 22:28–31

On the morning of the third day there was thunder and lightning, as well as a thick cloud on the mountain, and a blast of trumpet so loud that all the people who were in the camp trembled. Moses brought the people out of the camp to meet God. They took their stand at the foot of the mountain. Now Mount Sinai was wrapped in smoke, because the LORD had descended upon it in fire; the smoke went up like the smoke of a kiln, while the whole mountain shook violently. As the blast of the trumpet grew louder, Moses would speak and God would answer him in thunder. When the LORD descended upon Mount Sinai to the top of the mountain, the LORD summoned Moses to the top of the mountain, and Moses went up. Then the LORD said to Moses, "Go down and warn the people not to break through to the LORD to look; otherwise many of them will perish. Even the priests who approach the LORD must consecrate themselves or the LORD will break out against them." . . .

Then God spoke all these words: I am the LORD your God, who brought you out of the land of Egypt, out of the house of slavery; you shall have no other gods before me.

You shall not make for yourself an idol, whether in the form of anything that is in heaven above, or that is on the earth beneath, or that is in the water under the earth. You shall not bow down to them or worship them; for I the LORD your God am a jealous God, punishing the children for the iniquity of the parents, to the third and the fourth generation of those who reject me, but showing steadfast love to the thousandth generation of those who love me and keep my commandments.

You shall not make wrongful use of the name of the LORD your God, for the LORD will not acquit anyone who misuses his name.

Remember the Sabbath day, and keep it holy. Six days you shall labor and do all your work. But the seventh day is a sabbath to the LORD your God; you shall not do any work—you, your son or your daughter, your male or female slave, your livestock, or the alien resident in your towns. For in six days the LORD made heaven and earth, the sea, and all that is in them, but rested the seventh day; therefore the LORD blessed the Sabbath day and consecrated it.

Honor your father and your mother, so that your days may be long in the land that the LORD your God is giving you.

You shall not murder.

You shall not commit adultery.

You shall not steal.

You shall not bear false witness against your neighbor.

You shall not covet your neighbor's house; you shall not covet your neighbor's wife, or male or female slave, or ox, or donkey, or anything that belongs to your neighbor.

When all the people witnessed the thunder and lightning, the sound of the trumpet, and the mountain smoking, they were afraid and trembled and stood at a distance, and said to Moses, "You speak to us, and we will listen; but do not let God speak to us, or we will die." Moses said to the people, "Do not be afraid; for God has come only to test you and to put the fear of him upon you so that you do not sin." The people stood at a distance, while Moses drew near to the thick darkness where God was. . . .

These are the ordinances that you shall set before them:

When you buy a male Hebrew slave, he shall serve six years, but in the seventh he shall go out a free person, without debt. If he comes in single, he shall go out single; if he comes in married, then his wife shall go out with him. If his master gives him a wife and she bears him sons or daughters, the wife and her children shall be her master's and he shall go out alone. But if the slave declares, "I love my master, my wife, and my children; I will not go out a free person," then his master shall bring him before God. He shall be brought to the door or the doorpost; and his master shall pierce his ear with an awl; and he shall serve him for life. . . .

Whoever strikes a person mortally shall be put to death. If it was not premeditated, but came about by an act of God, then I will appoint for you a place to which the killer may flee. But if someone willfully attacks and kills another by treachery, you shall take the killer from my altar for execution. . . .

When people who are fighting injure a pregnant woman so that there is a miscarriage, and yet no further harm follows, the one responsible shall be fined what the woman's husband demands, paying as much as the judges determine. If any harm follows, then you shall give life for life, eye for eye, tooth for tooth, hand for hand, foot for foot, burn for burn, wound for wound, stripe for stripe.

When a slaveowner strikes the eye of a male or female slave, destroying it, the owner shall let the slave go, a free person, to compensate for the eye. If the owner knocks out a tooth of a male or female slave, the slave shall be let go, a free person, to compensate for the tooth. . . .

You shall not wrong or oppress a resident alien, for you were aliens in the land of Egypt. You shall not abuse any widow or orphan. If you do abuse them, when they cry out to me, I will surely heed their cry; my wrath will burn, and I will kill you with the sword, and your wives shall become widows and your children orphans. . . .

You shall not revile God, or curse a leader of your people.

You shall not delay to make offerings from the fullness of your harvest and from the outflow of your presses.

The firstborn of your sons you shall give to me. You shall do the same with your oxen and with your sheep: seven days it shall remain with its mother; on the eighth day you shall give it to me.

You shall be people consecrated to me; therefore you shall not eat any meat that is mangled by beasts in the field; you shall throw it to the dogs.

The Torah concludes with the Book of Deuteronomy, presented as a lengthy series of speeches by Moses to Israel on the east bank of the Jordan river. Moses, facing the end of his life and contemplating Israel's imminent passage into the land promised to Abraham, is most pointed in his description of the challenges that will face Israel as it attempts to fulfill the Torah in the new land.

1.1G DEUTERONOMY 30:11–20

Surely, this commandment that I am commanding you today is not too hard for you, nor is it too far away. It is not in heaven, that you should say, "Who will go up to heaven for us, and get it for us so that we may hear it and observe it?" Neither is it beyond the sea, that you should say, "Who will cross to the other side of the sea for us, and get it for us so that we may hear it and observe it?" No, the word is very near to you; it is in your mouth and in your heart for you to observe.

"See, I have set before you today life and prosperity, death and adversity. If you obey the commandments of the LORD your God that I am commanding you today, by loving the LORD your God, walking in his ways, and observing his commandments, decrees, and ordinances, then you shall live and become numerous, and the LORD your God will bless you in the land that you are entering to possess.

"But if your heart turns away and you do not hear, but are led astray to bow down to other gods and serve them, I declare to you today that you shall perish; you shall not live long in the land that you are crossing the Jordan to enter and possess.

"I call heaven and earth to witness against you today that I have set before you life and death, blessings and curses. Choose life so that you and your descendants may live, loving the LORD your God, obeying him and holding fast to him; for that means life to you and length of days, so that you may live in the land that the LORD swore to give to your ancestors, to Abraham, to Isaac, and to Jacob."

The Hebrew Bible's most complete summary of Israel's history is found in a speech ascribed to the post-exilic priest and scribe Ezra. The setting for the speech is a covenant-renewal ceremony in Persian-controlled Jerusalem. After reading the Torah in public, Ezra recounts the entire history of Israel's covenantal relationship with God. Note the persistent theme of Israel's rebelliousness in the past and commitment to a penitential turning in the future.

1.1H NEHEMIAH 9:1–37

Now on the twenty-fourth day of this month the people of Israel were assembled with fasting and sackcloth, and with earth on their heads. Then those of Israelite descent separated themselves from all foreigners, and stood and confessed their sins and the iniquities of their ancestors. They stood up in their place and read from the book of the Torah of the LORD their God for a fourth part of the day, and for another fourth they made confession and worshipped the LORD their God. . . . Then the Levites . . . said, "Stand up and bless the LORD your God from everlasting to everlasting. Blessed be your glorious name, which is exalted above all blessing and praise."

And Ezra said: "You are the LORD, you alone; you have made heaven, the heaven of heavens, with all their host, the earth and all that is on it, the seas and all that is in them. To all of them you give life, and the host of heaven worships you. You are the LORD, the God who chose Abram and brought him out of Ur of the Chaldeans and gave him the name Abraham; and you found his heart faithful before you, and made with him a covenant to give to his descendants the land of the Canaanite, the Hittite, the Amorite, the Perizzite, the Jebusite, and the Girgashite; and you have fulfilled your promise, for you are righteous.

"And you saw the distress of our ancestors in Egypt and heard their cry at the Red Sea. You performed signs and wonders against Pharoah and all his servants and all the people of his land, for you knew that they acted insolently against our ancestors. You made a name for yourself, which remains to this day. . . . You came down upon Mount Sinai, and spoke with them from heaven and gave them right ordinances and true laws, good statutes and commandments, and you made known your holy sabbath to them and gave them commandments and statutes and a Torah through your servant Moses. For their hunger you gave them bread from heaven, and for their thirst you brought water for them out of the rock, and you told them to go in to possess the land that you swore to give them.

"But they and our ancestors acted presumptuously and stiffened their necks and did not obey your commandments; they refused to obey, and were not mindful of the wonders that you performed among them; but they stiffened their necks and determined to return to their slavery in Egypt. But you are a God ready to forgive, gracious and merciful, slow to anger and abounding in steadfast love, and you did not forsake them. . . .

"Forty years you sustained them in the wilderness so that they lacked nothing; their clothes did not wear out and their feet did not swell. And you gave them kingdoms and peoples, and allotted to them every corner, so they took possession of the land of King Sihon of Heshbon and the land of King Og of Bashan. You multiplied their descendants like the stars of the heaven, and brought them into the land that you had told their ancestors to enter and possess. So the descendants went in and possessed the land, and you subdued before them the inhabitants of the land, the Canaanites, and gave them into their hands, with their kings and the peoples of the land, to do with them as they pleased. . . .

"Nevertheless they were disobedient and rebelled against you and cast your law behind their backs and killed your prophets, who had warned them in order to turn them back to you, and they committed great blasphemies. Therefore you gave them into the hands of their enemies, who made them suffer. Then in the time of their suffering they cried out to you and you heard them from heaven, and according to your great mercies you gave them saviors who saved them from the hands of their enemies. But after they had rest, they again did evil before you, and you abandoned them to the hands of their enemies, so that they had dominion over them; yet when they turned and cried to you, you heard from heaven, and many times you rescued them according to your mercies. And you warned them in order to turn them back to your law. . . . Many years you were patient with them, and warned them by your spirit through your prophets; yet they would not listen. Therefore, you handed them over to the peoples of the lands. Nevertheless, in your great mercies you did not make an end of them or forsake them, for you are a gracious and merciful God.

"Now therefore, our God . . . do not treat lightly all the hardship that has come upon us, upon our kings, our officials, our priests, our prophets, our ancestors, and all your people, since the time of the kings of Assyria until today. You have been just in all that has come upon us, for you have dealt faithfully and we have acted wickedly; our kings, our officials, our priests, and our ancestors have not kept your Torah or heeded the commandments and the warnings that you gave them. Even in their own kingdom, and in the great goodness you bestowed on them, and in the large and rich land that you set before them, they did not serve

you and did not turn from their wicked works. Here we are, slaves to this day—
slaves in the land that you gave to our ancestors to enjoy its fruit and its good gifts.
Its rich yield goes to the kings whom you have set over us because of our sins; they
have the power also over our bodies and over our livestock at their pleasure, and
we are in distress.

"Because of all this we make a firm agreement in writing, and on that sealed
document are inscribed the names of our officials, our Levites, and our priests."

1.2 The Literature of Oral Torah

Since the Middle Ages, Jewish tradition has held that the written versions of rabbinic texts reflect ancient oral traditions extending back to the Mosaic period. The
Mishnah's tractate Avot, probably compiled in the middle of the third century,
provides the earliest assertion that rabbinic tradition originates in teachings received from Moses at Sinai, although it does not mention a specifically "oral"
Torah. The passage to follow traces the main figures, linking Rabbi Judah the Patriarch, the editor of the Mishnah, to the Mosaic tradition.

1.2a Mishnah Avot 1:1–2:1

Moses received Torah from Sinai and transmitted it to Joshua, and Joshua to the Elders, and the Elders to the Prophets, and the Prophets transmitted it to the Men of
the Great Assembly. They said three things: Be deliberate in judgment; raise up
many disciples; and make a hedge around the Torah.

Shimon the Righteous was of the last members of the Great Assembly. He
would say: Upon three things the world is maintained: Upon the Torah; upon the
sacrificial service of the Temple; and upon reciprocal kindness among people.

Antigonus of Sokho received from Shimon the Righteous. He would say: Do
not be like servants who serve the master in order to receive a reward. Rather, be
like servants who serve the master not in order to receive a reward. And let the fear
of Heaven be upon you.

Yose ben Yoezer of Zeredah and Yose ben Yohanan of Jerusalem received
from them. Yose ben Yoezer says: May your house be a meeting place for Sages,
and become filthy with the dust of their feet, and thirstily drink in their words.

Yose ben Yohanan of Jerusalem says: May your house be opened so wide that
the poor become members of your household. And do not extend idle conversation with a woman. He said this regarding his own wife; all the more so with regard to another's wife. On this basis Sages said: As long as a man extends idle conversation with a woman he causes himself harm by ignoring words of Torah. And
his end is to inherit Gehenna.

Joshua ben Perakhyah and Nittai the Arbelite received from them. Joshua
ben Perakhyah says: Establish a Master for yourself, and acquire a study partner,
and judge each person on the scale of merit.

Nittai the Arbelite says: Distance yourself from a wicked neighbor, and don't associate with an evil person, and do not despair of divine retribution.

Judah ben Tabbai and Shimon ben Shetakh received from them. Judah ben Tabbai says: Do not behave like one who influences judges; and when litigants stand before you regard them as if they were guilty; but when they are discharged from before you, regard them as innocents who have accepted the judgment upon themselves.

Shimon ben Shetakh says: Take pains to question witnesses; and watch your words, lest from them they learn to give false testimony.

Shemaiah and Avtalion received from them. Shemaiah says: Love labor but hate authority, and don't become intimate with the government.

Avtalion says: Sages! Watch your words lest you become guilty of exile and be banished to a place of evil waters. For your disciples might drink after you and die, desecrating the Name of Heaven.

Hillel and Shammai received from them. Hillel says: Be among the disciples of Aaron, loving peace and pursuing peace, loving humanity and bringing it to Torah.

He would say: One who enhances his reputation loses it; and one who does not increase his learning diminishes it; and one who does not study is worthy of death; and one who makes worldly use of the Crown of Torah shall perish.

He would say: If I am not for myself, who will be for me? But when I am only for myself, what am I? And if not now, when?

Shammai says: Make your Torah study a habit; say little and do much; and receive each person with a pleasant expression.

Rabban Gamaliel says: Establish a Master for yourself; and remove yourself from doubt; and don't get used to tithing by a rough guess.

Shimon his son says: All my life I grew up among Sages, and I found nothing better for the body than silence. And interpreting the commandments is not the main thing, but the doing. And whoever talks too much introduces sin.

Rabban Shimon ben Gamaliel says: Upon three things the world is maintained: Upon judgment, upon truth, and upon peace, as it is said in Scripture: "Truth and the judgment of peace shall you execute in your gates" (Zech. 8:16).

Rabbi (Judah the Patriarch) says: Which is the true path that a person should choose? Whatever enhances the doer and elicits enhanced regard from others. Be just as careful in performing a trivial commandment as an important one, for you cannot know the reward of a commandment. And calculate the financial loss of performing a commandment against its spiritual profit, and the financial profit of a transgression against its spiritual loss. And pay attention to three things so that you don't fall into the hands of transgression: Know what is above you—an all-seeing eye and an all-hearing ear. And all your actions are recorded in a book.

The Mishnah is believed in later Jewish tradition to constitute the Oral Torah par excellence. Except for Tractate Avot, the Mishnah addresses details of law. For the most part, mishnaic law reveals close reflection upon biblical legal texts. Nevertheless, as in many other legal traditions grounded in sacred scriptures, the Mishnah's legal results are not always harmonious with explicit statements of scriptural law. What follows is an example from the Mishnah's tractate on lawsuits over personal or property damage (Tractate Bava Kamma). Behind the Mishnah's law lies the Torah's explicit ruling (see Exodus 21:22 ff. earlier) that bodily damages shall be repaid "eye for eye, tooth for tooth." The Mishnah, however, takes for granted that the Torah's rule actually refers to financial compensation. Here, then, is a case in which written law and oral legal tradition seem quite at odds.

1.2B MISHNAH BAVA KAMMA 8:1

One who causes damage to his neighbor must compensate him on five counts: for damages; for pain; for healing; for loss of time; and for humiliation.

How do they compute compensation for damages? If he blinded his neighbor's eye, cut off his hand, broke his leg—they view the injured party as if he were a slave sold in the market and estimate how much he was worth before the injury and how much he is worth now.

How do they compute compensation for pain? If he burned his neighbor with a spit or a stake, even on his nail or other place which yields no wound—they estimate how much a person of similar status would demand to suffer that much pain.

How do they compute compensation for healing? If he struck his neighbor—he is obliged to pay for his healing. If sores appeared on his body—if they were caused by the blow, he must pay for the healing; if not, he is exempt from payment. If the wound healed and then opened repeatedly—he is obliged to pay for his healing. Once it has healed completely, he is no longer obliged for his healing.

How do they compute compensation for loss of time? They view him as if he guarded cucumber patches for a living, for the damager has already given him compensation for his hand or leg.

How do they compute compensation for humiliation? All depends upon the status of the humiliator and the humiliated. One who humiliates a naked person (whose very nakedness is itself humiliating); one who humiliates a blind person (who cannot see that he is being humiliated); one who humiliates a sleeping person (who is unaware of the humiliation)—he is obliged to compensate him. But a sleeping person who humiliates another is exempt. If he fell from a roof, causing damages and humiliation—he is obliged to compensate the damage, but is exempt from compensating the humiliation, for it is said in Scripture: "And she put forth her hand and grabbed his shameful parts" (Deut. 25:21). He is obliged to compensate for humiliation only if he does so intentionally.

Rabbinic midrash (biblical interpretation) normally falls into two genres, midrash halakhah (interpretation of biblical law) or midrash aggadah (homiletical or historical interpretation of the Bible). The major assumption of midrash halakhah is that the laws of the Written Torah and those of the Mishnah and other rabbinic traditions are part of a single legal and conceptual framework. A principal task for the legal interpreter, then, is to show how the halakhic principles of the rabbinic oral tradition correlate with the biblical statutes. The following example from Mekhilta of Rabbi Ishmael, a midrashic commentary on the book of Exodus, is grounded in the same assumptions about compensation for damages taken for granted by Mishnah Bava Kamma (see earlier discussion). The midrashic editor, accordingly, links his citations from Exodus 21:23–25 and other biblical texts to those assumptions. A common trait of all midrashic texts, exemplified here as well, is the formulation of statements in a kind of argumentative style. As you read, try to imagine how the reciter of such a text might dramatize the point and counterpoint of the arguments.

1.2c MEKHILTA OF RABBI ISHMAEL, MISHPATIM 8 (EXOD. 21:23–25)

"You shall give life for life" (Exod. 21:23)—this means that you must compensate a life for a life, but you may not compensate a life with money.

Rabbi (Judah the Patriarch) says: "You shall give life for life"—this implies monetary compensation!

You claim this implies monetary compensation? Perhaps it permits only death?

(Said Rabbi:) Just attend to Scripture's terminology: here, in discussing compensation, the term "determine" is used (Exod. 21:22) and elsewhere (Exod. 21:30, where monetary compensation is permitted for damages caused by cattle) "determine" is used. Just as there the reference is to monetary compensation, so here!

"Eye for eye" (Exod. 21:24)—this means monetary compensation.

You say monetary compensation? Perhaps it really means taking out his eye?

Rabbi Ishmael would say: Indeed, Scripture says: "One who kills an animal shall make restitution for it; but one who kills a human being shall be put to death" (Lev. 24:21). Scripture has juxtaposed damages to a human with damages to cattle, and damages to cattle with damages to a human. Accordingly, just as damages to cattle are compensated with money, so too damages to humans (other than death itself) are compensated by money!

Rabbi Isaac says: Indeed (right after specifying that a goring ox must be killed), Scripture says: "If a ransom is imposed upon the owner" (Exod. 21:30). Now this yields a clear inference. Just as where Scripture imposes the death penalty it makes room for monetary compensation, in the present case (of bodily harm), where death is not mentioned, it is reasonable to suppose that the only compensation is monetary!

Rabbi Eliezer says: "Eye for eye"—shall I conclude that whether the damage is intentional or unintentional he only compensates with money? But, indeed, Scripture singles out one who intends to cause bodily harm, specifying that he must compensate in kind (by a wound to himself). For it is said: "Anyone who injures another shall suffer the same injury in return" (Lev. 24:19)—this is the general principle. "Eye for eye" (Lev. 24:20)—this is a specification. Where a general principle is immediately followed by a specification, the application of the principle is limited to the case stated in the specification.

Yet when it continues to say "the injury inflicted is the injury to be suffered" (Lev. 24:20) a general principle is restated.

Perhaps the point is that the two general principles are redundant?

Absolutely not! Rather, where a general principle introduces a specification which is then followed by another general principle, you can only draw inferences that have analogies to the specification. Just as the specification here is clear that wounds that are permanent, affecting major organs, are visible, and inflicted intentionally must be compensated only with money—so we conclude that all wounds that are permanent, affecting major organs, are visible, and inflicted intentionally are compensated with money!

Scripture says: "The injury inflicted is the injury to be suffered" (Lev. 24:20)—this applies only where he intended to harm him.

Structured as a massive Mishnah commentary, the Babylonian Talmud is the most comprehensive collection of rabbinic perspectives on biblical and mishnaic law. In many cases, the Talmud's commentary is built upon the citation and expansion of earlier halakhic midrash, such as the one you have just read. In other cases, the Talmud raises its own legal questions independently. What follows is part of the Talmud's discussion of Mishnah Bava Kamma 8:1. Here the Talmud raises one of its characteristic questions—which Tannaitic authority stands behind a principle articulated anonymously in the Mishnah? The passage begins with a citation from the Mishnah you have already studied and proceeds to compare it with another extra-mishnaic source from the larger oral tradition. Notice the persistence of the argumentative, dialogical style. I have reproduced the quoted sources in boldface to distinguish them from the surrounding talmudic discussion.

1.2D BABYLONIAN TALMUD, BAVA KAMMA 86A

How do they compute compensation for humiliation? All depends upon the status of the humiliator and the humiliated.

Whose view is represented in the mishnaic tradition? It is neither that of Rabbi Meir nor that of Rabbi Judah. Rather, it is that of Rabbi Shimon.

For oral tradition transmits the following: **They view all injured Jews as if they were freemen who lost their property, for they are the children of Abraham, Isaac and Jacob—these are the words of Rabbi Meir.**

Rabbi Judah says: They compensate a great person in accord with his greatness and an insignificant person in accord with his insignificance.

Rabbi Shimon says: The rich are viewed as if they were freemen who lost their property; the poor are viewed as the least of these.

Now, in the light of this, who stands behind our mishnaic tradition? If you claim Rabbi Meir—our mishnaic tradition teaches **all depends upon the status of the humiliator and the humiliated,** but Rabbi Meir holds that they are all to be treated equally! And if you claim Rabbi Judah—our mishnaic tradition teaches **one who humiliates a blind person is obliged to compensate him,** but Rabbi

Judah elsewhere holds that humiliation does not apply to the blind! Therefore, mustn't our authority be Rabbi Shimon?

You could even say that our mishnaic tradition is Rabbi Judah's! For when Rabbi Judah said that humiliation does not apply to the blind, he meant only that we do not hold him liable for humiliation, but he certainly is due compensation for humiliation!

But consider what is transmitted at the end of our mishnaic tradition: **One who humiliates a sleeping person is obliged to compensate him; but a sleeping person who humiliates another is exempt.** Note that it does not transmit that a blind person who humiliates another is exempt. This implies that there is no difference one way or another with regard to a blind person (contrary to Rabbi Judah's view). Obviously, our mishnaic tradition represents the view of Rabbi Shimon!

Our final samples of rabbinic literature come from the genre of midrash aggadah, or homiletic/historical exegesis of Scripture. Midrash aggadah, like rabbinic literature in general, is dialogical and argumentative. A key trait is the breaking of biblical verses into smaller units without reference to the meaning of the verse in its scriptural context. The contextual meaning of verses is further obscured by the assumption that any verse in Scripture can, at least in principle, be read meaningfully in conjunction with any other verse. This permits the midrashist to construct interpretations that are free of the restrictions imposed by narrow contextual readings of Scripture. It also enables rabbinic interpreters to weave rabbinic traditional wisdom into the scriptural text rather seamlessly. The first example following is from a Palestinian midrashic compilation on the book of Genesis. It speaks of redemptive events that were set in place prior to the creation of the world. The second selection comes from the Palestinian Talmud. It is one of the classic rabbinic "proofs" that the Oral Torah is already included in Moses' teaching.

1.2e Bereshit Rabbah 1:4 (Gen. 1:1)

"In the beginning when God created the heavens and the earth" (Gen. 1:1).

Six things preceded the creation of the world. And some of them were actually created and some of them were conceived for creation in the future.

The Torah and the Throne of Glory were created. We know this of the Torah since it is written in Scripture: "The LORD created me at the beginning of his work" (Prov. 8:22). We know this of the Throne of Glory since it is written in Scripture: "Your throne is established from of old" (Ps. 93:2).

The Patriarchs (Abraham, Isaac and Jacob) were conceived for creation in the future, since it is written in Scripture: "Like the first fruit on the fig tree in its first season I saw your ancestors" (Hos. 9:10).

Israel was conceived for creation in the future, since it is written in Scripture: "Remember your congregation which you acquired long ago" (Ps. 74:2).

The Temple was conceived for creation in the future, since it is written in

Scripture: "O glorious throne, exalted from the beginning, the place of our sanctuary" (Jer. 17:12).

The Messiah's name was conceived for creation in the future, since it is written in Scripture: "May his name endure forever, his fame continue as long as the sun" (Ps. 72:17).

Rabbi Ahava ben Rabbi Zeira said: Also repentence, as it is written in Scripture: "Before the mountains were formed . . ." (Ps. 90:2)—from that moment, "you turn us back to dust and say, 'Turn back you mortals' " (Prov. 90:3).

But still, I don't know if the Torah preceded the Throne of Glory or the Throne of Glory preceded the Torah.

Said Rabbi Abba bar Kahana: The Torah preceded the Throne of Glory, since it is said: "The LORD created me at the beginning of his work, the first of his acts of long ago" (Prov. 8:22). And this act preceded that of which it is written: "Your throne is established from of old" (Ps. 93:2).

Rabbi Huna, Rabbi Jeremiah in the name of Rabbi Samuel ben Rabbi Isaac: The conception of Israel preceded them all. It is like a King who was married to a Lady from whom he had not received a son. One time the King was passing through the market and said: Take these inks, pen-holders and pens for my son. They said: He has no son. Why does he want inks, pen-holders and pens? Reconsidering, they said: The King is an astrologer, and he has foreseen that he will receive a son. Thus, if the Holy One Blessed is He had not foreseen that in twenty-six generations Israel would accept the Torah, he wouldn't have written in it: "Command the children of Israel"!

1.2F PALESTINIAN TALMUD, PEAH 2:6, 17A

Said Rabbi Zeira in the name of Rabbi Yohanan: If a halakhic ruling comes to your attention and you cannot discern its nature, do not set it aside for another matter. For, indeed, many halakhic rulings were stated to Moses on Sinai, and all of them are imbedded in the mishnaic tradition! . . .

Rabbi Zeira in the name of Rabbi Eleazar: "Though I write for him the majority of my Torah, they are regarded as a strange thing" (Hos. 8:12). Now is the majority of the Torah written down? Rather the point is that truths derived from the interpretation of what is written exceed in quantity truths derived from the interpretation of what is oral.

Is that so? Rather it should be put this way: Truths derived from the interpretation of what is oral are more dear then truths derived from the interpretation of what is written. . . .

Said Rabbi Avin: Render the verse as follows: "Had I written the majority of my Torah, wouldn't they [i.e., Israel] have been considered like strangers?" What distinguishes us from the nations of the world? They present their books and we present our books, and they present their records and we present our records!

Rabbi Haggai in the name of Rabbi Samuel bar Nahman: Some things were stated orally and some were stated in writing, but we do not know which are more precious. But, on the basis of what is written in Scripture: "In accordance with [literally: "by the mouth" of] these words I have made a covenant with you and with Israel" (Exod. 34:27), it seems that the oral truths are more precious.

Rabbi Yohanan and Rabbi Yudan ben Rabbi Shimon transmitted renderings of this verse. One said: "If you have preserved what is rendered orally and preserved what is rendered in writing I shall make a covenant with you. But if not, I will not make a covenant with you." The other said: "If you have preserved what is rendered orally and established what is rendered in writing you shall be rewarded. But if not, you shall not be rewarded."

Rabbi Joshua ben Levi said (of the verse: "And on them were written as all the words that the LORD had spoken to you at the mountain" [Deut. 9:10]): Instead of "on them" it says "*and* on them"; instead of "all" it says "*as* all"; instead of "words" it says "*the* words." These extraneous grammatical items imply that Scripture, mishnaic tradition, dialectical studies and aggadic tradition—even what a trained disciple will in the future teach before his Master—was already transmitted to Moses on Sinai.

What's the proof for this opinion? "Is there a thing of which it is said, 'See, this is new'?" One will reply: "It has already been, in the ages before us" (Eccles. 1:10).

1.3 A KARAITE VIEW OF RABBINIC TRADITION

The Karaite attack against the rabbinic oral tradition is usually said to have begun with the eighth-century Baghdadi scholar Anan ben David. The Karaite polemic reached its most brilliant height in the work of the tenth-century historian and biblical exegete Jacob al-Kirkisani. Writing on the history of Jewish sectarianism, he portrayed the religion of the rabbis of his own day as just one more expression of false sectarian Judaism that had plagued Israel since the time of the death of King Solomon in biblical times. Note how his conception of rabbinic Judaism depends upon and recontextualizes material transmitted in such rabbinic works as Mishnah Avot.

1.3A A BOOK OF LIGHTS AND WATCH-TOWERS

After the Samaritans there appeared the Chiefs of the Community, who are the original Rabbanites; this was in the days of the second Temple. The first of them to be recorded was Shimon, whom they call Shimon the Righteous; they say that he was one of the remaining members of the Great Assembly. These, they say, lived in the time of Ezra and Nehemiah. The Rabbanites acknowledged the authority of the Chiefs of the Community solely because they followed the practices and the indulgences inherited from Jeroboam (the original schismatic after King Solomon's death). In particular, they sustained and confirmed these practices, supplied them with argumentative proofs, and wrote down the interpretation of them in the Mishnah and in other works. At times one or another among them did set forth the true meaning of a biblical ordinance, but they invariably banished him and sought to do him injury, as was, for example, the case of Gamaliel who fixed the date of holidays on the basis of the appearance of the new moon, or of Eliezer ben Hyrcanus, who disagreed with them in the matter of uncleanness of vessels the construction of which has not been completed; they excommunicated him and kept away from him, despite miraculous proofs of the truth of his opinion. . . .

The Rabbanites subsequently split into two factions, called the House of Hillel and the House of Shammai. The Rabbanites of Iraq followed the practice of the House of Hillel, while those in Syria followed that of the House of Shammai. Hillel and Shammai received their learning from Shemaiah and Avtalion. The conflict between the House of Hillel and the House of Shammai broke out on the third day of the month of Adar, and a number of adherents of each school was slain.

1.4 A KABBALISTIC VIEW OF RABBINIC TRADITION

In contrast to the Karaites, kabbalists of the Middle Ages and after were convinced that their mystical traditions of the Torah were part of the original Oral Torah of Moses. Their task, accordingly, was to explain how this was so. Rabbi Meir ben Gabbai, a Turkish scholar of the sixteenth century, provided an exhaustive explanation in his treatise *Sacred Service*. An excerpt, translated by Gershom Scholem in his book *The Messianic Idea in Judaism,* follows. Note how the mystical writer links all sources of Written and Oral Torah to a supernal source in the divine emanations, the "hidden Eden." You will also observe that, in this text, the Written and Oral Torah are not only historical traditions, but elements of God himself!

1.4A SACRED SERVICE

The highest wisdom . . . contains as the foundation of all emanations pouring forth out of the hidden Eden the true fountain from which the Written and the Oral Torah emanate and are impressed. . . . This fountain is never interrupted; it gushes forth in constant production. Were it to be interrupted for even a moment, all creatures would sink back into their non-being; for the gushing forth is the cause of God's great name appearing in its oneness and in its glory. . . . On this fountain rests the continued existence of all creatures; it is said of it (Ps. 36:10): "For with

From Rabbi Meir ben Gabbai, *Sacred Service,* translated by Gershom Scholem in *The Messianic Idea in Judaism and Other Essays on Jewish Spirituality.* Copyright © 1971 by Schocken Books, Inc. Reprinted with the permission of Schocken Books, distributed by Pantheon Books, a division of Random House, Inc., and Routledge.

Thee is the fountain of life." And this is a life that has no measure and no end, no death or dissolution. Now, since the nature of the original source is also preserved in what was formed from it, it necessarily follows that the Torah, arising out of this source, also never has an interruption within itself. Rather, its fountain always gushes forth, to indicate the source whence it was formed. We learn this from the prayer which designates God as The One Who "gives the Torah." For that great voice with which He gave it has not ceased. After He gave us His holy words and caused us to hear them as the very essence of the whole Torah, He did not cease to let us hear its details through His prophet, the trusted one of His house [i.e., Moses]. . . .

That great voice sounds forth without interruption; it calls with that eternal duration that is its nature; whatever the prophets and scholars of all generations have taught, proclaimed, and produced, they have received precisely out of that voice which never ceases, in which all regulations, determinations, and decisions are implicitly contained, as well as everything new that may ever be said in any future. In all generations, these men stand in the same relationship to that voice as the trumpet to the mouth of a man who blows into it and brings forth sound. In that process, there is no production from their own sense and understanding. Instead, they bring out of potentiality into actuality that which they received from that voice when they stood at Sinai. . . .

That great voice is the gate and portal of all the other voices, and that is [the meaning of] "fence of unity," and the reference of the verse in the Psalms: "This is the gate of the LORD," the gate representing the Oral Torah which leads to God, Who is the Written Torah, guarded by the Oral Torah. This is the reason for the fences and limitations with which the scholars enclose the Torah. But since that voice is never interrupted and that fountain always gushes forth, the deliberations of the scholars in the Talmud were necessary. . . .

If new teachings (regarding the understanding of the Torah) are produced daily, this proves that the fountain ever gushes and that the great voice sounds forth without interruption. For that reason, the deliberations upon the Torah may not suffer any interruptions, nor the production of new teachings and laws and incisive discussion. But the authority of the prophets and scholars who know the secret is nothing but the authority of that voice from which they have received all they have produced and taught, which in no way arose out of their own mind and out of their rational investigations.

SCRIPTURE AND TRADITION

CHAPTER 2
IN CHRISTIANITY

2.1 OLD AND NEW REVELATIONS

The earliest Christian community saw itself as a continuation and fulfillment of Judaism, and it interpreted many texts of the Hebrew scriptures—especially the books of the prophets—as an accurate prediction of everything Jesus would accomplish and as conclusive proof of his messianic identity. The gospel of Luke and the Acts of the Apostles were written by the same author in the late first century for a non-Jewish (Gentile) community. In the following texts, an intrinsic progression is established between the old and new revelations of God: Jesus is proclaimed as Messiah and as revealer of the hidden truths of Scripture; in addition, the apostles are proclaimed as the legitimate successors of Jesus and as the Spirit-inspired accurate interpreters of revelation.

2.1A THE GOSPEL ACCORDING TO LUKE 24:1–53

VII. After the Resurrection

The Empty Tomb. The Angel's Message

On the first day of the week, at the first sign of dawn, they went to the tomb with the spices they had prepared. They found that the stone had been rolled away from the tomb, but on entering discovered that the body of the Lord Jesus was not there. As they stood there not knowing what to think, two men in brilliant clothes suddenly appeared at their side. Terrified, the women lowered their eyes. But the two men said to them, "Why look among the dead for someone who is alive? He is not here; he has risen. Remember what he told you when he was still in Galilee: that the Son of Man had to be handed over into the power of sinful men and be crucified, and rise again on the third day." And they remembered his words.

The Apostles Refuse to Believe the Women

When the women returned from the tomb they told all this to the Eleven and to all the others. The women were Mary of Magdala, Joanna, and Mary the mother of James. The other women with them also told the apostles, but this story of theirs seemed pure nonsense, and they did not believe them.

Peter at the Tomb

Peter, however, went running to the tomb. He bent down and saw the binding cloths but nothing else; he then went back home, amazed at what had happened.

The Road to Emmaus

That very same day, two of them were on their way to a village called Emmaus seven miles from Jerusalem, and they were talking together about all that had happened. Now as they talked this over, Jesus himself came up and walked by their side; but something prevented them from recognizing him. He said to them, "What matters are you discussing as you walk along?" They stopped short, their faces downcast.

Then one of them, called Cleopas, answered him. "You must be the only person staying in Jerusalem who does not know the things that have been happening there these last few days." "What things?" he asked. "All about Jesus of Nazareth," they answered, "who proved he was a great prophet by the things he said and did in the sight of God and of the whole people; and how our chief priests and our leaders handed him over to be sentenced to death, and had him crucified. Our own hope had been that he would be the one to set Israel free. And this is not all: two whole days have gone by since it all happened; and some women from our group have astounded us: they went to the tomb in the early morning, and when they did not find the body, they came back to tell us they had seen a vision of angels who declared he was alive. Some of our friends went to the tomb and found everything exactly as the women had reported, but of him they saw nothing."

Then he said to them, "You foolish men! So slow to believe the full message of the prophets! Was it not ordained that the Christ should suffer and so enter into his glory?" Then, starting with Moses and going through all the prophets, he explained to them the passages throughout the scriptures that were about himself.

When they drew near to the village to which they were going, he made as if to go on; but they pressed him to stay with them. "It is nearly evening," they said, "and the day is almost over." So he went in to stay with them. Now while he was with them at table, he took the bread and said the blessing; then he broke it and handed it to them. And their eyes were opened and they recognized him; but he had vanished from their sight. Then they said to each other, "Did not our hearts burn within us as he talked to us on the road and explained the scriptures to us?"

They set out that instant and returned to Jerusalem. There they found the Eleven assembled together with their companions, who said to them, "Yes, it is true. The Lord has risen and has appeared to Simon." Then they told their story of what had happened on the road and how they had recognized him at the breaking of bread.

Jesus Appears to the Apostles

They were still talking about all this when he himself stood among them and said to them, "Peace be with you!" In a state of alarm and fright, they thought they were seeing a ghost. But he said, "Why are you so agitated, and why are these doubts rising in your hearts? Look at my hands and feet; yes, it is I indeed. Touch me and see for yourselves; a ghost has no flesh and bones as you can see I have." And as he said this he showed them his hands and feet. Their joy was so great that they still could not believe it, and they stood there dumfounded; so he said to them, "Have you anything here to eat?" And they offered him a piece of grilled fish, which he took and ate before their eyes.

Last Instructions to the Apostles

Then he told them, "This is what I meant when I said, while I was still with you, that everything written about me in the Law of Moses, in the Prophets and in the Psalms, has to be fulfilled." He then opened their minds to understand the scriptures, and he said to them, "So you see how it is written that the Christ would suffer and on the third day rise from the dead, and that, in his name, repentance for the forgiveness of sins would be preached to all the nations, beginning from Jerusalem. You are witnesses to this.

"And now I am sending down to you what the Father has promised. Stay in the city then, until you are clothed with the power from on high."

The Ascension

Then he took them out as far as the outskirts of Bethany, and lifting up his hands he blessed them. Now as he blessed them, he withdrew from them and was carried up to heaven. They worshiped him and then went back to Jerusalem full of joy; and they were continually in the Temple praising God.

2.1B THE ACTS OF THE APOSTLES 2:1–41

Pentecost

When Pentecost day came around, they had all met in one room, when suddenly they heard what sounded like a powerful wind from heaven, the noise of which filled the entire house in which they were sitting; and something appeared to them that seemed like tongues of fire; these separated and came to rest on the head of each of them. They were all filled with the Holy Spirit, and began to speak foreign languages as the Spirit gave them the gift of speech.

Now there were devout men living in Jerusalem from every nation under heaven, and at this sound they all assembled, each one bewildered to hear these men speaking his own language. They were amazed and astonished. "Surely," they said, "all these men speaking are Galileans? How does it happen that each of us hears them in his own native language? Parthians, Medes and Elamites; people from Mesopotamia, Judaea and Cappadocia, Pontus and Asia, Phrygia and Pamphylia, Egypt and the parts of Libya around Cyrene; as well as visitors from Rome—Jews and proselytes alike—Cretans and Arabs; we hear them preaching in our own language about the marvels of God." Everyone was amazed and unable to explain it; they asked one another what it all meant. Some, however, laughed it off. "They have been drinking too much new wine," they said.

Peter's Address to the Crowd

Then Peter stood up with the Eleven and addressed them in a loud voice:

"Men of Judaea, and all you who live in Jerusalem, make no mistake about this, but listen carefully to what I say. These men are not drunk, as you imagine; why, it is only the third hour of the day. On the contrary, this is what the prophet spoke of:

> In the days to come—it is the Lord who speaks—
> I will pour out my spirit on all mankind.
> Their sons and daughters shall prophesy,
> your young men shall see visions,
> you old men shall dream dreams.
> Even on my slaves, men and women,
> in those days, I will pour out my spirit.
> I will display portents in heaven *above*
> and *signs* on earth *below*.
> The sun will be turned into darkness
> and the moon into blood
> before the great Day of the Lord dawns.
> All who call on the name of the Lord will be saved. (Joel 3:1–5)

"Men of Israel, listen to what I am going to say: Jesus the Nazarene was a man commended to you by God by the miracles and portents and signs that God worked through him when he was among you, as you all know. This man, who was put into your power by the deliberate intention and foreknowledge of God, you took and had crucified by men outside the Law. You killed him, but God raised him to life, freeing him from the pangs of Hades; for it was impossible for him to be held in its power since, as David says of him:

> *I saw the Lord before me always.*
> *for with him at my right hand nothing can shake me.*
> *So my heart was glad*

and my tongue cried out with joy;
my body, too, will rest in the hope
that you will not abandon my soul to Hades
nor allow your holy one to experience corruption.
You have made known the way of life to me,
you will fill me with gladness through your presence. (Psalm 16:8–11)

"Brothers, no one can deny that the patriarch David himself is dead and buried: his tomb is still with us. But since he was a prophet, and knew that God *had sworn him* an oath *to make one of his descendants succeed him on the throne,* what he foresaw and spoke about was the resurrection of the Christ: he is the one who was *not abandoned to Hades,* and whose body did not *experience corruption.* God raised this man Jesus to life, and all of us are witnesses to that. Now raised to the heights by God's right hand, he has received from the Father the Holy Spirit, who was promised, and what you see and hear is the outpouring of that Spirit. For David himself never went up to heaven; and yet these words are his:

The Lord said to my Lord:
Sit at my right hand
until I make your enemies
a footstool for you. (Psalm 110:1)

"For this reason the whole House of Israel can be certain that God has made this Jesus whom you crucified both Lord and Christ."

The First Conversions

Hearing this, they were cut to the heart and said to Peter and the apostles, "What must we do, brothers?" "You must repent," Peter answered, "and every one of you must be baptized in the name of Jesus Christ for the forgiveness of your sins, and you will receive the gift of the Holy Spirit. The promise that was made is for you and your children, and for all *those who are far away, for all those whom the Lord* our God *will call to himself.*" He spoke to them for a long time using many arguments, and he urged them, "Save yourselves from this perverse generation." They were convinced by his arguments, and they accepted what he said and were baptized. That very day about three thousand were added to their number.

Paul, former Pharisee and persecutor of the early Christian church, zealous convert to Christianity, and missionary to the Gentiles, wrote this letter to the Roman Christian community sometime in the late fifties CE. The church at Rome was apparently composed of both Jews and Gentiles, and the two groups were not getting along. The three main questions addressed here were pressing ones for the first generation of Christians (whether Jewish or Gentile): (1) If Jesus were indeed the Messiah, then why was he not universally acclaimed as such by the Jewish people? (2) How would the rejection of the genuine Messiah affect the status of the Jews as God's chosen people? (3) What did this situation imply for the trustworthiness of God's promises?

2.1c Saint Paul's Letter to the Romans 9:1–33

What I want to say now is no pretense; I say it in union with Christ—it is the truth—my conscience in union with the Holy Spirit assures me of it too. What I want to say is this: my sorrow is so great, my mental anguish so endless, I would willingly be condemned and be cut off from Christ if it could help my brothers of Israel, by own flesh and blood. They were adopted as sons, they were given the glory and the covenants; the Law and the ritual were drawn up for them, and the promises were made to them. They are descended from the patriarchs and from their flesh and blood came Christ who is above all, God forever blessed! Amen.

God Has Kept His Promise

Does this mean that God has failed to keep his promise? Of course not. Not all those who descend from Israel are Israel; not all the descendants of Abraham are his true children. Remember: *It is through Isaac that your name will be carried on,* which means that it is not physical descent that decided who are the children of God; it is only the children of the promise who will count as the true descendants. The actual words in which the promise was made were: *I shall visit you* at such and such a time, *and Sarah will have a son.* Even more to the point is what was said to Rebecca when she was pregnant by our ancestor Isaac, but before her twin children were born and before either had done good or evil. In order to stress that God's choice is free, since it depends on the one who calls, not on human merit, Rebecca was told: *the elder shall serve the younger,* or as scripture says elsewhere: *I showed my love for Jacob and my hatred for Esau.* (Gen. 21:12, 18:10, 25:23; Malachi 1:2–3)

God Is Not Unjust

Does it follow that God is unjust? Of course not. Take what God said to Moses: *I have mercy on whom I will, and I show pity to whom I please.* In other words, the only thing that counts is not what human beings want or try to do, but the mercy of God. For in scripture he says to Pharoah: *It was for this I raised you up, to use you as a means of showing my power and to make my name known throughout the world.* In other words, when God wants to show mercy he does, and when he wants to harden someone's heart he does so. (Exod. 33:19, 9:16)

You will ask me, "In that case, how can God ever blame anyone, since no one can oppose his will?" But what right have you, a human being, to cross-examine God? *The pot has no right to say to the potter: Why did you make me this shape?* Surely a potter can do what he likes with the clay? It is surely for him to decide whether he will use a particular lump of clay to make a special pot or an ordinary one? (Isa. 29:116)

Or else imagine that although God is ready to show his anger and display his power, yet he patiently puts up with the people who make him angry, however much they deserve to be destroyed. He puts up with them for the sake of those other people, to whom he wants to be merciful, to whom he wants to reveal the richness of his glory, people he had prepared for this glory long ago. Well, we are those people; whether we were Jews or pagans we are the ones he has called.

All Has Been Foretold in the Old Testament

That is exactly what God says in Hosea: *I shall say to a people that was not mine, "You are my people," and to a nation I never loved, "I love you." Instead of being told, "You are no people of mine," they will now be called the sons of the living God.* Referring to Israel Isaiah had this to say: *Though Israel should have as many descendants as there are grains of sand on the seashore, only a remnant will be saved, for without hesitation or delay the Lord will execute his sentence on the earth.* As Isaiah foretold: *Had the Lord of hosts not left us some descendants we should now be like Sodom, we should be like Gomorrah.*

From this it follows that the pagans who were not looking for righteousness found it all the same, a righteousness that comes of faith, while Israel, looking for a righteousness derived from law failed to do what that law required. Why did they fail? Because they relied on good deeds instead of trusting in faith. In other words, they *stumbled over the stumbling stone* mentioned in scripture: *See how I lay in Zion a stone to stumble over, a rock to trip men up—only those who believe in him will have no cause for shame.* (Hos. 2:25, 2:1; Isa. 10:22–23, 28:16)

The Infancy Gospel of Thomas was probably written around the middle of the second century by a Gentile author who was not well acquainted with Judaism. It is a good example of the kind of "sacred" texts that were competing with those of the orthodox Christian community and that were rejected by it. The gospel's purpose was to fill in the details of Jesus' childhood, which cannot be found in the orthodox gospels. The divine child depicted here, however, is a holy terror: a capricious, impulsive, conceited, and vindictive deity who displays his awesome powers with nary a trace of love and compassion. The communities that accepted this text as sacred scripture obviously found this kind of savior more appealing than the meek one of Matthew, Mark, Luke, and John. Notice, however, that one story from the canonical gospels is embedded in this text and that it is not altogether out of character with the rest of the narrative: this is, of course, the story of Jesus the twelve year old worrying his family and amazing the elders and teachers at Jerusalem.

2.1D The Infancy Gospel of Thomas

Thomas the Israelite, announce and make known to all you brethren from the Gentiles the childhood and great deeds of our Lord Jesus Christ, which he did when he was born in our country. This is the beginning.

From David R. Carthridge and David L. Duncan, eds. and trans., *Documents for the Study of the Gospels.* Copyright © 1980 by David R. Carthridge and David L. Duncan. Reprinted with the permission of Augsburg Fortress.

When this child Jesus was five years old he was playing at the ford of a stream. He made pools of the rushing water and made it immediately pure; he ordered this by word alone. He made wet clay and modeled twelve sparrows from it. It was the Sabbath when he did this. There were many other children playing with him. A certain Jew saw what Jesus did while playing on the Sabbath. He immediately went and announced to his father Joseph, "See, your child is at the stream, and has taken clay and modeled twelve birds; he has profaned the Sabbath." Joseph came to the place and seeing what Jesus did he cried out: "Why do you do on the Sabbath what it is not lawful to do?" Jesus clapped his hands and cried to the sparrows, "Be gone." And the sparrows flew off chirping. The Jews saw this and were amazed. They went away and described to their leaders what they had seen Jesus do.

The son of Annas the scribe was standing there with Joseph. He took a branch of a willow and scattered the water which Jesus had arranged. Jesus saw what he did and became angry and said to him, "You unrighteous, impious ignoramus, what did the pools and the water do to harm you? Behold, you shall also wither as a tree, and you shall not bear leaves nor roots nor fruit." And immediately that child was all withered. Jesus left and went to the house of Joseph. The parents of the withered one bore him away, bemoaning his lost youth. They led him to Joseph and reproached him, "What kind of child do you have who does such things?"

Once again he was going through the village, and a child who was running banged into his shoulder. Jesus was angered and said to him, "You shall go no further on your way." And immediately the child fell down dead. Some people saw this happen and said, "From whence was this child begotten, for his every word is an act accomplished?" The parents of the dead boy went to Joseph and blamed him: "Because you have such a boy, you cannot live with us in the village; your alternative is to teach him to bless and not to curse, for he is killing our children."

Joseph took the child aside privately and warned him, saying, "Why do you do such things? These people are suffering and they hate us and are persecuting us!" Jesus said, "I know that these are not your words, but on account of you I will be silent. However, they shall bear their punishment." Immediately, those who accused him were blinded. Those who saw were very frightened and puzzled, and they said about him, "Every word he speaks, whether good or evil, happens and is a miracle." When he saw what Jesus had done, Joseph arose and took hold of Jesus' ear and pulled it hard. The child was angry and said to him, "It is fitting for you to seek and not find. You have acted very stupidly. Do you not know I am yours? Do not vex me."

A man named Zaccheus, a teacher, was standing there and he heard, in part, Jesus saying these things to his father. He was greatly astonished that he said such things, since he was just a child. And after a few days he approached Joseph and said to him, "You have a smart child, and he has a mind. Come, hand him over to me so that he may learn writing. I will give him all understanding with the letters, and teach him to greet all the elders and to honor them as grandfathers and fathers and to love his peers." He told him all the letters from the Alpha to the Omega plainly, with much discussion. But Jesus looked at Zaccheus the teacher, and said to him, "You do not know the Alpha according to nature, how do you teach others the Beta? You hypocrite! First, if you know it, teach the Alpha, then we shall believe you about the Beta." Then he began to question the teacher about the first letter and he could not answer him. Many heard as the child said to Zaccheus, "Listen, teacher, to the order of the first element, and pay attention to this, how it has lines, and a central mark which goes through the two lines you see, they converge, go up, again come to head, become the same three times, subordinate, and hypostatic, isometric . . . [the text is unreliable.] You now have the lines of Alpha."

When the teacher, Zaccheus, heard so many such allegories of the first letter spoken by the child, he was puzzled about such expoundings and his teaching. He said to those present, "Woe is me, I am wretched and puzzled; I have shamed myself trying to handle this child. I beg you, brother Joseph, take him away. I cannot bear the severity of his glance. I cannot understand his speech at all. This child is not earthborn; he is able to tame even fire. Perhaps he was begotten before the world's creation. What belly bore him, what womb nurtured him, I do not know. Woe is me, friend, he completely confuses me. I cannot follow his understanding. I have fooled myself; I am thrice wretched. I worked anxiously to have a disciple, and I found myself with a teacher. I consider my shame, friends; I am an old man and have been conquered by a child; for at this hour I cannot look into his gaze. When they all say that I have been conquered by a little child, what can I say? What can I discuss about the lines of the first element he spoke to me? I do not know, O friends, for I do not know its beginning and end. Therefore, I beg you, brother Joseph, take him into your house. He is something great: a God, an angel, or what I should say I do not know." . . .

When he was twelve his parents, according to custom, went to Jerusalem to the Passover with their traveling companions. After the Passover they returned to their house. While they were going home, the child Jesus went back to Jerusalem. His parents thought that he was in the caravan. After a day's travel, they sought him among their kinfolk and when they did not find him they were troubled. They returned again to the city to seek him. After three days they found him in the Temple, seated in the midst of the teachers, listening and questioning them. They all were attentive and amazed at how he, being a child, could argue with the elders and teachers of the people, solving the chief problems of the Law and the parables of the prophets. His mother, Mary, came up and said to him, "How can you have done this to us, child? Behold, we have looked everywhere for you, grieving." And Jesus said to them, "Why did you look for me? Do you not know that I must be in my Father's house?" The scribes and Pharisees said, "Are you the mother of this child?" She said, "I am." They said to her, "You are blessed among women, because God has blessed the fruit of your womb. We have never before seen or heard such glory or such excellence and wisdom." Jesus arose and followed his mother and was obedient to his parents. But his mother kept in her heart all that had happened. Jesus grew in wisdom and stature and grace. Glory be to him for ever and ever. Amen.

2.2 INTERPRETING SCRIPTURE

Origen (ca. 185–254), an Egyptian Christian from Alexandria, was deeply influenced by the Hellenistic philosophical and theological currents that thrived in his city's many academies. He was especially attracted to Platonism and to its metaphysical understanding of material reality as subservient to a higher spiritual realm. Origen's *On First Principles* provided Christians with their first systematic hermeneutical treatise. In this section, Origen outlines the ways in which the sacred texts of the Bible are to be approached on different levels, proposing that there is an inexhaustible depth of meaning in each and every utterance, no matter how seemingly mundane. Though he was eventually condemned for other teachings (such as the eternity of creation, the reincarnation of human souls, and the ultimate redemption of all of creation, including Satan and the fallen angels), he bequeathed to orthodox Christians an impressive and useful set of interpretive tools. His approach to each text on three levels—literal, moral, and allegorical—was wholeheartedly embraced and became the foundation of Christian theologizing up to the Enlightenment of the eighteenth century. Among some Christians, Origen's approach is still followed today.

2.2A ORIGEN, *ON FIRST PRINCIPLES*, Book IV

Chapter Two:
That Many by Not Understanding the Scriptures
Spiritually and by Badly Understanding Them Fall
into Heresies

Now that we have briefly discussed the inspiration of divine Scripture by the Holy Spirit, it seems necessary also to explain how certain people by failing to read or understand Scripture correctly have given themselves up to a great many errors, since the way one ought to approach the understanding of divine letters is unknown to a great many people. And so, the Jews, through the hardness of their heart and because they wish to seem wise in themselves, have not believed in our Lord and Savior. They suppose that what was prophesied of Him should be understood according to the letter, that is, that He ought to have "proclaimed release to the captives" (Is. 61:1; cf. Lk. 4:19) in a perceptible and visible way, and that He ought first to have built the city that they think is truly the city of God and at the same time to have "cut off the chariot from Ephraim and the war horse from Jerusalem" (Zech. 9:10; cf. Ezek. 48:15ff.; Ps. 46:4). He should have "eaten butter and

From Origen, *An Exhortation to Martyrdom, On Prayer, and Selected Works*, translated by Rowan A. Greer, *Classics of Western Spirituality*. Copyright © 1979 by The Missionary Society of Saint Paul the Apostle in the State of New York. Reprinted with the permission of Paulist Press.

honey before He knew how to refuse the evil and choose the good" (Is. 7:15). And they suppose that the wolf, that four-footed animal, as was prophesied for the coming of Christ, ought to have "fed with the lambs, and the leopard lie down with the kids, and the calf and bull together feed with the lions and be led to pastures by a little child, and the ox and the bear lie down together in fields and their young be brought up in common, and the lions stand in the mangers with the oxen and eat straw" (Is. 11:6–7). Thus, since they see that none of these things that were prophesied of Him have happened according to the narrative meaning of Scripture,[1] and since they hold the belief that in them especially the signs of the coming of Christ were to be observed, they have been unwilling to accept the presence of our Lord Jesus Christ. On the contrary, against law and divine right, that is, against the faith of prophecy, they crucified Him as though He had taken the name of Christ for Himself.

Now the reason those we have just mentioned have a false understanding of these matters is quite simply that they understand Scripture not according to the spiritual meaning but according to the sound of the letter. For this reason, as far as our modest perception admits, we shall address those who believe the sacred Scriptures were not composed by any human words but were written by the inspiration of the Holy Spirit and were also delivered and entrusted to us by the will of God the Father through His Only Begotten Son Jesus Christ. And we shall try to make clear to them what seems to us the right way of understanding Scripture, observing that rule and discipline[2] which was delivered by Jesus Christ to the apostles and which they delivered in succession to their followers who teach the heavenly Church.

Now the fact that certain mysterious dispensations are disclosed by the holy Scriptures is something everyone, I think, even the more simple believers, will admit. But what they are or of what sort is something anyone of a right mind and who is not plagued with the vice of boasting will confess in the spirit of true religion he does not know. For if someone, for example, points out to us the stories of Lot's daughters and their apparently unlawful intercourse with their father, or of Abraham's two wives, or of the two sisters who married Jacob, or of the two maidservants who increased the number of his sons, what else can we answer than that these are certain mysteries and types of spiritual matters, but that we do not know of what sort they are? Moreover, when we read of the building of the tabernacle, we are, of course, certain that the things that have been described are types of certain obscure matters. But I think it is extremely difficult, I might almost say impossible, to fit them to their own measures and to uncover and describe each one of them. Nevertheless, as I have said, the fact that the description is filled with mysteries does not escape even an ordinary understanding. Indeed, the entire narrative, which seems to be written about weddings or the births of sons or different battles or whatever other stories one wishes, what else must it be believed to be

---

[1] Latin, *historia*. "Narrative meaning" will be adopted as the translation throughout.
[2] The Rule of Faith.

than the forms and types of hidden and sacred matters? But either because people bring too little zeal to the training of their minds or because they think they know before they have learned, it happens that they never begin to learn. On the other hand, if neither zeal nor a teacher is actually lacking and if these matters are sought after as divine and not as though they were human, that is religiously and piously and as matters we hope to be revealed in as many cases as possible through God's revelation, since they are, of course, extremely difficult and obscure for human perception, then perhaps the person who seeks this way will at last find what is right to find.

But perhaps this difficulty will be supposed present only in the prophetic words, since it is certainly clear to everyone that the prophetic style is always strewn with types and enigmas. What shall we say when we come to the Gospels? Does not an inner meaning, the Lord's meaning, also lie hidden there that is revealed only by the grace he received who said, "But we have the mind of Christ . . . that we might understand the gifts bestowed upon us by God. And we impart this in words not taught by human wisdom but taught by the Spirit" (1 Cor. 2:16, 12–13)? And if anyone reads the revelations made to John, how can he fail to be amazed at how great an obscurity of ineffable mysteries is present there? It is evident that even those who cannot understand what lies hidden in them nevertheless understand that something lies hidden. And indeed, the letters of the apostles, which do seem to some clearer, are they not so filled with profound ideas that through them, as through some small opening, the brightness of an immense light seems to be poured forth for those who can understand the meaning of divine wisdom? Since all this is the case and since there are many in error in this life, I do not think that anyone can without danger proclaim that he knows or understands those things that require "the key of knowledge" before they can be opened. This key the Savior said was with those skilled in the Law. At this point, granted it is something of a digression, I think the question should nonetheless be put to those who say that before the coming of the Savior there was no truth with those acquainted with the Law, how it could be said by our Lord Jesus Christ that the "keys of knowledge" are with those who held in their hands the books of the Law and the prophets. For this is what the Lord said, "Woe to you, teachers of the Law, for you have taken away the key of knowledge; you did not enter yourselves, and you hindered those who wanted to enter" (Lk. 11:52).

But, of course, we must not ignore the fact that there are certain passages in Scripture in which what we have called the body, that is a logically coherent narrative meaning, is not always to be found, as we shall show in what follows. And there are places where only what we have called the soul and the spirit may be understood. I think this is also indicated in the Gospels, when "six stone jars" are said to be "standing there, for the Jewish rites of purification, each holding two or three measures" (Jn. 2:6). As I have said, this verse in the Gospel seems to refer to those whom the Apostle calls "Jews inwardly" (Rom. 2:29), because they are purified by the word of Scripture, sometimes holding "two measures," that is, receiving the meanings of the soul and of the spirit, according to what we have just said, and sometimes holding "three measures," when a reading for edification can keep the bodily meaning, which is the narrative meaning. And "six stone jars" are mentioned because they bear a logical relation to those who are placed in this world to be purified. For we read that in six days (which is a perfect number[3]) this world and everything in it were finished.

Chapter Three:
Examples from the Scriptures of How Scripture Should Be Understood

So that what we say may be understood quite concretely, let us now bring the argument to bear upon actual passages in Scripture. To what person of intelligence, I ask, will the account seem logically consistent that says there was a "first day" and a "second" and "third," in which also "evening" and "morning" are named, without a sun, without a moon, and without stars, and even in the case of the first day without a heaven (Gen. 1:5–13)? And who will be found simple enough to believe that like some farmer "God planted trees in the garden of Eden, in the east" and that He planted "the tree of life" in it, that is a visible tree that could be touched, so that someone could eat of this tree with corporeal teeth and gain life, and, further, could eat of another tree and receive knowledge "of good and evil" (Gen. 2:8–9)? Moreover, we find that God is said to stroll in the garden in the afternoon and Adam to hide under a tree (cf. Gen. 3:8). Surely, I think no one doubts that these statements are made by Scripture in the form of a type by which they point toward certain mysteries. Also Cain's going away "from the face of God" (Gen. 4:16) obviously stirs the wise reader to ask what "the face of God" is and how any one could "go away" from it. But there is no need for us to enlarge the discussion too much beyond what we have in hand, since it is quite easy for everyone who wishes to collect from the holy Scriptures things that are written as though they were really done, but cannot be believed to have happened appropriately and reasonably according to the narrative meaning. And this form of Scripture also finds abundant and copious expression in the Gospels, when, for example, the devil is said to have placed Jesus on "a very high mountain" to show Him from there "all the kingdoms of the world and the glory of them" (Mt. 4:8). How could it possibly happen according to the letter either that the devil led Jesus to a very high mountain or that to His fleshly eyes he "showed," as though they were below and next to that one mountain, "all the kingdoms of the world," that is, the kingdoms of the Persians, the Scythians, the Indians, and how their kings are glorified by men? Moreover, whoever reads with special care will find a great many other passages like this in the Gospels. In this way he will notice that into these accounts that seem to have been described according to the letter there have been

---

[3] Cf. Philo, *De op. mund.* 3. Six is perfect because it is the sum of its parts, 1 + 2 + 3.

sown in and woven together things that the narrative meaning will not admit but that preserve the spiritual meaning.

And now if we look for similar examples from the Gospels, how will it fail to seem ridiculous if we understand according to the letter the statement "Salute no one on the road" (Lk. 10:4)? For certain of the simpler believers think that our Savior gave the apostles this order. Moreover, how will it be possible, especially in those places where an extremely harsh winter is rough with icy frosts (cf. Vergil, *Geor.* II.263), to observe the commandment that no one should have "two tunics or sandals" (Mt. 10:10)? And what about the commandment that the person struck on the right cheek should offer also the left one, since anyone who struck with the right hand would hit the left cheek (cf. Mt. 5:39; Lk. 6:29)? Also to be considered one of the impossibilities is the verse in the Gospel "If your right eye has offended, let it be plucked out" (cf. Mt. 5:29, 18:9). For even if we refer the saying to fleshly eyes, how will it appear logical that the blame for the offense is referred to one eye, the right one, when a person sees with both eyes? Or who would be considered innocent of a great crime if he laid hands on himself?

Perhaps the letters of the Apostle Paul will appear free from these difficulties. But consider what he says, "Was any one at the time of his call already circumcised? Let him not seek uncircumcision" (1 Cor. 7:18). In the first place, if one examines the passage carefully, it will not appear addressed to the subjects that are being discussed in the context. For Paul's discussion concerns instructions for marriage and chastity, and the verse that has been cited will appear beside the point in such matters. Second, what would be the objection if someone could return to uncircumcision in order to escape the disfigurement that comes from circumcision? Third, this certainly cannot be done by any manner of means.

Now we have brought all these examples in order to show that the aim of the Holy Spirit, who thought it right to give us the divine Scriptures, is not that we might be able to be edified by the letter alone or in all cases, since we often discover that the letter is impossible or insufficient in itself because by it sometimes not only irrationalities but even impossibilities are described. But the aim of the Holy Spirit is that we should understand that there have been woven into the visible narrative truths that, if pondered and understood inwardly, bring forth a law useful to men and worthy of God.

With the battle cry of "Scripture alone!," Martin Luther (1483–1546) brought about a change and renewal in the interpretation of the Bible among European Christians of the sixteenth century. Over and against the papal claim that all true theology was founded on the revelations contained in Scripture as interpreted by the hierarchy of the Catholic Church, Luther proposed a more immediate and radical biblicism. Theology and piety should be based directly on the Word of God, said Luther, not on "human" traditions of interpretation. Anything that did not square with Scripture, he concluded, must be false. But did this mean that the Bible spoke unequivocally to each and every Christian or that a church was unnecessary? Certainly not. Luther believed the existence of the church was proposed by Scripture itself, and he defined the church as that institution in which "the Word of God is purely preached." But preaching purely did not come naturally; it required the proper kind of education. In his prefaces to the New Testament, Luther briefly outlined how Scripture was to be approached and taught. Toward the end of this text, he laid bare one of his guiding exegetical principles: the notion of a "canon within the canon," that is, a hierarchical arrangement of the books of Scripture, in which some books are to be accepted as superior to others, serving as lenses through which the Bible as a whole is to be read and understood.

2.2B LUTHER, PREFACES TO THE NEW TESTAMENT 1546 (1522)

[It would be right and proper for this book to go forth without any prefaces or extraneous names attached and simply have its own say under its own name. However many unfounded interpretations and prefaces have scattered the thought of Christians to a point where no one any longer knows what is gospel or law, New Testament or Old. Necessity demands, therefore, that there should be a notice or preface, by which the ordinary man can be rescued from his former delusions, set on the right track, and taught what he is to look for in this book, so that he may not seek laws and commandments where he ought to be seeking the gospel and promises of God.

Just as the Old Testament is a book in which are written God's laws and commandments, together with the history of those who kept and of those who did not keep them, so the New Testament is a book in which are written the gospel and the promises of God, together with the history of those who believe and of those who do not believe them.

For "gospel" [*Euangeleium*] is a Greek word and means in Greek a good message, good tidings, good news, a good report, which one sings and tells with gladness. For example, when David overcame the great Goliath, there came among the Jewish people the good report and encouraging news that their terrible enemy had been struck down and that they had been rescued and given joy and peace; and they sang and danced and were glad for it [I Sam. 18:6].

Thus this gospel of God or New Testament is a good story and report, sounded forth into all the world by the apostles, telling of a true David who strove with sin, death, and the devil, and overcame them, and thereby rescued all those who were captive in sin, afflicted with death, and overpowered by the devil. Without any merit of their own he made them righteous, gave them life, and saved them, so that they were given peace and brought back to God. For this they sing, and thank and praise God, and are glad forever, if only they believe firmly and remain steadfast in faith.

This report and encouraging tidings, or evangelical and divine news, is also called a New Testament. For it is a testament when a dying man bequeaths his property, after his death, to his legally defined heirs. And Christ, before his death, commanded and ordained that his gospel be preached after his death in all the world [Luke 24:44–47]. Thereby he gave to all who believe, as their possession, everything that he had. This included: his life, in which he swallowed up death; his righteousness, by which he blotted out sin; and his salvation, with which he overcame everlasting damnation. A poor man, dead in sin and consigned to hell, can hear nothing more comforting than this precious and tender message about Christ; from the bottom of his heart he must laugh and be glad over it, if he believes it true.

Now to strengthen this faith, God has promised this gospel and testament in many ways, by the prophets in the Old Testament, as St. Paul says in Romans 1[:1], "I am set apart to preach the gospel of God which he promised beforehand through his prophets in the holy scriptures, concerning his Son, who was descended from David," etc.

The gospel, then, is nothing but the preaching about Christ, Son of God and of David, true God and man, who by his death and resurrection has overcome for us the sin, death, and hell of all men who believe in him. Thus the gospel can be either a brief or a lengthy message; one person can write of it briefly, another at length. He writes of it at length, who writes about many words and works of Christ, as do the four evangelists. He writes of it briefly, however, who does not tell of Christ's works, but indicates briefly how by his death and resurrection he has overcome sin, death, and hell for those who believe in him, as do St. Peter and St. Paul.

See to it, therefore, that you do not make a Moses out of Christ, or a book of laws and doctrines out of the gospel, as has been done heretofore and as certain prefaces put it, even those of St. Jerome. For the gospel does not expressly demand works of our own by which we become righteous and are saved; indeed it condemns such works. Rather the gospel demands faith in Christ: that he has overcome for us sin, death, and hell, and thus gives us righteousness, life, and salvation not through our works, but through his own works, death, and suffering, in order that we may avail ourselves of his death and victory as though we had done it ourselves.

To be sure, Christ in the gospel, and St. Peter and St. Paul besides, do give many commandments and doctrines, and expound the law. But these are to be counted like all Christ's other works and good deeds. To know his works and the things that happened to him is not yet to know the true gospel, for you do not yet thereby know that he has overcome sin, death, and the devil. So, too, it is not yet knowledge of the gospel when you know these doctrines and commandments, but only when the voice comes that says, "Christ is your own, with his life, teaching, works, death, resurrection, and all that he is, has, does, and can do."

Thus we see also that he does not compel us but invites us kindly and says, "Blessed are the poor," etc. [Matt. 5:3]. And the apostles use the words, "I exhort," "I entreat," "I beg," so that one sees on every hand that the gospel is not a book of law, but really a preaching of the benefits of Christ, shown to us and given to us for our own possession, if we believe. But Moses, in his books, drives, compels, threatens, strikes, and rebukes terribly, for he is a law-giver and driver.

Hence it comes that to a believer no law is given by which he becomes righteous before God, as St. Paul says in I Timothy 1[:9], because he is alive and righteous and saved by faith, and he needs nothing further except to prove his faith by works. Truly, if faith is there, he cannot hold back; he proves himself, breaks out into good works, confesses and teaches this gospel before the people, and stakes his life on it. . . .

That is what Christ meant when at the last he gave no other commandment than love, by which men were to know who were his disciples [John 13:34–35] and true believers. For where works and love do not break forth, there faith is not right, the gospel does not yet take hold, and Christ is not rightly known. See, then, that you so approach the books of the New Testament as to learn to read them in this way.

Which are the true and noblest books of the New Testament?

From all this you can now judge all the books and decide among them which are the best. John's Gospel and St. Paul's epistles, especially that to the Romans, and St. Peter's first epistle are the true kernel and marrow of all the books. They ought properly to be the foremost books, and it would be advisable for every Christian to read them first and most, and by daily reading to make them as much his own as his daily bread. For in them you do not find many works and miracles of Christ described, but you do find depicted in masterly fashion how faith in Christ overcomes sin, death, and hell, and gives life, righteousness, and salvation. This is the real nature of the gospel, as you have heard.

If I had to do without one or the other—either the works or the preaching of Christ—I would rather do without the works than without his preaching. For the works do not help me, but his words give life, as he himself says [John 6:63]. Now John writes very little about the works of Christ, but very much about his preaching, while the other evangelists write much about his works and little about his preaching. Therefore John's Gospel is the one, fine, true, and chief gospel, and is far, far to be preferred over the other three and placed high above them. So, too, the epistles of St. Paul and St. Peter far surpass the other three gospels, Matthew, Mark, and Luke.

In a word St. John's Gospel and his first epistle, St. Paul's epistles, especially Romans, Galatians, and Ephesians, and St. Peter's first epistle are the books that show you Christ and teach you all that is necessary and salvatory for you to know, even if you were never to see or hear any other book or doctrine. Therefore St. James' epistle is really an epistle of straw, compared to these others, for it has nothing of the nature of the gospel about it.

2.3 The Catholic Church Defends Its Interpretation of the Scriptures

Wishing to uphold the Catholic Church's traditional understanding of the Holy Scriptures in the light of the Protestant challenge, the Council of Trent issued the following decree in 1563. Here, as in most of the decrees of this council, compromises with Protestantism are avoided. Several Old Testament books that Protestants had rejected as uncanonical, or apocryphal, were here defended as truly biblical: Esdras, Tobias, Judith, Esther, Baruch, Ecclesiasticus, Wisdom, and Maccabees. Moreover, the Latin translation of Jerome, known as the Vulgate edition, was reconfirmed as authoritative and unerring and proclaimed as the only proper text for teaching and preaching in the Catholic Church. Careful regulations were also set in place for the publication and distribution of printed Bibles. Implicitly, this decree frowns on translations into vernacular languages and discourages private reading by the laity.

2.3A The Canons and Decrees of the Council of Trent, A.D. 1563

Third Session,
Celebrated on the Fourth Day of February, 1546

Decree Concerning the Symbol of Faith

In the name of the holy and undivided Trinity, Father, Son, and Holy Ghost.

This holy, ecumenical and general Council of Trent, lawfully assembled in the Holy Ghost, the same three legates of the Apostolic See presiding, considering the magnitude of the matters to be dealt with, especially those comprised under the two heads, the extirpation of heresies and the reform of morals, for which purposes it was chiefly assembled, and recognizing with the Apostle that its *wrestling is not against flesh and blood, but against the spirits of wickedness in high places*, exhorts with the same Apostle each and all above all things to be *strengthened in the Lord and in the might of his power, in all things taking the shield of faith, wherewith they may be able to extinguish all the fiery darts of the most wicked one, and to take the helmet of the hope of salvation and the sword of the spirit, which is the word of God.* . . . (Eph. 6:12–17)

Fourth Session,
Celebrated on the Eighth Day of April, 1546

Decree Concerning the Canonical Scriptures

The holy, ecumenical and general Council of Trent, lawfully assembled in the Holy Ghost, the same three legates of the Apostolic See presiding, keeps this con-

From John Leith, ed., *Creeds of the Church: A Reader in Christian Doctrine from the Bible to the Present,* Revised Edition. Copyright © 1973, 1982 by John Leith. Reprinted with the permission of Westminster John Knox Press.

stantly in view, namely, that the purity of the Gospel may be preserved in the Church after the errors have been removed. This [Gospel], of old promised through the Prophets in the Holy Scriptures, our Lord Jesus Christ, the Son of God, promulgated first with His own mouth, and then commanded it to be preached by His Apostles to every creature as the source at once of all saving truth and rules of conduct. It also clearly perceives that these truths and rules are contained in the written books and in the unwritten traditions, which, received by the Apostles from the mouth of Christ Himself, or from the Apostles themselves, the Holy Ghost dictating, have come down to us, transmitted as it were from hand to hand. Following, then, the examples of the orthodox Fathers, it receives and venerates with a feeling of piety and reverence all the books both of the Old and New Testaments, since one God is the author of both; also the traditions, whether they relate to faith or to morals, as having been dictated either orally by Christ or by the Holy Ghost, and preserved in the Catholic Church in unbroken succession. . . .

Decree Concerning the Edition and Use of the Sacred Books

Moreover, the same holy council considering that not a little advantage will accrue to the Church of God if it be made known which of all the Latin editions of the sacred books now in circulation is to be regarded as authentic, ordains and declares that the old Latin Vulgate Edition, which, in use for so many hundred years, has been approved by the Church, be in public lectures, disputations, sermons and expositions held as authentic, and that no one dare or presume under any pretext whatsoever to reject it.

Furthermore, to check unbridled spirits, it decrees that no one relying on his own judgment shall, in matters of faith and morals pertaining to the edification of Christian doctrine, distorting the Holy Scriptures in accordance with his own conceptions, presume to interpret them contrary to that sense which holy mother Church, to whom it belongs to judge of their true sense and interpretation, has held and holds, or even contrary to the unanimous teaching of the Fathers, even though such interpretations should never at any time be published. . . .

Furthermore, wishing to repress that boldness whereby the words and sentences of the Holy Scriptures are turned and twisted to all kinds of profane usages, namely, to things scurrilous, fabulous, vain to flatteries, detractions, superstitions, godless and diabolical incantations, divinations, the casting of lots and defamatory libels, to put an end to such irreverence and contempt, and that no one may in the future date use in any manner the words of Holy Scripture for these and similar purposes, it is commanded and enjoined that all people of this kind be restrained by the bishops as violators and profaners of the word of God, with the penalties of the law and other penalties that they may deem fit to impose. . . .

2.4 New Revelations: The Case of the Mormons

Joseph Smith, a young farmer in upstate New York, learned from an angel named Moroni in 1823 the location of gold plates buried in the ground nearby. Smith excavated the plates and translated them, publishing them in 1840 as the *Book of Mormon*, a history of various Hebraic-American peoples. The Mormon (or Latter-Day Saints) religion that subsequently emerged around Smith and the book recognizes several collections of revelations to Smith and others as Scripture, along with the Old and New Testaments "properly translated." Mormonism, moreover, accepts as Scripture the revelations received by the church's presidents. Accordingly, Mormonism keeps the canon open. The relation of Mormonism to Christianity is complex, but Mormons perceive themselves as the only true Christians. The following excerpt from *The Book of Mormon* includes references to Jesus, Moses, Isaiah, and other figures familiar to Christians.

2.4A The Book of Mormon

Chapter 11

Jacob saw his Redeemer—The law of Moses typifies Christ and proves he shall come.

AND now, Jacob spake many more things to my people at that time; nevertheless only these things have I caused to be written, for the things which I have written sufficeth me.

2 And now I, Nephi, write more of the words of Isaiah, for my soul delighteth in his words. For I will liken his words unto my people, and I will send them forth unto all my children, for he verily saw my Redeemer, even as I have seen him.

3 And my brother, Jacob, also has seen him as I have seen him; wherefore, I will send their words forth unto my children to prove unto them that my words are true. Wherefore, by the words of three, God hath said, I will establish my word. Nevertheless, God sendeth more witnesses, and he proveth all his words.

4 Behold, my soul delighteth in proving unto my people the truth of the coming of Christ; for, for this end hath the law of Moses been given; and all things which have been given of God from the beginning of the world, unto man, are the typifying of him.

5 And also my soul delighteth in the covenants of the Lord which he hath made to our fathers; yea, my soul delighteth in his grace, and in his justice, and power, and mercy in the great and eternal plan of deliverance from death.

6 And my soul delighteth in proving unto my people that save Christ should come all men must perish.

7 For if there be no Christ there be no God; and if there be no God we are not, for there could have been no creation. But there is a God, and he is Christ, and he cometh in the fulness of his own time.

8 And now I write some of the words of Isaiah, that whoso of my people shall see these words may lift up their hearts and rejoice for all men. Now these are the words, and ye may liken them unto you and unto all men.

Chapter 12

Isaiah sees the latter-day temple, gathering of Israel, and millennial judgment and peace— The proud and wicked shall be brought low at the Second Coming—Compare Isaiah 2.

THE word that Isaiah, the son of Amoz, saw concerning Judah and Jerusalem:

2 And it shall come to pass in the last days, when the mountain of the Lord's house shall be established in the top of the mountains, and shall be exalted above the hills, and all nations shall flow unto it.

3 And many people shall go and say, Come ye, and let us go up to the mountain of the Lord, to the house of the God of Jacob; and he will teach us of his ways, and we will walk in his paths; for out of Zion shall go forth the law, and the word of the Lord from Jerusalem.

4 And he shall judge among the nations, and shall rebuke many people: and they shall beat their swords into plow-shares, and their spears into pruning-hooks—nation shall not lift up sword against nation, neither shall they learn war any more.

5 O house of Jacob, come ye and let us walk in the light of the Lord; yea, come, for ye have all gone astray, every one to his wicked ways.

6 Therefore, O Lord, thou hast forsaken thy people, the house of Jacob, because they be replenished from the east, and hearken unto soothsayers like the Philistines, and they please themselves in the children of strangers.

7 Their land also is full of silver and gold, neither is there any end of their treasures; their land is also full of horses, neither is there any end of their chariots.

8 Their land is also full of idols; they worship the work of their own hands, that which their own fingers have made.

9 And the mean man boweth not down, and the great man humbleth himself not, therefore, forgive him not.

10 O ye wicked ones, enter into the rock, and hide thee in the dust, for the fear of the Lord and the glory of his majesty shall smite thee.

11 And it shall come to pass that the lofty looks of man shall be humbled, and the haughtiness of men shall be bowed down, and the Lord alone shall be exalted in that day.

12 For the day of the Lord of Hosts soon cometh upon all nations, yea, upon every one; yea upon the proud and lofty, and upon every one who is lifted up, and he shall be brought low.

13 Yea, and the day of the Lord shall come upon all the "cedars of Lebanon," for they are high and lifted up; and upon all the oaks of Bashan;

14 And upon all the high mountains, and upon all the hills, and upon all the nations which are lifted up and upon every people;

15 And upon every high tower, and upon every fenced wall;

16 And upon all the ships of the sea, and upon all the ships of Tarshish, and upon all pleasant pictures.

17 And the loftiness of man shall be bowed down, and the haughtiness of men shall be made low; and the Lord alone shall be exalted in that day.

18 And the idols he shall utterly abolish.

19 And they shall go into the holes of the rocks, and into the caves of the earth, for the fear of the Lord shall come upon them and the glory of his majesty shall smite them, when he ariseth to shake terribly the earth.

20 In that day a man shall cast his idols of silver, and his idols of gold, which he hath made for himself to worship, to the moles and to the bats;

21 To go into the clefts of the rocks, and into the tops of the ragged rocks, for the fear of the Lord shall come upon them and the majesty of his glory shall smite them, when he ariseth to shake terribly the earth.

22 Cease ye from man whose breath is in his nostrils; for wherein is he to be accounted of?

Chapter 13

Judah and Jerusalem shall be punished for their disobedience—The Lord pleads for and judges his people—The daughters of Zion are cursed and tormented for their worldliness— Compare Isaiah 3

FOR behold, the Lord, the Lord of Hosts, doth take away from Jerusalem, and from Judah, the stay and the staff, the whole staff of bread, and the whole stay of water—

2 The mighty man, and the man of war, the judge, and the prophet, and the prudent, and the ancient;

3 The captain of fifty, and the honorable man, and the counselor, and the cunning artificer, and the eloquent orator.

4 And I will give children unto them to be their princes, and babes shall rule over them.

5 And the people shall be "oppressed, every one by another, and every one by his neighbor; the child shall behave himself proudly against the ancient, and the base against the honorable."

6 When a man shall take hold of his brother of the house of his father, and shall say: Thou hast clothing, be thou our ruler, and let not this ruin come under thy hand—

7 In that day shall he swear, saying: I will not be a healer; for in my house there is neither bread nor clothing; make me not a ruler of the people.

8 For Jerusalem is ruined, and Judah is fallen, because their tongues and their doings have been against the Lord, to provoke the eyes of his glory.

9 The show of their countenance doth witness against them, and doth declare their sin to be even as Sodom, and they cannot hide it. Wo unto their souls, for they have rewarded evil unto themselves!

10 Say unto the righteous that it is well with them; for they shall eat the fruit of their doings.

11 Wo unto the wicked, for they shall perish; for the reward of their hands shall be upon them!

12 And my people, children are their oppressors, and women rule over them. O my people, they who lead thee cause thee to err and destroy the way of thy paths.

13 The Lord standeth up to plead, and standeth to judge the people.

14 The Lord enter into judgment with the ancients of his people and the princes thereof; for ye have eaten up the vineyard and the spoil of the poor in your houses.

15 What mean ye? Ye beat my people to pieces, and grind the faces of the poor, saith the Lord God of Hosts.

16 Moreover, the Lord saith: Because the daughters of Zion are haughty, and walk with stretched-forth necks and wanton eyes, walking and mincing as they go, and making a tinkling with their feet—

17 Therefore the Lord will smite with a scab the crown of the head of the daughters of Zion, and the Lord will discover their secret parts.

18 In that day the Lord will take away the bravery of their tinkling ornaments, and cauls, and round tires like the moon;

19 The chains and the bracelets, and the mufflers;

20 The bonnets, and the ornaments of the legs, and the headbands, and the tablets, and the ear-rings;

21 The rings, and nose jewels;

22 The changeable suits of apparel, and the mantles, and the wimples, and the crisping-pins;

23 The glasses, and the fine linen, and hoods, and the veils.

24 And it shall come to pass, instead of sweet smell there shall be stink; and instead of a girdle, a rent; and instead of well set hair, baldness; and instead of a stomacher, a girding of sackcloth; burning instead of beauty.

25 Thy men shall fall by the sword and thy mighty in the war.

26 And her gates shall lament and mourn; and she shall be desolate, and shall sit upon the ground.

SCRIPTURE AND TRADITION

Chapter 3
In Islam

3.1 Pre-Islamic Arabia

Poetry was the pre-Islamic Arabs' main art form. Much historical, genealogical, cultural, and social lore is preserved in the poetry that has survived. The following poem is known in Arabic as a *qaṣīda,* meaning "ode." According to folklore, seven famous odes were honored by being hung in the Ka'aba sanctuary in Mecca before the coming of Islam. Whatever the truth of that, the typical pre-Islamic Arabic ode celebrated the virtues of desert life and the love of the pure Arabic language among pastoral nomads. Imr al-Qais, pseudonym for a noble Arab of the sixth century named Hunduj, writes autobiographically, to a degree. In any event, his great ode displays key aspects of the qasida, which was a highly stereotyped form of poetry around which bardic tournaments were organized. Typically, an ode contained an "amatory prelude": the expression of a sense of longing and loss when the former encampment where the hero and his beloved had met is discovered; boasting about amatory exploits; doting description of one's riding beast, whether horse or camel; praise of one's patron and derision of his enemies; and, finally, a tour de force description of something, in this case a desert thunderstorm.

3.1A THE ODE OF IMR AL-QAIS

Halt, friends both! Let us weep, recalling a love and a lodging
by the rim of the twisted sands between Ed-Dakhool and Haumal,
Toodih and El-Mikrát, whose trace is not yet effaced
for all the spinning of the south winds and the northern blasts;
there, all about its yards, and away in the dry hollows
you may see the dung of antelopes spattered like peppercorns.
Upon the morn of separation, the day they loaded to part,
by the tribe's acacias it was like I was splitting a colocynth;
there my companions halted their beasts awhile over me
saying, 'Don't perish of sorrow; restrain yourself decently!'
Yet the true and only cure of my grief is tears outpoured:
what is there left to lean on where the trace is obliterated?

Even so, my soul, is your wont; so it was with Umm al-Huwairith
before her, and Umm ar-Rabát her neighbour, at Ma'sal;
when they arose, the subtle musk wafted from them
sweet as the zephyr's breath that bears the fragrance of cloves.
Then my eyes overflowed with tears of passionate yearning
upon my throat, till my tears drenched even my sword's harness.

Oh yes, many a fine day I've dallied with the white ladies,
and especially I call to mind a day at Dára Juljul,
and the day I slaughtered for the virgins my riding-beast
(and oh, how marvellous was the dividing of its loaded saddle),
and the virgins went on tossing its hacked flesh about
and the frilly fat like fringes of twisted silk.
Yes, and the day I entered the litter where Unaiza was
and she cried, 'Out on you! Will you make me walk on my feet?'

She was saying, while the canopy swayed with the pair of us,
'There now, you've hocked my camel, Imr al-Kais. Down with you!'
But I said, 'Ride on, and slacken the beast's reins,
and oh, don't drive me away from your refreshing fruit.
Many's the pregnant woman like you, aye, and the nursing mother
I've night-visited, and made her forget her amuleted one-year-old;
whenever he whimpered behind her, she turned to him
with half her body, her other half unshifted under me.'

Ha, and a day on the back of the sand-hill she denied me
swearing a solemn oath that should never, never be broken.
'Gently now, Fátima! A little less disdainful:
even if you intend to break with me, do it kindly.
If it's some habit of mine that's so much vexed you

just draw off my garments from yours, and they'll slip away.
Puffed-up it is it's made you, that my love for you's killing me
and that whatever you order my heart to do, it obeys.
Your eyes only shed those tears so as to strike and pierce
with those two shafts of theirs the fragments of a ruined heart.
Many's the fair veiled lady, whose tent few would think of seeking,
I've enjoyed sporting with, and not in a hurry either,
slipping past packs of watchmen to reach her, with a whole tribe
hankering after my blood, eager every man-jack to slay me,
what time the Pleiades showed themselves broadly in heaven
glittering like the folds of a woman's bejewelled scarf.
I came, and already she'd stripped off her garments for sleep
beside the tent-flap, all but a single flimsy slip;
and she cried, "God's oath, man, you won't get away with this!
The folly's not left you yet; I see you're as feckless as ever."
Out I brought her, and as she stepped she trailed behind us
to cover our footprints the skirt of an embroidered gown.

But when we had crossed the tribe's enclosure, and dark about us
hung a convenient shallow intricately undulant,
I twisted her side-tresses to me, and she leaned over me;
slender-waisted she was, and tenderly plump her ankles,
shapely and taut her belly, white-fleshed, not the least flabby,
polished the lie of her breast-bones, smooth as a burnished mirror.
She turns away, to show a soft cheek, and wards me off
with the glance of a wild deer of Wajra, a shy gazelle with its fawn;
she shows me a throat like the throat of an antelope, not ungainly
when she lifts it upwards, neither naked of ornament;
she shows me her thick black tresses, a dark embellishment
clustering down her back like bunches of a laden date-tree—
twisted upwards meanwhile are the locks that ring her brow,
the knots cunningly lost in the plaited and loosened strands;
she shows me a waist slender and slight as a camel's nose-rein,
and a smooth shank like the reed of a watered, bent papyrus.
In the morning the grains of musk hang over her couch,
sleeping the forenoon through, not girded and aproned to labour.
She gives with fingers delicate, not coarse; you might say
they are sand-worms of Zaby, or tooth-sticks of ishil-wood.
At eventide she lightens the black shadows, as if she were
the lamp kindled in the night of a monk at his devotions.
Upon the like of her the prudent man will gaze with ardour
eyeing her slim, upstanding, frocked midway between matron and maiden;
like the first egg of the ostrich—its whiteness mingled with yellow—
nurtured on water pure, unsullied by many paddlers.
Let the follies of other men forswear fond passion,
my heart forswears not, nor will forget the love I bear you.

Many's the stubborn foe on your account I've turned and thwarted
sincere though he was in his reproaches, not negligent.'

Oft night like a sea swarming has dropped its curtains
over me, thick with multifarious cares, to try me,
and I said to the night, when it stretched its lazy loins
followed by its fat buttocks, and heaved off its heavy breast,
'Well now, you tedious night, won't you clear yourself off, and let
dawn shine? Yet dawn, when it comes, is no way better than you.
Oh, what a night of a night you are! It's as though the stars
were tied to the Mount of Yadhbul with infinite hempen ropes;
as though the Pleiades in their stable were firmly hung
by stout flax cables to craggy slabs of granite.'

Many's the water-skin of all sorts of folk I have slung
by its strap over my shoulder, as humble as can be, and humped it;
many's the valley, bare as an ass's belly, I've crossed,
a valley loud with the wolf howling like a many-bairned wastrel
to which, howling, I've cried, 'Well, wolf, that's a pair of us,
pretty unprosperous both, if you're out of funds like me.
It's the same with us both—whenever we get aught into our hands
we let it slip through our fingers; tillers of our tilth go pretty thin.'
Often I've been off with the morn, the birds yet asleep in their nests,
my horse short-haired, outstripping the wild game, huge-bodied,
charging, fleet-fleeing, head-foremost, headlong, all together
the match of a rugged boulder hurled from on high by the torrent,
a gay bay, sliding the saddle-felt from his back's thwart
just as a smooth pebble slides off the rain cascading.
Fiery he is, for all his leanness, and when his ardour
boils in him, how he roars—a bubbling cauldron isn't in it!
Sweetly he flows, when the mares floundering wearily
kick up the dust where their hooves drag in the trampled track;
the lightweight lad slips landward from his smooth back,
he flings off the burnous of the hard, heavy rider;
very swift he is, like the toy spinner a boy will whirl
plying it with his nimble hands by the knotted thread.
His flanks are the flanks of a fawn, his legs like an ostrich's;
the springy trot of the wolf he has, the fox's gallop;
sturdy his body—look from behind, and he bars his legs' gap
with a full tail, not askew, reaching almost to the ground;
his back, as he stands beside the tent, seems the pounding-slab
of a bride's perfumes, or the smooth stone a colocynth's broken on;
the blood of the herd's leaders spatters his thrusting neck
like expressed tincture of henna reddening combed white locks.
A flock presented, itself to us, the cows among them
like Duwár virgins mantled in their long-trailing draperies;
turning to flee, they were beads of Yemen spaced with cowries
hung on a boy's neck, he nobly uncled in the clan.
My charger thrust me among the leaders, and way behind him
huddled the stragglers herded together, not scattering;
at one bound he had taken a bull and a cow together
pouncing suddenly, and not a drop of sweat on his body.

Busy then were the cooks, some roasting upon a fire
the grilled slices, some stirring the hasty stew.
Then with the eve we returned, the appraising eye bedazzled
to take in his beauty, looking him eagerly up and down;
all through the night he stood with saddle and bridle upon him,
stood where my eyes could see him, not loose to his will.

Friend, do you see yonder lightning? Look, there goes its glitter
flashing like two hands now in the heaped-up, crowned stormcloud.
Brilliantly it shines—so flames the lamp of an anchorite
as he slops the oil over the twisted wick.
So with my companions I sat watching it between Dárij
and El-Odheib, far-ranging my anxious gaze;
over Katan, so we guessed, hovered the right of its deluge,
its left dropping upon Es-Sitár and further Yadhbul.
Then the cloud started loosing its torrent about Kutaifa
turning upon their beards the boles of the tall kanahbals;
over the hills of El-Kanán swept its flying spray
sending the white wild goats hurtling down on all sides.
At Taimá it left not one trunk of a date-tree standing,
not a solitary fort, save those buttressed with hard rocks;
and Thabeer—why, when the first onrush of its deluge came
Thabeer was a great chieftain wrapped in a striped jubba.
In the morning the topmost peak of El-Mujaimir
was a spindle's whorl cluttered with all the scum of the torrent;
it had flung over the desert of El-Ghabeet its cargo
like a Yemeni merchant unpacking his laden bags.
In the morning the songbirds all along the broad valley
quaffed the choicest of sweet wines rich with spices;
the wild beasts at evening drowned in the furthest reaches
of the wide watercourse lay like drawn bulbs of wild onion.

Muslim tradition has referred to pre-Islamic Arabia as an era of ignorance, cruelty, and irreligion. The following essay is a celebrated note on what the term *al-jāhilīya* (usually translated as the "age of ignorance") applied to that period could have meant according to its own terms, as discovered, for example, in poetry. Ignaz Goldziher (1850–1921) is the founder of modern scientific Islamic studies. He was a Jew from Budapest, Hungary, who excelled in studies of the Bible and Middle Eastern studies. His writings on many aspects of Islam continue today to be mined for their excellent use of sources and their brilliant and judicious interpretations. Some of the technical content and references have been deleted from the following selection.

3.1B WHAT IS MEANT BY 'AL-JĀHILIYYA'

From Islam's earliest times, Muslims have tried to bring order into the narrow picture of the historical development of humanity offered them by their religious view by marking the critical points of history, to delimit historical epochs and divide that development into periods. No comprehensive and self-conscious view of life can forgo this analytical task which for the first time expresses an awareness of the difference between its own essence and past preparatory stages of development.

The division into periods which the Muslims undertook is by its nature concerned only with the religious development of humanity, and takes account only of elements which Islam believes to have been its own preparation. The periods of Judaism, Christianity and Islam are the three epochs which are differentiated as phases in the development of the history of the world, or rather of religions. The Muslims express this sequence by the simile of morning, noon, and evening prayer. The duration of the world is taken to be a day. 'Your relation to the owners of the two books,' the Prophet is made to say to true believers, 'can be illustrated by the following parable: A certain man hired workers and told them: He who works the whole day will receive a certain sum in wages. A few of them worked only till noon (these are the Jews) and said: We will not work any longer, we renounce the agreed wages, and what we have done up to now shall be done for nothing. When they were not to be persuaded to finish their work and gain their full wages the employer hired other men for the rest of the day to whom he promised, on completion of the work, the full reward promised to the first group. But these people too (they are the Christians) stopped work in the afternoon and gave up their wages, even after they were told that they had but a few more hours' work before gaining the whole reward. Now new workers were yet again engaged, the Muslims, who worked until sunset and gained the whole reward.'

This division, however, refers only to the development of Islamic monotheism, and only considers its preparatory stages; the heathen world does not appear in it at all. The consideration of the relationship of Islam to previous, more especially Arab, paganism, resulted in the well-known division, which also is hinted at in the Koran, of the history of the Arab people into two periods: that of the Jāhiliyya and that of Islam. The whole of the pagan, pre-Islamic time is al-Jāhiliyya. Between these two periods there is the *Nubuwwa*, i.e. the time of Muhammed's appearance as prophet and of his missionary work. For the sake of completeness it might be mentioned that the Jāhiliyya is subdivided into two periods: the older period (i.e. the time from Adam to Noah or Abraham—according to others from Noah to Idrīs) and the more recent one (from Jesus to Muhammed).

This, as we see, rather unclear sub-division arose owing to misunderstanding of the Koranic passage 33:33 where Muhammed says to the women that they should not flirt as was customary in the days of the 'first Jāhiliyya'.

Following the general Muslim explanation we tended to think of the 'Jāhiliyya', in contrast to 'Islam', as 'the time of ignorance.' This conception is wrong. When Muhammed contrasted the change brought about by his preaching with earlier times he did not seek to describe those times as times of ignorance, since in that case he would not have opposed ignorance with devotion to God and confidence in God but with al-'ilm, 'knowledge.' In this book we have explained the word al-Jāhiliyya as 'time of barbarism' because Muhammed wanted to contrast the Islam that he preached with barbarism.

Though it may seem trivial and pedantic to put so much stress on the mere translation of a word, we do think that a proper definition of the concept of Jāhiliyya is important for these studies, since it aids us in finding the correct point of view for the understanding of Muslim opinion about pagan times. Therefore it will be well worth the space needed to give at length the reasons for our opinion.

Muhammed presumably did not intend to express anything else by Jāhiliyya than the condition which in the poetical documents of the time preceding him is described with the verb *jhl*, the substantive *jahl*, and the *nomen agentis, jāhil*. It is true that in the old language, too, we find the concept of knowledge (*'ilm*) contrasted to *jahl*, but this opposition is founded on a secondary meaning of *jhl*. The original meaning is seen in an antithesis of this word group, much more common in the older language, with *ḥlm, ḥilm* and *ḥalīm*. According to their etymological meaning these words describe the concept of firmness, strength, physical integrity and health, and in addition moral integrity, the 'solidity' of a moral character, unemotional, calm deliberation, mildness of manner. A *ḥalīm* is what we would call a civilized man. The opposition to all this is the *jāhil*, a wild, violent and impetuous character who follows the inspiration of unbridled passion and is cruel by following his animal instincts; in one word, a barbarian. 'May no one act wildly against us (*lā yajhalan*) because we then would excel the wildness of those acting wildly (*jahl al-jāhilīna*).' The kind of character and manner of action against which 'Amr b. Kulthūm wishes to protect himself by threatening revenge in the way of the Jāhiliyya is usually contrasted to *al-ḥilm*, i.e. mildness—and not *al-'ilm. Wā-law shā'a qawmī kāna ḥilmiya fīhimī / wa-kāna 'alā juhhāli a'dā'ihim jahlī*, 'If my tribe would have it I would show mildness to them—and practise my wildness against its wild enemies'. . . .

The false assumption that *jāhil* is the opposite to 'knowing' and that therefore *istajhala* means 'to consider someone ignorant' has misled the translators. Freytag, who misunderstood al-Tabrīzī's and al-Marzūqī's *scholia* which lead to the proper meaning; translates: *Mansuetudinem meam in causa fuisse puto cur gens contra me ageret et fit interdum ut mansuetus ignorans habetur.* E. Rehatshek translates: 'I think [my] meekness instigated my people against me, and verily a meek man is considered a fool.' Here also Rückert rightly understood what Qays meant to say (I, p. 135) *Ich denk', um Mässigung (ḥilm) kann mein Volk mich loben, Doch der Gemässigste (ḥalīm) gereizt mag toben*, i.e, literally: 'A wild man can be brought to wild excesses.'

Istajhala means: to display the manner of a *jāhil*, here in the passive: to be roused to such wild behaviour. The second line fits in with this: 'I tested the men and they tested me—there were amongst them some who showed themselves crooked (brutal and unjust) to me and some who behaved straight (well and justly).' This contrast of 'crooked' and 'straight' (*muʿawwaj* and *mustaqīm*) corresponds also elsewhere in the poetry of Arab heroes to the contrast of *jāhil* with *ḥalīm*.

> *Fa-in kuntu muḥtājan ilaʾl-ḥilmi innanī / ilaʾl-jahli fī baʿḍiʾl-aḥāyīni aḥwaju*
> *Wa-lī farasun liʾl-ḥilmi biʾl-ḥilmi muljamu / wa-lī farasun liʾl-jahli biʾl-jahli musraju*
> *Fa-man rāma taqwīmī fa-innī muqawwamun / wa-man rāma taʿwījī fa-innī muʿawwaju.*

> Though I need mildness, at times I need wildness (*jahl*) even more.
> I have a horse bridled with mildness and I have another bridled with wildness.
> He who wants me to be straight, to him I am straight, but he who desires my
>   crookedness, for him I am crooked.

The pagan hero al-Shanfarā says in his famous *Lāmiyyat al-ʿArab*, v. 53: 'The wild desires (*al-ajhālu*) do not overwhelm my mild sentiment (*ḥilmī*) and one does not see me looking for bad news and slandering.' This shows how the Arab made from *jahl* the plural *ajhāl* in order to express the multitude of evil passions and the various points of bestial brutality; a similar plural was formed from *ḥilm* (*aḥlām*).

Ṭarafa describes the virtue of noble Arabs: 'They suppress brutality (*al-jahla*) in their circles and come to the aid of the man of discretion (*dhiʾl-ḥilmi*), the noble one' and in the same sense another poet says: 'If you come to them you will find round their houses circles in which brutality is cured by their good nature (*majālisa qad yushfā bi-aḥlāmihaʾl-jahlu*.)'

Jahl thus was neither a virtue to the Arabs of an older time—it was appropriate to a young and impetuous character—nor was it entirely condemned. Part of the *muruwwa* (i.e., "manliness") was knowing when mildness was not befitting the character of a hero and when *jahl* was indicated: 'I am ferocious (*jahūl*) where mildness (*taḥallum*) would make the hero despicable, meek (*ḥalīm*) when ferocity (*jahl*) would be unfitting to a noble', or, as is said in the spirit of paganism: 'Some meekness is shame (*inna minaʾ l-ḥilmi dhullun*) as you well know, but mildness when one is able (to be ferocious) is honourable.'

Another poet, expressing the same thought, tells under what circumstances *ḥilm* would be shameful and base:

> The wild man amongst us is ferocious (*jāhil*) in the defence of his guest;
> The ferocious man is mild (*ḥalīm*) when insulted by him (the guest).

This *jahl* is expressed not in rough words but in powerful deeds: 'We act wildly with our hands (*tajhalu aydīnā*) but our mind is meek, we scorn with deeds and not with talk.'

Examples could be multiplied and a number of examples from more recent poetry could be cited to elucidate this antithesis. *Jāhil* and *ḥalīm* are two groups in one or the other of which every man belongs: *wa-maʾl-nāsu illā jāhilun wa-ḥalīmu*.

We will just refer to some old proverbs where the contrast is shown: *al-ḥalīm maṭiyyat al-jahūl*, 'the meek is the pack animal of the ferocious,' i.e. he allows himself to be ruthlessly used without *ḥasbu'l-ḥalīmi anna'l-nāsa anṣāruhu 'ala'l-jāhili*, 'It is a satisfaction for a decent man that his fellow-man help him against the *jāhil*.' In none of these examples can *jāhil* mean ignorant, nor can it do so in the proverb (lacking in al-Maydānī): *ajhalu min al-namr*, 'more ferocious than the tiger.' In the same way a saying of the Prophet, transmitted by Abū Hurayra, demands of him who is fasting *wa-lā yajhal*, i.e., that he should not be roused to deeds of brutality; 'if someone wishes to fight or insult him he should say: I am fasting.'

When, therefore, Muhammed and his first successors refer to the pre-Islamic times as the Jāhiliyya we must not take this in the sense of the χρόνους τῆς ἀγνοίας ["time of ignorance"], which, according to the Apostle, preceded Christianity, since for this ἀγνοία [ignorance] Muhammed used the Arab term *dalāl* (error), which he contrasts with his *hudā* (right guidance). The Jāhiliyya in this context is nothing but the time in which *jahl*—in the sense which we have seen—was prevalent, i.e. barbarism and cruelty. When the proponents of Islam say that it has ended the customs and habits of the Jāhiliyya, they are thinking of these barbaric customs and the wild mentality which distinguish Arab paganism from Islam, and through the abolition of which Muhammed intended to become the reformer of his people's morality—the arrogance of the Jāhiliyya (*ḥamiyyat al-Jāhiliyya*) [Sura 48:26], the tribal pride and the eternal feuds, the cult of revenge, rejection of forgiveness, and all the other particularities of Arab paganism which were to be superseded by Islam. 'If one does not turn from the lying speech and the *jahl* (i.e. wild habits),' transmits Abū Hurayra, 'verily, God does not require one to restrict one's food and drink.' This tradition clearly shows that in early Islamic times *jahl* was understood in the same way as in old Arabic poetry. 'Previously we were a people, men of the Jāhiliyya,' Ja'far b. Abī Ṭālib is made to say to the Ethiopian prince: 'we prayed to idols, ate carrion and committed shameful deeds; we disrespected the ties of kinship and violated the duty of faithfulness; the strong among us oppressed (ate up) the weaker ones. Thus we were, until God sent a Prophet from our midst, whose descent and justice, righteousness and virtue are known to us. He called us to God so that we might recognise His unity and pray to Him and cast aside what our parents adored: stones and idols; he commanded us to speak the truth, be faithful and respect ties of blood, fulfill our duties of protection and keep away from forbidden things and bloodshed. He forbade evil vices and unjust talk, squandering the goods of orphans, slandering innocent people, etc.' In the invitations to pagans to be converted to Islam, almost exclusively moral—not ritual—observances are demanded; thus, for example, the homage of the twelve neophytes at the 'Aqaba takes place under the following conditions: that they will put no one on a level with God, will not steal, commit adultery or infanticide or be arrogant. This is the point of view from which older Islam contrasts the Jāhiliyya with Islam. The ritual laws of Islam are also mentioned, but the main point in a life contrary to the Jāhiliyya lies in turning away from worshipping lifeless things and more especially putting an end to immoral and cruel actions in which the Prophet and his apostles see the main characteristics of the Jāhiliyya. From this point of view the Jāhiliyya is the contrast to what is called *dīn* [professing] in a religious sense, and the opposition of the two words is attested from the earliest days in Islam.

What Islam attempted to achieve was, after all, nothing but a *ḥilm* of higher nature than that taught by the code of virtues of pagan days. Many a virtue of Arab paganism was—as we have seen—reduced to the level of a vice by Muhammed, and on the other hand many a social act, considered dishonourable by Arabs, was now elevated to the status of a virtue. He is fond of calling people *ḥalīm* who practise forgiveness and leniency. With this in mind he [the Qur'an] often calls Allah *ḥalīm*, a title which he gives with preference to Ibrāhīm amongst the prophets.

Muhammed's teaching thus brought about a change in the meaning of *ḥilm* and hence we can understand that his pagan fellow-citizens, who opposed his teaching, constantly accuse the reformer of declaring their *ḥilm* to be folly (*yusaffih aḥlāmanā*) branding as barbaric acts (*Jāhiliyya*) deeds which in their eyes were of the highest virtue. The word *safīh*, fool, is a synonym of the word *jāhil* and belongs to that group of words which, like *kesīl* and *sākhāl* (in Hebrew), describe not only fools but also cruel and unjust men.

Accordingly, when Zayd b. ʿAmr b. Nufayl is converted to Islam and renounces paganism he says: 'I will no longer pay homage to (the idol) Ghanm, who was God to us when my *ḥilm* was small,' i.e. when I was still *jāhil*, in the time of the Jāhiliyya. The latter word is thus also in the early days of Islam, as in pagan times, the conceptual opposite of *ḥilm* and not yet of *ʿilm* (science). These two are well differentiated. 'There are people', says a tradition of ʿUbāda b. al-Ṣāmit, 'who had science and *ḥilm* and others who had but one of the two.'

Because Islamic ethics restricted the idea of *ḥalīm* to such men as were virtuous in the Islamic sense, it was quite possible for *muʾmin*, right believer, to be used as the opposite of *jāhil*, i.e., from the point of view of Islam, a man acting according to God's will in practical things as well as in the dogmatic sense. Thus Rabīʿ b. Khaytham speaks of two kinds of men: one is either *muʾmin*—and such a one must not be harmed—or *jāhil*—to whom one must not be cruel. Profane literature also shows this contrast, which is also projected back into earlier times. It is told of Qays b. ʿĀṣim, whom his contemporary, the Prophet, called 'master of all tent dwellers' (*sayyid ahl al-wabar*), that he belonged 'to the *ḥulamāʾ* of the Banū Tamīm and abstained from drinking wine even in pagan days.'

3.2 MUHAMMAD

The biography of Muhammad is drawn from a variety of original sources. The most authoritative narrative biography is the *Sirat Rasul Allah* of Ibn Ishaq (d. ca. 767), which collects most of what is known about the Prophet. The following selections are from Alfred Guillaume's translation of Ibn Ishaq and cover Muhammad's call to be a prophet, the Hijra or "emigration" from Mecca to Medina in 622, and Muhammad's death.

3.2A *The Life of Muhammad*

The Prophet's Mission

When Muhammad the apostle of God reached the age of forty God sent him in compassion to mankind, 'as an evangelist to all men.' Now God had made a covenant with every prophet whom he had sent before him that he should believe in him, testify to his truth and help him against his adversaries, and he required of them that they should transmit that to everyone who believed in them, and they carried out their obligations in that respect. God said to Muhammad, 'When God made a covenant with the prophets (He said) this is the scripture and wisdom which I have given you, afterwards an apostle will come confirming what you know that you may believe in him and help him.' He said, 'Do you accept this and take up my burden?' i.e. the burden of my agreement which I have laid upon you. They said, 'We accept it.' He answered, 'Then bear witness and I am a witness with you.' Thus God made a covenant with all the prophets that they should testify to his truth and help him against his adversaries and they transmitted that obligation to those who believed in them among the two monotheistic religions. . . .

Al-Zuhrī related from 'Urwa b. Zubayr that 'Ā'isha told him that when Allah desired to honour Muhammad and have mercy on His servants by means of him, the first sign of prophethood vouchsafed to the apostle was true visions, resembling the brightness of daybreak, which were shown to him in his sleep. And Allah, she said, made him love solitude so that he liked nothing better than to be alone.

'Abdu'l-Malik b. 'Ubaydullah b. Abū Sufyān b. al-'Ala' b. Jariya the Thaqafite who had a retentive memory related to me from a certain scholar that the apostle at the time when Allah willed to bestow His grace upon him and endow him with prophethood would go forth for his affair and journey far afield until he reached the glens of Mecca and the beds of its valleys where no house was in sight; and not a stone or tree that he passed by but would say, 'Peace unto thee, O apostle of Allah.' And the apostle would turn to his right and left and look behind him and he would see naught but trees and stones. Thus he stayed seeing and hearing so long as it pleased Allah that he should stay. Then Gabriel came to him with the gift of God's grace whilst he was on Ḥirā' in the month of Ramaḍān.

Wahb b. Kaisān a client of the family of al-Zubayr told me: I heard 'Abdullah b. al-Zubayr say to 'Ubayd b. 'Umayr b. Qatāda the Laythite, 'O 'Ubayd tell us how began the prophethood which was first bestowed on the apostle when Gabriel came to him.' And 'Ubayd in my presence related to 'Abdullah and those with him as follows: The apostle would pray in seclusion on Ḥirā' every year for a month to practise *taḥannuth* as was the custom of Quraysh in heathen days. *Taḥannuth* is religious devotion. Abū Ṭālib said:

From "Muhammad and the Qur'an: The Life of Muhammad" in Alfred Guillaume, *The Life of Muhammad: A Translation of Ibn Ishaq's Sirat Rasul Allah.* Copyright © 1967. Reprinted with the permission of Oxford University Press (Pakistan).

By Thaur and him who made Thabīr firm in its place
And by those going up to ascend Ḥirā' and coming down.[1]

Wahb b. Kaisān told me that 'Ubayd said to him: Every year during that month the apostle would pray in seclusion and give food to the poor that came to him. And when he completed the month and returned from his seclusion, first of all before entering his house he would go to the Ka'ba and walk round it seven times or as often as it pleased God; then he would go back to his house until in the year when God sent him, in the month of Ramaḍān in which God willed concerning him what He willed of His grace, the apostle set forth to Ḥirā' as was his wont, and his family with him. When it was the night on which God honoured him with his mission and showed mercy on His servants thereby, Gabriel brought him the command of God. 'He came to me,' said the apostle of God, 'while I was asleep, with a coverlet of brocade whereon was some writing, and said, "Read!" I said, "What shall I read?" He pressed me with it so tightly that I thought it was death; then he let me go and said, "Read!" I said, "What shall I read?" He pressed me with it again so that I thought it was death; then he let me go and said "Read!" I said, "What shall I read?" He pressed me with it the third time so that I thought it was death and said "Read!" I said, "What then shall I read?"—and this I said only to deliver myself from him, lest he should do the same to me again. He said:

"Read in the name of thy Lord who created,
Who created man of blood coagulated.
Read! Thy Lord is the most beneficent,
Who taught by the pen,
Taught that which they knew not unto men" (96:1–5).

So I read it, and he departed from me. And I awoke from my sleep, and it was as though these words were written on my heart. Now none of God's creatures was more hateful to me than an (ecstatic) poet or a man possessed: I could not even look at them. I thought, Woe is me poet or possessed—Never shall Quraysh say this of me! I will go to the top of the mountain and throw myself down that I may kill myself and gain rest. So I went forth to do so and then when I was midway on the mountain, I heard a voice from heaven saying, "O Muhammad! thou art the apostle of God and I am Gabriel." I raised my head towards heaven to see (who was speaking), and lo, Gabriel in the form of a man with feet astride the horizon, saying, "O Muhammad! thou art the apostle of God and I am Gabriel." I stood gazing at him, moving neither forward nor backward; then I began to turn my face away from him, but towards whatever region of the sky I looked, I saw him as before. And I continued standing there, neither advancing nor turning back, until Khadīja sent her messengers in search of me and they gained the high ground above Mecca and returned to her while I was standing in the same place; then he parted from me and I from him, returning to my family. And I came to Khadīja and

---

[1] Thaur and Thabir are mountains near Mecca.

sat by her thigh and drew close to her. She said, "O Abū'l-Qāsim, where hast thou been? By God, I sent my messengers in search of thee, and they reached the high ground above Mecca and returned to me." I said to her, "Woe is me poet or possessed." She said, "I take refuge in God from that O Abū'l-Qāsim. God would not treat you thus since he knows your truthfulness, your great trustworthiness, your fine character, and your kindness. This cannot be, my dear. Perhaps you did see something." "Yes, I did," I said. Then I told her of what I had seen; and she said, "Rejoice, O son of my uncle, and be of good heart. Verily, by Him in whose hand is Khadīja's soul, I have hope that thou wilt be the prophet of this people.'" Then she rose and gathered her garments about her and set forth to her cousin Waraqa b. Naufal b. Asad b. 'Abdu'l-'Uzzā b. Quṣayy, who had become a Christian and read the scriptures and learned from those that follow the Torah and the Gospel. And when she related to him what the apostle of God told her he had seen and heard, Waraqa cried, 'Holy! Holy! Verily by Him in whose hand is Waraqa's soul, if thou hast spoken to me the truth, O Khadīja, there hath come unto him the greatest Nāmūs (meaning Gabriel) who came to Moses aforetime, and lo, he is the prophet of this people. Bid him be of good heart.' So Khadīja returned to the apostle of God and told him what Waraqa had said. And when the apostle of God had finished his period of seclusion and returned (to Mecca), in the first place he performed the circumambulation of the Ka'ba, as was his wont. While he was doing it, Waraqa met him and said, 'O son of my brother, tell me what thou hast seen and heard.' The apostle told him, and Waraqa said, 'Surely, by Him in whose hand is Waraqa's soul, thou art the prophet of this people. There hath come unto thee the greatest Nāmūs, who came unto Moses. Thou wilt be called a liar, and they will use thee despitefully and cast thee out and fight against thee. Verily, if I live to see that day, I will help God in such wise as He knoweth.' Then he brought his head near to him and kissed his forehead; and the apostle went to his own house. (Waraqa's words added to his confidence and lightened his anxiety.)

Ismā'īl b. Abū Ḥakīm, a freedman of the family of al-Zubayr, told me on Khadīja's authority that she said to the apostle of God, 'O son of my uncle, are you able to tell me about your visitant, when he comes to you?' He replied that he could, and she asked him to tell her when he came. So when Gabriel came to him, as he was wont, the apostle said to Khadīja, 'This is Gabriel who has just come to me.' 'Get up, O son of my uncle,' she said, 'and sit by my left thigh.' The apostle did so, and she said, 'Can you see him?' 'Yes,' he said. She said, 'Then turn round and sit on my right thigh.' He did so, and she said, 'Can you see him?' When he said that he could she asked him to move and sit in her lap. When he had done this she again asked if he could see him, and when he said yes, she disclosed her form and cast aside her veil while the apostle was sitting in her lap. Then she said, 'Can you see him?' And he replied, 'No.' She said, 'O son of my uncle, rejoice and be of good heart, by God he is an angel and not a satan.'

I told 'Abdullah b. Ḥasan this story and he said, 'I heard my mother Fāṭima, daughter of Ḥusayn, talking about this tradition from Khadīja, but as I heard it she made the apostle of God come inside her shift, and thereupon Gabriel departed, and she said to the apostle of God, "This verily is an angel and not a satan."'

The Beginning of the Sending Down of the Qurān

The apostle began to receive revelations in the month of Ramaḍān. In the words of God, 'The month of Ramaḍān in which the Qurān was brought down as a guidance to men, and proofs of guidance and a decisive criterion' (Sura 2:185). And again, 'Verily we have sent it down on the night of destiny, and what has shown you what the night of destiny is? The night of destiny is better than a thousand months. In it the angels and the spirit descend by their Lord's permission with every matter. It is peace until the rise of dawn' (Sura 97). Again, '. . . by the perspicuous book, verily we have sent it down in a blessed night. Verily, we were warning. In it every wise matter is decided as a command from us. Verily we sent it down.' And again, 'Had you believed in God and what we sent down to Our servant on the day of decision, the day on which the two parties met' (Sura 44:1–5), i.e. the meeting of the apostle with the polytheists in Badr. Abū Jaʿfar Muhammad b. ʿAlī b. al-Ḥusayn told me that the apostle of God met the polytheists in Badr on the morning of Friday, the 17th of Ramaḍān.

Then revelation came fully to the apostle while he was believing in Him and in the truth of His message. He received it willingly, and took upon himself what it entailed whether of man's goodwill or anger. Prophecy is a troublesome burden—only strong, resolute messengers can bear it by God's help and grace, because of the opposition which they meet from men in conveying God's message. The apostle carried out God's orders in spite of the opposition and ill treatment which he met with.

The Hijra of the Prophet

After his companions had left, the apostle stayed in Mecca waiting for permission to migrate. Except for Abū Bakr and ʿAlī, none of his supporters were left but those under restraint and those who had been forced to apostatize. The former kept asking the apostle for permission to emigrate and he would answer, 'Don't be in a hurry; it may be that God will give you a companion.' Abū Bakr hoped that it would be Muhammad himself.

When the Quraysh saw that the apostle had a party and companions not of their tribe and outside their territory, and that his companions had migrated to join them, and knew that they had settled in a new home and had gained protectors, they feared that the apostle might join them, since they knew that he had decided to fight them. So they assembled in their council chamber, the house of Quṣayy b. Kilāb where all their important business was conducted, to take counsel what they should do in regard to the apostle, for they were now in fear of him.

One of our companions whom I have no reason to doubt told me on the authority of ʿAbdullah b. Abū Najīḥ from Mujāhid b. Jubayr father of al-Ḥajjāj; and another person of the same character on the authority of ʿAbdullah b. ʿAbbās told me that when they had fixed a day to come to a decision about the apostle, on the morning of that very day which was called the day of al-Zaḥma the devil came to them in the form of a handsome old man clad in a mantle and stood at the door of the house. When they saw him standing there they asked him who he was and he told them that he was a shaykh from the highlands who had heard of their intention and had come to hear what they had to say and perhaps to give them counsel and advice. He was invited to enter and there he found the leaders of Quraysh [a listing is provided]. . . . and others including some who were not of Quraysh.

The discussion opened with the statement that now that Muhammad had gained adherents outside the tribe they were no longer safe against a sudden attack and the meeting was to determine the best course to pursue. One advised that they should put him in irons behind bars and then wait until the same fate overtook him as befell his like, the poets Zuhayr and Nābigha, and others. The shaykh objected to this on the ground that news would leak out that he was imprisoned, and immediately his followers would attack and snatch him away; then their numbers would so grow that they would destroy the authority of Quraysh altogether. They must think of another plan. Another man suggested that they should drive him out of the country. They did not care where he went or what happened to him once he was out of sight and they were rid of him. They could then restore their social life to its former state. Again the shaykh objected that it was not a good plan. His fine speech and beautiful diction and the compelling force of his message were such that if he settled with some Beduin tribe he would win them over so that they would follow him and come and attack them in their land and rob them of their position and authority and then he could do what he liked with them. They must think of a better plan.

Thereupon Abū Jahl said that he had a plan which had not been suggested hitherto, namely that each clan should provide a young, powerful, well-born, aristocratic warrior; that each of these should be provided with a sharp sword; then that each of them should strike a blow at him and kill him. Thus they would be relieved of him, and responsibility for his blood would lie upon all the clans. The B. 'Abdu Manāf could not fight them all and would have to accept the blood-money which they would all contribute to. The shaykh exclaimed: 'The man is right. In my opinion it is the only thing to do.' Having come to a decision the people dispersed.

Then Gabriel came to the apostle and said: 'Do not sleep tonight on the bed on which you usually sleep.' Before much of the night had passed they assembled at his door waiting for him to go to sleep so that they might fall upon him. When the apostle saw what they were doing he told 'Alī to lie on his bed and to wrap himself in his green Ḥaḍramī mantle; for no harm would befall him. He himself used to sleep in this mantle.

Yazīd b. Ziyād on the authority of Muhammad b. Ka'b. al-Qurazī told me that when they were all outside his door Abū Jahl said to them: 'Muhammad alleges that if you follow him you will be kings of the Arabs and the Persians. Then after death you will be raised to gardens like those of the Jordan. But if you do not follow him you will be slaughtered, and when you are raised from the dead you will be burned in the fire of hell.' The apostle came out to them with a handful of dust saying: 'I do say that. You are one of them.' God took away their sight so that they could not see him and he began to sprinkle the dust on their heads as he recited these verses: 'Ya Sīn, by the wise Quran. Thou art of those that art sent on a straight path, a revelation of the Mighty the Merciful' as far as the words 'And we covered them and they could not see' (Sura 36:2–10). When he had finished reciting not one of them but had dust upon his head. Then he went wherever he wanted to go and someone not of their company came up and asked them what they were waiting for there. When they said that they were waiting for Muhammad he said: 'But good heavens Muhammad came out to you and put dust on the head of every single man of you and then went off on his own affairs. Can't you see what has happened to you?' They put up their hands and felt the dust on their heads. Then they began to search and saw 'Alī on the bed wrapped in the apostle's mantle and said, 'By God it is Muhammad sleeping in his mantle.' Thus they remained until the morning when 'Alī rose from the bed and then they realized that the man had told them the truth.

Among the verses of the Quran which God sent down about that day and what they had agreed upon are: 'And when the unbelievers plot to shut thee up or to kill thee or to drive thee out they plot, but God plots also, and God is the best of plotters' (Sura 8:30); and 'Or they say he is a poet for whom we may expect the misfortune of fate. Say: Go on expecting for I am with you among the expectant' (Sura 52:31).

It was then that God gave permission to his prophet to migrate. Now Abū Bakr was a man of means, and at the time that he asked the apostle's permission to migrate and he replied 'Do not hurry; perhaps God will give you a companion,' hoping that the apostle meant himself he bought two camels and kept them tied up in his house supplying them with fodder in preparation for departure.

A man whom I have no reason to doubt told me as from 'Urwa b. al-Zubayr that 'Ā'isha said: The apostle used to go to Abū Bakr's house every day either in the early morning or at night; but on the day when he was given permission to migrate from Mecca he came to us at noon, an hour at which he was not wont to come. As soon as he saw him Abū Bakr realized that something had happened to bring him at this hour. When he came in Abū Bakr gave up his seat to him. Only my sister Asmā' and I were there and the apostle asked him to send us away. 'But they are my two daughters and they can do no harm, may my father and my mother be your ransom,' said Abū Bakr. 'God has given me permission to depart and migrate,' he answered. 'Together?' asked Abū Bakr. 'Together,' he replied. And by God before that day I had never seen anyone weep for joy as Abū Bakr wept then. At last he said, 'O prophet of God, these are the two camels which I have held in readiness for this.' So they hired 'Abdullah b. Arqaṭ, a man of B. 'l-Di'l b. Bakr whose mother was a woman of B. Saham b. 'Amr, and a polytheist to lead them on the way, and they handed over to him their two camels and he kept them and fed them until the appointed day came.

According to what I have been told none knew when the apostle left except 'Alī and Abū Bakr and the latter's family. I have heard that the apostle told 'Alī about his departure and ordered him to stay behind in Mecca in order to return goods which men had deposited with the apostle; for anyone in Mecca who had property which he was anxious about left it with him because of his notorious honesty and trustworthiness.

When the apostle decided to go he came to Abū Bakr and the two of them left by a window in the back of the latter's house and made for a cave on Thaur, a mountain below Mecca. Having entered, Abū Bakr ordered his son 'Abdullah to listen to what people were saying and to come to them by night with the day's news. He also ordered 'Āmir b. Fuhayra, his freedman, to feed his flock by day and to bring them to them in the evening in the cave. Asmā' his daughter used to come at night with food to sustain them.

The two of them stayed in the cave for three days. When Quraysh missed the apostle they offered a hundred she-camels to anyone who would bring him back. During the day 'Abdullah was listening to their plans and conversation and would come at night with the news. 'Āmir used to pasture his flock with the shepherds of Mecca and when night fell would bring them to the cave where they milked them and slaughtered some. When 'Abdullah left them in the morning to go to Mecca, 'Āmir would take the sheep over the same route to cover his tracks. When the three days had passed and men's interest waned, the man they had hired came with their camels and one of his own. Asmā' came too with a bag of provisions; but she had forgotten to bring a rope, so that when they started she could not tie the bag on the camel. Thereupon she undid her girdle and using it as a rope tied the bag to the saddle. For this reason she got the name 'She of the girdle.'

When Abū Bakr brought the two camels to the apostle he offered the better one to him and invited him to ride her. But the apostle refused to ride an animal which was not his own and when Abū Bakr wanted to give him it he demanded to know what he had paid for it and bought it from him. They rode off, and Abū Bakr carried 'Āmir his freedman behind him to act as a servant on the journey.

I was told that Asmā' said, 'When the apostle and Abū Bakr had gone, a number of Quraysh including Abū Jahl came to us and stood at the door. When I went out to them they asked where my father was and when I said that I did not know Abū Jahl, who was a rough dissolute man, slapped my face so violently that my earring flew off. Then they took themselves off and we remained for three days without news until a man of the Jinn came from the lower part of Mecca singing some verses in the Arab way. And lo people were following him and listening to his voice but they could not see him, until he emerged from the upper part of Mecca saying the while:

> God the Lord of men give the best of his rewards
> To the two companions who rested in the two tents of Umm Ma'bad.
> They came with good intent and went off at nightfall.
> May Muhammad's companion prosper!
> May the place of the Banū Ka'b's woman bring them luck,
> For she was a look-out for the believers.

Asmā' continued: 'When we heard his words we knew that the apostle was making for Medina. There were four of them: the apostle, Abū Bakr, 'Āmir, and 'Abdullah b. Arqaṭ their guide.'

Yaḥya b. ʿAbbād b. ʿAbdullah b. al-Zubayr told me that his father ʿAbbād told him that his grandmother Asmāʾ said: 'When the apostle went forth with Abū Bakr the latter carried all his money with him to the amount of five or six thousand dirhams. My grandfather Abū Quḥāfa who had lost his sight came to call on us saying that he thought that Abū Bakr had put us in a difficulty by taking off all his money. I told him that he had left us plenty of money. And I took some stones and put them in a niche where Abū Bakr kept his money; then I covered them with a cloth and took his hand and said, "Put your hand on this money, father." He did so and said: "There's nothing to worry about; he has done well in leaving you this, and you will have enough." In fact he had left us nothing, but I wanted to set the old man's mind at rest.'

Al-Zuhrī told me that ʿAbduʾl-Rahmān b. Mālik b. Juʿshum told him from his father, from his uncle Surāqa b. Mālik b. Juʿshum: 'When the apostle migrated Quraysh offered a reward of a hundred camels to anyone who would bring him back. While I was sitting in my people's assembly one of our men came up and stopped saying, "By God, I've just seen three riders passing. I think they must be Muhammad and his companions." I gave him a wink enjoining silence and said "They are the so-and-so looking for a lost camel." "Perhaps so," he said and remained silent. I remained there for a short while; then I got up and went to my house and ordered my horse to be got ready, for it was tethered for me in the bottom of the valley. Then I asked for my weapons and they were brought from the back of the room. Then I took my divining arrows and went out, having put on my armour. Then I cast the divining arrows and out came the arrow which I did not want: "Do him no harm." I did the same again and got the same result. I was hoping to bring him back to Quraysh so that I might win the hundred camels reward.

'I rode in pursuit of him and when my horse was going at a good pace he stumbled and threw me. I thought this was somewhat unusual so I resorted to the divining arrows again and out came the detestable "Do him no harm." But I refused to be put off and rode on in pursuit. Again my horse stumbled and threw me, and again I tried the arrows with the same result. I rode on, and at last as I saw the little band my horse stumbled with me and its forelegs went into the ground and I fell. Then as it got its legs out of the ground smoke arose like a sandstorm. When I saw that I knew that he was protected against me and would have the upper hand. I called to them saying who I was and asking them to wait for me; and that they need have no concern, for no harm would come to them from me. The apostle told Abū Bakr to ask what I wanted and I said, "Write a document for me which will be a sign between you and me" and the apostle instructed Abū Bakr to do so.

'He wrote it on a bone, or a piece of paper, or a potsherd and threw it to me and I put it in my quiver and went back. I kept quiet about the whole affair until when the apostle conquered Mecca and finished with al-Ṭāʾif and Hunayn I went out to give him the document and I met him in al-Jiʿrāna.

'I got among a squadron of the Anṣār cavalry and they began to beat me with their spears, saying, "Be off with you; what on earth do you want?" However, I got near to the apostle as he sat on his camel and his shank in his stirrup looked to me like the trunk of a palm-tree. I lifted my hand with the document, saying what it was and what my name was. He said "It is a day of repaying and goodness. Let him come near." So I approached him and accepted Islam. Then I remembered something that I wanted to ask him. All I can remember now is that I said "Stray camels used to come to my cistern which I kept full for my own camels. Shall I get a reward for having let them have water?" "Yes," he said, "for watering every thirsty creature there is a reward." Then I returned to my people and brought my alms to the apostle.' ...

Muhammad b. Ja'far b. al-Zubayr from 'Urwa b. al-Zubayr from 'Abdu'l-Raḥmān b. 'Uwaymir b. Sā'ida told me, saying, 'Men of my tribe who were the apostle's companions told me, "When we heard that the apostle had left Mecca and we were eagerly expecting his arrival we used to go out after morning prayers to our lava tract beyond our land to await him. This we did until there was no more shade left and then we went indoors in the hot season. On the day that the apostle arrived we had sat as we always had until there being no more shade we went indoors and then the apostle arrived. The first to see him was a Jew. He had seen what we were in the habit of doing and that we were expecting the arrival of the apostle and he called out at the top of his voice 'O Banū Qayla your luck has come!' So we went out to greet the apostle who was in the shadow of a palm-tree with Abū Bakr who was of like age. Now most of us had never seen the apostle and as the people crowded round him they did not know him from Abū Bakr until the shade left him and Abū Bakr got up with his mantle and shielded him from the sun, and then we knew."' ...

'Alī stayed in Mecca for three days and nights until he had restored the deposits which the apostle held. This done he joined the apostle and lodged with him at Kulthūm's house. ...

The apostle stayed in Qubā' among B. 'Amr b. 'Auf from Monday to Thursday and then he laid the foundation of his mosque. Then God brought him out from them on the Friday. The B. 'Amr allege that he stayed longer with them, and God knows the truth of the matter. Friday prayer found the apostle among B. Sālim b. 'Auf and he prayed it in the mosque which is in the bottom of the Wādī Rānūnā'. This was the first Friday prayer that he prayed in Medina.

'Itbān b. Mālik and 'Abbās b. 'Ubāda b. Naḍla with some of B. Sālim b. 'Auf came and asked him to live with them and enjoy their wealth and protection, but he said, 'Let her go her way,' for his camel was under God's orders; so they let her go until she came to the home of B. Bayāḍa, where he was met by Ziyād b. Labīd and Farwa b. 'Amr with some of their clansmen. They gave the same invitation and met with the same reply. The same thing happened with B. Sā'ida when Sa'd b. 'Ubāda and al-Mundhir b. 'Amr invited him to stay; and with B. 'l-Ḥārith b. al-Khazraj represented by Sa'd b. al-Rabī' and Khārija b. Zayd and 'Abdullah b. Rawāḥa; and with B. 'Adīy b. al-Najjār (who were his nearest maternal relatives the mother of 'Abdu'l-Muṭṭalib Salmā d. 'Amr being one of their women), being represented by Salīṭ b. Qays and Abū Salīṭ and Usayra b. Abū Khārija. Finally the camel came to the home of B. Mālik b. al-Najjār when it knelt at the door of his mosque, which at that time was used as a drying-place for dates and belonged to two young orphans of B. al-Najjār of B. Mālik clan, who were under the protection of Muʿādh b. ʿAfrāʾ, Sahl and Suhayl the sons of ʿAmr. When it knelt the apostle did not alight, and it got up and went a short distance. The apostle left its rein free, not guiding it, and it turned in its tracks and returned to the place where it had knelt at first and knelt there again. It shook itself and lay exhausted with its chest upon the ground. The apostle alighted and Abū Ayyūb Khālid b. Zayd took his baggage into the house (Ṭ. The Anṣār invited him to stay with them, but he said 'A man (stays) with his baggage) and the apostle stayed with him. When he asked to whom the date-store belonged Muʿādh b. ʿAfrāʾ told him that the owners were Sahl and Suhayl the sons of ʿAmr who were orphans in his care and that he could take it for a mosque and he would pay the young men for it.

The apostle ordered that a mosque should be built, and he stayed with Abū Ayyūb until the mosque and his houses were completed.

Muhammad's Death

Al-Zuhrī said, Ḥamza b. ʿAbdullah b. ʿUmar told me that ʿĀʾisha said: 'When the prophet became seriously ill he ordered the people to tell Abū Bakr to superintend the prayers. ʿĀʾisha told him that Abū Bakr was a delicate man with a weak voice who wept much when he read the Quran. "You are like Joseph's companions; tell him to preside at prayers." My only reason for saying what I did was that I wanted Abū Bakr to be spared this task, because I knew that people would never like a man who occupied the apostle's place, and would blame him for every misfortune that occurred, and I wanted Abū Bakr to be spared this.'

Ibn Shihāb said, ʿAbdullah b. Abū Bakr b. ʿAbdu'l-Raḥmān b. al-Ḥārith b. Hishām told me from his father from ʿAbdullah b. Zamaʿa b. al-Aswad b. al-Muṭṭalib b. Asad that when the apostle was seriously ill and I with a number of Muslims was with him Bilāl called him to prayer, and he told us to order someone to preside at prayers. So I went out and there was ʿUmar with the people, but Abū Bakr was not there. I told ʿUmar to get up and lead the prayers, so he did so, and when he shouted Allah Akbar the apostle heard his voice, for he had a powerful voice, and he asked where Abū Bakr was, saying twice over, 'God and the Muslims forbid that.' So I was sent to Abū Bakr and he came after ʿUmar had finished that prayer and presided. ʿUmar asked me what on earth I had done, saying, 'When you told me to take the prayers I thought that the apostle had given you orders to that effect; but for that I would not have done so.' I replied that he had not ordered me to do so, but when I could not see Abū Bakr I thought that he was most worthy of those present to preside at prayers.

Al-Zuhrī said that Anas b. Mālik told him that on the Monday on which God took His apostle he went out to the people as they were praying the morning prayer. The curtain was lifted and the door opened and out came the apostle and stood at ʿĀʾisha's door. The Muslims were almost seduced from their prayers for joy at seeing him, and he motioned to them that they should continue their prayers. The apostle smiled with joy when he marked their mien in prayer, and I never saw him with a nobler expression than he had that day. Then he went back and the people went away thinking that the apostle had recovered from his illness. Abū Bakr returned to his wife in al-Sunḥ.

Muhammad b. Ibrāhīm b. al-Ḥārith told me from al-Qāsim b. Muhammad that when the apostle heard ʿUmar saying Allah Akbar in the prayer he asked where Abū Bakr was. 'God and the Muslims forbid this.' Had it not been for what ʿUmar said when he died, the Muslims would not have doubted that the apostle had appointed Abū Bakr his successor; but he said when he died, 'If I appoint a successor, one better than I did so; and if I leave them (to elect my successor) one better than I did so.' So the people knew that the apostle had not appointed a successor and ʿUmar was not suspected of hostility towards Abū Bakr.

Abū Bakr b. ʿAbdullah b. Abū Mulayka told me that when the Monday came the apostle went out to morning prayer with his head wrapped up while Abū Bakr was leading the prayers. When the apostle went out the people's attention wavered, and Abū Bakr knew that the people would not behave thus unless the apostle had come, so he withdrew from his place; but the apostle pushed him in the back, saying, 'Lead the men in prayer,' and the apostle sat at his side praying in a sitting posture on the right of Abū Bakr. When he had ended prayer he turned to the men and spoke to them with a loud voice which could be heard outside the mosque: 'O men, the fire is kindled, and rebellions come like the darkness of the night. By God, you can lay nothing to my charge. I allow only what the Quran allows and forbid only what the Quran forbids.'

When he had ended these words Abū Bakr said to him: 'O prophet of God, I see that this morning you enjoy the favour and goodness of God as we desire; today is the day of Bint Khārija. May I go to her?' The apostle agreed and went indoors and Abū Bakr went to his wife in al-Sunḥ.

Al-Zuhrī said, and ʿAbdullah b. Kaʿb b. Mālik from ʿAbdullah b. ʿAbbās told me: That day ʿAlī went out from the apostle and the men asked him how the apostle was and he replied that thanks be to God he had recovered. ʿAbbās took him by the hand and said, 'Alī, three nights hence you will be a slave. I swear by God that I recognized death in the apostle's face as I used to recognize it in the faces of the sons of ʿAbduʾl-Muṭṭalib. So let us go to the apostle; if authority is to be with us, we shall know it, and if it is to be with others we will request him to enjoin the people to treat us well.' ʿAlī answered: 'By God, I will not. If it is withheld from us none after him will give it to us.' The apostle died with the heat of noon that day.

Yaʿqūb b. ʿUtba from al-Zuhrī from ʿUrwa from ʿĀʾisha said: The apostle came back to me from the mosque that day and lay in my bosom. A man of Abū Bakr's family came in to me with a toothpick in his hand and the apostle looked at it in such a way that I knew he wanted it, and when I asked him if he wanted me to give it him he said Yes; so I took it and chewed it for him to soften it and gave it to him. He rubbed his teeth with it more energetically than I had ever seen him rub before; then he laid it down. I found him heavy in my bosom and as I looked into his face, lo his eyes were fixed and he was saying, 'Nay, the most Exalted Companion is of paradise.' I said, 'You were given the choice and you have chosen, by Him Who sent you with the truth!' And so the apostle was taken.

Yaḥyā b. ʿAbbād b. ʿAbdullah b. al-Zubayr from his father told me that he heard ʿĀʾisha say: The apostle died in my bosom during my turn: I had wronged none in regard to him. It was due to my ignorance and extreme youth that the apostle died in my arms. Then I laid his head on a pillow and got up beating my breast and slapping my face along with the other women.

Al-Zuhrī said, and Saʿīd b. al-Musayyib from Abū Hurayra told me: When the apostle was dead ʿUmar got up and said: 'Some of the disaffected will allege that the apostle is dead, but by God he is not dead: he has gone to his Lord as Moses b. ʿImrān went and was hidden from his people for forty days, returning to them after it was said that he had died. By God, the apostle will return as Moses returned and will cut off the hands and feet of men who allege that the apostle is dead.' When Abū Bakr heard what was happening he came to the door of the mosque as ʿUmar was speaking to the people. He paid no attention but went in to ʿĀʾisha's house to the apostle, who was lying covered by a mantle of Yamanī cloth. He went and uncovered his face and kissed him, saying, 'You are dearer than my father and mother. You have tasted the death which God had decreed: a second death will never overtake you.' Then he replaced the mantle on the apostle's face and went out. ʿUmar was still speaking and he said, 'Gently, ʿUmar, be quiet.' But ʿUmar refused and went on talking, and when Abū Bakr saw that he would not be silent he went forward to the people who, when they heard his words, came to him and left ʿUmar. Giving thanks and praise to God he said: 'O men, if anyone worships Muhammad, Muhammad is dead: if anyone worships God, God is alive, immortal.' Then he recited this verse: 'Muhammad is nothing but an apostle. Apostles have passed away before him. Can it be that if he were to die or be killed you would turn back on your heels? He who turns back does no harm to God and God will reward the grateful.' By God, it was as though the people did not know that this verse had come down until Abū Bakr recited it that day. The people took it from him and it was (constantly) in their mouths. ʿUmar said, 'By God, when I heard Abū Bakr recite these words I was dumbfounded so that my legs would not bear me and I fell to the ground knowing that the apostle was indeed dead.'

3.3 THE QUR'AN

The Prophet Receives the Revelation

The Islamic scripture is self-conscious about its being revealed as "an Arabic recitation" (12:1), bringing God's message of warning and good news to the Arabs in a manner that they could not ignore. Something of the marvelous quality of the Qurʾan and its awed reception may be seen in the following passage (17:105–110). The divine name Al-Raḥmān, "The Beneficent," was not acknowledged by the pagan Meccans, but it came to be a major way of understanding God's nature as merciful and compassionate. The ancient Arabs recognized Allah as the supreme deity, but not as the only god. Al-Raḥmān and other divine names came through the Qurʾan to characterize the many attributes of the one and only God.

3.3A SELECTIONS FROM THE QUR'AN

105. With truth have We sent it down, and with truth hath it descended. And We have sent thee as naught else save a bearer of good tidings and a warner.

106. And (it is) a Qur'ân that We have divided, that thou mayest recite it unto mankind at intervals, and We have revealed it by (successive) revelation.

107. Say: Believe therein or believe not, lo! those who were given knowledge before it, when it is read unto them, fall down prostrate on their faces, adoring,

108. Saying: Glory to our Lord! Verily the promise of our Lord must be fulfilled.

109. They fall down on their faces, weeping, and it increaseth humility in them.

110. Say (unto mankind): Cry unto Allah, or cry unto the Beneficent,[1] unto whichsoever ye cry (it is the same). His are the most beautiful names. And thou (Muhammad), be not loud voiced in thy worship nor yet silent therein, but follow a way between.

The first verses revealed to Muhammad are generally considered to be the opening five lines of Sura 96, "The Clot," which follows. The first word is "Read," which could also be rendered as "Recite!" from the same root that gives us Qur'an, meaning "Recitation." The next passages tell something about Muhammad's experience of revelation. The first, Sura 81, "The Overthrowing," opens with a typically Meccan warning of a coming judgment (1–14), which will be heralded by reversals in the natural order. The visionary verses then give way to an oath that Muhammad had indeed received true revelation (15–29). The "honored messenger" is held by exegetical tradition to be the angel Gabriel. The next example is a passage from Sura 53, "The Star," in which Muhammad's vision is described in greater detail in verses 1–18. The final passages come from Suras 74:1–5 and 73:1–9. Muhammad, at least during the early Meccan period of revelations, would cover himself with a cloak when Gabriel visited. An important Qur'anic direction concerning ritual recitation is 73:4, "and chant the Qur'an in measure."

96:1–5 The Clot

In the name of Allah, the Beneficent, the Merciful.

1. Read: In the name of thy Lord who createth,
2. Createth man from a clot.
3. Read: And thy Lord is the Most Bounteous,
4. Who teacheth by the pen,
5. Teacheth man that which he knew not.

---

[1] That is, *Al-Raḥmān.*

81:1–29 The Overthrowing

In the name of Allah, the Beneficent, the Merciful.

1. When the sun is overthrown,
2. And when the stars fall,
3. And when the hills are moved,
4. And when the camels big with young are abandoned,
5. And when the wild beasts are herded together,
6. And when the seas rise,
7. And when souls are reunited,
8. And when the girl-child that was buried alive is asked
9. For what sin she was slain,
10. And when the pages are laid open,
11. And when the sky is torn away,
12. And when hell is lighted,
13. And when the garden is brought nigh,
14. (Then) every soul will know what it hath made ready.
15. Oh, but I call to witness the planets,
16. The stars which rise and set,
17. And the close of night,
18. And the breath of morning
19. That this is in truth the word of an honoured messenger,
20. Mighty, established in the presence of the Lord of the Throne,
21. (One) to be obeyed, and trustworthy;
22. And your comrade is not mad.
23. Surely he beheld him on the clear horizon.
24. And he is not avid of the Unseen.
25. Nor is this the utterance of a devil worthy to be stoned.
26. Whither then go ye?
27. This is naught else than a reminder unto creation,
28. Unto whomsoever of you willeth to walk straight.
29. And ye will not, unless (it be) that Allah willeth, the Lord of Creation.

53:1–18 The Star

In the name of Allah, the Beneficent, the Merciful.

1. By the Star when it setteth,
2. Your comrade erreth not, nor is deceived;
3. Nor doth he speak of (his own) desire.
4. It is naught save an inspiration that is inspired,
5. Which one of mighty powers hath taught him,
6. One vigorous; and he grew clear to view
7. When he was on the uppermost horizon.
8. Then he drew nigh and came down
9. Till he was (distant) two bows' length or even nearer,
10. And He revealed unto His slave that which He revealed.

11. The heart lied not (in seeing) what it saw.
12. Will ye then dispute with him concerning what he seeth?
13. And verily he saw him yet another time
14. By the lote-tree of the utmost boundary,
15. Nigh unto which is the Garden of Abode.
16. When that which shroudeth did enshroud the lote-tree,
17. The eye turned not aside nor yet was overbold.
18. Verily he saw one of the greater revelations of his Lord.

74:1–5 The Cloaked One

In the name of Allah, the Beneficent, the Merciful.

1. O thou enveloped in thy cloak,
2. Arise and warn!
3. Thy Lord magnify,
4. Thy raiment purify,
5. Pollution shun!

73:1–6 The Enshrouded One

In the name of Allah, the Beneficent, the Merciful.

1. O thou wrapped up in thy raiment!
2. Keep vigil the night long, save a little—
3. A half thereof, or abate a little thereof
4. Or add (a little) thereto—and chant the Qur'ân in measure,
5. For We shall charge thee with a word of weight.
6. Lo! the vigil of the night is (a time) when impression is more keen and speech more certain.

Interpretation of the Qur'an

The science of Qur'anic interpretation is known in Arabic as *tafsīr al-Qur'ān*, lit. "interpretation of the Qur'an." Readers from Muhammad's time have needed explanations and commentary about the message's meaning. The prophetic *ḥadīth* contain much pertaining to interpretation, as do discourses from the founding community. Muhammad's cousin Ibn 'Abbās (d. ca. 688), who knew many of the first generation of Muslims, is thought to have composed the first commentary of the Qur'an. The development of tafsir may be traced to him. Over the centuries, this science developed in a number of directions. The central tradition is a somewhat literal and conservative type of commentary that carefully weighs alternatives before providing an opinion. In addition are mystical and philosophical exegesis that go beyond the external, obvious meanings. Further, the Shiites have developed their characteristic types of interpretation. And modern times have seen the introduction of new trends.

Our first example of tafsir is a combination of the traditional and philosophic type, by the Persian philologist and rationalist theologian al-Zamakhsharī (d. 1144) in his "The Unveiler of the Realities of the Secrets of Revelation" (Gätje, pp. 55–57) [3:5].

3.3B SOME EXAMPLES OF TAFSIR

Clarity and Ambiguity in the Revelation

Zamakhsharī on Sūra 3:7

> It is He who sent down upon thee the Book (*al-kitāb*), wherein are clear verses that are the *umm al-kitāb*, and others that are ambiguous. As for those in whose hearts is swerving, they follow the ambiguous part, desiring dissension, and desiring its interpretation. But none knows its interpretation, except God and those firmly rooted in knowledge. They say: 'We believe in it; all is from our Lord'; yet none remembers, but men of understanding.

Clear verses (*āyāt muḥkamāt*): those whose diction and meaning are clear to the extent that they are preserved from the possibility of various interpretations and from ambiguity. *And others that are ambiguous* (*mutashābihāt*): those (verses) which are ambiguous in that they allow various interpretations.

That are the umm al-kitāb: that is, the origin (*asl*) of the book, since the ambiguous (verses) are to be traced back to it and must be reconciled with it. Examples of it are the following: 'The vision reaches Him not, but He reaches the vision; He is the All-subtle, the All-aware' (Sūra 6 :103). 'Upon that day faces shall be radiant, gazing upon their Lord' (Sūra 75:22f.). 'And whenever they commit an indecency they say: "We found our fathers practising it, and God has commanded us to do it." Say: "God does not command indecency! What, do you say concerning God such things as you know not?"' (Sūra 7 :28/27). 'And when We desire to destroy a city, We command its men who live at ease, and they commit ungodliness therein. Then the word is realized against it, and We destroy it utterly' (Sūra 17:16/17). If one then asks whether the (meaning of the) entire Qur'ān might be (clearly) determined, (I answer that) men would (then) depend on it since it would be so easily accessible, and (in this manner) turn away from what they lack—research and meditation through reflection and inference. If they did that, then they would neglect the way by which alone one can reach the knowledge of God and his unity (*tauḥīd*). (Further grounds are the following): In the ambiguous verses lie a trial and a separation between those who stand firm in the truth and those who waver regarding it. And great advantages, including the noble sciences and the profit of higher orders, are given by God, when the scholars stimulate each other and develop their natural abilities, arriving at the meanings of the ambiguous verses and reconciling these with the (clearly) determined verses. Further, if the believer is firmly convinced that no disagreement or contradiction can exist in God's words (that is, the Qur'an), and then he notices something that in outward appearance seems to be a contradiction, and he then zealously seeks some means by which he can bring it into harmony, treating it according to a uniform principle, and he reflects upon it, coming to an insight about himself and other things and being inspired by God, and (in this manner) he acquires a clear perception of the harmony which exists between the ambiguous verses and the (clearly) determined verses, then, his certainty regarding the contents of his conviction and the intensity of his certitude increase.

As for those in whose hearts is swerving: These are the people who introduce (heretical) innovations (*bida'*, sing. *bid'a*).

They follow the ambiguous part: They confine themselves to the ambiguous verses, which (on the one hand) allow the point of view of the (heretical) innovations without harmonizing them with the (clearly) determined verses. However (on the other hand), (these verses) also allow an interpretation which agrees with the views of the orthodox (*ahl al-ḥaqq*).

Desiring dissension: seeking to lead the people into error and divert them from their religion.

And desiring its interpretation: and seeking the interpretation they wanted it to have.

And none knows its interpretation, except God and those firmly rooted in knowledge: Only God and his servants who have a firmly-rooted knowledge, that is, those who are firm in knowledge and thereby 'bite with the sharp molar,' come to the correct interpretation, according to which one must necessarily explain it. Some people place a pause after *except God* and begin a new sentence with *and those firmly rooted in knowledge . . . say.* They interpret the ambiguous verses as those concerning which God reserves to himself alone the knowledge of their meaning and the cognizance of the wisdom present in them, as is the case with the exact number of the executioners of hell and similar questions. The first (interpretation regarding where the sentence should end) is correct. A new statement begins with *they say,* setting forth the situation of those who have a firmly-rooted knowledge, namely, in the following sense: These who know the meaning say *we believe in it,* that is, in the ambiguous verses.

All is from our Lord: that is, every ambiguous verse and every (clearly) determined verse is from him. Or, not only the ambiguous verses in the Book but also the (clearly) determined verses are from God, the Wise One, in whose words there is no contradiction and in whose Book there is no discrepancy. . . .

Our second selection is also from al-Zamakhsharī.

Methods of Divine Inspiration

Zamakhsharī on Sūra 42:51/50f.

> It belongs not to any mortal that God should speak to him, except by inspiration (*waḥy*), or from behind a veil, or that He should send a messenger and he reveal whatsoever He will, by His leave; surely He is All-high, All-wise.

It belongs not to any mortal: it does not fall to any man's lot *that God should speak to him, except* in three ways:

1. With the help of suggestion, that is, inspiration (*ilhām*), and lowering into the heart, or visions, just as God inspired the mother of Moses and commanded Abraham through inspiration to sacrifice his son. From Mujāhid (it is related) that God inspired David by placing the Psalms in his heart. . . .

2. In such a way that God causes man to hear his words, which he creates within someone's body, without the hearer seeing the one who speaks to him—since in his essence God is invisible. God's expression *from behind a veil* is a simile. That is, (he speaks to him) like a king who is hidden behind a veil when he converses with one of his eminent people, so that this person hears his voice but cannot see his figure. In the same manner God spoke with Moses and speaks with the angels.

3. In such a way that God sends an angel to man as a messenger to inspire him, just as the prophets were inspired, with the exception of Moses.
Some say: *by inspiration,* just as God inspired the messengers through the mediation of angels. *Or that He should send a messenger,* that is, a prophet, just as God spoke to the peoples of the prophets in their own languages. . . .

It is related: The Jews said to the Prophet: 'If you are a prophet, can you not speak with God and see him like Moses did? We will not believe in you until you do this.' To this the Prophet answered: 'Moses did not see God.' Then the present verse came down.
From 'Ā'isha (is related): Whoever asserts that Muhammad saw his Lord perpetrates an evil slander against God. Then she said: 'Have you not heard your Lord say . . .' and recited this verse.
Surely He is All-high above the qualities of his creatures and *All-wise:* he causes his acts to occur according to the requisites of wisdom and speaks sometimes indirectly and sometimes directly, (that is,) it might be through inspiration or through speech.

The third selection is from the orthodox Sunni exegete, al-Bayḍāwī (d. ca. 1286), whose commentary depends heavily upon al-Zamakhsharī's but excludes the rationalist (Mu'tazilite) theological interpretations. It deals with Sura 12, "Joseph," a retelling of the story of the biblical Joseph and the migration of the Israelites to Egypt.

Concerning the Concept Qur'an

Baiḍāwī on Sūra 12:1–3

> Alif Lam Ra
>> These are the signs of the clear Book.
>> We have sent it down as an Arabic Qur'ān; perhaps you will understand.
>> We will relate to thee the fairest of stories in that we have
>> revealed to thee this Qur'ān, though before it thou wast one of the heedless.

These are the signs (or 'verses', āyāt) of the clear Book: (the word) 'these' (*tilka*) is a demonstrative pronoun referring to the (following) verses of the sūra. By the 'book' here is meant the sūra itself. The meaning is (therefore): These verses constitute the verses of the sūra which presents itself clearly as inimitability (*i'jāz*); or, as that of which the meanings are clear; or, as that which makes clear (*bayyana*) to anyone who reflects upon it that it comes from God; or, that which makes clear to the Jews what they have asked about. It is related that the learned men among the Jews said to the leaders of the polytheists: 'Ask Muḥammad why the family of Jacob moved from Syria to Egypt, and (ask him) about the story of Joseph!' Thereupon this sūra was sent down. . . .

As an Arabic Qur'ān: This part (of the whole revelation) is designated here as *qur'ān*. In origin this word is a generic noun which is applicable to the whole (of the class) as well as to a part of it. It then became predominant as a proper name referring to the whole. . . .

Perhaps you will understand: This is the reason why God sent down the Book in this (Arabic) form. The meaning is (therefore): We have sent it down to you as something that is composed in your own language or can be recited in your own language, so that you will be able to understand it and grasp its meanings; or, that you will employ your intellect and (through it) discover that the account, out of the mouth of a man like this who could not produce a (comparable) account (previously), is a matchless miracle (*mu'jiz*) which one can conceive only as having been revealed.

We will relate to thee the fairest of stories: (We will relate) in the best manner, since the account is given in the finest linguistic form; or, (we will relate) the best account (regarding its content), since it contains marvellous things, wisdom, signs (*āyāt*), and admonitions. . . .

Though before it thou wast one of the heedless of this account, since it had never come to your mind, nor had you ever heard of it. It is for this reason that the account must have been inspired

The next example is not of tafsir, as such, but about interpreting the Qur'an by personal opinion (*bi al-ra'y*). It is by the great orthodox Sunni theologian and mystic al-Ghazali (d. 1111), who in his lifetime fashioned a synthesis of Islamic theology, law, and Sufism in his magisterial multivolumed work *The Revival of the Sciences of Religion,* from which the following selection is taken.

The Outer and Inner Meanings

Ghazzālī on Interpretation According to Individual Opinion

... The Prophet said: 'Whoever interprets the Qur'ān according to his own opinion (*bi-ra'yihī*) is to receive his place in the hell-fire.' The people who are acquainted with only the outer aspect of exegesis (*tafsīr*) have for this reason discredited the mystics in so far as they have been involved with exegesis, because they explain (*ta'wīl*) the wording of the Qur'ān other than according to the Tradition of Ibn ʿAbbās and the other interpreters. They have thus advocated the view that what is involved here is unbelief. If the advocates of (the traditional) exegesis are correct, then the understanding of the Qur'ān consists in nothing else than that one knows its interpretation outwardly. But if they are not right, then what is the meaning of the Prophet's words: 'Whoever interprets the Qur'ān according to his own opinion is to receive his place in the hell-fire'?

One should note: When someone maintains that the Qur'ān has no other meaning than that expressed by the outer aspect of exegesis, then by doing so he manifests his own limitation (*ḥadd*). With this confession about himself he hits upon what is absolutely correct (for his own situation); however, he errs in his opinion that the entire creation is to be regarded as being on his level, that is, restricted to his limitation and situation. Rather, the commentaries and Traditions show that the meanings contained in the Qur'ān exhibit a wide scope for experts in the field. Thus, ʿAlī said (that a specific meaning can be grasped) only when God grants to one (*ʿabdan*) understanding for the Qur'ān. (But) if nothing else is present than the interpretation which has been handed down, then this is not understanding. (Further) the Prophet said that the Qur'ān had a literal meaning (*ẓāhir*), an inner meaning (*bāṭin*), a terminal point (of understanding) (*ḥadd*), and a starting point (for understanding) (*muṭṭalaʿ*). .... According to the opinion of some scholars, every verse can be understood in sixty thousand ways, and what then still remains unexhausted (in its meaning) is more numerous (*akthar*). Others have maintained that the Qur'ān contains seventy-seven thousand and two hundred (kinds of) knowledge, since every word constitutes one (kind of) knowledge. This then increases fourfold since every word has a literal meaning, an inner meaning, a terminal point (of understanding), and a starting point (for understanding). ....

Ibn Masʿūd said: Whoever wishes to obtain knowledge about his ancestors and descendants should meditate upon the Qur'ān. This knowledge does not appear, however, if one restricts the interpretation of the Qur'ān to the outer meaning. All in all, every kind of knowledge is included in the realm of actions and attributes of God, and the description of the nature of the actions and attributes of God is contained in the Qur'ān. These kinds of knowledge are unending; yet, in the Qur'ān is found (only) an indication of their general aspects. Thereby, the (various) degrees (*maqāmāt*) of the deeper penetration into the particulars of knowledge are traced back to the (actual) understanding of the Qur'ān. The mere outer aspect of interpretation yields no hint of this knowledge. Rather, the fact is that the

Qur'ān contains indications and hints, which certain select people with (correct) understanding can grasp, concerning all that remains obscure of the theoretical way of thinking and that about which the creatures (*al-khalā'iq*) disagree regarding the theoretical sciences and rational ideas. How is the interpretation and explanation of the outer meaning of the Qur'ān to be sufficient for this? . . .

Regarding the words of the Prophet 'Whoever interprets the Qur'ān according to his own opinion', and the prohibition concerning this, . . . one can conclude as follows: Either, restriction to the Tradition (*ḥadīth*) and what can be learned (from other sources), and (thus) the renunciation of inference and independent understanding, is meant; or, something else is meant. For the following reasons (*wujūh*), it has been decided that it is wrong to conclude that what is meant is that concerning the Qur'ān one is allowed only the outer meaning, which he has heard:

1. One would then be restricted to what was stated (in the time of the Prophet) and can be traced back to him (through statements of suitable authorities). But this seldom occurs with (interpretations of) the Qur'ān. . . .

2. The Companions of the Prophet and the exegetes are in disagreement concerning the interpretation of certain verses and advance differing statements about them which cannot be brought into harmony with one another. That all of these statements have been heard from the mouth of the Messenger of God is absurd. One was obliged to learn of one of these statements of the Messenger of God in order to refute the rest, and then it became clear that, concerning the meaning (of the passage of the Qur'ān in question), every exegete expressed what appeared to him to be evident through his inference. This went so far that seven different kinds of interpretations, which cannot be brought into harmony with one another, have been advanced concerning the (mysterious) letters at the beginning of (some of) the sūras. . . .

3. The Messenger of God prayed for Ibn 'Abbās: 'God instruct him in the religion and teach him the interpretation!' But if one had heard the interpretation in the same way (that he heard the recitation of the Qur'ān) and could preserve it in his memory just as it was revealed, then what could this statement (of Muhammad) mean, since it was intended especially for Ibn 'Abbās? . . .

4. God has said: '. . . those of them whose task it is to investigate would have come to know the matter' (Sūra 4:83). Thus he has granted a disclosure to people with knowledge, and it is certain that the disclosure surpasses what is heard (of the doctrines which have been handed down). All of the reports which we have mentioned concerning the understanding of the Qur'ān stand in opposition to this notion (*khayāl*) (of a restriction of interpretation to what is heard from earlier sources), and consequently it is senseless to make hearing (*samā'*) a condition for the interpretation (*ta'wīl*). (Rather) it is permitted to everyone to draw conclusions from the Qur'ān according to the measure of his understanding and according to the scope of his reason.

The prohibition (against interpreting the Qur'ān according to individual opinion) involves the following two reasons for its having been sent down: The first is that someone may have an opinion (*ra'y*) about something, and through his nature as well as his inclination he may shelter a bias for it and then interpret the Qur'ān in accordance with his opinion and bias, in order thereby to obtain arguments to prove his view to be correct. Moreover, the meaning (which he links with his view) could not at all appear to him from the Qur'ān if he did not have (preconceived) opinion and bias. This sometimes happens consciously, as perchance in the case of those who use individual verses of the Qur'ān as arguments for the correctness of a (heretical) innovation (*bid'a*) and thus know that this is not in accordance with what is meant by the verse. They want rather to deceive their opponents. Sometimes (however) it (also) happens unconsciously. For instance, when a verse allows various meanings, a man inclines in his understanding to that which corresponds with his own opinion. Then, he settles the issue according to his opinion and inclination and thus interprets according to 'individual opinion'. That is: It is 'individual opinion' which drives one to such an interpretation. If one did not have this opinion, then that possibility of interpretation (to which one is inclined) would not have gained predominance. . . .

The second reason is that someone may come to an interpretation of the Qur'ān prematurely on the basis of the outer meaning of the Arabic language, without receiving the assistance of hearing (*samā'*) and the Tradition for what is involved with passages of the Qur'ān which are difficult to understand, for the obscure and ambiguous (*mubdal*) expressions which are found in the Qur'ān, and for abbreviations, omissions, implications (*iḍmār*), anticipations, and allusions which are contained in it. Whoever has not mastered the outer aspect of exegesis, but solely on the basis of his understanding of the Arabic language proceeds hastily to the conclusion of the meaning (of the Qur'ān), commits many errors and aligns himself thereby to the group of those who interpret (the Qur'ān) according to individual opinion. The Tradition and hearing (*samā'*) are indispensable for the outer aspect of exegesis, first of all in order to make certain thereby against the opportunities for error, but then also in order to extend the endeavour to understand and to reach conclusions. The obscure passages which cannot be understood without hearing are in fact numerous. . . .

The next example is of allegorical exegesis, by the theosophically oriented follower of the great Spanish Sufi Ibn 'Arabī, 'Abd al-Razzāq al-Kāshānī (d. ca. 1330).

Kāshānī on Sūra 20:12

> (A voice cried out: 'Moses,) I am thy Lord! Take off thy sandals. Thou art in the holy valley, Tuwā.'

Take off thy sandals: namely, your soul and your body, or your two (temporal) forms of existence, since when one is free from soul and body, one is free from both (temporal) forms of existence. That is: As soon as one is free, through the spirit (*rūh*) and the inner mystery (*sirr*), from the properties and characteristics of the soul and the body, so that one is united with the holy spirit, then one is free from the soul and the body (also) through the heart (*qalb*) and the breast (*ṣadr*), since the general connection (with them) is severed, their actions are released, and one has escaped their properties and activities. God calls the soul and the body sandals and not garments. If one were not free from intimate contact with both, one could not become united with the sacred sphere. The condition (however, on which it depends) is that of becoming united. God gives to Moses the command that he is to devote himself exclusively to him, in the sense of his words: 'And remember the name of thy Lord, and devote thyself completely to Him' (Sūra 73:8). It is therefore almost as if the connection of Moses with the sandals (of the soul and the body) still exists. This connection permits his feet, that is, the lower self, just as the breast designates the place of the heart, to sink into the ground. Consequently, they stand back away from the spiritual and inner turning-point to the holy, and for this reason God commands Moses to free himself from them in order to enter the realm of the spirit. Appropriately, God gives a reason for the necessity of removing the sandals, in his words: *Thou art in the holy valley, Ṭuwā*, that is, in the world of the spirit, which is free from the actions of linking (through the soul and the body) the characteristics of transient things and the material bonds. This world is called Ṭuwā because the stages of the kingdom of God (*malakūt*) are concealed (*ṭawā*) in it, while the heavenly and earthly bodies stand under it. . . .

Our final example of tafsir is from the modernist commentary of Muhammad 'Abduh (d. 1905), the great theologian and activist who reformed Cairo's ancient Azhar University as its rector and struggled to update Islamic legal, theological, and social discourse.

Polygamy

Muhammad ʿAbduh on Sūra 4:3

> If you fear that you will not be able to act justly towards orphans (who are to be the first choice in marriage, then instead of them) marry two, three, or four of such women as seem good to you, but if you fear you will not be equitable, then (marry) only one, or what your right hands own (as slaves). Thus it will be more likely that you will not be partial.

. . . The Ustādh-Imām (Muhammad ʿAbduh has said): Polygamy is mentioned in connection with the words (of the present verse) concerning orphans and with the prohibition against spending all their wealth, even though it be through marriage. He said: If you feel within yourself the fear that by marrying the orphaned girl (*al-yatīma*) you will spend all her wealth, then you may (choose) not (to) marry her, since here God has given to you a possibility of avoiding (your duty) concerning (marriage to) the orphan. He has given you the choice of marrying other wives, up to (the number of) four. If you fear, however, that you will not be able to treat two or more wives justly, you must restrict yourself to one. Moreover, (justifiable) fear that a proper act will not be done is present whenever there is adequate presumption and adequate doubt, indeed even when there is adequate suspicion. The law may nevertheless justify suspicion since where knowledge of this kind of thing exists there is seldom freedom from it. The marriage of two or more wives is therefore allowed as an option (only) to one who has the conviction in himself that he will deal justly, (indeed) in such a way that he has no doubt about it, or that he suspects it but shelters (only) a small doubt about it.

Muhammad 'Abduh has said: After God said *But if you fear you will not be equitable, then (marry) only one,* he gives a reason for this in his words: *Thus, it will be more likely that you will not be partial,* that is, thus you will come more closely to the condition in which neither injustice nor oppression will occur. Consequently, God has made the condition that one keep far from injustice to be the basis for his giving of a law (concerning marriage). This confirms the fact that justice is enjoined as a condition and that duty consists in striving for it. Further, it shows that justice is something difficult to attain. God says in another verse of this sūra: 'You will not be able to treat your wives equally, regardless of how eager you are (to do so)' (Sūra 4:129). This refers to justice in the inclination of the heart, since otherwise the two verses taken together would have the result that there would be no permission for polygamy at all. And then also the meaning of his words in (another) part of the verse just cited, (namely) 'Yet do not follow your inclination to the extreme (thus completely severing your relations with any of them) so that you leave her as it were deserted' (Sūra 4:129), would not be clear. God forgives the servant when something in the inclination of his heart goes beyond his power, even as, towards the end of his life, the Prophet felt a stronger inclination for 'Ā'isha than for his other wives. To be sure, he did not treat her with any distinction above them, that is, not without their consent and authorization. He used to say: 'God, this is my share of what lies in my power. Do not call me to account for what does not lie in my power!' That is: (This is my share) regarding the inclination of the heart.

Muhammad 'Abduh has said: Whoever considers the two verses correctly acknowledges that permission for polygamy in Islam applies (only) with the most severe restriction. Polygamy is like one of those necessities which is permitted to the one to whom it is allowed (only) with the stipulation that he act fairly with trustworthiness and that he be immune from injustice (*al-jaur*). In view of this restriction, when one now considers what corruption results from polygamy in modern times, then one will know for certain that a people (*umma*) cannot be trained so that their remedy lies in polygamy, since, in a family in which a single man has two wives, no beneficial situation and no order prevail. Rather, the man and his wives each mutually assist in the ruin of the family, as if each of them were the enemy of the other; and also the children then become enemies to one another. The corruption or polygamy carries over from the individual to the family and from the family to the (entire) people.

Muhammad 'Abduh has said: Polygamy had advantages in the early period of Islam, among the most important at that time being that it brought about
the bond of blood relationship and of relationship by marriage, so that the
feeling of tribal solidarity was strengthened. Also, at that time it did not lead to
the same harm (*ḍarar*) that it does today, since at that time the religion was
firmly rooted in the souls of women and men, and the insult (*adhan*) of taking
an additional wife (*ḍarra*) did not go beyond her rival (in its effect). Today, on
the other hand, the harm (*ḍarar*) of every additional wife (*ḍarra*) carries over to
her child, its father, and its other relatives. The wife stirs up enmity and hatred
among them; she incites her child to enmity against his brothers and sisters,
and she incites her husband to suppress the rights of the children which he has
from the other wives. The husband, on the other hand, follows in the folly of
the wife whom he loves the most, and thus ruin creeps into the entire family.
If one wished to enumerate specifically the disadvantages and mishaps that
result from polygamy, then one would present something that would cause the
blood of the believers to curdle. This includes theft and adultery, lies and deceit, cowardice and deception, indeed even murder, so that the child kills the
father, the father kills the child, the wife kills the husband, and the husband kills
the wife. All this is tangible and is demonstrated from the (records of the) courts of
justice.

It may suffice here to refer to the (poor) education of the (modern) woman,
who knows neither the worth (*qūma*) of the husband nor that of the child and
finds herself in ignorance concerning herself and her religion, knowing of religion only legends and errors which she has snatched up from others like herself
and which are not found either in the scriptures or in (the sayings of) the prophets
who have been sent. If women had the benefit of a proper religious education,
so that religion had the highest power over their hearts and would prevail
over jealousy, then no harm would grow out of polygamy for the people today,
but the harm would remain limited as a rule to the women (who are concerned).
However, since the matter now stands as we see and hear it, there is no possibility of educating the people so long as polygamy is widespread among them. Thus,
it is the duty of scholars to investigate this problem, (that is) especially the
Hanafite scholars, in whose hand the matter lies (in the Ottoman empire and
its sphere of influence), and whose opinion is determinative (here). They do not
deny that religion was sent down for the use and benefit of mankind and that it
belongs to the principles of religion to prevent harm and injury. Now if at a
(certain) time (that is, the present), corruption results from something that was
not connected with it earlier, it is without doubt necessary to alter the laws and
to adapt them to the actual situation, that is, according to the principle that
one must prevent the deterioration beforehand in order then to bring about the
well-being (of the community). Muhammad 'Abduh has said: Hence, it is recognized that polygamy is strictly forbidden when the fear exists that one cannot act
fairly.

The Collection of the Qur'an

The following selection, by a leading contemporary Egyptian Qur'an scholar and sociologist, Labib as-Said, clearly recounts the somewhat complex story of how (and why) the materials revealed to Muhammad were collected into an official recension in a single volume.

3.3c THE COMPILATION OF THE WRITTEN TEXT: CRISIS AND RESPONSE

There is good reason to believe that virtually all of the Koran was committed to writing during the lifetime of the Prophet. We are told that the Prophet kept scribes in his service and that whenever he taught a portion of the Koran to his Companions—and it was his custom to do so soon after each portion was revealed—these scribes, themselves Companions, would in accordance with his wishes write down what was so taught. The materials upon which they wrote were those common to the Arabs at that time: thin flat stones, leafless palm branches, shoulder bones of camels or sheep, pieces of hide, parts of camel saddles, and pieces of tanned leather.

Nonetheless the Koran was not actually compiled as a single unified text during the lifetime of the Prophet. What the scribes wrote down appears to have remained fragmentary, waiting to be assembled by later hands. There is evidence that the Prophet undertook to compile sūras and that he indicated to his Companions their correct order; but that he compiled a complete and unified text is out of the question. Zayd ibn Thābit testified that "the Prophet, peace and blessing be upon him, died and the Koran had not yet been compiled."

In all probability the reason for this omission was that the Koran was delivered to Muslims piecemeal over a twenty-year period and could not, so long as the Prophet lived and the possibility of fresh revelation existed, be considered complete, a closed book as it were, ready for final compilation. Moreover, during the years of revelation, certain verses were abrogated by subsequent revelation; had the Koran been compiled as a unified text during those years, this abrogation would have caused much confusion and uncertainty. Still further, and perhaps most significantly, so long as the Prophet lived, the Community had in him an infallible guide as to the correct recitation of the Koran. The Prophet was granted special protection against forgetfulness, as the Koran itself indicates:

> By degrees shall we teach thee to declare (the message), so thou shalt not forget, except as God wills. (87:6–7)

From *The Recited Koran: A History of the First Recorded Version,* translated and adapted by Bernard M. Weiss, M. A. Rauf, and Morroe Berger. Copyright © 1975. Reprinted with the permission of The Darwin Press, Inc.

As the Koran was in essence an orally transmitted Word from God, to be heard and repeated and thus stored in the heart, there was no need for an authoritative written text so long as Muslims could be certain that their Koranic recitation was correct. We are told that the Companions consulted the Prophet regularly on matters relating to the Koran and that many of them made a practice of reciting the Koran in his presence.

It was not until some months after the Prophet's death that a serious effort was made, under the auspices of the Caliph Abū Bakr, to gather together all the written fragments of the Koran and compile a complete, continuous text. Zayd ibn Thābit, himself a principal figure in this undertaking, recounts in the following words how this came about:

> Abū Bakr, on hearing of the heavy losses at al-Yamāma, sent for me, 'Umar ibn al-Khaṭṭāb being present with him. Said Abū Bakr (God bless his soul): "Verily 'Umar has come to me saying, 'In truth death has claimed many lives from amongst the Koran-readers on the day of al-Yamāma, and I greatly fear that death shall claim many more lives of these readers in other places, and that much of the Koran will be lost. I therefore advise that you order the making of a (written) compilation of the Koran.' I said to 'Umar, 'How do you dare to do something the Prophet did not do?' 'Umar answered: 'Because, by God, it is a good thing (to do).' And 'Umar continued to urge me until God opened my heart to the idea, and I came to share 'Umar's opinion."
>
> Abū Bakr continued saying, "You are a wise young man, and we trust you. You used to write down the revelations for the Prophet, peace and blessing be upon him. Therefore, go and find (all the scattered written fragments of) the Koran, and assemble them together."
>
> By God, I felt as if I had been asked to move a mountain. So I said, "How do you dare to do something the Prophet himself did not do?" Abū Bakr answered, "Because, by God, it is a good thing (to do)." And Abū Bakr continued to urge me until God opened my heart to the idea, as He had opened the hearts of Abū Bakr and 'Umar to it.
>
> And so I proceeded with the task, searching for and collecting the fragments of the Koran, whether written on leafless palm-branches or thin stones or preserved in the hearts of men, until finally I found the very last fragment, namely the concluding lines of (the sūra entitled) *al-Tawba*, which was in the possession of Abū Khuzayma al-Anṣārī, whose testimony the Prophet counted as equal to that of two others. This fragment I put in its proper place. The final complete compilation was entrusted to Abū Bakr until his death, then to 'Umar, and finally, upon the death of the latter, to Ḥafṣa, 'Umar's daughter (Bukhārī).

Two significant points may be drawn from this account. The first is that the decision to compile the Koran was clearly a response to a definite crisis, which had been created by the death in battle of a large number of persons who knew the Koran by heart. The tragedy aroused the fear that if such persons continued to perish in this manner, portions of the Koran might ultimately be lost. The second point is that the project of compilation was initially regarded as an audacious undertaking, there being no clear mandate for it from the Prophet. It is 'Umar who prevails over the misgivings of his comrades by insisting, so we may gather, that in the light of the crisis at hand it is the expedient thing to do, the thing which the welfare of the community requires.

The possibility of error on the part of those who worked on the compilation was extremely remote from the start. The entire company of Companions had attended the recitation of the Koran by the Prophet during the twenty-year era of revelation. Many of them, including Zayd ibn Thābit, had committed the entire Koran to memory; their devotion and faithfulness to the letter of the Koran have never been questioned. Consequently, no error could have occurred unnoticed.

Nonetheless, the compilers, in examining written material submitted to them, insisted on certain principles as a safeguard against error. Only material which met the following conditions was accepted for inclusion: (1) It must have been originally written down in the presence of the Prophet; nothing written down later on the basis of memory alone was to be accepted. (2) It must be confirmed by two witnesses, that is to say, by two trustworthy persons testifying that they themselves had heard the Prophet recite the passage in question. (3) It must clearly not represent portions of the Koran subsequently abrogated by the Prophet.

As the narrative of Zayd ibn Thābit indicates, the completed text was kept in the private possession first of Abū Bakr and then, upon the latter's death, of the second Caliph 'Umar. When 'Umar died and 'Uthmān became the Caliph, it was entrusted to Ḥafṣa, who besides being the daughter of 'Umar was also a wife of the Prophet. There is no indication that either Abū Bakr or 'Umar after him attempted to establish this first recension of the text as a *sole* authorized canon or that any effort was made to prevent various Companions from keeping in their possession other recensions which they themselves had compiled for their own private use, and which differed at points from the caliphal recension. Such differences, as we shall have the occasion to point out again in a later chapter, do not really imply contradictory views as to the correct rendering of the authentic text. A tradition of the Prophet affirms that the Koran was originally revealed in seven dialects (*aḥruf*), thus testifying to a degree of variation in the original *verbum dei* delivered to the Prophet. As a result of this variation, not all of the early Muslims recited the Koran in a manner fully consistent with the recension of Abū Bakr. One cannot conclude therefore that divergent readings were incorrect, since such readings could well have originated in the Revelation itself. Evidently the reason why the recension of Abū Bakr was not given the status of a sole authorized canon was that the need for standardization was not yet felt. Abū Bakr's purpose was simply to produce, in response to the crisis posed by the death of many Koranic readers, a text which was indisputably authentic and publicly endorsed as such, as a safeguard against the possible loss of other Koran-readers. Standardization as such was not among his objectives.

The expansion of Islam into territories beyond the Arabian Peninsula precipitated a new crisis with respect to the Koran, which first became evident during the reign of the third Caliph, 'Uthmān. It is related that the governor of al-Madā'in, Ḥudhayfa ibn al-Yamān, who was among the more eminent of the Companions, complained to the Caliph that factions in the Muslim army were disputing over various Koranic passages and urged him to take steps to end the disagreement, which was undermining the unity of the Muslim community. "The Syrians," we are told, "contended with the 'Irāqīs, the former following the reading of Ubayy ibn Ka'b," the latter that of 'Abd Allāh ibn Mas'ūd, each party accusing the other of unbelief (*kufr*)." Not infrequently the recitation of the Holy Book was made the subject of boasting. The people of Ḥimṣ, for example, boasted that their way of reciting the Koran, which was adopted from al-Miqdād, was superior to that of the Baṣrites, who had learned the Koran from Abū Mūsā, whose written compilation they acclaimed as "the Heart of Hearts."

It is said that one day, in disgust, Ḥudhayfa had stood up to speak and, after having offered the usual prayers, had declared: "Thus did your pagan ancestors squabble and bicker. By God, I shall go to the Commander of the Faithful about this!" Upon arriving in Medina, he had gone directly to 'Uthmān—before even greeting his own kinsmen, it is said—beseeching him, "O Commander of the Faithful! Save this people (*umma*) before it is torn asunder in strife over the Holy Book."

'Uthmān, having himself noticed disputes over the recitation of the Koran in Medina, lent receptive ears to this plea. If those near at hand were disputing so, he reasoned, how much greater must be the disputing among those scattered in far-away places. Realizing that nothing less than the unity of the Muslim community was at stake, 'Uthmān turned to the Companions who were with him, saying "Muslims are saying to each other, 'My recitation is better than yours.' What do you say of this? This is almost unbelief (*kufr*)."

The Companions answered, "What is your opinion?"

To this 'Uthmān replied, "We must unite the community by means of a single, authorized text."

They said, approvingly, "That is an excellent opinion."

Thus did 'Uthmān, in response to what was clearly a threat to Muslim unity and strength, undertake that which had seemed unnecessary to his predecessors, namely, the standardization of the written text of the Koran through the institution of a sole authorized canon.

The new recension was based heavily on the earlier one. In fact, to a very great extent the task of the compilers appointed by 'Uthmān was simply to copy and distribute the earlier text. However, the elimination of some reading variants of the text was called for. It was 'Uthmān's wish that that canonical text conform as fully as possible to the dialect of the Quraysh, which was the dialect spoken by the Prophet himself. Since the earlier text reflected some of the dialectal variation of the Koran as originally revealed, this standardization required that non-Quraysh elements be abandoned in favor of Qurayshite variants. To deliberately suppress in this manner material which the Prophet himself had sanctioned was, needless to say, an audacious undertaking, but the exigencies of the situation required that this be done. The use of various dialectal versions of the Koran had originally been intended to solve a practical problem in the rapidly expanding community—the inability of Arabs of certain tribes to master the dialect of Quraysh. Multiple versions of the Revelation made possible a more rapid assimilation of the Koran by tribesmen speaking different dialects. By the time of 'Uthmān, however, the Arabs in general had become accustomed to the dialect of

Quraysh and thus the need for the several dialectal versions, by its very nature temporary, no longer existed. More importantly, under the circumstances arising after the expansion of Islam, the continued use of these versions, whatever its earlier benefits might have been, would do more harm than good to the community, undermining and perhaps ultimately destroying its essential unity. Such considerations can only have argued in favor of 'Uthmān's policy of uniting the Muslim community around a text conforming to the Qurayshite dialect.

Ibn al-Qayyim al-Jawzīya suggests the following parable as justification of 'Uthmān's action. "A house may have a number of roads leading to it. If it is the ruler's judgment that allowing people to use all the roads causes conflict and confusion, then he may decide to permit the use of one road only, forbidding the others. He does not thereby abolish the other roads as such, as they could still lead to the house; he merely forbids their use."

The renowned Egyptian essayist and scholar Ṭāhā Ḥusayn has described 'Uthmān's action as a mighty deed the audaciousness of which was exceeded only by its profound wisdom. "Had 'Uthmān suffered the people to go on reciting the Koran in so many ways, using diverse dialects, each with its distinctive vocabulary, there is no doubt that this variety would have been a source of sharp schism. Neither is there doubt that, after the age of the expansion was over and whole new peoples had become arabized and bedouins in remote places had begun to recite the Koran, this schism over the vocabulary of the Koran would have led to more serious schism over its meaning."

The work on the new recension was carried on by a council of prominent men appointed by the Caliph. The first members of this council were Zayd ibn Thābit, 'Abd Allāh ibn al-Zubayr, Sa'īd ibn al-'Āṣ and 'Abd al-Raḥmān ibn al-Ḥārith ibn Hishām. It is related that 'Uthmān first asked, "Who is the best copyist?" He was told, "The scribe of the Messenger of God, peace and blessing be upon him, namely, Zayd ibn Thābit." He then asked, "Who is linguistically most proficient?" The answer was: "Sa'īd ibn al-Ās." "Then let Sa'īd dictate and Zayd write," said 'Uthmān. He further instructed the three Qurayshite members of the council . . . as follows: "If you differ with Zayd over something, follow the dialect of Quraysh, for the Koran was (first) revealed in their tongue."

Later a number of others were added to the council to assist in the task of producing copies to be forwarded to the various regions. They included Mālik ibn Abī 'Āmir (grandfather of Mālik ibn Anas), Kathīr ibn Aflaḥ, Ubayy ibn Ka'b, Anas ibn Mālik and 'Abd Allāh ibn 'Abbās. Very likely these were added also in order further to guarantee the trustworthiness of the results, all of them being renowned for exactness and wide knowledge.

The work of the council proceeded in accordance with the following general principles:

1. The earlier recension was to serve as the principal basis of the new one, since it in turn had been made up of original materials written down during the lifetime of the Prophet. Thus no one in the future would be able to accuse the council of ignoring the work done under the first Caliph.

2. Additional written material not previously submitted was solicited, so that a wider range of material could be considered. Material thus submitted and duly authenticated provided a valuable confirmation of the earlier recension, as well as in some cases a valuable supplement in the way of authentic variants.

3. Variants conforming to the dialect of Quraysh were to be chosen over all others, for reasons already given.

4. The entire community was to be apprised of what was submitted, so that the work of final recension would be in effect a collective enterprise, and no one who possessed a portion of the Koran would be passed over. This would leave no ground for doubt concerning the reliability of the text, or for a possible claim that it was the product of individual effort rather than communal action.

5. Any doubt that might be raised as to the phrasing of a particular passage in the written text was to be dispelled by summoning persons known to have learned the passage in question from the Prophet. Thus, as before, the written text was to be confirmed by oral tradition.

6. The Caliph himself was to supervise the work of the council.

When the final recension was completed, 'Uthmān sent a copy to each of the main divisions of the Muslim army. The common view is that the number of copies sent out was five, though some have set the number at four. At the same time, 'Uthmān ordered that all other copies or fragments of the Koran be burned. A message conveyed to the major garrison-towns called upon Muslims to emulate the Commander of the Faithful himself. "I have done away with what is in my vicinity," he declared. "See that you do away with what is in your vicinity."

This action, though obviously drastic, was unanimously approved by the Companions, who realized, as Ibn al-Qayyim al-Jawzīya points out, that it was done for the welfare of the community. Zayd ibn Thābit is reported to have said: "I saw the Companions of Muhammad (going about) saying, 'By God, 'Uthmān has done well! By God, 'Uthmān has done well!'" The esteemed Companion Mus'ab ibn Sa'd ibn Abī Waqqās is said on good authority to have testified: "I saw the people assemble in large number at 'Uthmān's burning of the proscribed copies (of the Koran), and they were all pleased with his action; not a one spoke out against him." Even 'Alī ibn Abī Ṭālib commented: "If I were in command in place of 'Uthmān, I would have done the same."

PART II
MONOTHEISM

CHAPTER 4
IN JUDAISM

4.1 THE DIVERSITY OF MONOTHEISTIC CONCEPTIONS

The idea of the God of Israel as a world-creating judge of all humanity and the particular covenant partner of Israel is, of course, the fundamental assumption of the Hebrew Bible. We now turn to various refractions of these assumptions in ancient Judaism. Our first selections are from the preeminent intellectual of first-century CE Alexandrian Judaism, Philo. His thorough commitment to monotheistic belief is rooted in biblical images but is expressed in terms of Greek philosophical ideas about the source of the world in a single divine Mind or Word. We begin with his reflections on the creation narrative of Genesis 1:1 ff., as found in his work *On The Account of the World's Creation Given by Moses*. Note Philo's fundamental faith that the Torah expresses truths of a philosophical character. The second selection is from Philo's discussion of biblical laws, *On the Special Laws III*. The selection represents Philo's thought on the biblical law of personal damages, "an eye for an eye." In contrast to the rabbinic material we reviewed in the previous chapter, Philo takes the law to mean just what it says. But its ultimate significance is philosophical rather than juristic.

4.1a On the Account of the World's Creation

While among other lawgivers some have nakedly and without embellishment drawn up a code of the things held to be right among their people, and others, dressing up their ideas in much irrelevant and cumbersome matter, have befogged the masses and hidden the truth under their fictions, Moses, disdaining either course, the one as devoid of the philosopher's painstaking effort to explore his subject thoroughly, the other as full of falsehood and imposture, introduced his laws with an admirable and most impressive exordium . . . It consists of an account of the creation of the world, implying that the world is in harmony with the Law, and Law with the world, and that the man who observes the law is constituted thereby a loyal citizen of the world, regulating his doings by the purpose and will of Nature, in accordance with which the entire world itself also is administered. . . .

There are some people who, having the world in admiration rather than the Maker of the world, pronounce it to be without beginning and everlasting, while with impious falsehood they postulate in God a vast inactivity; whereas we ought on the contrary be astonished at his powers as Maker and Father, and not to assign to the world a disproportionate majesty. Moses, both because he had attained the very summit of philosophy, and because he had been divinely instructed in the greater and most essential part of Nature's lore, could not fail to recognize that the universal must consist of two parts, one part active Cause and the other passive object; and that the active Cause is the perfectly pure and unsullied Mind of the universe, transcending virtue, transcending knowledge, transcending the good itself and the beautiful itself; while the passive part is in itself incapable of life and motion, but, when set in motion and shaped and quickened by Mind, changes into the most perfect masterpiece, namely this world. . . . for it stands to reason that what has been brought into existence should be cared for by its Father and Maker. For, as we know, it is a father's aim in regard of his handiwork to preserve them, and by every means to fend off from them aught that may entail loss or harm. He keenly desires to provide for them in every way all that is beneficial and to their advantage: but between that which has never been brought into being and one who is not its Maker no such tie is formed. . . . It is a worthless and baleful doctrine, setting up anarchy in the well-ordered realm of the world, leaving it without protector, arbitrator, or judge, without anyone whose office it is to administer and direct all its affairs.

Not so Moses. That great master, holding the unoriginate to be of a different order from that which is visible, . . . assigned to that which is invisible and an object of intellectual apprehension the infinite and undefinable as united with it by closest tie; but on that which is an object of the senses he bestowed "genesis," "becoming," as its appropriate name. Seeing then that his world is both visible and perceived by the senses, it follows that it must also have had an origin. Whence it

Excerpts from Philo, *On the Account of the World's Creation Given by Moses*, translated by F. H. Colson and G. H. Whitaker, from *Philo, Volume 1* and *Volume 7* (Cambridge: Harvard University Press, 1929). Reprinted with the permission of the Loeb Classic Library and the publishers.

was entirely to the point that he put on record that origin, setting forth in its true grandeur the work of God. . . .

4.1b On the Special Laws

The legislators deserve censure who prescribe for malefactors punishments which do not resemble the crime, such as monetary fines for assaults, disfranchisement for wounding or maiming another, expulsion from the country and perpetual banishment for willful murder or imprisonment for theft. For inequality and unevenness is repugnant to the commonwealth which pursues truth. Our law exhorts us to equality when it ordains that the penalties inflicted on offenders should correspond to their actions, that their property should suffer if the wrongdoing affected their neighbor's property, and their bodies if the offence was a bodily injury, the penalty being determined according to the limb, part or sense affected, while if his malice extended to taking another's life his own life should be the forfeit. . . . [Having established the justice of the general principle of exact retaliation, Philo continues now to reflect upon the notion (Exod. 21:22 ff.) that one who damages another's eye must lose his own.]

Now as for the services and benefits which the eyes render to the human race, it would take a long time to enumerate them, but one, the best, must be mentioned. Philosophy was showered down by heaven and received by the human mind, but the guide which brought the two together was sight, for sight was the first to discern the high roads which lead to the upper air. . . . Now let us describe the way in which sight acted as guide to philosophy; sight looked up to the ethereal region and beheld the sun and moon and the fixed and wandering stars, the host of heaven in all its sacred majesty, a world within a world; then their risings and settings, their ordered rhythmic marchings, their conjunctions as the appointed times recur, their eclipses, their reappearances; then the waxing and waning of the moon, the courses of the sun from side to side . . .

The mind, having discerned through the faculty of sight what of itself it was not able to apprehend, did not simply stop short at what it saw, but, drawn by its love of knowledge and beauty and charmed by the marvellous spectacle, came to the reasonable conclusion that all these were not brought together automatically by unreasoning forces, but by the mind of God Who is rightly called their Father and Maker; . . . also that the Father Who begat them according to the law of nature takes thought for His offspring, His providence watching over both the whole and the parts. . . .

We may well ask what title we can give to research into these matters but philosophy and what more fitting name than philosopher to their investigator. For to make a study of God and the Universe embracing all that is therein, both animals and plants, and of the conceptual archetypes and also the works which they produce for sense to perceive, and of the good and evil qualities in every created thing—shows a disposition which loves to learn, loves to contemplate and is truly wisdom-loving or philosophical. This is the greatest boon which sight bestowed on human life, and I think that this pre-eminence has been awarded to it because it is more closely akin to the soul than the other senses. . . . If, then, anyone has maliciously injured another in the best and lordliest of his senses, sight, and is proved to have struck out his eye, he must in his turn suffer the same, if the other is a free man, but not if he is a slave.

Philo's ethnic pride in the Torah as the greatest of philosophical documents is expressed in the universalist language of Greco-Roman philosophy. When we enter the world of rabbinic theological thought, the ethnic self-confidence seems almost entirely untempered by universalist pronouncements. Here the God of Israel is, to be sure, the creator of heaven and earth and judge of humanity. But he is, above all the God of *Israel!* The first selection to follow is a midrashic passage that exemplifies the tendency of rabbinic parables to image God as a cosmic version of the Roman emperor. It is presented here in the translation of David Stern (*Parables in Midrash*, p. 29) from its source in a midrashic compilation on the book of Lamentations (*Ekhah Rabbah* 4:11). How does this passage make sense of God's apparent desire to destroy his Temple in Jerusalem?

The second passage is an aggadic reflection from the Babylonian Talmud's tractate on idolatry (*Avodah Zarah* 2a–2b). What attitude does it embody regarding the relation of Israel to God and God to the rest of the world? What function does the Torah play in these relationships?

4.1c EKHAH RABBAH 4:11

"And He has kindled a fire in Zion, which has devoured the foundations thereof" (Lam. 4:11). It is written: "A song of Asaph. O God, heathens have entered Your domain" (Ps. 79:1). Should not the verse have said, "A weeping of Asaph," or "a lament of Asaph," or "a dirge of Asaph"? And you say "a song of Asaph"?

But it is like a king who made a bridal-chamber for his son, and plastered, cemented, and decorated it. The son turned to wickedness. Immediately the king went up to the bridal-chamber, and tore its curtains, and broke its supports. The pedagogue took a tube of reeds and began to sing. [People] said to him: The king has destroyed his son's bridal-chamber, and you sit and sing! He said to them: I sing because he has destroyed his son's bridal-chamber, and he has not poured out his anger upon his son.

Similarly, they said to Asaph: The Holy One, blessed be He, has destroyed His sanctuary and temple, and you sit and sing! He said to them: I sing because the Holy One, blessed be He, poured out his anger upon wood and stones, and did not pour out His anger upon Israel.

This is what is written: "And He has kindled a fire in Zion, which has devoured the foundations thereof" (Lam. 4:11).

4.1D AVODAH ZARAH 2A–2B

Rabbi Hanina bar Pappa expounded; and some say it was Rabbi Simlai: In the coming time the Holy One Blessed is He brings a scroll of the Torah and sets it against his breast and says: Let whoever has busied himself with this come and receive his reward! Immediately all those in the world who serve stars and constellations gather together, as it is said in Scripture: "Let the nations gather together" (Isa. 43:9). The Holy One says to them: Don't press against me in a confused throng! Rather, let each nation and its teachers gather in sequence, as it is said in Scripture: "Let the peoples assemble" (Isa. 43:9). . . .

The Roman Empire enters first. Why? Because it is the most important. . . . The Holy One says to them: What have you done with yourselves? They say before him: Lord of the World! We have established great markets and built many baths, and much silver and gold have we accumulated. And we did all of it for Israel's sake, so that they may engage in the study of Torah! Says the Holy One to them: You worldly idiots! Whatever you did you did for your own benefit. You made markets to set up brothels within them, baths to preen yourselves in, and, as for the silver and gold—it's mine! As it is said: "Mine is the gold, mine is the silver, says the LORD of hosts" (Hag. 2:8). Do you have among you this teacher? And "this" refers only to the Torah, as it is said: "This is the Torah which Moses set before the Israelites" (Deut. 4:44)! Immediately, they leave crestfallen.

Rome leaves and the Persian Empire enters after it. Why? Because it is next in importance. . . . The Holy One says to them: What have you done with yourselves? They say before him: Lord of the World! We have constructed many bridges, conquered numerous cities and waged many wars. And we did it all for the sake of Israel, so that they may engage in the study of Torah! Says the Holy One to them: Whatever you did you did for your own benefit. You made bridges to collect tolls, conquered cities to raise forced-labor gangs and, as for wars, I waged them! As it is said: "The LORD is a warrior" (Exod. 15:3). Do you have among you this teacher? And "this" refers only to the Torah, as it is said: "And this is the Torah which Moses set before the Israelites!" Immediately, they leave crestfallen.

[The pattern continues with other nations until all leave crestfallen. Then the nations address God collectively.] They say to him: Lord of the World! Did you even offer the Torah to us? And did we refuse it? [The Talmud asks:] Now, how could they say such a thing? Well, isn't it written: "The LORD comes from Sinai, dawned upon us from Seir" (Deut. 33:2), and it is written: "God shall come from Teman, the Holy One from Mt. Paran" (Hab. 3:3). Why does Scripture mention Seir and Paran? Said Rabbi Yohanan: This proves that the Holy One went around to every nation and tongue with the Torah, and they didn't accept it. Then he finally got to Israel—they accepted it.

What the nations really say is: Did we accept it and then fail to fulfill it (like Israel has done)? [The Talmud asks:] That's a defense? Why didn't they simply accept it? Rather, this is what they say before him: Lord of the Worlds! Did you hold the mountain above us like a canopy, and did we fail to accept it as you did with Israel? For it is written: "And they stood together underneath the mountain"

(Exod. 19:17). And Rav Dimi bar Hama said: This proves that the Holy One turned the mountain like a canopy above Israel and said to them: If you accept the Torah, fine; and if not, let this be your grave! Says the Holy One to the nations: The first ones shall hear us, as it is said: "and the first ones shall hear us" (Isa. 43:9). The seven commandments of Noah which you did accept—did you ever fulfill even those?

We turn now to a world of thought close to that of the talmudic literature in temper but far more explicit than any talmudic text about the possibility for particularly pious Jews to have an actual experience of the heavenly domain beyond the material world. This body of literature, dealing largely in speculation about the nature of the heavenly palaces (*hekhalot*) and the divine chariot (*merkavah*) at their summit, comes from the same era as much of the rabbinic literature. Although the famous first-century rabbis Akiva and Ishmael figure in the action, the degree to which this text represents the views of the talmudic rabbis remains a question of scholarly debate. This translation of a text called *Maaseh Merkavah* ("The Ascent to the Chariot") is based on the translation of Michael Swartz in his study, *Mystical Prayer in Ancient Judaism*, pp. 231–234. The capitalized letters represent unpronounceable hidden names of God.

4.1E ASCENT TO THE CHARIOT

Rabbi Akiva said: Who can contemplate the seven Hekhalot, and gaze at the highest heavens, and see the inner chambers, and say, "I have seen the chambers of YH?" . . .

In the first Hekhal, Merkavot of fire say, "Holy, holy, holy is YHWH of Hosts, the whole earth is full of His Glory" (Isa. 6:3) and their flames spread out and gather together to the second Hekhal, and say, "Holy, holy, holy." In the second Hekhal, Merkavot of fire say, "Holy, holy, holy"; and their flames gather together and spread out to the third Hekhal and say, "Holy, holy, holy." In the third Hekhal, Merkavot of fire say: "Blessed is the name of His Majesty's Glory forever and ever from the place of His Presence"; and their flames gather together and spread out to the fourth Hekhal and say, "Blessed is the name of His Majesty's Glory forever and ever." In the fourth Hekhal, Merkavot of fire say, "Blessed is YY, living and enduring forever and ever, magnificent over all the Merkavah"; and their flames gather together and spread out to the fifth Hekhal and say, "Blessed is YHWH, living and enduring forever and ever." In the fifth Hekhal, Merkavot of fire say, "Blessed is the Holiness of His Majesty from the place of His Presence"; and their flames gather together and spread out to the sixth Hekhal and say, "Blessed is the Holiness of His Majesty from the place of His Presence." In the sixth Hekhal, Merkavot of fire say, "Blessed is YHWH, Lord of all power, Who creates power,

Translated by Michael Swartz.

and Ruler over all the Merkavah"; and their flames gather together and spread out to the seventh Hekhal and say, "Blessed is YHWH, Lord of all might, and Ruler over all the Merkavah. In the seventh Hekhal, Merkavot of fire say: "Blessed be the King of Kings, YY, Lord of all power. Who is like God, great and enduring? His praise is in the heavens' heaven, the holiness of His majesty is in the highest chambers. . . .

Rabbi Ishmael said: When Rabbi Nehuniah my teacher told me the secret of the chambers of the Hekhal and the Hekhal of the Merkavah, I saw the King of the universe sitting on a throne high and exalted, and all the chambers of the holiness of His name and His power were sanctifying His name in His praise, as it is said: "They called one to another and said, Holy, Holy, Holy, is YHWH of Hosts, the whole earth is full of His Glory": . . .

Rabbi Ishmael said: I asked Rabbi Akiva: What is the distance from one bridge to another? Rabbi Akiva said to me: There must be righteousness and piety in your heart, and you will know the measurements in heaven. He said to me: When I was in the first Hekhal, I was pious; in the second Hekhal, I was pure; in the third Hekhal, I was righteous; in the fourth Hekhal, I was perfect; in the fifth Hekhal, I presented a sanctified praise before the King of Kings, blessed be He. In the sixth Hekhal, I recited a sanctified praise before the One who spoke and formed, and He commanded all the creatures that the Ministering Angels should not kill me. In the seventh Hekhal, I stood before Him with all my strength and trembled in all my limbs, and said: Living and Enduring God, who formed the heaven and earth: besides You there is no rock, the Troops of above shall glorify Your remembrance forever, the work of Your hands in Your inhabited world. Great God, Maker of all, magnificent in greatness, beloved in might, the Mighty Ones of strength render thanks before You, who stand before You in truth and justice. Do justice in your world and in the justice of Your name, save me; and I will magnify the blessing of Your glory forever. Blessed are You, magnificent in the chambers of greatness.

With the advent of modernity, the potent theological images of divine kingship characteristic of premodern Judaism became difficult to accept for many Jews as accurate descriptions of the universe. For the past two centuries, modern Jewish thinkers have attempted to affirm divine unity in ways more acceptable to modern conceptions of the universe. Leo Baeck, an important twentieth-century figure in the Reform movement of Germany, spoke for many Western European Jews in conceiving the unity of God in essentially historical and ethical—rather than in metaphysical or cosmological—terms. In Baeck's view, Judaism's early insistence upon monotheism is the result of the emerging moral maturation of humanity within the process of history. The following passage is from his immensely popular book, *The Essence of Judaism*, pp. 95–97.

4.1F *THE ESSENCE OF JUDAISM*

To make the ethical the center of religion is the special characteristic of monotheism. The prophetic knowledge of God springs from the fundamental religious experience that God is different from all creation and evolution and from the earthly and the profane. . . . Since he is indeed the One, man shall decide for him above and against everything. Man may serve him alone. . . . In the good and the ethical, man experiences something that is different from this world and is not a part of nature. Thereby man can reach to the One God who "pronounces to a man and demands of him." As the ethical becomes man's possession in his innermost self, he feels its difference from nature and fate: he feels himself called by the One, by God, and led toward him. . . . Only when the moral unity rose to man's consciousness could he comprehend the unity of God. It is clear therefore that one and the same thing separated Judaism from all mythology and made of it a monotheistic religion. . . .

The religious value of monotheism consists not in its numerical unity, but in the reason for its unity: the content of its idea of God. The God of Israel is not One merely because he alone can accomplish what all the gods of polytheism can together accomplish. He is different from them all, he acts differently from them all. Not only is he more exalted than they; he really cannot be compared with them. For he alone is the creating and commanding God whose nature it is that he can be served by man only by the fulfillment of moral demands. Hence, monotheism was not a mere development from previous beliefs; it was rather their great contradictory, the revelation of the other principle: "Thus saith the Lord, the King of Israel and its redeemer, the Lord of Hosts: I am the first, and I am the last, and beside me there is no God" (Isa. 44:6).

4.2 MESSIANIC SPECULATION AND MOVEMENTS

By the late Second Temple period, earlier hopes for the restoration of the Davidic dynasty over Israel had broadened beyond the purely political. Increasingly, as one can see from the biblical book of Daniel (7:1–12:12), the return of the son of David was interpreted as part of a dramatic or violent conclusion to all of world history. Jewish literature from this period reveals a dazzling variety of speculation about the events of the end of time, the nature of the messianic figures expected (including, among some, a priestly Messiah of Aaronide ancestry; among others, a Messiah, son of Joseph), and the identities of the communities to be singled out as the True Israel and its enemies. The following text, called the Second Book of Baruch, was probably written shortly after the destruction of Jerusalem in 70 CE. It reflects common expectations of a final judgment, resurrection of the dead, and the coming of an anointed redeemer. The setting of the vision is Baruch's interview with a voice coming from the heavens.

4.2A II BARUCH 29–30

And he answered and said to me: That which will happen at that time bears upon the whole earth. Therefore, all who live will notice it. For at that time I shall only protect those found in this land at that time. And it will happen that when all that which should come to pass in these parts has been accomplished, the Anointed One will begin to be revealed. And Behemoth will reveal itself from its place, and Leviathan will come from the sea, the two great monsters which I created on the fifth day of creation and which I shall have kept until that time. And they will be nourishment for all who are left. The earth will also yield fruits ten thousandfold. And on one vine will be a thousand branches, and one branch will produce a thousand clusters, and one cluster will produce a thousand grapes, and one grape will produce a cor of wine. And those who are hungry will enjoy themselves and they will, moreover, see marvels every day. . . .

And it will happen after these things when the time of the appearance of the Anointed One has been fulfilled and he returns in glory, that then all who sleep in hope of him will rise. And it will happen at that time that those treasuries will be opened in which the number of the souls of the righteous were kept, and they will go out and the multitudes of the souls will appear together, in one assemblage, of one mind. And the first ones will enjoy themselves and the last ones will not be sad. For they know that the time has come of which it is said that it is the end of times. But the souls of the wicked will the more waste away when they shall see all these things. For they know that their torment has come and that their perditions have arrived.

In the classical rabbinic literature, attitudes toward the coming of the Messiah range from eager expectation to wary caution. The following passages from the Babylonian Talmud's tractate on the functions of the rabbinic High Court (San. 96b–98a) are representative of the rabbinic literature as a whole.

4.2B SANHEDRIN 96B–98A

Said Rav Nahman to Rabbi Isaac: Do you have a tradition about when the Son of the Fallen One will come? He said to him: Who is the Son of the Fallen One? He said to him: It is the Messiah. He replied: You call him Messiah, Son of the Fallen One? He said: Yes, for it is written in Scripture: On that day I will raise up the tabernacle of David, the Fallen One" (Amos 9:11). He said to him: Thus said Rabbi Yohanan: In the generation to which the Son of David comes, the disciples of Sages grow fewer; and as for the rest, their eyes grow dim through suffering and sighing, and troubles will multiply and harsh decrees will be promulgated so quickly that the latest will overtake its predecessor. . . .

Excerpts from the Second Book of Baruch, translated by A. F. J. Klijn from James H. Charlesworth, ed., *The Old Testament Pseudepigrapha, Vol. 1.* Copyright © 1983, 1985 by James H. Charlesworth. Reprinted with the permission of Doubleday, a division of Bantam Doubleday Dell Publishing Group, Inc.

A tradition from the disciples of Elijah: For six thousand years the world will exist. For two thousand it will be desolate, for two thousand Torah will reign, and two thousand will be the Days of the Messiah. But because of our many sins, what has been lost of the latter period is lost for good. . . .

Rabbi Joshua ben Levi found Elijah, the Prophet, standing at the entrance of the tomb of Rabbi Shimon bar Yohai. He said to him: Will I reach the World to Come? He said to him: If the gentleman so wishes! Said Rabbi Joshua ben Levi: Two have I seen, but the voice of a third did I hear! He said to him: When is the Messiah coming? He said to him: Go ask him yourself! He said: Where is he residing? He replied: At the gate of the city. He replied: What are his distinguishing features? He replied: He is sitting among the diseased poor. All of them untie and tie their bandages together, but he unties and ties them one by one, thinking: Should I be summoned, I don't want to delay. He went to the Messiah and said: Peace to you, my Master and Teacher! He replied: Peace to you, ben Levi! He said to him: When is the Master coming? He said to him: Today! Rabbi Joshua ben Levi returned to Elijah, who said: What did he say to you? He said: Peace to you, ben Levi! He replied: He thus promised you and your father the World to Come! He replied: But he lied to me, for he said: I am coming today—but he did not come! He replied: This is what he meant: "Today, if you will obey his voice" (Ps. 95:7). . . .

Said Ulla: Let him come, but let me not see him! And so said Rabba: Let him come, but let me not see him! Rav Joseph said: Let him come, and may I have the merit to sit in the shade of the dung of his donkey! Said Abbaye to Rabbah: Why this reluctance? Can it be because of the birthpangs of the Messiah? And so is it transmitted in oral tradition: His disciples asked Rabbi Eleazer, What should someone do to be spared the birthpangs of the Messiah? He replied: Let him engage in Torah study and acts of reciprocal kindness. But, as for Master, indeed he has both Torah and acts of reciprocal kindness (—so why is he reluctant to witness the Messiah)? He replied: Perhaps his sins will intervene (and cause him to suffer), as Rabbi Jacob bar Idi taught. For Rabbi Jacob bar Idi compared two verses as follows—It is written of Jacob: "And behold, I am with you and will keep you wherever you go" (Gen. 28:15), and it is written: "Then Jacob was greatly afraid" (Gen. 32:8). For Jacob was afraid that his sins would intervene. This accords with what is transmitted orally: "Till your people pass over, O LORD, till our people pass over, whom you have acquired" (Exod. 15:16). "Till your people pass over" refers to the first entry into the Land of Israel. "Till your people pass over whom you acquired" refers to the second entry. Learn from this that Israel would have been worthy to have a miracle performed for them upon the second entry as at the first entry—but sin intervened.

Messianic activism among the Jewish masses of medieval Islamic lands is well documented by Jewish, Muslim, and Karaite writers of the time. One such movement, around the figure of Daud ibn al-Ruhi (i.e., "David, Son of the Spirit"), reached its climax in the middle of twelfth-century Persia. The following account is written by Samuel ibn Abbas, a Jewish convert to Islam. He regards the movement around ibn al-Ruhi as a farce and probably embellishes the affair, but his account gives a rich sense of the passions aroused.

4.2C SILENCING OF THE JEWS AND THE CHRISTIANS THROUGH RATIONAL ARGUMENTS

We are going to tell a story of the haste with which the Jews accepted the false and the fictitious, which shows how little discernment they have. The following incident happened in our time among the finest, cleverest, and shrewdest among them, namely, the Jews of Baghdad. A swindler, a young Jew, a man of fine features, whose name was Menachem ben Solomon but who was known by the name of ibn al-Ruhi, grew up in the neighborhood of Mosul. . . . [Ibn Abbas goes on to describe the messianic movement as ibn al-Ruhi's plot to secure political power for himself by claiming to release the Jews from the domination of Muslims. The reaction of Baghdadi Jewry to al-Ruhi's claims is of great interest.] About the time that the people in Baghdad heard of Menachem, two crafty deceivers among the Jewish scholars of the city forged letters in his name in which they announced to the Jews of Baghdad the redemption which they had been awaiting of old and designated a night in which they would all fly to Jerusalem together. The Baghdad Jews . . . listened to this and allowed themselves to be misled into accepting it as truth. Their wives brought their possessions and jewelry to both men, in order that these might distribute them in their name to those who in their judgment were worthy of them. In this manner the Jews spent the largest portion of their fortune. . . . They procured green garments for themselves, and they came together that night on the roofs, waiting for the moment, when, as they hoped, they would fly from there to Jerusalem on angels' wings. . . . The women began to scream because of their suckling infants, for fear that they would fly away before their children, or their children before them, and thus the little ones, because of delay in getting suck, would suffer hunger. The Muslims there were amazed at this, wondering what could have happened to the Jews, and did not oppose them until they discovered to what unbelievable assurances the Jews had surrendered themselves. . . . The Jews continued to move to and fro in preparation for their flight until they were disillusioned by the break of dawn and by the departure of the deceivers who had already left with their riches. Now the deception was clear to them, and they realized how far these men had carried their villainy. This year was called the "Year of Flying Away," and both old and young date from it.

The thirteenth-century Zohar, which came to constitute the primary text of kabbalistic tradition, accepts with absolute seriousness the diverse tradition of messianic speculation preserved in earlier rabbinic sources. But, as with everything else kabbalists inherited from earlier Jewish thought, the Zohar uses midrashic methods to recast traditional ideas within its own metaphysical system of divine emanations, the Sefirot. For the Zohar, the Messiah as a figure is generally of less

Excerpts from Samuel ibn Abbas, from Jacob R. Marcus, *The Jew in the Medieval World.* Copyright 1938 by the Union of American Hebrew Congregations. Reprinted with the permission of The Jewish Publication Society of America.

interest than the sefirotic processes that will set the stage for the messianic transformation of reality—when the present distress of all being is healed. The following passage (*Akharei Mot*, III:77b) discusses the redemption in terms of the marital
union of Matronita with the King. The Matronita, also called "The Lady" or
"Shekhinah" (Divine Presence), is the last of the ten Sefirot. The King, also called
"Tiferet," represents the central sefirotic power that divides the upper from the
lower Sefirot. The Matronita and the King also stand for the first two letters of the
Divine Name (Y and H), which must be brought into unity with the last two (W
and H) in the Heavenly Realm in order for redemption to appear on the Earthly
Realm.

4.2D ZOHAR, AKHAREI MOT, III:77B

Y must be joined to H and H must be joined to W; W must be joined to H, and H
must be joined to all of them. Then they comprise a single entity, one Word that can
never be sundered for all eternity. One who (through sin in the Earthly Realm)
causes such a separation (in the Heavenly Realm) is, as it were, like one who has
destroyed the world and brought shame upon all!

In the Coming Time, the Holy One Blessed is He will restore the Shekhinah
to her place (in Heaven), so that all shall be joined in a single union, as it is written
in Scripture: "In that day the LORD will be one and his name one" (Zech. 14:9). Now
do you say: Is he not one now? No! For these days the wicked of the world are responsible for the fact that he is not one. For, indeed, the Matronita is in alienation
from the King, and they are no longer in conjugal union. Consequently, the Heavenly Mother [i.e., the Sefirah Understanding] is in alienation from her King and
does not nurse him. Now, since the King is deprived of his Matronita, he is also no
longer crowned with the crowns of the Heavenly Mother as he had been when he
was joined to the Matronita, who had crowned him with many crowns and glorious, holy, heavenly diadems, as it is written: "Go out, daughters of Zion, and see
upon King Solomon the crown with which his mother crowned him" (Song 3:11).
When he was in conjugal union with the Matronita—only then did the Heavenly
Mother properly crown him. But now, since the King is not with the Matronita, the
Heavenly Mother has removed her crowns and has withheld from him the up-
surge of the streams (of blessing), and he cannot be brought into a single unity.
Therefore, so to speak, he is not one! But when the Matronita returns to her Hekhal
[i.e., the Heavenly Sefirotic order], and the King joins her in conjugal union, then
all things will be joined into a unity, without separation.

And this is what is meant in Scripture: "In that day the LORD will be one and
his name one. "In *that* day"—only at the time that the Matronita returns to her
Hekhal; but now there is no unity without separation. Rather, now: "And the redeemed will climb Mt. Zion to judge Mt. Esau" (Obad. 1:21). And this is in line
with what oral tradition transmits: Said Rabbi Shimon: The Matronita will not go
up to her Temple in joy until the Kingdom of Esau is shattered and vengeance is
exacted for having caused all this. Only thereafter will the King join her in conju-

gal union in perfected joy, as it is written: "And the redeemed will climb Mt. Zion to judge Mt. Esau." This verse refers to the first act of the drama. Only thereafter: "And the kingdom will be God's" (Obad. 1:21). Who is this Kingdom? This is the Matronita, (which is obvious) if you render the verse: "She shall be to God as a Kingdom." Afterwards they will join together in a single conjugal union. This is just as is written: "And the LORD will be king over all the world. In that day the LORD will be one and his name one."

The seventeenth-century messianic movement surrounding Shabbatai Zvi drew much of its symbolic images from the Zoharic tradition as interpreted by later kabbalists, such as Rabbi Isaac Luria. The greatest challenge to the Shabbateans was to explain how the Messiah could become an apostate, a convert to Islam. The following letter from Zvi's major spokesman, Nathan of Gaza, draws upon this tradition to place the Messiah's shocking decision in proper context. The letter was written to believers on the Greek island of Zante in 1668. References to the *Ra'ya Mehemna* and the *Tiqqunim* are to portions of the Zohar.

4.2E LETTER OF NATHAN OF GAZA

Know therefore . . . that (it is) he and no other, and besides him there is no Savior of Israel. And although he has put the fair miter (the turban) on his head, his holiness is not profaned, for God has sworn with His right hand and He will not deceive. This is one of God's mysteries, and no one who has any knowledge of the mysteries of the Torah will consider it strange. For although nothing of the kind is indicated in the plain sense of Scripture, yet we have seen that the sayings of the ancient rabbis on these (eschatological) matters are obscure and utterly inexplicable. . . . Nevertheless, he who has eyes to see . . . can find (sufficient) proof for these things . . . and not speak falsely against the holiness of the Sabbath (that is, Sabbatai Sevi), for whoever inveighs against him no doubt his soul is of the "mixed multitude," as is evident from what is said in the holy book *Ra'ya Mehemna,* which . . . also speaks of the true Redeemer. There it is said that "Thou art wounded because of the guilt of the people and I suffer great pain as it is said "and they made his grave with the wicked" (Isa. 53:9), and they do not recognize me and I am accounted in their eyes like the stinking carcass of a dog.". . . No doubt the *Ra'ya Mehemna* has revealed that (the Messiah) would do strange things and be accounted therefore like a dead dog, as we have, indeed, seen it happening these days with some people who have removed their trust from the Lord (Messiah). A further definite proof can be found in the *Tiqqunim* where it is said, . . . "good from the inside, but his garment is bad—this refers to the lowly one, riding on an ass

(Zech. 9:9). Here you only need to understand the ordinary, plain sense, . . . for the "bad garment" refers to the turban which he donned. . . . Yet we (the true believers) have learned that the Sabbath has not been profaned because of his donning the turban, . . . but he had to act thus because of the sins of Israel. . . . Wherefore, my brethren and all faithful believers in Israel who stand and wait and tremble at these words, be strong and of good courage, be not affrighted nor dismayed, turn unto the Lord your God with all your heart and all your soul and give thanks unto His great name, for verily we shall behold what our ancestors have not seen. And although people may say that these words of comfort are mere vanity because I am unable, at present, to work a miracle, yet I shall not desist from comforting the downcast that tremble at this word, that ask of me righteous ordinances and desire to draw near to God, the poor and the needy who are in trouble and distress for the holiness of God's name.

By the nineteenth century, many Western European Jews who considered themselves loyal to Judaism nevertheless found traditional images of the Messiah difficult to accept. Literal belief in eschatological miracles seemed unscientific, and literal belief in the political restoration of Israel to its land seemed unpatriotic. The early German Reform movement took the lead in reconceiving messianic ideas in historical and ethical terms as the hoped-for unity of humanity. The following passage records a speech of Rabbi David Einhorn, an early Reform leader, speaking in 1845 at a rabbinical conference in Frankfurt.

4.2f PROTOCOLS OF THE SECOND RABBINIC CONFERENCE

The decline of Israel's political independence was at one time deplored, but in reality it was not a misfortune, but a mark of progress; not a degradation, but an elevation of our religion, through which Israel has come closer to fulfilling its vocation. . . . At one time I took the concept of the Messiah to be a substitute for the idea of immortality, but now I no longer think so. I rather consider it as a hope of both worldly and heavenly salvation. Neither this idea nor the concept of the Chosen People contain anything reprehensible. The concept of the Chosen People, in fact, offers the undeniable advantage, for it creates a beneficial self-consciousness in the face of the ruling church. I vote for the renunciation of all petitions for the restoration of the sacrifices and our political independence. I should prefer our prayers for the Messiah to express a hope for *a spiritual renaissance and the unification of all men* in faith and in love through the agency of Israel [italics in original].

Excerpts from a speech by Rabbi David Einhorn, from Paul Mendes-Flohr and Judah Reinharz, eds., *The Jew in the Modern World* (New York: Oxford University Press, 1980), pp. 163–164.

Despite nearly two centuries in which modern forms of Judaism have sought to reinterpret the messianic ideas of rabbinic tradition in terms of modern historical and ethical categories, there remain Jews who choose to retain premodern conceptions of a miraculous, world-transforming advent of the Son of David. Recently, the Habad-Lubavitch movement within Hasidism has played a central role in urging Jews to see in current historical events signs of the messianic conclusion of world history. Prior to his death in 1994, some followers argued that the Lubavitcher Rebbe, Rabbi Menachem Mendel Schneerson, would soon be designated as Messiah. The years since his death have seen a continued adherence to this belief in some Habad circles. The following excerpt, written by Rabbi Immanuel Schochet, was written prior to the Rebbe's death. It appeals to classical and modern halakhic authorities, arguing that the messianic hope in its premodern form is an essential element of Jewish belief and ought to be actively promoted in that form by contemporary Jews. Note that Rabbi Schochet's imagined opponents in this article are not Reform or Conservative Jews, but other Orthodox Jews who question the propriety of explicitly messianic action.

4.2G THE PRINCIPLE OF MASHIACH AND MESSIANIC ACTIVISM

Some object: "Messianic activism" is something novel, not seen among our predecessors; thus, "why now?" There are several simple answers.

1. Many sages throughout the ages are known to have made all kinds of efforts to bring about Mashiach. Any change, therefore, is only quantitative, in terms of the extent to involve *klal Yisrael*, but not in the principle *per se* (especially after the thousand-year ban on pressing for the end has passed).

Moreover, the Chafetz Chaim already established the precedent for our times to do so publicly, seeking over-all involvement. Like perhaps none before him, he spoke, admonished, issued letters, proclamations and special works urging Israel to ready itself for the imminent redemption, to await and demand it. He innovated a renewal of intensive study of laws relating to the service in the *Bet Hamikdash* in anticipation of imminent application.

2. Our predecessors, though far superior, did not succeed in bringing Mashiach. Thus, we must go beyond them. Extra measures are needed, in line with the homily which (by changing one vowel) reads *Leviticus* 19:31 as, "Do not turn to the *avot* (fathers)" i.e., do not restrict yourself to the measures of your predecessors.

To undertake new measures within the boundaries of *Halachah*, let alone when such are suggested by *Halachah* itself, is always a legitimate exercise. Moreover,

From Rabbi Immanuel Schochet, "The Principle of Mashiach and Messianic Activism" from *Jewish Action* (Winter 1991–1992). Copyright © 1992 by Union of Orthodox Jewish Congregations of America. Reprinted with the permission of the author and *Jewish Action*.

even if "Messianic activism" were a "novel" approach, it is certainly appropriate in view of Ramban and Abarbanel's premise that this is a case of *nishtanu ha-itim* (a historical change of conditions).

3. Our predecessors were indeed superior. Nonetheless, we have two advantages: (a) there is an automatic progression of time that brought us that much closer to the 'final end'; (b) we are much more likely to actualize the earlier 'potential ends' *by virtue of our predecessors;* we are like "a midget standing on the shoulders of a giant" because of the accumulative merit of our ancestors accruing to our credit along with our own *mitzvot* and good deeds.

On the very day that the *Bet Hamikdash* was destroyed, was born one fit to be the redeemer. In every generation thereafter, there is a *tzaddik* who has, what Rambam calls, *chezkat Mashiach*. Because of our sins, many such *tzaddikim* passed away in the past. We did not merit that the Messianic spirit was bestowed upon them. They were fit and ready for this, but their generations were not fit.

Mashiach is thus alive and present in our very midst, ready to be revealed at a moment's notice. The Chafetz Chaim, the most widely acclaimed *posek* of his day, ruled explicitly that even the primary condition of *t'shuvah* has already been fulfilled. As all the 'ends' have passed, why then has the scion of David not yet come?

The Chafetz Chaim answers: if we truly and sincerely awaited and longed for Mashiach, he would have come already!

All of us believe in Mashiach. The doctrine is affirmed, but mostly as an abstract theorem rather than a practical issue of immediate relevance. *Halachah* ordains that every day one is to consider Mashiach's coming on that very day, as evident from the *Gemara.* When not sensing it that way, "it follows that the belief in Mashiach is extremely weak. All our talk is but outwardly, while our heart is not with us . . ."

"Whenever *you* want, [God] wants! If you want to make your request to hasten the end, request!" The coming of Mashiach and the Messianic era now depend on the "Messianic activism" of Israel demanding the redemption. "*Today,* if you will listen to His voice!"

MONOTHEISM

CHAPTER 5
IN CHRISTIANITY

5.1 ESTABLISHING THE IDENTITY OF JESUS CHRIST

Since the second century, Christian authors have claimed that the writer of this Gospel was John the Apostle, the son of Zebedee, Jesus' "beloved" disciple. Many modern scholars propose that it was probably written at the end of the first century by disciples of John. This, the fourth of the Gospels, is the most overtly theological and mystical. Since much of its thought is centered on the mystery of the Incarnation and the divine personhood of Jesus, it became a singularly important book for the development of Christian thinking on God, the Trinity, and the person and work of Jesus Christ. The following selections from John's Gospel highlight its proclamation of the divine nature of Jesus, the incarnate God, and its avowal of a close relation between Jesus the Messiah and his heavenly Father.

5.1A THE GOSPEL ACCORDING TO SAINT JOHN 1:1–1:18

Prologue

> In the beginning was the Word:
> the Word was with God
> and the Word was God.

He was with God in the beginning.
Through him all things came to be,
not one thing had its being but through him.
All that came to be had life in him
and that life was the light of men,
a light that shines in the dark,
a light that darkness could not overpower.

A man came, sent by God.
His name was John.
He came as a witness,
as a witness to speak for the light,
so that everyone might believe through him.
He was not the light,
only a witness to speak for the light.

The Word was the true light
that enlightens all men;
and he was coming into the world.
He was in the world
that had its being through him,
and the world did not know him.
He came to his own domain
and his own people did not accept him.
But to all who did accept him
he gave power to become children of God,
to all who believe in the name of him
who was born not out of human stock
or urge of the flesh
or will of man
but of God himself.
The Word was made flesh,
he lived among us,
and we saw his glory,
the glory that is his as the only Son of the Father,
full of grace and truth.

"This is the one of whom I said:
He who comes after me
ranks before me
because he existed before me."

Indeed, from his fullness we have, all of us, received—
yes, grace in return for grace,
since, though the Law was given through Moses,
grace and truth have come through Jesus Christ.
No one has ever seen God;
it is the only Son, who is nearest to the Father's heart,
who has made him known. . . .

5.1B THE GOSPEL ACCORDING TO SAINT JOHN 7:12–7:20

When Jesus spoke to the people he said:

> "I am the light of the world;
> anyone who follows me will not be walking in the dark;
> he will have the light of life." . . .

At this the Pharisees said to him, "You are testifying on your own behalf; your testimony is not valid." Jesus replied:

> "It is true that I am testifying on my own behalf,
> but my testimony is still valid,
> because I know
> where I came from and where I am going;
> but you do not know
> where I come from or where I am going.
> You judge by human standards;
> I judge no one,
> but if I judge,
> my judgment will be sound,
> because I am not alone:
> that the testimony of two witnesses is valid.
> I may be testifying on my own behalf,
> but the Father who sent me is my witness too."

They asked him, "Where is your Father?" Jesus answered:

> "You do not know me, nor do you know my Father;
> if you did know me, you would know my Father as well."

He spoke these words in the Treasury, while teaching in the Temple. No one arrested him, because his time had not yet come. . . .

5.1C THE GOSPEL ACCORDING TO SAINT JOHN 8:52–8:59

The Jews said, "Now we know for certain that you are possessed. Abraham is dead, and the prophets are dead, and yet you say, 'Whoever keeps my word will never know the taste of death.' Are you greater than our father Abraham, who is dead? The prophets are dead too. Who are you claiming to be?" Jesus answered:

> "If I were to seek my own glory
> that would be no glory at all;
> my glory is conferred by the Father,
> by the one of whom you say, 'He is our God,'
> although you do not know him.

> But I know him,
> and if I were to say: I do not know him,
> I should be a liar, as you are liars yourselves.
> But I do know him, and I faithfully keep his word.
> Your father Abraham rejoiced
> to think that he would see my Day;
> he saw it and was glad."

The Jews then said, "You are not fifty yet, and you have seen Abraham!" Jesus replied:

> "I tell you most solemnly,
> before Abraham ever was,
> I Am."

At this they picked up stones to throw at him; but Jesus hid himself and left the Temple.

5.1D THE GOSPEL ACCORDING TO SAINT JOHN 10:22–10:33

VI. The Feast of Dedication

Jesus Claims to Be the Son of God

It was the time when the feast of Dedication was being celebrated in Jerusalem. It was winter, and Jesus was in the Temple walking up and down in the Portico of Solomon. The Jews gathered around him and said, "How much longer are you going to keep us in suspense? If you are the Christ, tell us plainly." Jesus replied:

> "I have told you, but you do not believe.
> The works I do in my Father's name are my witness;
> but you do not believe,
> because you are no sheep of mine.
> The sheep that belong to me listen to my voice;
> I know them and they follow me.
> I give them eternal life;
> they will never be lost
> and no one will ever steal them from me.
> The Father who gave them to me is greater than anyone,
> and no one can steal from the Father.
> The Father and I are one."

The Jews fetched stones to stone him, so Jesus said to them, "I have done many good works for you to see, works from my Father; for which of these are you stoning me?" The Jews answered him, "We are not stoning you for doing a good work but for blasphemy: you are only a man and you claim to be God."

5.2 Paul's Letters

The following selections from Paul's letters focus on descriptions of the person and work of Christ. These texts have all figured prominently in the development of Christian thinking on salvation (soteriology), Christ (Christology), and the Trinity.

Philipians

Written around 56–57 CE, this letter is not usually known for doctrinal expositions. It does, however, contain a most significant passage on Christ and his work, which many experts think could be an early Christian hymn.

Ephesians

This epistle was probably written around 61–63 CE—while Paul was under arrest in Rome—not just for the Christians of Ephesus, to whom it is addressed, but for wider circulation. This selection contains some of Paul's most significant Christological and soteriological thinking. In other words, Paul makes a sustained attempt at explaining who Jesus is and what he can do for those who accept him as the Christ.

Colossians

This was also written from prison in Rome around 61–63 CE, shortly before Paul's martyrdom. The passages here focus on the divinity of Christ and on the redemption now revealed to the Gentiles.

5.2A Philipians 2:1–2:11

If our life in Christ means anything to you, if love can persuade at all, or the Spirit that we have in common, or any tenderness and sympathy, then be united in your convictions and united in your love, with a common purpose and a common mind. That is the one thing which would make me completely happy. There must be no competition among you, no conceit; but everybody is to be self-effacing. Always consider the other person to be better than yourself, so that nobody thinks of his own interests first but everybody thinks of other people's interest instead. In your minds you must be the same as Christ Jesus:

His state was divine,
yet he did not cling
to his equality with God
but emptied himself
to assume the condition of a slave,
and became as men are;
and being as all men are,
he was humbler yet,
even to accepting death,
death on a cross.
But God raised him high
and gave him the name
which is above all other names
so that *all beings*
in the heavens, on earth and in the underworld,
should bend the knee at the name of Jesus
and that every tongue should acclaim
Jesus Christ as Lord,
to the glory of God the Father.

5.2B EPHESIANS 1:1–1:13, 2:1–2:10

Address and Greetings

From Paul, appointed by God to be an apostle of Christ Jesus, to the saints who are faithful to Christ Jesus: Grace and peace to you from God our Father and from the Lord Jesus Christ.

I. The Mystery of Salvation and of the Church

God's Plan of Salvation

Blessed be God the Father of our Lord Jesus Christ,
who has blessed us with all the spiritual blessings of heaven in Christ.
Before the world was made, he chose us, chose us in Christ,
to be holy and spotless, and to live through love in his presence,
determining that we should become his adopted sons, through Jesus Christ
for his own kind purposes,
to make us praise the glory of his grace,
his free gift to us in the Beloved,
in whom, through his blood, we gain our freedom, the forgiveness of our sins.
Such is the richness of the grace
which he has showered on us
in all wisdom and insight.
He has let us know the mystery of his purpose,
the hidden plan he so kindly made in Christ from the beginning
to act upon when the times had run their course to the end:

that he would bring everything together under Christ, as head,
everything in the heavens and everything on earth.
And it is in him that we were claimed as God's own,
chosen from the beginning,
under the predetermined plan of the one who guides all things
as he decides by his own will;
chosen to be,
for his greater glory,
the people who would put their hopes in Christ before he came.
Now you too, in him,
have heard the message of the truth and the good news of your salvation,
and have believed it;

And you were dead, through the crimes and the sins in which you used to live when you were following the way of this world, obeying the ruler who governs the air, the spirit who is at work in the rebellious. We all were among them too in the past, living sensual lives, ruled entirely by our own physical desires and our own ideas; so that by nature we were as much under God's anger as the rest of the world. But God loved us with so much love that he was generous with his mercy: when we were dead through our sins, he brought us to life with Christ—it is through grace that you have been saved—and raised us up with him and gave us a place with him in heaven, in Christ Jesus.

This was to show for all ages to come, through his goodness toward us in Christ Jesus, how infinitely rich he is in grace. Because it is by grace that you have been saved, through faith; not by anything of your own, but by a gift from God; not by anything that you have done, so that nobody can claim the credit. We are God's work of art, created in Christ Jesus to live the good life as from the beginning he had meant us to live it.

5.2c Colossians 1:3–1:7, 1:9–1:20

Preface

We have never failed to remember you in our prayers and to give thanks for you to God, the Father of our Lord Jesus Christ, ever since we heard about your faith in Christ Jesus and the love that you show toward all the saints because of the hope which is stored up for you in heaven. It is only recently that you heard of this, when it was announced in the message of the truth. The Good News which has reached you is spreading all over the world and producing the same results as it has among you ever since the day when you heard about God's grace and understood what this really is. . . . we have never failed to pray for you, and what we ask God is that through perfect wisdom and spiritual understanding you should reach the fullest knowledge of his will. So you will be able to lead the kind of life which the Lord expects of you, a life acceptable to him in all its aspects; showing the results in all the good actions you do and increasing your knowledge of God. You will have in you the strength, based on his own glorious power, never to give in, but to bear anything joyfully, thanking the Father who has made it possible for you to join the saints and with them to inherit the light.

Because that is what he has done: he has taken us out of the power of darkness and created a place for us in the kingdom of the Son that he loves, and in him, we gain our freedom, the forgiveness of our sins.

I. Formal Instruction

Christ is the Head of All Creation

> He is the image of the unseen God
> and the first-born of all creation,
> for in him were created
> all things in heaven and on earth:
> everything visible and everything invisible,
> Thrones, Dominations, Sovereignties, Powers—
> all things were created through him and for him.
> Before anything was created, he existed,
> and he holds all things in unity.
> Now the Church is his body,
> he is its head.
>
> As he is the Beginning,
> he was first to be born from the dead,
> so that he should be first in every way;
> because God wanted all perfection
> to be found in him
> and all things to be reconciled through him and for him,
> everything in heaven and everything on earth,
> when he made peace
> by his death on the cross.

5.3 THE LETTER TO THE HEBREWS

The most theological book of the New Testament, this document was written for Jewish Christians around 67 CE. Long attributed to Saint Paul, this epistle is now generally considered the work of someone else who might have been influenced by Paul. Its main concern is the work of redemption effected by Jesus Christ, which is explained largely through references to the rituals performed by the levitical priests at the Temple in Jerusalem. The author of *Hebrews* here proposes that the former sacrifices of the old covenant have been replaced by the unique sacrifice of Christ on the cross, in which as both victim and priest, the God-man made effective the forgiveness of sins once and for all.

5.3A A Letter Addressed to a Jewish-Christian Community
1:1–1:4, 2:3–2:18, 4:12–4:18, 5:1–5:9

Prologue

The Greatness of the Incarnate Son of God

At various times in the past and in various different ways, God spoke to our ancestors through the prophets; but in our own time, the last days, he has spoken to us through his Son, the Son that he has appointed to inherit everything and through whom he made everything there is. He is the radiant light of God's glory and the perfect copy of his nature, sustaining the universe by his powerful command; and now that he has destroyed the defilement of sin, he has gone to take his place in heaven at the right hand of divine Majesty. So he is now as far above the angels as the title which he has inherited is higher than their own name. . . .

He did not appoint angels to be rulers of the world to come, and that world is what we are talking about. Somewhere there is a passage that shows us this. It runs: *What is man that you should spare a thought for him, the son of man that you should care for him? For a short while you made him lower than the angels; you crowned him with glory and splendor. You have put him in command of everything.* Well then, if he has *put him in command of everything*, he has left nothing which is not under his command. At present, it is true, we are not able to see that *everything has been put under his command*, but we do see in Jesus one who was *for a short while made lower than the angels* and is now *crowned with glory and splendor* because he submitted to death; by God's grace he had to experience death for all mankind. (Ps. 8:4–6)

As it was his purpose to bring a great many of his sons into glory, it was appropriate that God, for whom everything exists and through whom everything exists, should make perfect, through suffering, the leader who would take them to their salvation. For the one who sanctifies, and the ones who are sanctified, are of the same stock; that is why he openly calls them *brothers* in the text: *I shall announce your name to my brothers, praise you in full assembly;* or the text: *In him I hope;* or the text: *Here I am with the children whom God has given me.* (Ps. 22:22; Isa. 8:17)

Since all the *children* share the same blood and flesh, he too shared equally in it, so that by his death he could take away all the power of the devil, who had power over death, and set free all those who had been held in slavery all their lives by the fear of death. For it was not the angels that he took to himself; he took to himself *descent from Abraham.* It was essential that he should in this way become completely like his brothers so that he could be a compassionate and trustworthy high priest of God's religion, able to atone for human sins. That is, because he has himself been through temptation he is able to help others who are tempted.

The word of God is something alive and active: it cuts like any double-edged sword but more finely: it can slip through the place where the soul is divided from the spirit, or joints from the marrow; it can judge the secret emotions and thoughts. No created thing can hide from him; everything is uncovered and open to the eyes of the one to whom we must give account of ourselves.

Since in Jesus, the Son of God, we have the supreme high priest who has gone through to the highest heaven, we must never let go of the faith that we have professed. For it is not as if we had a high priest who was incapable of feeling our weaknesses with us; but we have one who has been tempted in every way that we are, though he is without sin. Let us be confident, then, in approaching the throne of grace, that we shall have mercy from him and find grace when we are in need of help.

Every high priest has been taken out of mankind and is appointed to act for men in their relations with God, to offer gifts and sacrifices for sins; and so he can sympathize with those who are ignorant or uncertain because he too lives in the limitations of weakness. That is why he has to make sin offerings for himself as well as for the people. No one takes this honor on himself, but each one is called by God, as Aaron was. Nor did Christ give himself the glory of becoming high priest, but he had it from the one who said to him: *You are my son, today I have become your father,* and in another text: *You are a priest of the order of Melchizedek, and for ever.* During his life on earth, he offered up prayer and entreaty, aloud and in silent tears, to the one who had the power to save him out of death, and he submitted so humbly that his prayer was heard. Although he was Son, he learned to obey through suffering; but having been made perfect, he became for all who obey him the source of eternal salvation. (Ps. 2:7; 110:4)

5.4 SOME OBSERVATIONS ON THE HUMANITY AND DIVINITY OF JESUS

Saint Irenaeus of Lyons, *Against Heresies*

Whereas gnosticism offered redemption *from* the material world, orthodox Christianity promised the redemption *of* material existence. Among the early Christian writers, few rival Ireneaus of Lyons (ca. 130–200) in his defense of the reality of God's incarnation as a human being and in his vision of the promised redemption of God's material creation. Irenaeus' *Against Heresies,* written in the latter part of the second century, took dead aim against gnostic dualism. This selection highlights Irenaeus' defense of apostolic tradition against gnostic claims of a secret oral tradition that revealed Christ as totally otherworldly and less than fully human. Against these gnostic beliefs in a Christ who could not condescend to take on a "disgusting" human body, Irenaeus proposes an enfleshed divinity who redeems a fallen world precisely because of his corporality.

5.4A IRENAEUS CHALLENGES GNOSTICISM

The apostolic tradition is preserved in the Church and has come down to us. Let us turn, then, to the demonstration from the Writings of those apostles who recorded the gospel, in which they recorded their conviction about God, showing that our Lord Jesus Christ is the Truth, and in him is no lie—as also David said when he prophesied his birth of a virgin and the resurrection of the dead, "Truth has come forth from the earth."[1] The apostles, being disciples of the truth, are apart from every lie. For a lie has no fellowship with the truth, any more than light with darkness, but the presence of one excludes the other.[2] . . . manifestation of the truth. Therefore the Lord imparted knowledge of the truth to his disciples, by which he cured those who were suffering, and restrained sinners from sin. So he did not speak to them in accordance with their previous ideas, nor answer in accordance with the presumptions of inquirers, but in accordance with the sound teaching, without any pretense or respect for persons.

Doctrine of Redemption in Reply to the Gnostics

We could in no other way have learned the things of God unless our Teacher, being the Word, had been made man. For none could declare to us the things of the Father, except his own Word. For who else has known the mind of the Lord, or who has become his counselor?[3] Nor again could we have learned in any other way than by seeing our Teacher, that we might become imitators of his works and doers of his words, and so have communion with him, receiving our increase from him who is perfect and before all creation. We were but recently made by him who is the highest and best, by him who is able to bestow the gift of incorruptibility, made according to the image which is with him and predestined according to the foreknowledge of the Father to be what we were not yet. Made the beginning of [his new] creation, we have received [this gift] in times foreknown by the dispensation of the Word, who is perfect in all things, for he is the mighty Word, and true man. Redeeming us by his blood in accordance with his reasonable[4] nature, he gave himself a ransom for those who had been led into captivity. Since the apostasy tyrannized over us unjustly, and when we belonged by nature to God Almighty had unnaturally alienated us, God's Word, mighty in all things, [reclaimed us], making us his own disciples. Not failing in his quality of justice, he acted justly against the apostasy itself, not redeeming his own

---

[1] Ps. 85 (84):11; "truth" is used practically as a name of Christ, as later not uncommonly by Latin Fathers (especially Augustine and Gregory the Great).

[2] II Cor. 6:14; I John 1:6; Irenaeus' combinations of passages from either Testament or both in such allusive references are an interesting aspect of his use of the Bible.

[3] Rom. 11:34.

[4] The Logos acted *logikos,* a play on words which cannot be rendered exactly in either Latin or English.

From St. Irenaeus of Lyons, *Against Heresies,* in Cyril Richardson, *Early Christian Fathers.* Reprinted with the permission of Westminster John Knox Press.

from it by force, although it at the beginning had merely tyrannized over us, greed-ily seizing the things that were not its own, but by persuasion, as it is fitting for God to receive what he wishes by gentleness and not by force.[5] So neither was the stan-dard of what is just infringed nor did the ancient creation of God perish.

So, then, since the Lord redeemed us by his own blood, and gave his soul for our souls, and his flesh for our bodies, and poured out the Spirit of the Father to bring about the union and communion of God and man—bringing God down to men by [the working of] the Spirit, and again raising man to God by his incarna-tion—and by his coming firmly and truly giving us incorruption, by our commu-nion with God, all the teachings of the heretics are destroyed. Vain are those who say that his appearance [on earth] was a mere fiction. These things did not take place fictitiously but in reality. If he had appeared as man when he was not really human, the Spirit of God could not have rested on him, as was the case, since the Spirit is invisible,[6] nor would there have been any truth in him, what was [then tak-ing place] not being what it seemed to be. As I said before, Abraham and the other prophets saw him prophetically, prophesying by vision what was to be. If he then had appeared without really being what he appeared to be, this would have been just another prophetic vision for men, and they would have had to wait for another coming, in which he would be indeed what now was seen prophetically. I have shown too that to say that his appearance was only seeming is the same as to say that he took nothing from Mary. He would not have had real flesh and blood, by which he paid the price [of our salvation], unless he had indeed recapitulated in himself the ancient making of Adam. Vain therefore are the Valentinians who teach this, and so reject the [new] life of the flesh and scorn what God has made. . . .

Vain above all are they who despise the whole dispensation of God, and deny the salvation of the flesh and reject its rebirth, saying that it is not capable of incorruption. For if this [mortal flesh] is not saved, then neither did the Lord re-deem us by his blood, nor is the cup of the Eucharist the communion of his blood, and the bread which we break the communion of his body. For blood is only to be found in veins and flesh, and the rest of [physical] human nature, which the Word of God was indeed made [partaker of, and so] he redeemed us by his blood. So also his apostle says, "In whom we have redemption by his blood, and the remis-sion of sins."[7] For since we are his members, and are nourished by [his] creation—and he himself gives us this creation, making the sun to rise, and sending the rain as he wills—he declares that the cup, [taken] from the creation, is his own blood, by which he strengthens our blood, and he has firmly assured us that the bread, [taken] from the creation, is his own body, by which our bodies grow. For when the mixed cup and the bread that has been prepared receive the Word of God, and be-come the Eucharist, the body and blood of Christ,[8] and by these our flesh grows

---

[5] Cf. Diog. 7:4; Irenaeus here avoids referring to the prince of the apostasy, but in the process al-most personifies the *apostasia* itself.

[6] And therefore presumably could "rest" only on a visible being, not on another invisible one.

[7] Col. 1:14.

[8] "And blood" lacking in Greek (quoted here by John of Damascus), but doubtless correctly present in Latin; Irenaeus thinks of consecration of the Eucharist by the power of the Word (as in the Eucharistic prayer of Sarapion), or perhaps by the divinely ordered pattern of prayer (cf. Justin, Apol. I, ch. 66).

and is confirmed, how can they say that flesh cannot receive the free gift of God, which is eternal life, since it is nourished by the body and blood of the Lord, and made a member of him? As the blessed Paul says in the Epistle to the Ephesians, that we are members of his body, of his flesh and his bones.[9] He does not say this about a [merely] spiritual and invisible man, for the spirit has neither bones nor flesh, but about [God's] dispensation for the real man, [a dispensation] consisting of flesh and nerves and bones, which is nourished by his cup, which is his blood, and grows by the bread which is his body.

And just as the wooden branch of the vine, placed in the earth, bears fruit in its own time—and as the grain of wheat, falling into the ground and there dissolved, rises with great increase by the Spirit of God, who sustains all things, and then by the wisdom of God serves for the use of men, and when it receives the Word of God becomes the Eucharist, which is the body and blood of Christ—so also our bodies which are nourished by it, and then fall into the earth and are dissolved therein, shall rise at the proper time, the Word of God bestowing on them this rising again, to the glory of God the Father. It is he who indeed grants to this mortal immortality, and gives to the corruptible the gracious gift of incorruption, for God's power is made perfect in weakness, so that we should not be puffed up as if we had life from ourselves, and be exalted against God, developing ungrateful minds. But we learn by experience that our survival forever comes from his greatness, not from our nature, so that we may neither ignore the glory that surrounds God as he is nor be ignorant of our own nature, but may see what it is that God can do, and what man receives as a gift [from him], and so may not wander from the true conception of the reality of things, with reference to both God and man. May it not be, as I have said, that God allows our dissolution into the earth for this very purpose, that being instructed in every way we should for the future be quite definite about all [these] things, being ignorant neither of God nor of ourselves?

5.5 SAINT ATHANASIUS, *ON THE INCARNATION*

Athanasius (ca. 296–373), bishop of Alexandria, was one of the most formidable opponents of Arianism. Arian Christians proposed that Christ, the Son of God, was a lesser deity than God the Father. Arianism attained a large following and at times even the upper hand, gaining the support of some emperors. Dubbed "the black dwarf" by his Arian opponents and forcibly exiled from Alexandria five times, Athanasius stood firm against them, proposing instead the paradox that Christ the Son was fully divine, co-eternal with the Father and the Holy Spirit, *and* also fully human. *On the Incarnation* was written sometime between 318 and 338 as a defense of this paradoxical teaching. In this treatise, Athanasius explains how by becoming a man (Jesus), God the Word (*Logos*) restored to a fallen humanity the image of God in which it had been created.

---

[9] Eph. 5:30.

5.5A Defining the Triune God

For, men's mind having finally fallen to things of sense, the Word disguised himself by appearing in a body, that he might, as man, transfer men to himself, and center their senses on himself, and, men seeing him thenceforth as man, persuade them by the works he did that he is not man only, but also God, and the Word and wisdom of the true God. This too is what Paul means to point out when he says: "That ye, being rooted and grounded in love, may be strong to apprehend with all the saints what is the breadth and length, and height and depth, and to know the love of Christ which passeth knowledge, that ye may be filled unto all the fullness of God."[1] For by the Word revealing himself everywhere, both above and beneath, and in the depth and in the breadth—above, in the creation; beneath, in becoming man; in the depth, in Hades; and in the breadth, in the world—all things have been filled with the knowledge of God. Now for this cause, also, he did not immediately upon his coming accomplish his sacrifice on behalf of all, by offering his body to death and raising it again, for by this means he would have made himself invisible. But he made himself visible enough by what he did, abiding in it, and doing such works, and showing such signs, as made him known no longer as man, but as God the Word. For by his becoming man, the Saviour was to accomplish both works of love: first, in putting away death from us and renewing us again; secondly, being unseen and invisible, in manifesting and making himself known by his works to be the Word of the Father, and the ruler and king of the universe.

For he was not, as might be imagined, circumscribed in the body, nor, while present in the body, was he absent elsewhere; nor, while he moved the body, was the universe left void of his working and providence; but, thing most marvelous, Word as he was, so far from being contained by anything, he rather contained all things himself; and just as while present in the whole of creation, he is at once distinct in being from the universe, and present in all things by his own power—giving order to all things, and over all and in all revealing his own providence, and giving life to each thing and all things, including the whole without being included, but being in his own Father alone wholly and in every respect—thus, even while present in a human body and himself quickening it, he was, without inconsistency, quickening the universe as well, and was in every process of nature, and was outside the whole, and while known from the body by his works, he was none the less manifest from the working of the universe as well. Now, it is the function of the soul to behold even what is outside its own body, by acts of thought, without, however, working outside its own body, or moving by its presence things remote from the body. Never, that is, does a man, by thinking of things at a distance, by that fact either move or displace them; nor if a man were to sit in his own house

---

[1] Eph. 3:17–19.

From St. Athanasius, *On the Incarnation* from Edward R. Hardy, ed., *Christology of the Later Fathers.* Reprinted with the permission of Westminster John Knox Press.

and reason about the heavenly bodies, would he by that fact either move the sun or make the heavens revolve. But he sees that they move and have their being, without being actually able to influence them. Now, the Word of God in his man's nature was not like that; for he was not bound to his body, but was rather himself wielding it, so that he was not only in it, but was actually in everything, and while external to the universe, abode in his Father only. And this was the wonderful thing that he was at once walking as man, and as the Word was quickening all things, and as the Son was dwelling with his Father. So that not even when the Virgin bore him did he suffer any change, nor by being in the body was [his glory] dulled: but, on the contrary, he sanctified the body also. For not even by being in the universe does he share in its nature, but all things, on the contrary, are quickened and sustained by him. For if the sun, too, which was made by him, and which we see as it revolves in the heaven, is not defiled by touching the bodies upon earth, nor is it put out by darkness, but on the contrary itself illuminates and cleanses them also, much less was the all-holy Word of God, maker and lord also of the sun, defiled by being made known in the body; on the contrary, being incorruptible, he quickened and cleansed the body also, which was in itself mortal: "who did," for so it says, "no sin, neither was guile found in his mouth."[2] . . .

Now, if they ask, Why, then, did he not appear by means of other and nobler parts of creation, and use some nobler instrument, as the sun, or moon, or stars, or fire, or air, instead of man merely? let them know that the Lord came not to make a display, but to heal and teach those who were suffering. For the way for one aiming at display would be, just to appear, and to dazzle the beholders; but for one seeking to heal and teach the way is, not simply to sojourn here, but to give himself to the aid of those in want, and to appear as they who need him can bear it; that he may not, by exceeding the requirements of the sufferers, trouble the very persons that need him, rendering God's appearance useless to them. Now, nothing in creation had gone astray with regard to their notions of God, save man only. Why, neither sun, nor moon, nor heaven, nor the stars, nor water, nor air had swerved from their order; but knowing their artificer and sovereign, the Word, they remain as they were made. But men alone, having rejected what was good, then devised things of nought instead of the truth, and have ascribed the honor due to God, and their knowledge of him, to demons and men in the shape of stones. With reason, then, since it were unworthy of the divine goodness to overlook so grave a matter, while yet men were not able to recognize him as ordering and guiding the whole, he takes to himself as an instrument a part of the whole, his human body, and unites himself with that, in order that since men could not recognize him in the whole, they should not fail to know him in the part; and since they could not look up to his invisible power, might be able, at any rate, from what resembled themselves to reason to him and to contemplate him. For, men as they are, they will be able to know his Father more quickly and directly by a body of

[2] I Peter 2:22.

like nature and by the divine works wrought through it, judging by comparison that they are not human but the works of God which are done by him. . . .

But perhaps, shamed into agreeing with this, they will choose to say that God, if he wished to reform and to save mankind, ought to have done so by a mere fiat, without his Word taking a body, in just the same way as he did formerly, when he produced them out of nothing. To this objection of theirs a reasonable answer would be: that formerly, nothing being in existence at all, what was needed to make everything was a fiat and the bare will to do so. But when man had once been made, and necessity demanded a cure, not for things that were not, but for things that had come to be, it was naturally consequent that the physician and Saviour should appear in what had come to be, in order also to cure the things that were. For this cause, then, he has become man, and used his body as a human instrument. For if this were not the right way, how was the Word, choosing to use an instrument, to appear? or whence was he to take it, save from those already in being, and in need of his Godhead by means of one like themselves? For it was not things without being that needed salvation, so that a bare command should suffice, but man, already in existence, was going to corruption and ruin. It was then natural and right that the Word should use a human instrument.

5.6 CHRISTIAN MONOTHEISM AND ENLIGHTENMENT DOCTRINES OF REASON

Unitarianism repudiated the conceptualization of God as three persons and proposed instead the unity of God, arguing that Christ was distinct from and inferior to God. William Ellery Channing's 90-minute sermon "Unitarian Christianity," preached in Baltimore in 1819, outlined as well Unitarian opposition to the traditional Christian doctrine of the atonement. Exuding Enlightenment optimism about human nature, the sermon rejected the Calvinist doctrine of human depravity in favor of trust in human capability and potential. The significance of Christ accordingly lay not in his role as a savior—Unitarians were opposed to the view that Christ died as a sacrifice for human sinfulness—but rather in his example, ongoing intercession with God, and his benevolent justice in his dealings with the world, over which he has been given power.

5.6A CHANNING, UNITARIAN CHRISTIANITY

1. In the first place, we believe in the doctrine of God's UNITY, or that there is one God, and one only. To this truth we give infinite importance, and we feel our-

From William Ellery Channing, "Unitarian Christianity" in Sydney E. Ahlstrom and Jonathan S. Carey, eds., *An American Reformation: A Documentary History of Unitarian Christianity* (Middletown, Conn.: Wesleyan University Press, 1985). Copyright © 1985. Reprinted with the permission of University Press of New England.

selves bound to take heed, lest any man spoil us of it by vain philosophy. The proposition, that there is one God, seems to us exceedingly plain. We understand by it, that there is one being, one mind, one person, one intelligent agent, and one only, to whom underived and infinite perfection and dominion belong. We conceive, that these words could have conveyed no other meaning to the simple and uncultivated people who were set apart to be the depositaries of this great truth, and who were utterly incapable of understanding those hairbreadth distinctions between being and person, which the sagacity of later ages has discovered. We find no intimation, that this language was to be taken in an unusual sense, or that God's unity was a quite different thing from the oneness of other intelligent beings.

We object to the doctrine of the Trinity, that, whilst acknowledging in words, it subverts in effect, the unity of God. According to this doctrine, there are three infinite and equal persons, possessing supreme divinity, called the Father, Son, and Holy Ghost. Each of these persons, as described by theologians, has his own particular consciousness, will, and perceptions. They love each other, converse with each other, and delight in each other's society. They perform different parts in man's redemption, each having his appropriate office, and neither doing the work of the other. The Son is mediator and not the Father. The Father sends the Son, and is not himself sent; nor is he conscious, like the Son, of taking flesh. Here, then, we have three intelligent agents, possessed of different consciousnesses, different wills, and different perceptions, performing different acts, and sustaining different relations; and if these things do not imply and constitute three minds or beings, we are utterly at a loss to know three minds or beings are to be formed. It is difference of properties, and acts, and consciousness, which leads us to the belief of different intelligent beings, and, if this mark fails us, our whole knowledge falls; we have no proof, that all the agents and persons in the universe are not one and the same mind. When we attempt to conceive of three Gods, we can do nothing more than represent to ourselves three agents, distinguished from each other by similar marks and peculiarities to those which separate the persons of the Trinity; and when common Christians hear these persons spoken of as conversing with each other, loving each other, and performing different acts, how can they help regarding them as different beings, different minds?

We do, then, with all earnestness, though without reproaching our brethren, protest against the irrational and unscriptural doctrine of the Trinity. "To us," as to the Apostle and the primitive Christians, "there is one God, even the Father." With Jesus, we worship the Father, as the only living and true God. We are astonished, that any man can read the New Testament, and avoid the conviction, that the Father alone is God. We hear our Saviour continually appropriating this character to the Father. We find the Father continually distinguished from Jesus by this title. "God sent his Son." "God anointed Jesus." Now, how singular and inexplicable is this phraseology, which fills the New Testament, if this title belong equally to Jesus, and if a principal object of this book is to reveal him as God, as partaking equally with the Father in supreme divinity! We challenge our opponents to adduce one passage in the New Testament, where the word God means three persons, where it is not limited to one person, and where, unless turned from its usual sense by the connexion, it does not mean the Father. Can stronger proof be given, that the doctrine of three persons in the Godhead is not a fundamental doctrine of Christianity?

2. Having thus given our views of the unity of God, I proceed in the second place to observe, that we believe in the unity of Jesus Christ. We believe that Jesus is one mind, one soul, one being, as truly one as we are, and equally distinct from the one God. We complain of the doctrine of the Trinity, that, not satisfied with making God three beings, it makes Jesus Christ two beings, and thus introduces infinite confusion into our conceptions of his character. This corruption of Christianity, alike repugnant to common sense and to the general strain of Scripture, is remarkable proof of the power of a false philosophy in disfiguring the simple truth of Jesus.

According to this doctrine, Jesus Christ, instead of being one mind, one conscious intelligent principle, whom we can understand, consists of two souls, two minds; the one divine, the other human; the one weak, the other almighty; the one ignorant, the other omniscient. Now we maintain, that this is to make Christ two beings. To denominate him one person, one being, and yet to suppose him made up of two minds, infinitely different from each other, is to abuse and confound language, and to throw darkness over all our conceptions of intelligent natures. According to the common doctrine, each of these two minds in Christ has its own consciousness, its own will, its own perceptions. They have, in fact, no common properties. The divine mind feels none of the wants and sorrows of the human, and the human is infinitely removed from the perfection and happiness of the divine. Can you conceive of two beings in the universe more distinct? We have always thought that one person was constituted and distinguished by one consciousness. The doctrine, that one and the same person should have two consciousnesses, two wills, two souls, infinitely different from each other, this we think an enormous tax on human credulity.

We say, that if a doctrine, so strange, so difficult, so remote from all the previous conceptions of men, be indeed a part and an essential part of revelation, it must be taught with great distinctness, and we ask our brethren to point to some plain, direct passage, where Christ is said to be composed of two minds infinitely different, yet constituting one person. We find none. Other Christians, indeed, tell us, that this doctrine is necessary to the harmony of the Scriptures, that some texts ascribe to Jesus Christ human, and others divine properties, and that to reconcile these, we must suppose two minds, to which these properties may be referred. In other words, for the purpose of reconciling certain difficult passages, which a just criticism can in a great degree, if not wholly, explain, we must invent an hypothesis vastly more difficult, and involving gross absurdity. We are to find our way out of a labyrinth, by a clue which conducts us into mazes infinitely more inextricable.

Surely, if Jesus Christ felt that he consisted of two minds, and that this was a leading feature of his religion, his phraseology respecting himself would have been colored by this peculiarity. The universal language of men is framed upon the idea, that one person is one person, is one mind, and one soul; and when the multitude heard this language from the lips of Jesus, they must have taken it in its usual sense, and must have referred to a single soul all which he spoke, unless expressly instructed to interpret it differently. But where do we find this instruction? Where do you meet, in the New Testament, the phraseology which abounds in Trinitarian books, and which necessarily grows from the doctrine of two natures in Jesus? Where does this divine teacher say, "This I speak as God, and this as man; this is true only of my human mind, this only of my divine"? Where do we find in the Epistles a trace of this strange phraseology? Nowhere. It was not needed in that day. It was demanded by the errors of a later age.

We believe, then, that Christ is one mind, one being, and, I add, a being distinct from the one God. That Christ is not the one God, not the same being with the Father, is a necessary inference from our former head, in which we saw that the doctrine of three persons in God is a fiction. But on so important a subject, I would add a few remarks. We wish, that those from whom we differ, would weigh one striking fact. Jesus, in his preaching, continually spoke of God. The word was always in his mouth. We ask, does he, by this word, ever mean himself? We say, never. On the contrary, he most plainly distinguishes between God and himself, and so do his disciples. How this is to be reconciled with the idea, that the manifestation of Christ, as God, was a primary object of Christianity, our adversaries must determine.

If we examine the passages in which Jesus is distinguished from God, we shall see, that they not only speak of him as another being, but seem to labor to express his inferiority. He is continually spoken of as the Son of God, sent of God, receiving all his powers from God, working miracles because God was with him, judging justly because God taught him, having claims on our belief, because he was anointed and sealed by God, and as able of himself to do nothing. The New Testament is filled with this language.

Harriet Martineau (1802–1876) was born into a family of English Unitarians. Known for her ability to translate sophisticated philosophical and economic ideas into layperson's terms, she was the author of many works, including the nine-volume *Illustrations of Political Economy* (1832–1834) and her *Autobiography* (1877), of which an excerpt follows. Describing her tenuous religious belief at the age of 20 and then her eventual rejection of that belief as superstition, Martineau displayed the influence of Enlightenment criticism of Christian doctrines. Her conclusions that Christian doctrines about God and salvation were superstitions and that religion was merely a matter of "individual interpretation" subject to a person's "intellectual and moral taste" emerged in connection with her rejection of miracles as proof of the truth of doctrine.

5.6B *Harriet Martineau's Autobiography*

My religious belief, up to the age of twenty, was briefly this. I believed in a God, milder and more beneficent and passionless than the God of the orthodox, inasmuch

Harriet Martineau's Autobiography (Boston: J. R. Osgood, 1877).

as he would not doom any of his creatures to eternal torment. I did not at any time, I think, believe in the Devil, but understood the Scriptures to speak of Sin under that name, and of eternal detriment under the name of eternal punishment. I believed in inestimable and eternal rewards of holiness; but I am confident that I never in my life did a right thing, or abstained from a wrong one from any consideration of reward or punishment. To the best of my recollection, I always feared sin and remorse extremely, and punishment not at all; but, on the contrary, desired punishment or anything else that would give me the one good that I pined for in vain,—ease of conscience. The doctrine of forgiveness on repentance never availed me much, because forgiveness for the past was nothing without safety in the future; and my sins were not curable, I felt, by any single remission of their consequences,—if such remission were possible. If I prayed and wept, and might hope that I was pardoned at night, it was small comfort, because I knew I should be in a state of remorse again before the next noon. I do not remember the time when the forgiveness clause in the Lord's Prayer was not a perplexity and a stumblingblock to me. I did not care about being let off from penalty. I wanted to be at ease in conscience; and that could only be by growing good, whereas I hated and despised myself every day. My belief in Christ was that he was the purest of all beings, under God; and his sufferings for the sake of mankind made him as sublime in my view and my affections as any being could possibly be. The Holy Ghost was a mere fiction to me. I took all the miracles for facts, and contrived to worship the letter of the Scriptures long after I had, as desired, given up portions as 'spurious,' 'interpolations,' and so forth. I believed in a future life as a continuation of the present, and not as a new method of existence; and, from the time when I saw that the resurrection of the body and the immortality of the soul could not both be true, I adhered to the former,—after St. Paul. I was uncomfortably disturbed that Christianity had done so little for the redemption of the race: but the perplexity was not so serious as it would have been if I had believed in the perdition of the majority of men; and, for the rest, I contrived to fix my view pretty exclusively on Christendom itself,—which Christians in general find a grand resource in their difficulties. In this way, and by the help of public worship, and of sacred music, and Milton, and the Pilgrim's Progress, I found religion my best resource, even in its first inconsistent and unsatisfactory form, till I wrought my way to something better, as I shall tell by and by.

In the first place, it appeared to me when I was twenty, as it appears to me now, that the practice of prayer, as prevailing throughout Christendom, is wholly unauthorized by the New Testament. Christian prayer, as prevailing at this day, answers precisely to the description of that pharisaic prayer which Christ reprobated. His own method of praying, the prayer he gave to his disciples, and their practice, were all wholly unlike anything now understood by Christian prayer, in protestant as well as catholic countries. I changed my method accordingly,—gradually, perhaps, but beginning immediately and decidedly. Not knowing what was good for me, and being sure that every external thing would come to pass just the same, whether I liked it or not, I ceased to desire, and therefore to pray for, any thing external,—whether 'daily bread,' or health, or life for myself or others, or any thing whatever but spiritual good. There I for a long time drew the line. Many years after I had outgrown the childishness of wishing for I knew not what,—of praying for what might be either good or evil, I continued to pray for spiritual benefits.

It was a grand discovery to me when I somewhere met with the indication, (since become a rather favourite topic with Unitarian preachers) that the fact of the miracles has nothing whatever to do with the quality of the doctrine. When miracles are appealed to by the Orthodox as a proof of, not only the supernatural origin, but the divine quality of the doctrine, the obvious answer is that devils may work miracles, and the doctrine may therefore be from hell. Such was the argument in Christ's time; and such is it now among a good many protestants,—horrifying the Catholics and High-Churchmen of our time as much as it horrified the evangelists of old. The use to which it is turned by many who still call themselves Unitarians, and to which it was applied by me is,—the holding to Christianity in a manner as a revelation, after surrendering belief in the miracles. I suppose the majority of Unitarians still accept all the miracles (except the Miraculous Conception, of course)—even to the withering away of the fig-tree. Some hold to the resurrection, while giving up all the rest; and not a few do as I did,—say that the interior evidence of a divine origin of that doctrine is enough, and that no amount of miracles could strengthen their faith. It is clear however that a Christianity which never was received as a scheme of salvation,—which never was regarded as essential to salvation,—which might be treated, in respect to its records, at the will and pleasure of each believer,—which is next declared to be independent of its external evidences, because those evidences are found to be untenable,—and which is finally subjected in its doctrines, as in its letter, to the interpretation of each individual,—must cease to be a faith, and become a matter of speculation, of spiritual convenience, and of intellectual and moral test, till it declines to the rank of a mere fact in the history of mankind. These are the gradations through which I passed. It took many years to travel through them; and I lingered long in the stages of speculation and taste, intellectual and moral. But at length I recognized the monstrous superstition in its true character of a great fact in the history of the race, and found myself, with the last link of my chain snapped,—a free rover on the broad, bright breezy common of the universe.

Fanny Lewald-Starr (1811–1889) was born into a middle-class German Jewish family and was educated at a Christian Pietist school in Königsberg. Her brothers converted to Christianity in order to aid their careers. Fanny's father agreed to let her convert at the age of 17, probably as a consolation for his refusal to allow her a relationship with Leopold Bock, whom she had planned to marry. In these excerpts from her autobiography, she recounts her mounting discomfort with Christian "mysteries" and her dissatisfaction with "standard dogmas" and "forms" as she prepares for her baptism. Later, at the age of 34, she describes how she was drawn to the ideas of Baruch Spinoza. In these excerpts, we see first the disruptive, and then the constructive, effects of the Enlightenment upon the search for religious meaning.

5.6C *The Education of Fanny Lewald: An Autobiography*

In February, my teacher pronounced me sufficiently prepared to receive baptism. The twenty-fourth, my parents' wedding anniversary, was set for this religious ceremony, and Kähler now asked me to prepare a profession of faith, which I would acknowledge in the presence of the friends I had chosen as my witnesses.

I sat down to write this, when I suddenly realized, thinking to myself, that I did not believe anything of what constitutes the essence of ecclesiastical Christianity, of what forms the actual articles of faith (the Apostles' Creed). I did not believe in the divine parentage of the Savior, I did not believe in the "only Son our Lord, who was conceived by the Holy Ghost, born of the Virgin Mary, suffered under Pontius Pilate, was crucified, dead and buried; on the third day he arose again from the dead, he ascended into heaven, and sitteth at the right hand of God the Father Almighty; from thence he shall come to judge the quick and the dead." I did not believe in immortality, let alone the resurrection of the flesh; I believed neither in original sin, for which I, though I bore it without guilt, would have to atone, nor in the concept of being redeemed from a sin I had committed through my own volition by the death of a sinless ideal of mankind, crucified eighteen hundred years ago. I did not believe in the redemptive power of Holy Communion either. In short, I believed none of that I was soon formally to profess; I was in utter despair.

I had taken several days to compose my profession of faith, and every day that passed heightened my sense of futility. I was appalled at the thought of uttering a falsehood ceremoniously and of thus committing perjury at the baptism. I was also afraid to tell my revered teacher how far I had stretched the freedom of the rational, humanistic interpretation of Christianity to which he had generously attributed a certain amount of credit in his explanations. I imagined what an impression it would make on Leopold, if he learned—and he would undoubtedly, through the Kähler family—that I had refused finally to convert to Christianity. He would remember everything we had discussed. Everything I had often told him would seem a deliberate lie to him. He, my teacher, my parents, Mathilde—none of them would know what to make of me, and I did not know, either.

If you do not want to start doubting yourself in such situations, you end up doubting others, and my instinct for self-preservation led me in that direction. I began to ask myself if my teacher had really revealed the last inner core of his faith to me. Did the ministers of the Christian church act just like the heathen priests they deplored in respect to dogma and the mysteries, giving laymen the symbol instead of the truth? I asked myself how it was possible that a man of such sharp intellect as Kähler, a man who strove as earnestly after truth as Leopold, could believe in the mysteries of Christianity. This seemed impossible to me; so I told myself, audaciously, that it was obviously impossible for them, too, that they would have to acknowledge some other truth, see a deeper meaning within the standard dogmas or the pure spirit within the form. A religion which was based upon a mystery valid for every person must also allow each individual his own mystery. If the teachers of Christianity thought they could compromise by using silent knowledge equally with a spoken confession, why could I not do the same as they, if I found myself in a like position?

Soothing myself with such thoughts, I went to write my profession of faith. It was a sorry example of enthusiastic casuistry. I avoided, as best I could, making any positive declaration, and because of the vagueness with which young girls usually tend to express themselves about abstract matters, this probably seemed not very unusual. For me, however, who had achieved control over my thoughts and their expression even then, this profession was a product of pure calculation, and was so repugnant and alien to me in later years that I finally burned it so I would never have to look at this evidence against my honesty again.

Now came the day of my baptism. It was to take place, as had my brothers', in the Kählers' apartment, because we did not want to call attention to it at our house; an evening hour was set. I had chosen the witnesses myself: two older men, acquaintances of my parents', whom I cherished; Mrs. Kähler, the model of a noble and educated matron; and my friend Mathilde. My parents and brothers were there. The baptism and confirmation were celebrated in due form. My mother was very happy that she had saved one more of her children from Judaism, and my father said, "I hope this will be good for you." That was all.

As I stood there, however, taken into the covenant of the Christian community, as my friend and my brothers congratulated and embraced me, as I told myself that I was getting closer to Leopold with this step and further from my parents—I found that I had put more distance between Leopold and me by my lack of belief and was tied more closely to my father by my convictions than ever before. It was one of the few moments of my life when I felt in conflict with myself, and I was very unhappy because of it.

I was very conscious of the fact that I had carried out a decision, originally made with good faith, love, and confidence, with a hypocrisy usually foreign to me; but I lacked the courage to admit to a mistake and to place myself in direct opposition to those I loved most. I had trespassed against myself out of fear of others and love. Although I could not see any other positive purpose in that hour marking a definite stage in my life, I did vow to myself that this would be the first and last time I would stray from the God of truth and fearless veracity. I think I have kept that vow. The meaning and spirit of Christianity as the purest teaching of freedom and brotherhood only became apparent to me at a time when the days of my youth lay far behind me.

MONOTHEISM

CHAPTER 6
IN ISLAM

6.1 ISLAM AS A MONOTHEISTIC CREED

Although the Qur'an contains the fundamental teachings of Islamic monotheism, it is not a systematic treatise on theology; rather, it is the authoritative source for all theology and law. Following are some passages expressing aspects of the Islamic belief system. The first passage is the short prayer called "The Opening" (*al-fātiḥa*), with which the Qur'an begins. It clearly states God's supreme position in the universe and humankind's special, moral relationship with him. This sura, parallel to the Christian "Lord's Prayer" in that it is the perfect model of prayer, is known by heart by most Muslims and frequently recited, for example in each of the five daily prayer services as well as in private devotions. Following the first sura are the first five verses of the second sura, named "The Cow," which amount to a compact creed for Muslims. Whenever a recitation of the whole Qur'an is completed, the reciter(s) close by reciting "The Opening" and the first five verses of "The Cow," followed by a special litany of praise and thanksgiving.

6.1A THE OPENING

In the name of Allah, the Beneficent, the Merciful.

1. Praise be to Allah, Lord of the Worlds,
2. The Beneficent, the Merciful.
3. Owner of the Day of Judgment,

4. Thee (alone) we worship; Thee (alone) we ask for help.
5. Show us the straight path,
6. The path of those whom Thou hast favoured;
7. Not (the path) of those who earn Thine anger nor of those who go astray.

6.1B THE COW

In the name of Allah, the Beneficent, the Merciful.

1. Alif. Lâm. Mîm.
2. This is the Scripture whereof there is no doubt, a guidance unto those who ward off (evil).
3. Who believe in the unseen, and establish worship, and spend of that We have bestowed upon them;
4. And who believe in that which is revealed unto thee (Muhammad) and that which was revealed before thee, and are certain of the Hereafter.
5. These depend on guidance from their Lord. These are the successful.

Sura 112, known as "The Unity," is an uncompromising declaration of monotheism. The Prophet Muhammad declared that recitation of this sura is equal to reciting one third of the Qur'an.

6.1C THE UNITY

Revealed at Mecca

In the name of Allah, the Beneficent, the Merciful.

1. Say: He is Allah, the One!
2. Allah, the eternally Besought of all!
3. He begetteth not nor was begotten.
4. And there is none comparable unto Him.

Sura 2, verse 255, is one of the most often memorized passages in the Qur'an; it is known as the "Throne Verse." Following it (vs. 256) is a clear statement of religion as a voluntary matter.

6.1D THRONE VERSE

255. Allah! There is no God save Him, the Alive, the Eternal. Neither slumber nor sleep overtaketh Him. Unto Him belongeth whatsoever is in the heavens and whatsoever is in the earth. Who is he that intercedeth with Him save by His leave? He knoweth that which is in front of them and that which is behind them, while

they encompass nothing of His knowledge save what He will. His throne includeth the heavens and the earth, and He is never weary of preserving them. He is the Sublime, the Tremendous.

256. There is no compulsion in religion. The right direction is henceforth distinct from error. And he who rejecteth false deities and believeth in Allah hath grasped a firm handhold which will never break. Allah is Hearer, Knower.

Sura 3:101–104, 110 focuses on the nature and function of the umma as moral community.

6.1E THE MUSLIM COMMUNITY

101. How can ye disbelieve, when Allah's revelations are recited unto you, and His messenger is in your midst? He who holdeth fast to Allah, he indeed is guided unto a right path.

102. O ye who believe! Observe your duty to Allah with right observance, and die not save as those who have surrendered (unto Him);

103. And hold fast, all of you together, to the cable of Allah, and do not separate. And remember Allah's favour unto you: how ye were enemies and He made friendship between your hearts so that ye became as brothers by His grace; and (how) ye were upon the brink of an abyss of fire, and He did save you from it. Thus Allah maketh clear His revelations unto you, that haply ye may be guided,

104. And there may spring from you a nation who invite to goodness, and enjoin right conduct and forbid indecency. Such are they who are successful.

105. And be ye not as those who separated and disputed after the clear proofs had come unto them. For such there is an awful doom,

106. On the day when (some) faces will be whitened and (some) faces will be blackened; and as for those whose faces have been blackened, it will be said unto them: Disbelieved ye after your (profession of) belief? Then taste the punishment for that ye disbelieved. . . .

110. Ye are the best community [*umma*] that hath been raised up for mankind. Ye enjoin right conduct and forbid indecency; and ye believe in Allah. And if the People of the Scripture had believed it had been better for them. Some of them are believers; but most of them are evil-livers.

Sura 2:177 exhibits the essentially ethical doctrine of the Qur'an. The Arabic word translated as "righteousness" is *birr*.

6.1F A DEFINITION OF RIGHTEOUSNESS

177. It is not righteousness that ye turn your faces to the East and the West; but righteous is he who believeth in Allah and the Last Day and the angels and the

Scripture and the Prophets; and giveth his wealth, for love of Him, to kinsfolk and to orphans and the needy and the wayfarer and to those who ask, and to set slaves free; and observeth proper worship and payeth the poor-due. And those who keep their treaty when they make one, and the patient in tribulation and adversity and time of stress. Such are they who are sincere. Such are the God-fearing.

6.2 THE SCIENCE OF SPECULATIVE THEOLOGY

Jurisprudence is the chief religious science of Islam. But systematic theological discourse, known as *'ilm al-kalām,* has also been of great importance, for reasons given in the following selection from the great North African historiographer and cultural historian Ibn Khaldūn (d. 1406). Some venture to call Ibn Khaldūn the father of social science because of his acute, empirical observations on the cycles of empire and the various types of human societies that cause them. His theological views were cautious and conservative, as may be seen in this selection, taken from his famous introduction to the study of history, *The Muqqadimah,* which in the complete English translation fills three large volumes.

6.2A IBN KHALDŪN ON THEOLOGY

The Science of Speculative Theology

This is a science that involves arguing with logical proofs in defence of the articles of faith and refuting innovators who deviate in their dogmas from the early Muslims and Muslim orthodoxy.

The real core of the articles of faith is the oneness of God. Therefore, we shall present here, first, a nice specimen of logical argumentation that will show us the oneness of God in the most direct method and manner. We shall then return and give a correct description of speculative theology and the (subjects) it studies. We shall also indicate the reason why it developed in Islam and what it was that called for its invention.

We say: It should be known that the things that come into being in the world of existing things, whether they belong to essences or to either human or animal actions, require appropriate causes which are prior to (their existence). They introduce the things that come into being into the realm dominated by custom, and effect their coming into being. Each one of these causes, in turn, comes into being and, thus, requires other causes. Causes continue to follow upon causes in an ascending order, until they reach the Causer of causes, Him who brings them into existence and creates them.

In the process, the causes multiply and widen in extent vertically and horizontally. The intellect becomes confused in the attempt to perceive and enumerate them. Only a comprehensive knowledge can encompass them all, especially human and animal actions. Among the causes of (action), there evidently belong the various kinds of intention and volition, since no action can materialize except through volition and intention. The various kinds of intention and volition are matters pertaining to the soul. As a rule, they originate from previous consecutive perceptions. These perceptions cause the intention to act. The causes of such perceptions are, again, other perceptions. Now, the cause of all the perceptions taking place in the soul is unknown, since no one is able to know the beginnings or order of matters pertaining to the soul. They are consecutive notions that God puts into the mind of man, who is unable to understand their beginnings and ends. As a rule, man is able only to comprehend the causes that are natural and obvious and that present themselves to our perception in an orderly and well-arranged manner, because nature is encompassed by the soul and on a lower level than it. The range of perceptions, however, is too large for the soul, because they belong to the intellect, which is on a higher level than the soul. The soul, therefore, can scarcely perceive very many of them, let alone all of them. Man often stops (to speculate about causes); his feet slip, and he becomes one of those who go astray and perish.

One should not think that man has the power, or can choose at will, to stop or to retrace his steps. No, one must be on guard by completely abandoning any speculation about (causes).

Furthermore, the way in which causes exercise their influence upon the majority of things caused is unknown. They are only known through customary (experience) and through conclusions which attest to (the existence of an) apparent (causal) relationship. What that influence really is and how it takes place is not known. Therefore, we have been commanded completely to abandon and suppress any speculation about them and to direct ourselves to the Causer of all causes, so that the soul will be firmly coloured with the oneness of God.

A man who stops at the causes is frustrated. He is rightly (said to be) an unbeliever. If he ventures to swim in the ocean of speculation and of research, (seeking) each one of the causes that cause them and the influence they exercise, I can guarantee him that he will return unsuccessful. Therefore, we were forbidden by Muhammad to study causes. We were commanded to recognize the absolute oneness of God.

Man should not trust the suggestion his mind makes, that it is able to comprehend all existing things and their causes, and to know all the details of existence. Such a suggestion of the mind should be dismissed as stupid. Every person with perception has the superficial impression that the (whole of) existence is comprised by his perceptions, and that it does not extend beyond them. The matter is different in fact. The truth lies beyond that. One knows that a deaf person feels that the whole of existence is comprised in the perceptions of his four senses and his intellect. The whole group of audible things constitutes no part of existence for him. The same applies to a blind person. The whole group of visible things constitutes no part of existence for him. If (people with such defects) were not set right by their adherence to information they receive from their fathers and teachers and from the majority of people in general, they would not admit (the existence of those things). They follow the majority in admitting the existence of these groups (of *sensibilia*), but (the admission) is not in their natural disposition nor in the nature of their sense perception. If dumb animals were asked and could speak, we would find that they would ignore the whole group of *intelligibilia*. It would simply not exist for them.

Now, it might be assumed that there exists another kind of perception different from ours, since our sense perceptions are created and brought into existence. God's creation extends beyond the creation of man. Complete knowledge does not exist in man. The world of existence is too vast for him. Therefore, everyone should be suspicious of the comprehensiveness of his perceptions and the results of his perception. This does not speak against the intellect and intellectual perceptions. The intellect, indeed, is a correct scale. Its indications are completely certain and in no way wrong. However, the intellect should not be used to weigh such matters as the oneness of God, the other world, the truth of prophecy, the real character of the divine attributes, or anything else that lies beyond the level of the intellect. That would mean to desire the impossible. One might compare it with a man who sees a scale in which gold is being weighed, and wants to weigh mountains in it. The (fact that this is impossible) does not prove that the indications of the scale are not true. Thus, the intellect cannot comprehend God and His attributes. It is but one of the atoms of the world of existence which results from God.

If this is clear, it is possible that the ascending sequence of causes reaches the point where it transcends the realm of human perception and existence and thus ceases to be perceivable. The intellect would here become lost, confused, and cut off in the wilderness of conjectures. Thus, (recognition of the) oneness of God is identical with inability to perceive the causes and the ways in which they exercise their influence, and with reliance in this respect upon the Creator of the causes who comprises them. There is no maker but Him. All (causes) lead up to Him and go back to His power. We know about Him only inasmuch as we have issued from Him. This is the meaning of the statement transmitted on the authority of a certain truthful (person): 'The inability to perceive is perception.'

Such (declaration of the) oneness of God does not merely refer to faith, which is affirmation based upon judgment. The object of (all human) actions and divine worship is acquisition of the habit of obedience and submissiveness, and the freeing of the heart from all preoccupations save the worshipped Master, until the novice on the path to God becomes a holy person.

The difference between 'state' and knowledge in questions of dogma is the same as that between talking (about attributes) and having them. This may be explained as follows: Many people know that mercy to the orphans and the poor brings (a human being) close to God and is recommendable. They say so and acknowledge the fact. They quote the sources for it from the religious law. But if they were to see an orphan or a poor person they would run away from him and disdain to touch him, let alone show mercy to him. Their mercy for the orphan was the result of having reached the station of knowledge. It was not the result of the station of 'state' nor of an attribute of theirs. Now, there are people who, in addition to the station of knowledge and the realization of the fact that mercy to the poor brings one close to God, have attained another, higher 'station': they have attained the attribute and habit of mercy. When they see an orphan or a poor person, they approach him and show him (mercy). They wish to receive the (heavenly) reward for the compassion they show him.

The relationship of man's knowledge of the oneness of God to his possession of it as an attribute, is of the same character. Knowledge results by necessity from possession of an attribute. It is a kind of knowledge that exists on a more solid basis than knowledge attained previous to the possession of the attribute. An attribute is not obtained from knowledge alone. There must be an action, and it must be repeated innumerable times. Only this results in a firmly rooted habit, in the acquisition of the attribute and real (knowledge). Another kind of knowledge thus makes its appearance. It is the kind that is useful in the other world. The original knowledge which was devoid of being an attribute is of little advantage or use. It is the knowledge that most thinkers (possess). But the real object is knowledge as a 'state,' and it originates from divine worship.

It is clear that the object of all (religious) obligations is the acquisition of a habit firmly rooted in the soul, from which a necessary knowledge results for the soul. It is the (recognition of the) oneness of God which is the (principal) article of faith and the thing through which happiness is attained.

Faith, which is the basis and source of all (religious) obligations, has several degrees. The first degree is the affirmation by the heart of what the tongue says. The highest degree is the acquisition, from the belief of the heart and the resulting actions, of a quality that has complete control over the heart. It commands the actions of the limbs. Every activity takes place in submissiveness to it. Thus, all actions, eventually, become subservient to this affirmation by faith, and this is the highest degree of faith. It is perfect faith. The believer who has it will commit neither a great nor a small sin. . . .

In time, the science of logic spread in Islam. People studied it. They made a distinction between it and the philosophical sciences, in that logic was merely a norm and yardstick for arguments and served to probe the arguments of the (philosophical sciences) as well as (those of) all other (disciplines).

(Scholars) studied the basic premises the earlier theologians had established. They refuted most of them with the help of arguments leading them to (a different opinion). Many of these were derived from philosophical discussions of physics and metaphysics. When they probed them with the yardstick of logic, it showed that they were applicable only to those (other disciplines and not to theology, but) they did not believe that if the arguments were wrong, the thing proven (by the arguments) was also wrong. This approach differed in its technical terminology from the older one. It was called 'the school of recent scholars'. Their approach often included refutation of the philosophers where the (opinions of the) latter differed from the articles of faith. They considered the (philosophers) enemies of the articles of faith, because, in most respects, there is a relationship between the opinions of the innovators and the opinions of the philosophers.

The first (scholar) to write in accordance with the new theological approach was al-Ghazzâlî. He was followed by the imam Ibn al-Khatîb. A large number of scholars followed in their steps and adhered to their tradition.

The later scholars were very intent upon meddling with philosophical works. The subjects of the two disciplines (theology and philosophy) were thus confused by them. They thought that there was one and the same (subject) in both disciplines, because the problems of each discipline were similar.

The theologians most often deduced the existence and attributes of the Creator from the existing things and their conditions. As a rule, this was their line of argument. The physical bodies form part of the existing things, and they are the subject of the philosophical study of physics. However, the philosophical study of them differs from the theological. The philosophers study bodies in so far as they move or are stationary. The theologians, on the other hand, study them in so far as they serve as an argument for the Maker. In the same way, the philosophical study of metaphysics studies existence as such and what it requires for its essence. The theological study (of metaphysics), on the other hand, is concerned with the *existentia*, in so far as they serve as argument for Him who causes existence. In general, to the theologians, the object of theology is (to find out) how the articles of faith which the religious law has laid down as correct, can be proven with the help of logical arguments, so that innovations may be repulsed and doubts and misgivings concerning the articles of faith be removed.

If one considers how this discipline originated and how scholarly discussion was incorporated within it step by step, and how, during that process, scholars always assumed the correctness of the articles of faith and paraded proofs and arguments (in their defence), one will realize that the character of the subject of this discipline is as we have established it, and one will realize that (the discipline) cannot go beyond it. However, the two approaches have been mixed up by recent scholars. The problems of theology have been confused with those of philosophy. This has gone so far that the one discipline is no longer distinguishable from the other.

The approach of the early Muslims can be reconciled with the beliefs of the science of speculative theology only if one follows the old approach of the theologians (and not the mixed approach of recent scholars). In general, it must be known that this science—the science of speculative theology—is not something that is necessary to the contemporary student. Heretics and innovators have been destroyed. The orthodox religious leaders have given us protection against heretics and innovators in their systematic works and treatments.

However, the usefulness of speculative theology for certain individuals and students is considerable. Orthodox Muslims should not be ignorant of speculative argumentation in defence of the articles of orthodox faith.

6.3 A MUSLIM CREED

The closest thing to a universal, required creed in Islam is the Shahada: "There is no god but God; Muhammad is the Messenger of God." But various theologians compiled statements of faith in order to defend Islam against heresy and transmit its essentials in an advanced form of discourse. The following such statement was probably in circulation by the mid-tenth century and displays throughout a Sunni orthodoxy staunchly opposed to the rational theology of the Muʿtazilites, which had been politically dominant, at least, some two centuries before in Baghdad. The author of the *Fiqh Akbar II* ("Greater Understanding") is unknown, but the contents are heavily influenced by the teachings of the great Sunni theologian al-Ashʿarī (d. 935), a former Muʿtazilite who abandoned rational theology in favor of a Qurʾan-based orthodoxy that accepts difficult-to-understand points of doctrine "without [asking] how" (*bilā kayf*).

6.3A THE FIQH AKBAR II

Translation

Art. 1. The heart of the confession of the unity of Allah and the true foundation of faith consist in this obligatory creed: I believe in Allah, His angels, His books, His Apostles, the resurrection after death, the decree of Allah the good and the evil thereof, computation of sins, the balance, Paradise and Hell; and that all these are real.

Art. 2. Allah the exalted is one, not in the sense of number, but in the sense that He has no partner; He begetteth not and He is not begotten and there is none like unto Him. He resembles none of the created things, nor do any created things resemble Him. He has been from eternity and will be to eternity with His names and qualities, those which belong to His essence as well as those which belong to His action.

Those which belong to His essence are: life, power, knowledge, speech, hearing, sight and will. Those which belong to His action are: creating, sustaining, producing, renewing, making, and so on.

He has been from eternity and will be to eternity with His qualities and His names. None of His qualities or names has come into being; from eternity He knows by virtue of His knowledge, knowledge being an eternal quality; He is almighty by virtue of His power, His power being an eternal quality; He speaks by virtue of His speech, His speech being an eternal quality; He creates by virtue of His creative power, His creative power being an eternal quality; He acts by virtue of His power of action, His power of action being an eternal quality.

The agent is Allah and the product of His action is created, but the power of action of Allah is not created and His qualities are eternal; they have not come into being, nor have they been created. Whoso sayeth that they are created or have come into being, or hesitates or doubts regarding these two points, is an infidel in regard to Allah.

From A. J. Wensinck, *The Muslim Creed: Its Genesis and Historical Development.* Copyright 1932. Reprinted with the permission of Cambridge University Press.

Art. 3. The Kuran is the speech of Allah, written in the copies, preserved in the memories, recited by the tongues, revealed to the Prophet. Our pronouncing, writing and reciting the Kuran is created, whereas the Kuran itself is uncreated.

Whatever Allah quotes in the Kuran from Moses or other Prophets, from Pharaoh or from Satan, is the speech of Allah in relation to theirs. The speech of Allah is uncreated, but the speech of Moses and other creatures is created. The Kuran is the speech of Allah and as such from eternity, not theirs. Moses heard the speech of Allah, as the Kuran saith: And Allah spoke with Moses—Allah was speaking indeed before He spoke to Moses. For Allah was creating from eternity ere He had created the creatures; and when He spoke to Moses, He spoke to Him with His speech which is one of His eternal qualities.

All His qualities are different from those of the creatures. He knoweth, but not in the way of our knowledge; He is mighty, but not in the way of our power; He seeth, but not in the way of our seeing; He speaketh, but not in the way of our speaking; He heareth, but not in the way of our hearing. We speak by means of organs and letters, Allah speaks without instruments and letters. Letters are created, but the speech of Allah is uncreated.

Art. 4. Allah is thing, not as other things but in the sense of positive existence; without body, without substance, without *accidens.* He has no limit, neither has He a counterpart, nor a partner, nor an equal. He has hand, face and soul, for He refers to these in the Kuran; and what He saith in the Kuran regarding face, hand and soul, this belongs to His qualities, without how.[1] It must not be said that His hand is His power or His bounty, for this would lead to the annihilation of the quality. This is the view of the Kadarites and the Mu'tazilites. No, His hand is His quality, without how. Likewise His wrath and His good pleasure are two of His qualities, without how.

Art. 5. Allah has not created things from a pre-existent thing. Allah had knowledge concerning things before they existed, from eternity; He had so decreed and ordained them that nothing could happen either in this world or in the next except through His will, knowledge, decision, decree and writing on the preserved table. Yet His writing is of a descriptive, not of a decisive nature. Decision, decree and will are His eternal qualities, without how. Allah knoweth the non-existent things in the state of non-existence, as not existing; and He knoweth how they will be. And He knoweth the existing things in the state of existence, as existing; and He knoweth how their vanishing will be. Allah knoweth the rising in the state of His rising, as rising. And when He sitteth down, He knoweth Himself as sitting down, in the state of His sitting down, without a change in His knowing and without His getting knowledge. But change and difference come into being in creatures.

Art 6. Allah created the creatures free from unbelief and from belief. Then He addressed them and gave them commandments and prohibitions. Thereupon some turned to unbelief. And their denial and disavowal of the truth was caused

---

[1] That is, without either asking for or being granted an explanation *(bilā kayf).*

by Allah's abandoning them. And some of them believed—as appeared in their acting, consenting and declaring—through the guidance and help of Allah.

Allah took the posterity of Adam from his loins and endowed them with intellect. Thereupon He addressed them and commanded them to believe and to abstain from unbelief. Thereupon they recognized His lordship, and this was belief on their part. And in this religion [*fiṭra*] they are born. And whosoever became an unbeliever afterwards, deviated from this and changed, and whosoever believed and professed his belief, clung to it and adhered to this belief.

Allah did not compel any of His creatures to be infidels or faithful. And He did not create them either as faithful or infidels, but He created them as individuals, and faith and unbelief are the acts of men. Allah knoweth the man who turneth to belief as an infidel in the state of his unbelief; and if he turneth to belief afterwards, Allah knoweth him as faithful, in the state of his belief; and He loveth him, without change in His knowledge or His quality. All the acts of man—his moving as well as his resting—are truly his own acquisition, but Allah creates them and they are caused by His will, His knowledge, His decision, and His decree.

Art. 7. All acts of obedience are obligatory on account of Allah's command, wish, good pleasure, knowledge, will, decision and decree. All acts of disobedience happen through His knowledge, decision, decree, and will; not according to His wish, good pleasure, or command.

Art. 8. All the Prophets are exempt from sins, both light and grave, from unbelief and sordid deeds. Yet stumbling and mistakes may happen on their part.

Art. 9. Muhammad is His beloved, His servant, His Apostle, His Prophet, His chosen and elect. He did not serve idols, nor was he at any time a polytheist, even for a single moment. And he never committed a light or a grave sin.

Art. 10. The most excellent of men after the Apostle of Allah is Abū Bakr al-Siddīk; after him, 'Umar ibn al-Khaṭṭāb al-Fārūk; after him, 'Uthmān ibn 'Affān, he of the two lights; after him, 'Alī al-Murtaḍā, may Allah encompass all of them with His good pleasure, being His servants who persevere in truth and with truth. We cling to all of them and we name all the companions of Allah's Apostle in the way of praise only.

Art. 11. We declare no Muslim an infidel on account of any sin—even though a mortal one—if he does not declare it allowed. Neither do we banish him from the field of faith, nay, we call him really faithful; he may be faithful of bad behaviour, not an infidel.

Art. 12. The moistening of the shoes is commendable. The supererogatory prayers in the month of Ramadān are commendable.

Art. 13. Prayer behind every faithful man, be he of good or of bad behaviour, is valid.

Art. 14. We do not say that sins will do no harm to the Faithful; nor do we say that he will not enter the fire; nor do we say that he will remain therein for ever, although he should be of bad behaviour, after having departed this world as one of the Faithful. And we do not say—as the Murdjites do—that our good deeds are accepted and our sins forgiven. But we say, that when a man performs a good deed, fulfilling all its conditions so that it is free from any blame that might spoil it, without nullifying it by unbelief, apostasy or bad morals, until he departs this world as one of the Faithful—then Allah shall not overlook it but accept it from him and reward him on account of it. As to evil deeds—apart from polytheism and unbelief—if he who commits them does not repent ere he dies as one of the Faithful, he will be dependent on Allah's will: if He willeth He punisheth him in the fire, and if He willeth He forgiveth him without punishing him in any way in the fire.

Art. 15. If any work be mixed with ostentation, its reward is forfeited thereby, and likewise if it be mixed with vainglory.

Art. 16. The signs of the Prophets and the miracles of the saints are a reality. As to those which were performed by His [Allah's] enemies, such as Iblīs, Firʿawn and the Anti-Christ, and which, according to historical tradition, have taken place or will take place, we do not call them signs or miracles, but we call them the fulfilling of their wants. Allah fulfils the wants of His enemies, eluding them in this world and punishing them in the next. So they are betrayed and increase in error and unbelief.

All this is contingent and possible.

Allah was creator before He created, and sustainer before He sustained.

Art. 17. Allah will be seen in the world to come. The Faithful will see Him, being in Paradise, with their bodily eyes, without comparison or modality. And there will be no distance between Him and His creatures.

Art. 18. Faith consists in confessing and believing.

The faith of the inhabitants of heaven and earth does not increase or decrease.

The Faithful are equal in faith and in the confession of the unity of Allah; they are different in degree of superiority regarding works.

Islam is absolute agreement and compliance with the commands of Allah. Language distinguishes between faith and Islam. Yet there is no faith without Islam and Islam without faith cannot be found. The two are as back and belly. Religion [*dīn*] is a noun covering faith and Islam and all the commandments of the law.

Art. 19. We know Allah with adequate knowledge, as He describes Himself in His book, with all His qualities. Nobody, on the other hand, is able to serve Allah with adequate service, such as He may truly lay claim to. But man serves Him at His command, as He has ordered him in His book and in the *sunna* of His Apostle.

All the Faithful are equal as to knowledge, subjective certainty, trust, love, inner quiet, fear, hope and faith. They differ in all these, except in faith.

Allah lavishes His bounty on His servants and acts according to justice as well. He giveth them a reward twice as large as they have deserved, by grace, and He punisheth on account of sin, by justice. He forgiveth by grace.

Art. 20. The intercession of the Prophets is a reality.

The intercession of the Prophet on behalf of the Faithful who have committed sins, even grave sins, and who have deserved punishment, is an established reality.

Art. 21. The weighing of works in the balance on the day of resurrection is a reality.

The basin of the Prophet is a reality. Retaliation between litigants by means of good works on the day of resurrection is a reality. And if they do not possess good works, the wrongs, done by them to others, are thrown upon them; this is a reality.

Paradise and Hell are created, and are in existence at the present time; they will never cease to exist.

The black-eyed ones [the beautiful maidens of Paradise] will never die. Punishment and reward by Allah will never end.

Art. 22. Allah guideth whomsoever He pleaseth, by grace, and He leadeth astray whomsoever He pleaseth, by justice. His leading astray means His abandoning, and the explanation of "abandoning" is that He does not help a man by guiding him towards deeds that please Him. This is justice on His part, and so is His punishment of those who are abandoned on account of sin. We are not allowed to say that Satan deprives the Faithful of his faith by constraint and compulsion. But we say that man gives up his faith, whereupon Satan deprives him of it.

Art. 23. The interrogation of the dead in the tomb by Munkar and Nakīr is a reality and the reunion of the body with the spirit in the tomb is a reality. The pressure and the punishment in the tomb are a reality that will take place in the case of all the infidels, and a reality that may take place in the case of some sinners belonging to the Faithful.

Art. 24. It is allowable to follow scholars in expressing the qualities of Allah in Persian, in all instances except in the case of Allah's hand. It is allowable to say *rūyi khudāy*, without comparison or modality.

Art. 25. Allah's being near or far is not to be understood in the sense of a shorter or longer distance, but in the sense of man's being honoured or slighted. The obedient is near to Him, without how, and the disobedient is far from Him, without how. Nearness, distance and approach are applied to man in his intimate relation with Allah, and so it is with Allah's neighbourhood in Paradise, and with man's standing before Him, without modality.

Art. 26. The Kuran is revealed to the Apostle of Allah and it is written in the copies. The verses of the Kuran, being Allah's speech, are all equal in excellence and greatness. Some, however, have a pre-eminence in regard to recitation or to their contents, *e.g.* the verse of the Throne [2:255], because it deals with Allah's majesty, His greatness and His description. So in it are united excellence in regard to recitation and excellence in regard to its contents. Others possess excellence only in regard to recitation, such as the descriptions of the infidels, whereas those who are mentioned in them, that is, the infidels, have no excellence.

Likewise all of Allah's names and qualities are equal in greatness and excellence, without difference.

Art. 27. Ḳāsim, Ṭāhir and Ibrāhīm were the sons of the Apostle of Allah.

Fāṭima, Ruḳaiya, Zainab and Umm Kulthūm were all of them daughters of the Apostle of Allah.

Art. 28. When a man is uncertain concerning any of the subtleties of theology, it is his duty to cling for the time being to the orthodox faith. When he finds a scholar, he must consult him; he is not allowed to postpone inquiry and there is no excuse for him if he should persevere in his attitude of hesitation, nay, he would incur the blame of unbelief thereby.

Art. 29. The report of the ascension is a reality, and whosoever rejects it is an erring schismatic. The appearance of the Anti-Christ, Yādjūdj and Mādjūdj [Gog and Magog], the rising of the sun from the place where it sets, the descent of 'Isā [Jesus] from Heaven, as well as the other eschatological signs according to the description thereof in authentic Tradition, are a reality that will take place.

Allah guideth to the straight way whomsoever He willeth.

6.4 ISLAMIC MYSTICISM: THE SUFI WAY TO UNION WITH GOD

Islamic mysticism is definitively grounded in the Qur'an, although its many forms and expressions resulted from profound individual speculation and meditative disciplines that extended the horizons of spirituality among Muslims in important ways. Sufis see the Qur'an not as limited to its external meanings, but as a vehicle bestowed by God's grace to lift His servants—more to the point his "friends"—beyond *ḥayāt al-dunyā,* "the life of this world," to abiding union with God beginning in this life. "Die before ye die!" is the admonitory exclamation of the Sufi, who regards full spiritual awareness now as the necessary passage to authentic, lasting life. Following are several Qur'anic passages that Sufis hold up as particularly significant for their quest.

The first passage (7:172) tells of the primordial covenant that God made with the human race even before it was brought into this world. The great modern scholar of Sufism Annemarie Schimmel wrote, "The idea of this primordial covenant (*mīthāq*) has impressed the religious conscience of the Muslims, and especially the Muslim mystics, more than any other idea. Here is the starting point for their understanding of free will and predestination, of election and acceptance, of God's eternal power and man's loving response and promise. The goal of the mystic is to return to the experience of the 'Day of *Alastu,*' when only God existed, before He led future creatures out of the abyss of not-being and endowed them with life, love, and understanding so that they might face Him again at the end of time."

6.4A MYSTICAL DIMENSIONS OF ISLAM

172. And (remember) when thy Lord brought forth from the Children of Adam, from their reins, their seed, and made them testify of themselves, (saying): Am I not[1] your Lord? They said: Yea, verily. We testify. (That was) lest ye should say at the Day of Resurrection: Lo! of this we were unaware;

[1] *Alastu.*

Mystical Dimensions of Islam (Chapel Hill: University of North Carolina Press, 1975), 24.

Sura 24:35 is the well-known "Light Verse" that Sufis, indeed all Muslims, delight and find hope in.

35. Allah is the Light of the heavens and the earth. The similitude of His light is as a niche wherein is a lamp. The lamp is in a glass. The glass is as it were a shining star. (This lamp is) kindled from a blessed tree, an olive neither of the East nor of the West, whose oil would almost glow forth (of itself) though no fire touched it. Light upon light, Allah guideth unto His light whom He will. And Allah speaketh to mankind in allegories, for Allah is Knower of all things.

The Qur'an speaks in several passages about the "face" or "countenance" (*wajh*) of God, meaning His eternal essence as distinguished from the created realm.

2:115 Unto Allah belong the East and the West, and withersoever ye turn, there is Allah's Countenance. Lo! Allah is All-embracing, All-Knowing.

5:27 All that dwells upon the earth is perishing, yet still abides the Face of thy Lord, majestic, splendid [ed.'s tr.].

The characteristic meditation device of Sufis is *dhikr,* which means "remembrance, mentioning" of God. *Dhikr* came to be highly technical and formal, but its Qur'anic meaning is most often prayer and simple devout remembrance of God. Among the many Qur'anic references to *dhikr* are the following:

33:41 O ye who believe! Remember Allah with much remembrance (*dhikr*).

13:26 Allah enlargeth livelihood for whom He will, and straiteneth (it for whom He will); and they rejoice in the life of the world (*ḥayāt al-dunyā*), whereas the life of the world is but brief comfort as compared with the Hereafter. **27** Those who disbelieve say: If only a portent were sent down upon him and his Lord! Say Lo! Allah sendeth whom He will astray, and guideth unto Himself all who turn (unto Him), **28** Who have believed and whose hearts have rest in the remembrance (*dhikr*) of Allah. Verily in the remembrance of Allah do hearts find rest.

A particularly arresting Qur'anic passage describes the experience that any person—whether Sufi, ordinary Muslim, or anyone—can have when reading that scripture:

39:23 Allah hath (now) revealed the fairest of statements, a Scripture consistent, (wherein promises of reward are) paired (with threats of punishment), whereat doth creep the flesh of those who fear their Lord, so that their flesh and their hearts soften to Allah's reminder. Such is Allah's guidance, wherewith He guideth whom He will. And him whom Allah sendeth astray, for him there is no guide.

Finally, the Qur'an speaks of friendship between God and His servants. Sufis have focused on this idea more than any other Muslims, so that divine-human fellowship is the central characteristic of the mystical path in Islam. The Qur'anic term *walī* is usually translated as "friend," although it may also mean, depending on context, "patron, protector, kinsman." When applied to God it may be translated (as the Pickthall translation often does) "Protecting Friend." In later Islamic history, *walī* came also to mean something close to the Christian notion of "saint." The first passage indicates the boundaries of intimate association: a close triad of believers, God, and the Prophet.

> **5:55** Your friend can be only Allah: and His messenger and those who believe, who establish worship and pay the poor-due, and bow down (in prayer). **56** And whoso taketh Allah and His messenger and those who believe for friend (will know that), lo! the party of Allah, they are the victorious.

The next passage (10:63) is a more general declaration about the outcome of friendship with God.

> Lo! verily the friends of Allah are (those) on whom fear cometh not, nor do they grieve.

6.5 A TRADITIONAL SCHOLAR'S OVERVIEW OF SUFISM

Ibn Khaldūn also wrote the following sketch about Sufism in his *Muqaddimah.*

6.5A SUFISM

Sufism belongs to the sciences of the religious law that originated in Islam. It is based on the assumption that the practices of its adherents had always been considered by the important early Muslims, the men around Muhammad and the men of the second generation, as well as those who came after them, as the path of truth and right guidance. The Sufi approach is based upon constant application to divine worship, complete devotion to God, aversion to the false splendour of the world, abstinence from the pleasure, property, and position to which the great mass aspire, and retirement from the world into solitude for divine worship. These things were general among the men around Muhammad and the early Muslims.

Then, worldly aspirations increased in the second [eighth] century and after. At that time, the special name of Sufis was given to those who aspired to divine worship.

From Ibn Khaldūn, *The Muqqadimah: An Introduction to History,* translated by Franz Rosenthal, abridged and edited by N. J. Dawood. Copyright © 1967 by Princeton University Press. Reprinted with the permission of the publishers.

The Sufis came to represent asceticism. They developed a particular kind of perception which comes about through ecstatic experience, as follows. Man, as man, is distinguished from all the other animals by his ability to perceive. His perception is of two kinds. He can perceive sciences and matters of knowledge, and these may be certain, hypothetical, doubtful, or imaginary. Also, he can perceive 'states' persisting in himself, such as joy and grief, anxiety and relaxation, satisfaction, anger, patience, gratefulness, and similar things. The reasoning part active in the body originates from perceptions, volitions, and states. It is through them that man is distinguished from the other animals. Knowledge originates from evidence, grief and joy from the perception of what is painful or pleasurable, energy from rest, and inertia from being tired. In the same way, the exertion and worship of the Sufi novice must lead to a 'state' that is the result of his exertion. That state may be a kind of divine worship. Then, it will be firmly rooted in the Sufi novice and become a 'station' for him. Or, it may not be divine worship, but merely an attribute affecting the soul, such as joy or gladness, energy or inertia, or something else.

The 'stations' (form an ascending order). The Sufi novice continues to progress from station to station, until he reaches the (recognition of the) oneness of God and the gnosis (*ma'rifah*) which is the desired goal of happiness.

Thus, the novice must progress by such stages. The basis of all of them is obedience and sincerity. Faith precedes and accompanies all of them. Their result and fruit are states and attributes. They lead to others, and again others, up to the station of the (recognition of the) oneness of God and of gnosis (*'irfân*). If the result shows some shortcoming or defect, one can be sure that it comes from some shortcoming that existed in the previous stage. The same applies to the ideas of the soul and the inspirations of the heart.

The novice, therefore, must scrutinize himself in all his actions and study their concealed import, because the results, of necessity, originate from actions, and shortcomings in the results, thus, originate from defects in the actions. The Sufi novice finds out about that through his mystical experience, and he scrutinizes himself as to its reasons.

Very few people share the self-scrutiny of the Sufis, for negligence in this respect is almost universal. Pious people who do not get that far perform, at best, acts of obedience. The Sufis, however, investigate the results of acts of obedience with the help of mystical and ecstatic experience, in order to learn whether they are free from deficiency or not. Thus, it is evident that the Sufis' path in its entirety depends upon self-scrutiny with regard to what they do or do not do, and upon discussion of the various kinds of mystical and ecstatic experience that result from their exertions. This, then, crystallizes for the Sufi novice in a 'station.' From that station, he can progress to another, higher one.

Furthermore, the Sufis have their peculiar form of behaviour and a linguistic terminology which they use in instruction. Linguistic data apply only to commonly accepted ideas. When there occur ideas not commonly accepted, technical terms facilitating the understanding of those ideas are coined to express them.

Thus, the Sufis had their special discipline, which is not discussed by other representatives of the religious law. As a consequence, the science of the religious law came to consist of two kinds. One is the special field of jurists and muftis. It is concerned with the general laws governing the acts of divine worship, customary actions, and mutual dealings. The other is the special field of the Sufis. It is concerned with pious exertion, self-scrutiny with regard to it, discussion of the different kinds of mystical and ecstatic experience occurring in the course of (self-scrutiny), the mode of ascent from one mystical experience to another, and the interpretation of the technical terminology of mysticism in use among them.

When the sciences were written down systematically and when the jurists wrote works on jurisprudence and the principles of jurisprudence, on speculative theology, Qur'ân interpretation, and other subjects, the Sufis, too, wrote on their subject. Some Sufis wrote on the laws governing asceticism and self-scrutiny, how to act and not act in imitation of (saints).

Al-Ghazzâlî, in the *Kitāb al-Iḥyā,* dealt systematically with the laws governing asceticism and the imitation of models. Then, he explained the behaviour and customs of the Sufis and commented on their technical vocabulary.

The science of Sufism became a systematically treated discipline in Islam. Before that, mysticism had merely consisted of divine worship, and its laws had existed in the breasts of men. The same had been the case with all other disciplines, such as Qur'ân interpretation, the science of tradition, jurisprudence, and the principles of jurisprudence.

6.6 RUMI

One of the most influential Sufis was the Central Asian refugee from the Mongol invasions Jalāl al-Dīn Rūmī (d. 1273), who in Konya, Turkey, founded the Mawlawi order of Sufis, also known as "whirling dervishes" because of their ecstasy-producing ritual dance. Rumi was a religious scholar who lived an eventful life marked by intimate friendships with remarkable men in whom he sought the essence of divinity. His mystical poetry expressed a strong sense of longing for union with the Divine Beloved, Allah.

Rumi did not have a high opinion of professional religious scholars, who rely on rational proofs instead of love.

6.6A LOVE AND LOGIC (P. 165)

Learn from thy Father! He, not falsely proud,
With tears of sorrow all his sin avowed.[1]

[1] After his fall from Paradise Adam repented and took the blame on himself (*Qur'ān* VII, 22). It is said that he alighted in Sarandīb (Ceylon) and shed floods of tears which caused every valley to be filled with fragrant plants and spices.

From Reynold A. Nicholson, ed. and trans., *Rumi: Poet and Mystic, 1207–1273.* Copyright 1950 by Reynold A. Nicholson. Reprinted with the permission of HarperCollins Publishers, Ltd.

Wilt thou, then, still pretend to be unfree
And clamber up Predestination's tree?—
Like Iblīs and his progeny abhorred,
In argument and battle with their Lord.
The blest initiates *know:* what need to *prove?*
From Satan logic but from Adam love.

The famous saying of Muhammad, "die before you die" has inspired Sufis in all times and given them a strong sense of his authority for their mystic quest.

6.6B DIE BEFORE YOU DIE (P. 131)

The Prophet said, "O seeker of the mysteries, wouldst thou see a dead man living,
Walking on the earth, like living men; yet his spirit dwells in Heaven,
Because it has been translated before death and will not be translated when he
    dies—
A mystery beyond understanding, understood only by dying—
If any one wish to see a dead man walking thus visibly on the earth,
Let him behold Abū Bakr, the devout, who in virtue of being a true witness to God
    became the Prince of the resurrected."
Mohammed is the twice-born in this world: he died to all temporal losing and find-
    ing: he was a hundred resurrections here and now.

The surprising declaration of the mystic-martyr al-Hallaj, whom Rumi greatly admired, is the subject of the following meditation.

6.6C ONCE ONE KNOWS, PRAYER IS UNBELIEF! (P. 92)

Jalalu'l-dīn was asked, "Is there any way to God nearer than the ritual prayer?" "No," he replied; "but prayer does not consist in forms alone. Formal prayer has a beginning and an end, like all forms and bodies and everything that partakes of speech and sound; but the soul is unconditioned and infinite: it has neither beginning nor end. The prophets have shown the true nature of prayer. . . . Prayer is the drowning and unconsciousness of the soul, so that all these forms remain without. At that time there is no room even for Gabriel, who is pure spirit. One may say that the man who prays in this fashion is exempt from all religious obligations, since he is deprived of his reason. Absorption in the Divine Unity is the soul of prayer."[1]

Islam does not have a pervasive sense of human sinfulness, at least not in the sense that Christianity often does. But Rumi goes beyond sins or even Sin to a fundamental insight: that to praise God is nevertheless to assert one's own being, too.

---

[1] Şūfīs often describe "The naughting of self-consciousness (*fanā'u'l-ṣifāt*)" which results from intense concentration of every faculty on God in the performance of the ritual prayer (*ṣalāt*). The Prophet is said to have declared that no *ṣalāt* is complete without the inward presence of God. To him every *ṣalāt* was a new Ascension (*mi'rāj*), in which he left even Gabriel behind.

6.6D GOD BEYOND PRAISE (P. 94)

When beams of Wisdom strike on soils and clays
Receptive to the seed, Earth keeps her trust:
In springtime all deposits she repays,
Taught by eternal Justice to be just.

O Thou whose Grace informs the witless clod,
Whose Wrath makes blind the heart and eye within,
My praise dispraises Thee, Almighty God;
For praise is being, and to be is sin.

The following anecdote could apply in principle also to Judaism and Christianity. Al-Khadir is a legendary, mysterious holy person who lives from generation to generation interceding for people bent on spiritual questing. His name means "Evergreen." Ibn 'Arabi, the Spanish Sufi (and contemporary of Rumi) with monistic tendencies, claimed to have been confirmed in the Sufi way by al-Khadir.

6.6E THE PAIN OF UNANSWERED PRAYER (P. 91)

One night a certain man cried "Allah!" till his lips grew sweet with praising Him.
The Devil said, "O man of many words, where is the response 'Here am I' *(labbayka)*
  to all this 'Allah'?
Not a single response is coming from the Throne: how long will you say 'Allah' with
  grim face?"
He was broken-hearted and lay down to sleep: in a dream he saw Khaḍir amidst the
  verdure,
Who said, "Hark, you have held back from praising God: why do you repent of call-
  ing unto Him?"
He answered. "No 'Here am I' is coming to me in response: I fear that I am turned
  away from the Door."
Said Khaḍir, "Nay; God saith: That 'Allah' of thine is My 'Here am I,' and that sup-
  plication and grief
And ardour of thine is My messenger to thee. Thy fear and love are the noose to
  catch My Favour:
Beneath every 'O Lord' of thine is many a 'Here am I' from Me."

6.6F THE TRUE SUFI (P. 54)

What makes the Ṣūfī? Purity of heart;
Not the patched mantle and the lust perverse
Of those vile earth-bound men who steal his name.
He in all dregs discerns the essence pure:
In hardship ease, in tribulation joy.
The phantom sentries, who with batons drawn
Guard Beauty's palace-gate and curtained bower,
Give way before him, unafraid he passes,
And showing the King's arrow, enters in.

6.6G A VISION OF DIVINITY AS FEMININE (P. 44)

If you rule your wife outwardly, yet inwardly you are ruled by her whom you desire,

This is characteristic of Man: in other animals love is lacking, and that shows their inferiority.

The Prophet said that woman prevails over the wise, while ignorant men prevail over her; for in them the fierceness of the animal is immanent.

Love and tenderness are human qualities, anger and lust are animal qualities.

Woman is a ray of God: she is not the earthly beloved. She is creative: you might say she is not created.[1]

6.7 HAMZAH FANSURI

Islam spread to Southeast Asia by trade and was carried in personal ways through the Malaysian-Indonesian archipelago by Sufis. From its beginnings, Islam in Malaysia and Indonesia has had a strong mystical bent, partly because of the Sufis but also because of the Hindu-Buddhist traditions that had long flourished there, as well as the strongly mystical native temperament of Southeast Asians. The monistic, known as *wujūdīya,** theosophy influenced by Ibn 'Arabī and his popularizer al-Jīlī was carried to Melaka, Sumatra, and Java, where it has had a fascinating career to this day. Hamzah Fansuri, about whose life practically nothing is known, was probably active in the latter part of the sixteenth century and survived perhaps to 1630. He came from the town of Barus, famous as a producer of Camphor, on the west coast of Aceh in northern Sumatra. His mystical poems are considered to be the finest in Malay literature, which had reached its peak in that era. Hamzah's mystical—some have said pantheistic—views were stoutly challenged by the orthodox Indian-Arab Muslim scholar al-Raniri (d. 1658), who denounced them as heretical in an influential treatise written during his sojourn in Aceh in 1637–1644. A modern study** argues that far from espousing a crude pantheism,

> like Ibnu'l-'Arabi, Hamzah conceives Reality as having both aspects of transcendence (*tanzīh*) and immanence (*tashbīh*), and takes care to assert repeatedly that God is not everything and all things in the sense of being as aggregation of existents. Almost all of Raniri's attacks on Hamzah's "pantheism" seem to prove to be nothing beyond his own fallacy of jumping to conclusions in identifying what Hamzah means metaphorically with what Hamzah considers to be real. In this way it is the metaphors that are attacked and the picture of the real caricatured.

---

[1] Sweeping aside the veil of form, the poet beholds in woman the eternal Beauty, the inspirer and object of all love, and regards her, in her essential nature, as the medium through which that Beauty reveals itself and exercises creative activity. Ibnu'l-'Arabī went so far as to say that the most perfect vision of God is enjoyed by those who contemplate Him in woman.

*From the Arabic phrase *waḥdat al-wujūd,* that is, "oneness of being." It has not been discovered that Ibn 'Arabī, who is most often credited with the phrase, ever used it.

**Syed Muhammad Naguib al-Attas, *Rānirī and the Wujūdiyyah of 17th Century Aceh,* monographs of the Malaysian Branch of the Royal Asiatic Society, III (Singapore, 1966), p. 21.

Al-Raniri's attack on Hamzah and other holders of what the heretic hunter considered pantheistic and *wujūdī* (in the *non*-Muslim monist sense) doctrines was highly effective. The modern state Islamic university in Aceh carries al-Raniri's name, indicating the strong Sunni orthodoxy of today's Acehnese, who continue as before to refer to their beautiful country (actually a province of Indonesia) as "The Verandah of the Ka'aba."

6.7A OCEAN AND WAVES (NO. IV, PP. 51–55)

1. Oh all of us who worship the Name
   One should know what comes first
   For our Lord is the Eternal One
   Inclusive of His seven attributes

2. Among the attributes of our Lord, the possessor of Essence
   That of living ranks first
   His second attribute is that He knows all objects of knowledge as they are
   The third, that He is willing, (which comprises) all His acts of will

3. The fourth is that He is almighty
   The fifth is the attribute of speech
   The sixth, that of hearing, permanently operative
   The seventh, that He sees what is permitted and what is forbidden

4. These seven being eternally His
   He is fully conversant with the disposition of the universe
   Because these qualities are attended with perfect judiciousness
   He is named God the Merciful, the Compassionate

5. The 'Reality of Muhammad' is identical with His knowledge
   It is fully conditioned by the known (in God's knowledge)
   In this his Reality both fool and saint
   Are foreseen in every respect

6. Our Lord is possessed of perfection
   In His knowledge the known is forever present
   In 'Merciful' His entire aspect of Majesty is contained
   As is that of Beauty in 'Compassionate'

7. Our Lord, who is named the Exalted
   Is everlasting, with all His attributes
   Their effects are noticeable in the entire universe
   Hence the six directions do not apply to Him

From Hamzah Fansuri, *The Poems of Hamzah Fansuri*, edited and translated by G. W. J. Drewes and L. F. Brakel, Bibliotheca Indonesica, no. 26 (1986). Reprinted with the permission of Royal Institute of Linguistics and Anthropology, Leiden, The Netherlands.

8. The radiance of these effects will never be extinguished
   They give existence to the entire universe
   Day and night He is creating
   To all eternity, without coming to an end

9. Our Lord is comparable to the fathomless Ocean
   The waves of which are rolling on all sides
   Ocean and waves are constant companions
   And finally the waves will merge into the Ocean

10. The Ocean is the Knower, the waves are the known
    It is He who metes out, meted out are the waves
    The tempest is the Ruler, at His discretion are the engagements
    By which the course of the universe is settled

11. If you are sensible of the Being
    It is this you keep in view
    Free your person from all shackles
    So that you may be able to abide in the Self

12. In that Being you should subsist
    Give up your personality and name altogether
    Free yourself of the notion of Lord and servant
    So that you may achieve the final act

13. As long as you are not as solid as a rock
    The duality of servant and Lord will subsist
    Once you are dead to gold and carats (coin)
    You will be able to achieve union

14. As long as you have not disabused yourself of the hundreds and thousands
    How can you efface your being?
    Free yourself from the idea of material and immaterial
    So that whatever you say will be permissible

15. Hamzah Fansuri, although a mere nobody
    Intrinsically is close to the Exalted Essence
    Although materially nothing but a bubble
    He is in constant union with the Divine Ocean

6.7B THE "DEVICES" OF ALLAH (NO. XVIII, PP. 97–99)

1. In fact, the divine Sovereign
   Is always playing with His servants
   Since His names confirm themselves
   His countenance is everywhere

2. He is the greatest of kings
   Called the only mighty one
   Plotting and resourceful
   He constantly conceals Himself inside a servant

3. His devices are various
   He is both mother and father
   On account of His skilfulness
   The mass of mankind do not give heed to Him

4. After His very words His attributes
   Display themselves on the human stage
   That is why they are so much in evidence
   (Yet) their origin remains completely hidden

5. He is bent on veiling Himself
   Apart from His garment He is hidden
   But this is none other than He
   With Himself too He is playing

6. Now He is young and modest
   Now old and white-haired
   Going forth for months in seclusion
   Seeking the Lord in the wilderness

7. Now He is a mystic
   Now a passionate lover
   Then again a spiritual-minded person
   Going about peevish and wry-faced on this earth

8. Now He is competent and skilful
   Now He is hungry and thin
   Then again He is Jonah
   Confined in the inside of a fish

9. Now He is a stranger
   Now He is a fellow-tiller
   Then again He is in penurious circumstances
   Always running on the rocks

10. Now He is called a thunder
    Now a torch
    Then again He is an enemy
    Who permanently perturbs one's person .

11. Now He is an offering
    Now He is naked
    Then again He adduces decisive proof
    In Mecca, and verses of the Qor'ān

12. Now He is a seeker
    Now He is utterly obscure
    Then again He is a penitent
    His presence in this world is quite common

13. Like that is the supreme King
    Called the creative ruler
    He is the Beloved, He the Lover
    Constantly giving expression to Himself

14. His radiance is a blazing glow
    In all of us
    It is He who is the cup and the arak
    Do not look for Him far away, my boy

15. Hamzah Fansuri, you thoughtless fellow
    Under the delusion that your Beloved was veiled
    You always went up a dead-end road
    How then could you soon attain union?

6.7c A VISION OF GOD IN THE CHINA SEA (NO. XXXII, PP. 141–143)

1. How strange that the whale
   Having its habitat in the China Sea
   Looks for water on Mount Sinai
   Hence its efforts are worthless

2. The China Sea is unfathomable
   For this reason the population of the entire universe
   Jinn, angels and (the sons of) Adam
   All of us get submerged in that sea

3. Its reefs are numerous, its coasts extensive
   Its bays are fine, as it were enclosures
   Into that sea one must swim
   Then you will soon be able to see

4. A violent storm is continuously sweeping it
   Raging unremittedly
   You get submerged there entirely
   So that you may obtain a heavenly reward

5. Adam the mystic was confused by the Devil
   In the flower-decked Paradise
   He came down to the earth on a mountain in Ceylon
   Crazy about Eve, utterly bewildered

6. Do not disregard Adam
   In him God's supreme wisdom becomes apparent
   Let all who inquire after him show respect
   He was an eminent wave of the Ocean

7. Listen, you pious reciters of the Qorʾān
   Do not cast about far and wide
   Do not run away from the water
   So that you may become pure

8. The whale is swimming about
   In the Ocean in search of water
   Yet the sea is much in evidence
   To pious as well as to sinful people

9. Have done with soldiery and pageantry
   Dispense with money and bondmen
   Do your utmost to retire from this world
   Then you may grow regardful

10. Tell the malleable youngsters
    Do not be fickle
    This world is like a game of dice
    So how can you go on loving it?

11. Be indifferent to heat and cold
    Desist from cupidity and desire
    Have them melt away as wax
    Then your works will go smoothly

12. The whale is in close union
    With the shoreless Ocean
    Even so it is madly casting about for it, stupidly
    And so its efforts are idle

13. Hamzah of Shahr-i Naw is entirely effaced
    As wood burnt down altogether
    His origin is the unruffled Ocean
    He became camphor in Barus

6.8 SEJARAH MELAYU: *MALAY ANNALS*

The following episodes come from the greatest classic of Malay prose literature, *Sejarah Melayu*, the "Malay Annals," a work found in various versions that dates probably from 1612 and was composed for the Sultan who ruled Melaka, the great seaport on the straits separating the Malay Peninsula from Sumatra. The point of view throughout is that of cosmopolitan and sophisticated Melaka, which although comprised largely of Muslim Malays, was also a global crossroads of commerce and great-power politics because of its strategic position as a gateway between the Indian Ocean and the China Sea. There is a considerable amount of folklore in the Annals, as well as some sharp personality sketches. The work abounds in humor, too, which is even funnier in the original terse and subtle Malay language. Here and there may be seen references to Islam and its doctrines, as well as Muslim practices. But the work is mostly about kings and their courts, as it was intended to be.

Sultan Ahmad of Melaka mounts his battle elephant when leading his troops in the defense of their city against the Portuguese armada from the sea. He takes his court teacher of Islam with him to continue his studies in the mysteries of the Divine Unity (*tawḥīd*).

6.8A A DANGEROUS LESSON IN THE DIVINE UNITY (PP. 161–162)

Here now is a story of Fongso d'Albuquerque. At the end of his term of office as viceroy he proceeded to Pertugal and presenting himself before the Raja of Pertugal asked for an armada. The Raja of Pertugal gave him four carracks and five long galleys. He then returned from Pertugal and fitted out a fleet at Goa, consisting of three carracks, eight galeasses, four long galleys and fifteen foysts. There were thus forty (sic) craft in all. With this fleet he sailed for Malaka. And when he reached Malaka, there was great excitement and word was brought to Sultan Ahmad, "The Franks are come to attack us! They have seven carracks, eight galeasses, ten long galleys, fifteen sloops and five foysts." Thereupon Sultan Ahmad had all his forces assembled and he ordered them to make ready their equipment. And the Franks engaged the men of Malaka in battle, and they fired their cannon from their ships so that the cannon balls came like rain. And the noise of the cannon was as the noise of thunder in the heavens and the flashes of fire of their guns were like flashes of lightning in the sky: and the noise of their matchlocks was like that of ground-nuts popping in the frying-pan. So heavy was the gun-fire that the men of Malaka could no longer maintain their position on the shore. The Franks then bore down upon the bridge with their galleys and foysts. Thereupon Sultan Ahmad came forth, mounted on his elephant Jituji

The Sri Awadana was on the elephant's head, and to balance him on the packsaddle Sultan Ahmad took him Makhdum Sadar Jahan because he was studying the doctrine of the Unity of God with him. On the elephant's croup was Tun 'Ali Hati.

And the king went forth on to the bridge and stood there amid a hail of bullets. But Makhdum Sadar Jahan clasping the pannier with both hands cried out to

From C. C. Brown, trans., *Sejarah Mulayu or Malay Annals*. Reprinted with the permission of Oxford University Press, Singapore.

Sultan Ahmad Shah "Sultan, this is no place to study the Unity of God, let us go home!" Sultan Ahmad smiled and returned to the palace. And the Franks shouted from their ships, "Take warning, you men of Malaka, to-morrow we land!" And the men of Malaka answered, "Very well!"

6.8B SUFI CONUNDRUMS AND INTERNATIONAL RELATIONS (PP. 148–149)

It happened once that Sultan Mahmud Shah wished to send an envoy to Pasai to ask for the answer to a question in dispute between the divines of the Country beyond the River, the divines of Khurassan and the divines of Irak. And the king consulted with the Bendahara and the chiefs. "How are we going to send our message to Pasai?" he asked. "If we send it in writing, we shall certainly come off badly, for the men of Pasai have no scruples about altering the text of a letter. Even if the letter says 'greetings,' they still make it say 'obeisance.'" Then said Bendahara Sri Maharaja, "In that case all we have to do is this; we send an envoy but without a letter and we order the envoy to commit the message to memory." And Sultan Mahmud Shah replied, "Yes, that will do, but Tun Muhammad must be the envoy." Tun Muhammad having signified his compliance, the letter was borne in procession to the ship; and as presents to accompany the letter the king sent a cleaver of Pahang made with gold inlay, a white cockatoo and a purple cockatoo. Tun Muhammad then set forth and on the voyage he committed the contents of the letter to memory.

When Tun Muhammad reached Pasai, the Raja of Pasai was informed that an envoy was come from Malaka. The Raja of Pasai gave orders to his chiefs to fetch the letter with ceremony from the ship and bring it with drum, pipe, clarionet and kettledrums. And when they came to Tun Muhammad, the chiefs sent to welcome the letter said to him, "Where is the letter? Let us take it in procession." But Tun Muhammad answered, "I am the letter! Take me in procession!" He was accordingly mounted on an elephant and taken in procession to the hall of audience. When the procession arrived at the hall, Tun Muhammad dismounted from the elephant and standing at the place where letters were read, he proceeded to recite the letter, as follows:—

"Greetings and prayers to God from the elder brother to his younger brother Sri Sultan the Exalted, the Honoured King, Shadow of God in the World. The elder brother's reason for sending his chiefs, Tun Muhammad and Tun Bija Wangsa, to present themselves before his younger brother is that the elder brother wishes to know the explanation of this difficulty—first *man kala, Inna'llaha ta'ala khalikun' warazkun fi'l-azali fakad kafara,* that is to say 'whoever declares God to be the creator and preserver to eternity is verily an infidel'; and second *man kala Inna'llaha ta'ala lam yakun khalikan warazikan fi'l-azali fakad kafara,* that is to say 'whoever declares that God is not the creator and preserver to eternity is verily an infidel.' It is desired that the younger brother should give the explanation." The Raja of Pasai assembled all the divines of Pasai and bade them give the required explanation but not one of them could do so. The Raja of Pasai then bade Tun Muhammad approach and when he was close to him the Raja of Pasai told him the (? explanation of the) difficulty, saying "This is the explanation that our brother in Malaka desires." This answer satisfied Tun Muhammad and he said, "It is as your Highness has said." Tun Muhammad then sought leave to return to Malaka and the Raja of Pasai had a letter written in reply to that from the Raja of Malaka: this letter was borne in procession to Tun Muhammad's ship.

Tun Muhammad then set out for Malaka, where he arrived in due course. The letter from Pasai was borne in procession according to ancient custom to the hall of audience where it was read, and Tun Muhammad related to the king what the Raja of Pasai had said and all that had happened at Pasai. Sultan Mahmud Shah was well pleased with Tun Muhammad's account, and the answer the Sultan of Pasai had given met with his approval. And Tun Muhammad and Tun Bija Wangsa were presented by him with robes of honour with accessories such as are worn by princes and they received other rich rewards.

God knoweth the truth.

This story of the "Letter" contains a difficult riddle. Sir Richard Winstedt, the great master of Malay studies, attempted to provide a solution: "The answer to the first problem Malays found in the popular *Insan al-Kamil* or Perfect Man of al-Jili [a famous Arab Sufi, d. ca. 1417; a disciple of the teachings of Ibn ʿArabi], who held that the sufferers' power of endurance being a divine gift extinguished the fire or else that their torment was changed to pleasure. To the second question, the Malay knew two answers, the orthodox one that spirit (*ruh*) is not eternal but created, and the unorthodox one that the word of creation merely raised what was already existent though not manifest."

Sultan Mahmud Shah, like other rulers in traditional Southeast Asia, wanted to keep abreast of learning, especially as it related to values and religious realities. In this charming episode, his first lesson is in how to approach a holy man for instruction. Maulana (meaning "Our Master") Yusuf had become a "fakir" (Arabic *faqir*), that is, a renunciate who has embarked on the way of Sufism. The term *faqīr* is related to *faqr*, "spiritual poverty," which is a sort of total emptying of the worldly self and an opening to God's guidance and grace. Maulana Yusuf, clearly, is one who feared only God. Sultan Mahmud proves to be a promising student. The detail about the kites would appeal to a Malay audience, because making and flying colorful, elaborate kites is a cherished pastime of traditional Malays.

6.8c How to Approach a Sufi Teacher (pp. 124–125)

Now Sultan Mahmud Shah wished to receive instruction in the sciences from Maulana Yusuf. [He (Maulana Yusuf) had become a recluse. If people flew kites over the roof of his house, he would order them to be shot down [with a catapult]:

and when he got one, he would order the cord of the kite to be wound in, saying, "How dare people fly kites over my house!" That was how he behaved. He had ceased to be Kadli, having been succeeded in that office by his son, Kadli Menawar Shah. In pursuance of this intention Sultan Mahmud Shah set out for the house of Maulana Yusuf: he was mounted on his elephant and escorted by his retainers. When they reached the fence round Maulana Yusuf's house, the retainers said to the gatekeeper, "Tell Maulana Yusuf that Sultan Mahmud Shah, the Ruler, is here." But when this message was brought to Maulana Yusuf, he said, "Shut the gate! What business has Sultan Mahmud Shah to come to a fakir's house?" When Sultan Mahmud Shah was told what Maulana Yusuf had said, he returned to the palace. But when night fell, he dismissed his retainers and when he was alone, he set out again for Maulana Yusuf's house, this time with no one but a boy for escort and himself carrying his book. On arriving at the gate the king said to the gatekeeper, "Tell Maulana Yusuf that Mahmud the fakir is come." And the gatekeeper opened the gate, thinking it was only right that one fakir should come to another fakir's house. Forthwith Maulana Yusuf came out and brought Sultan Mahmud Shah into the house and bade him be seated. Sultan Mahmud Shah then had his lesson (? in the sciences) with Maulana Yusuf.

PART III
AUTHORITY
AND COMMUNITY

CHAPTER 7
IN JUDAISM

7.1 BIBLICAL MODELS OF RELIGIOUS LEADERSHIP

Although many types of individuals bear the designation "prophet" in the biblical canon, Moses is represented in the Torah as the paradigm of what the prophet is as a religious leader. His prophetic role consists primarily in his function as a means by which the God of Israel communicates His will to the people of Israel. These communications, as well as the book Moses is said to have written, are called Torah, "teaching." The following passages are representative of the Torah's portrayal of Moses as a prophetic intercessor and teacher of Torah. In the first selection, Moses, at the end of his forty-day communion with God on Sinai, averts God's anger after Israel betrays the covenant by worshiping the image of a calf. The second, set during the forty years of wilderness wandering, describes Moses as an administrator of the divine laws, procuring from God new revelations about a legal question not included in the revelation at Sinai.

7.1A EXODUS 32:7–14

The LORD said to Moses, "Go down at once! Your people, whom you brought up out of Egypt, have acted perversely; they have been quick to turn aside from the way that I commanded them; they have cast for themselves an image of a calf, and have worshipped it and sacrificed to it, and said, 'These are your gods, O Israel, who brought you up out of the land of Egypt!'" The LORD said to Moses, "I have seen this people, how stiff-necked they are. Now let my wrath burn hot against them and I may consume them; and of you I will make a great nation." But Moses implored the LORD his God, and said, "O LORD, why does your wrath burn hot against your people, whom you brought out of the land of Egypt with great power and with a mighty hand? Why should the Egyptians say, 'It was with evil intent that he brought them out to kill them in the mountains, and to consume them from the face of the earth'? Turn from your fierce wrath; change your mind and do not bring disaster on your people. Remember Abraham, Isaac and Israel, your servants, how you swore to them by your own self, saying to them, 'I will multiply your descendants like the stars of heaven, and all this land that I have promised I will give to your descendants, and they shall inherit forever.'" And the LORD changed his mind about the disaster that he planned to bring on his people.

7.1B NUMBERS 27:1–11

Then the daughters of Zelophehad had come forward. . . . They stood before Moses, Eleazar the priest, the leaders, and all the congregation, at the entrance of the tent of meeting, and they said, "Our father died in the wilderness; he was not among the company of those who gathered themselves together against the LORD in the company of Korah, but died for his own sins, and he had no sons. Why should the name of our father be taken away from his clan because he had no sons? Give to us a possession among our father's brothers." Moses brought their case before the LORD. And the LORD spoke to Moses, saying: The daughters of Zelophehad are right in what they are saying; you shall indeed let them possess an inheritance among their father's brothers and pass the inheritance of their father on to them. You shall also say to the Israelites, "If a man dies, and has no son, then you shall pass his inheritance on to his daughter. If he has no daughter, then you shall give his inheritance to his brothers. If he has no brothers, then you shall give his inheritance to his father's brothers. And if his father has no brothers, then you shall give his inheritance to the nearest kinsman of his clan, and he shall possess it. It shall be for the Israelites a statute and ordinance, as the LORD commanded Moses."

The richest representation of priestly leadership in the Hebrew Bible is found in the Torah's depictions of Aaron and his sons as they perform their sacrificial duties in the Tent of Meeting or Tabernacle. These sacrifices invoke the divine presence in the Tent and thus ensure His protection of the entire encampment in the wilderness. The first passage to follow describes the inauguration of the sacrificial service. Note the careful procedure of the sacrifice itself, the first appearance of the divine glory in the Tabernacle, and finally, the devastating power unleashed upon anyone bringing any but the prescribed offerings to the altar. The second passage, concluding a description of the sacrificial rite of the Day of Atonement, spells out the priestly role in achieving purification and atonement before God on behalf of the people.

7.1c Leviticus 9:1–10:3

On the eighth day Moses summoned Aaron and his sons and the elders of Israel. He said to Aaron, "Take a bull calf for a sin offering and a ram for a burnt offering, without blemish, and offer them before the LORD.". . . They brought what Moses commanded to the front of the tent of meeting; and the whole congregation drew near and stood before the LORD. And Moses said, "This is the thing that the LORD commanded you to do, so that the glory of the LORD may appear to you." Then Moses said to Aaron, "Draw near to the altar and sacrifice your sin offering and your burnt offering, and make atonement for yourself and for the people; and sacrifice the offering of the people, and make atonement for them as the LORD has commanded."

Aaron drew near to the altar, and slaughtered the calf of the sin offering, which was for himself. The sons of Aaron presented the blood to him, and he dipped his finger in the blood and put it on the horns of the altar; and the rest of the blood he poured out at the base of the altar. But the fat, the kidneys, and the appendage of the liver from the sin offering he turned into smoke on the altar, as the LORD commanded Moses; and the flesh and the skin he burned with fire outside the camp. Then he slaughtered the burnt offering. Aaron's sons brought him the blood and he dashed it against all sides of the altar. And they brought him the burnt offering piece by piece, and the head, which he turned into smoke on the altar. He washed the entrails and the legs and, with the burnt offering, turned them into smoke on the altar. . . .

Aaron lifted his hands toward the people and blessed them; and he came down after sacrificing the sin offering, the burnt offering, and the offering of well-being. Moses and Aaron entered the tent of meeting, and then came out and blessed the people; and the glory of the LORD appeared to all the people. Fire came out from the LORD and consumed the burnt offering and the fat on the altar; and when all the people saw it, they shouted and fell on their faces.

Now Aaron's sons, Nadab and Abihu, each took his censer, put fire in it, and laid incense on it; and they offered unholy fire before the LORD, such as he had not commanded them. And fire came out from the presence of the LORD and consumed them, and they died before the LORD. Then Moses said to Aaron, "This is what the LORD meant when he said, 'Through those who are near me I will show myself holy, and before all the people I will be glorified.'" And Aaron was silent.

7.1d Leviticus 16:29–34

This shall be a statute to you forever: In the seventh month, on the tenth day of the month, you shall deny yourselves, and shall do no work, neither the citizen nor the alien who resides among you. For on this day atonement shall be made for you, to cleanse you; from all your sins you shall be cleansed before the LORD. It is a sabbath of complete rest to you, and you shall deny yourselves; it is a statute forever. The priest who is anointed and consecrated as priest in his father's place shall make atonement wearing the linen vestments, the holy vestments. He shall make atonement for the sanctuary, and he shall make atonement for the priests and for all the people of the assembly. This shall be an everlasting statute for you, to make atonement for the people of Israel once in the year for all their sins. And Moses did as the LORD commanded him.

In the historical narrative of the Hebrew Bible's prophetic canon, the figure of David looms as the ideal king against whom all others are measured. But he is also portrayed as a complex, lusty person not above sin and self-interest. The Bible's final historical judgment, however, is that David's reign is represented as a high point of ancient Israelite history, the restoration of which is eagerly anticipated in the future. The first passage to follow summarizes David's character, as the author of the post-exilic book of Chronicles wanted it to be remembered. The second shows how, in the imagination of the exilic prophet Ezekiel, the restoration of the Davidic line is part of God's larger plan of reconciliation with Israel and forgiveness of its sins.

7.1E I CHRONICLES 28:2–8, 29:20–22, 29:26–30

Then King David rose to his feet and said: "Hear me, my brothers and my people. I had planned to build a house of rest for the ark of the covenant of the LORD, for the footstool of our God; and I made preparations for the building. But God said to me, 'You shall not build a house for my name, for you are a warrior and have shed blood.' Yet the LORD God of Israel chose me from all my ancestral house to be king over Israel forever; for he chose Judah as leader, and in the house of Judah my father's house, and among my father's sons he took delight in making me king over all Israel. He said to me, 'It is your son Solomon who shall build my house and my courts, for I have chosen him to be a son to me, and I will be a father to him. I will establish his kingdom forever if he continues resolute in keeping my commandments and my ordinances, as he is today.' Now therefore in the sight of all Israel, the assembly of the LORD, and in the hearing of our God, observe and search out all the commandments of the LORD your God; that you may possess this good land, and leave it for an inheritance to your children after you forever.". . .

Then David said to the whole assembly, "Bless the LORD your God." And all the assembly blessed the LORD, the God of their ancestors, and bowed their heads and prostrated themselves before the LORD and the King. On the next day they offered sacrifices and burnt offerings to the LORD, a thousand bulls, a thousand rams, and a thousand lambs, with their libations, and sacrifices in abundance for all Israel; and they ate and drank before the LORD on that day with great joy. . . .

Thus David son of Jesse reigned over all Israel. The period that he reigned over Israel was forty years; he reigned seven years in Hebron, and thirty-three years in Jerusalem. He died in a good old age, full of days, riches, and honor; and his son Solomon succeeded him. Now the acts of King David, from first to last, are written in the records of the seer Samuel, and in the records of the prophet Nathan, and in the records of the seer Gad, with accounts of all his rule and his might and of the events that befell him and Israel and all the kingdoms of the earth.

7.1F EZEKIEL 34:20–31

Therefore, thus says the LORD God to them: I myself will judge between the fat sheep and the lean sheep. . . . I will save my flock, and they shall no longer be ravaged; and I will judge between sheep and sheep. I will set up over them one shepherd, my servant David, and he shall feed them; he shall feed them and be their shepherd. And I, the LORD, will be their God, and my servant David shall be prince among them; I, the LORD, have spoken.

I will make them a covenant of peace and banish wild animals from the land, so that they may lie in the wild and sleep in the woods securely. I will make them and the region round my hill a blessing; and I will send down the showers in their season; they shall be showers of blessing. The trees of the field shall yield their fruit, and the earth shall yield its increase. They shall be secure on their soil; and they shall know that I am the LORD, when I break the bars of their yoke, and save them from the hands of those who enslaved them. . . . They shall know that I, the LORD their God, am with them, and that they, the house of Israel, are my people, says the LORD God. You are my sheep, the sheep of my pasture and I am your God, says the LORD God.

In the biblical literature, King Solomon, the son of David, looms as the paradigm of the wise sage. The book of Ecclesiastes, ascribed to an anonymous author called "Koheleth (Teacher), son of David," is regarded by later tradition to be of Solomonic authorship. The following passage records a wise sage's reflections upon the approach of death and a concluding admonishment to attend to sages' words.

7.1G ECCLESIASTES 12:1–14

Remember your creator in the days of your youth, before the days of trouble come, and the years draw near when you will say, "I have no pleasure in them" before the sun and the light and the moon and the stars are darkened and the clouds return with the rain; in the day when the guards of the house tremble, and the strong men are bent, and the women who grind cease working because they are few, and those who look through the windows see dimly; when the doors on the street are shut, and the sound of the grinding is low, and one rises up at the sound of a bird, and all the daughters of song are brought low; when one is afraid of heights, and terrors are in the road; the almond tree blossoms, the grasshopper drags itself along and desire fails; because all must go to their eternal home, and the mourners will go about the streets; before the silver cord is snapped, and the golden bowl is broken, and the pitcher is broken at the fountain, and the wheel broken at the cistern, and the dust returns to the earth as it was, and the breath returns to God who gave it. Vanity of vanities, says the Teacher; all is vanity.

Besides being wise, the Teacher also taught the people knowledge, weighing and studying and arranging many proverbs. The Teacher sought to find pleasing words, and he wrote words of truth plainly. The sayings of the wise are like goads, and like nails firmly fixed are the collected sayings that are given by one shepherd. Of anything beyond these, my child, beware. Of making many books there is no end, and much study is a weariness of flesh. The end of the matter; all has been heard. Fear God, and keep his commandments; for that is the whole duty of everyone. For God will bring every deed into judgment, including every secret thing, whether good or evil.

7.2 COMMUNITY AND AUTHORITY: THE YAKHAD AND THE RABBINIC SAGES

Members of the community gathered in Qumran—the Yakhad—regarded themselves as penitents who had converted to a way of truth after a lifetime of living sinfully. New members, accordingly, had to serve a period of training and trial before full entry. Upon entry, new members gave all their possessions to the community, committed themselves to follow the Yakhad's ritual procedures of purification, and were permitted to participate in communal meals. The selection to follow is from a document called by archeologists the Community Rule (columns V and VIII), an important Dead Sea text. It describes expected behavior of members and procedures for disciplining full members.

7.2A COMMUNITY RULE V–VIII

And this is the Rule for the men of the Community who have freely pledged themselves to be converted from all evil and to cling to all His commandments according to His will.

They shall separate from the congregation of the men of falsehood and shall reunite, with respect to the Law and possessions, under the authority of the sons of Zadok, the Priests who keep the Covenant. Every decision concerning doctrine, property and justice shall be determined by them.

They shall practice truth and humility in common, and justice and uprightness and charity and modesty in all their ways. No man shall walk in the stubbornness of his heart so that he strays after his heart and eyes and evil inclination, but he shall circumcise in the Community the foreskin of evil inclination and of stiffness of neck that they may lay a foundation of truth for Israel, for the Commu-

Excerpts from Geza Vermes, *The Dead Sea Scrolls in English, Third Edition*, translated by G. Vermes. Copyright © 1962, 1965, 1968, 1975, 1987 by G. Vermes. Reprinted with the permission of Penguin Books, Ltd.

nity of the everlasting Covenant. They shall atone for all those in Aaron who have freely pledged themselves to the House of Truth, and for those who join them to live in community and to take part in the trial and judgement and condemnation of all those who transgress the precepts.

On joining the Community, this shall be their code of behaviour with respect to all these precepts. Whoever approaches the Council of the Community shall enter the Covenant of God in the presence of all who have freely pledged themselves. He shall undertake by a binding oath to return with all his heart and soul to every commandment of the Torah of Moses in accordance with all that has been revealed of it to the sons of Zadok, the Keepers of the Covenant and Seekers of His will, and to the multitude of the men of their Covenant who together have freely pledged themselves to His truth and to walking in the way of His delight. And he shall undertake by the Covenant to separate from all the men of falsehood who walk in the way of wickedness. . . .

And these are the rules which the men of perfect holiness shall follow in their commerce with one another.

Every man who enters the Council of Holiness, (the Council of those) who walk in the way of perfection as commanded by God, and who deliberately or through negligence transgresses one word of the Torah of Moses, on any point whatever, shall be expelled from the Council of the Community and shall return no more; no man of holiness shall be associated in his property or counsel in any matter at all. But if he has acted inadvertently, he shall be excluded from the pure Meal and the Council and they shall interpret the rule (as follows). For two years he shall take no part in judgment or ask for counsel; but if, during that time, his way becomes perfect, then he shall return to the (Court of) Inquiry and the Council, in accordance with the judgement of the Congregation, provided that he commit no further inadvertent sin during two full years.

At the center of the Yakhad stood an inspired interpreter of Scripture. Whether terms such as Teacher of Righteousness or Interpreter of the Torah refer to one or numerous individuals, it is likely that this person's function was to deliver prophetically inspired interpretations of the Torah's message for the life of the Yakhad. The following passage from the Damascus Rule (columns V–VI) offers an example of such interpretation of an enigmatic verse in Numbers 21:18. The exegete interprets the Torah as an allusion to the origins of the Yakhad, in a "time of desolation," among "men of discernment and wisdom" who unite around an "Interpreter of the Torah" (Vermes, p. 87).

7.2b Damascus Rule, V–VI

And at the time of the desolation of the Land there arose removers of the bound who led Israel astray. And the land was ravaged because they preached rebellion against the commandments of God given by the hand of Moses and of His holy anointed ones, and because they prophesied lies to turn Israel away from following God. But God remembered the Covenant with the forefathers, and he raised from Aaron men of discernment and from Israel men of wisdom, and He caused them to hear. And they dug the Well: "the well which the princes dug, which the nobles of the people delved with the stave" (Numbers 21:18).

"The well" is the Torah, and those who dug it were the converts of Israel who went out of the land of Judah to sojourn in the land of Damascus [i.e., Qumran]. God called them "princes" because they sought Him, and their renown was disputed by no man. "The stave" is the Interpreter of the Torah of whom Isaiah said: "He makes a tool for His work" (Isa. 54:16); and "the nobles of the people" are those who come to dig "the well" with the staves with which "the stave" ordained that they should walk in all the age of wickedness . . . until he comes who shall teach righteousness at the end of days.

As in the Yakhad, entry into the early rabbinic communities involved a period of discipleship and training in the lore and rules of the group. Some rabbinic texts preserve memories that a principal criterion of membership was a commitment to abide by certain rules of ritual purity that permitted a person to share common meals with others in the community. The following passage from the Tosefta (*Tractate Demai*, 2:9–13), a document edited slightly later than the Mishnah, seems to assume that these requirements were met only by a small group ("association": *khavurah*) within the larger community of disciples of sages (*talmidei khakhamim*). Note the idea, expressed early in the passage, that joining the association was akin to religious conversion.

7.2c Tractate Demai 2:9–13

Regarding all those who recanted membership in the association, they never accept them again—words of Rabbi Meir. Rabbi Judah says: If they recanted in public, they accept them; if in secret, they do not accept them. Rabbi Shimon and Rabbi Joshua ben Korha say: In either case they accept them, as it is written: "Repent O faithless children!" (Jer. 3:14)

He who comes to accept the discipline of the association—if he had previously performed it in private, they accept him and afterwards instruct him; and if not, they instruct him and afterwards accept him. Rabbi Shimon says: In either case they accept him and then instruct him progressively.

And they accept him first in matters pertaining to the purity of his hands, and afterwards in matters pertaining to food which must be prepared in a state of purity. If he said: I accept upon myself only matters pertaining to the purity of my hands—they accept him. If he accepted upon himself matters pertaining to the purity of foods, but did not accept upon himself matters pertaining to purity of the hands, he also is not deemed trustworthy regarding the purity of food.

How long before they accept him? The House of Shammai say: Regarding trustworthiness to preserve the purity of liquids, thirty days; regarding the purity of clothing, twelve months. And the House of Hillel say: For both, thirty days.

He who comes to accept upon himself the discipline of the association—even a disciple of the sages must accept this upon himself through a formal oath. But a sage who sits on the court does not have to accept this upon himself through an oath, for he has already accepted this upon himself from the moment that he entered the court. Abba Saul says: Rather a disciple of the sages does not have to accept this upon himself through an oath. And furthermore, others accept it upon themselves through an oath made before him.

A fundamental aspect of rabbinic discipleship was tutelage in the rabbinic Oral Torah. This could be learned only from a rabbinic sage. Mastery of this Oral Torah not only served as one's credential for membership in the sages' community, but also gave one access to a tradition of learning believed to stem from Sinai. What follows is an example of how the sages imagined Moses' original establishment of the procedures for memorizing Oral Torah.

7.2D BABYLONIAN TALMUD, *ERUVIN* 54B

Our rabbis transmitted as oral tradition: How was oral teaching (*mishnah*) conducted? Moses learned from the mouth of the Power (that is, God). Then Aaron entered and Moses reviewed his portion for him. Aaron stepped aside and sat at the left of Moses. Aaron's sons entered and Moses reviewed their portion for them. They stepped aside, Elazar sitting to the right of Moses and Itamar to the left of Aaron. . . .

The elders entered, and Moses reviewed their portion for them. They stepped aside. All the people entered, and Moses reviewed their portion for them. Thus Aaron heard it four times, his sons three times, the elders twice and all the people once. Then Moses stepped aside and Aaron reviewed his portion with them. Then Aaron stepped aside and his sons reviewed their portion with them. Then his sons stepped aside and the elders reviewed their portion with them. It turns out, then, that everyone heard it a total of four times.

On this basis said R. Eliezer: A man is obliged to review with his disciples four times. . . . R. Aqiva says: How do we know that a man is obliged to review with his disciples until he teaches them? For it is said: "Teach the children of Israel" (Deut. 31:19). . . . And how do we know that he does so until it is commanded orally? For it is said: "Place it in their mouths" (Deut. 31:19).

Among the sages whose traditions are preserved in the Babylonian Talmud, the rabbi was viewed as a powerful figure whose knowledge of Written and Oral Torah afforded him great influence on earth and in heaven. In the following passage (*Bava Metzia* 86a), Rabbah bar Nahmani is presented as a consultant to the divine court on a difficult halakhic matter. His Torah is so powerful that it forestalls even the Angel of Death who has come to take him above. Note how rabbinic disciples, a non-Jew, and heavenly beings all respond to his death.

7.2E *BAVA METZIA* 86A

Rabbah was sitting on the trunk of a palm and studying. In the heavenly academy they were then arguing this: If a bright spot (indicating an impure blemish) precedes a white hair, it is unclean, and if the white hair precedes the bright spot, it is clean. When in doubt, the Holy One, blessed be He, says it is clean, and the entire heavenly academy says it is unclean. Who will decide the matter? Let Rabbah bar Nahmani decide it, for Rabbah bar Nahmani said: I am uniquely qualified to decide cases of law relating to skin diseases and corpse contamination.

The heavenly court sent a messenger after him. The angel of death could not come near him, because his mouth did not cease from repeating words of Torah. Meanwhile a wind blew and caused a rustling in the branches. Rabbah feared that was a band of cavalry. He said: Let my soul die, but let me not be given into the hand of the government. While dying, Rabbah said: Clean! Clean!

A heavenly echo went forth and said: Happy are you, Rabbah bar Nahmani, that your body is clean, and your soul went forth in speaking of cleanness! A slip of paper fell from heaven into Pumbedita on which was written: Rabbah bar Nahmani has been summoned to the heavenly academy.

Abbaye and Rava and all the rabbis went out to attend to him, but they did not know his place. They went to Agma and saw birds hovering and overshadowing the corpse. They said: So he is there. They mourned him three days and three nights. A slip of paper fell: Whoever holds aloof from lamenting will be under a ban! They mourned seven more days. A slip of paper fell: God home in peace!

On that day a hurricane lifted an Arab camel-driver from one side of the Papa canal to the other. The Arab said: What is this? He was told: Rabbah bar Nahmani has died. He cried: Lord of the World! The whole world is yours, and Rabbah bar Nahmani is yours. You are Rabbah's and Rabbah is yours. Why do you destroy the world! The storm subsided.

7.3 THE TZADDIK OR REBBE IN HASIDIC COMMUNITIES

Many of the classical images of the Hasidic Tzaddik or Rebbe are vividly drawn in a famous collection of tales about the Baal Shem Tov, published early in the nineteenth century. In the passage to follow, the focus is upon the Besht's power to intercede with heavenly powers—the Messiah himself—on behalf of Israel. The theme goes as far back as the early rabbinic literature but is presented here in the distinctive garb of heavenly journeys inherited by Hasidism from the medieval kabbalah. The story is set on the Day of Atonement, as the Besht intuits that Israel's prayers are not ascending to Heaven.

Excerpts from Babylonian Talmud (*Bava Metzia* 86a), adapted from Jacob Neusner, *There We Sat Down: Talmudic Judaism in the Making.* Copyright © 1971 by Jacob Neusner. Reprinted with the permission of the author.

7.3A In Praise of the Baal Shem Tov

The Besht began to make terrible gestures, and he bent backwards until his head came close to his knees, and everyone feared that he would fall down. . . . His eyes bulged and he sounded like a slaughtered bull. He kept this up for about two hours. Suddenly he stirred and straightened up. He prayed in a great hurry and finished the prayer.

[In explanation of the event, the Besht said:] "In the spoken eighteen benedictions I also continued to move until I came to one palace. I had but one more gate to pass through to appear before God, blessed be He. In that palace I found all the prayers of the past fifty years that had not ascended, and now, because on this Yom Kippur we prayed with proper intention, all the prayers ascended. Each prayer shone as the bright dawn. I said to those prayers: 'Why did you not ascend before?' And they said, 'We were instructed to wait for you, sir, to lead us.' I told them: 'Come along with me.' And the gate was open. . . . When we started to accompany the prayers, one angel came and closed the door, and he put a lock on the gate. . . . And I began to turn the lock to open it, but I could not do it. So I ran to my rabbi . . . and I said: 'The people of Israel are in great trouble and now they will not let me in. At another time I would not have forced my way in.' My rabbi said: 'I shall go without and if there is a possibility to open the gate for you I shall open it.' And when he came he turned the lock, but he could not open it either. Then he said to me: '. . . You and I will go to the palace of the Messiah. Perhaps there will be some help there.'

"With a great outcry I went to the palace of the Messiah. When our righteous Messiah saw me from afar he said to me, 'Don't shout.' He gave me two holy letters of the alphabet. I went to the gate, and I led in all the prayers. Because of the great joy when all the prayers ascended, the Accuser became silent, and I did not need to argue. The decree was cancelled and nothing remained of it but an impression of the decree."

The biblical commentaries of the eighteenth- and nineteenth-century Hasidic leaders of Eastern Europe are rich in efforts to link the Tzaddik to any available biblical models of authority. The materials to follow are written by men who, as Hasidic communal leaders themselves, have a deep stake in linking their authority to biblical images. The first passage, by Rabbi Elimelekh of Lizensk (*Noam Elimelekh, Tazri'a*), focuses upon the priestly functions of the Tzaddik, here taking the priestly diagnoses of a skin eruption as a metaphor for the Tzaddik's diagnoses of a spiritual blemish in the Hasid.

7.3B *Noam Elimelekh, Tazriʻa*

When a man has in his skin . . . a leprous sore, he shall be brought to Aaron the priest or to one of his sons the priests, and the priest shall look at the sore . . . and if the hair in the sore be turned white or the sore appears to be deeper than the skin, it is leprosy. The priest shall look at it and proclaim him unclean" (Lev. 13:2–3). The letters NeGaʻ ("sore") are the same as those of ʻoNeG ("joy"); if one does not take care, however, this sore becomes "leprous." Scripture then speaks of what one should do to set one's deeds aright. "He shall be brought to the priest"— the perfect Tzaddik is called a priest; he should attach himself to the Tzaddikim. "The priest shall look . . . and if the hair on the sore be turned white"—the Tzaddik must see the condition of the sore. He must determine whether the white divine fluid of compassion has been turned "by a hair," by one of those minor sins which are like "mountains hanging by a hair," or whether the "sore appears to be deeper than the skin," the affliction, heaven forfend, be more than skin-deep. In either case, it is "a leprous sore; the priest shall look at it and proclaim him unclean"; he must show him to understand the great damage he has wrought in all this, teaching him the ways of return and true penitence so that he make good all those bad and shameful qualities that he bears.

A disciple of Elimelekh of Lizensk, Rabbi Kalonymos Kalman Epstein of Cracow developed his teacher's thought on the Tzaddik in important directions. In this selection (*Maor vaShemesh, Shofetim*), the Tzaddik is portrayed as the successor of both the Davidic king and the rabbinic sage. Epstein begins his comment on Scripture in venerable rabbinic fashion, citing and disputing the great medieval biblical exegete, Rashi.

7.3C *Maor vaShemesh, Shofetim*

"Set a king over yourself, as the Lord your God chooses. . . . As he sits upon his throne he shall write out his second Torah in a book, before the Levitical priests" (Deut. 17:15–18). Rashi comments on this "second Torah" that the king is to write two Torah scrolls, one to remain in his treasury and the other to be carried with him to and fro. . . . Of what value to him is the scroll that just lies in his treasury?

We know, however, the statement "Who are the kings? The rabbis." The sages are truly kings, as Scripture says: "Through me [wisdom or Torah] do kings rule" (Prov. 8:15). But the fact is that even if a person learns the whole Torah and all the holy volumes and teachings of the sages, this still will not bring him to repentance or remove the curtain that separates him from God, not until he cleaves

"The Tzaddik or Rebbe in Hasidic Communities," from Rabbi Elimelkh, translated by Arthur Green in "Typologies of Religious Leadership and the Hasidic Zaddiq" from Arthur Green, ed., *Jewish Spirituality From the Sixteenth Century Revival Until the Present* (New York: Crossroad, 1986), pp. 141, 143.

to God's holy ones, the Tzaddikim of the generation. Thus have I heard from my master and teacher, the man of God Elimelelch, of blessed and sainted memory; a person must choose one Tzaddik in his generation to be his master. And who is the one he should choose as a master, teacher and intimate? When he sees a Tzaddik all of whose comings and goings are conducted in accord with the holy Torah, who is lax neither in the Torah's own commands nor in matters ordained by the rabbis, while in his heart there burns a pillar of fire as he performs the unifications, this thought being visible in his deeds—such a one should he choose as a master.

This is the meaning of "set a king over yourself;" "King" here refers to rabbis. "As the Lord your God chooses"—whom should you choose? Scripture goes on to answer this by the words "he shall write this second Torah," according to Rashi's interpretation. He should have two scrolls, the one that is "carried with him to and fro" refers to the justice of his deeds and the way he conducts himself. The "treasury" in which the other scroll remains refers to his heart, burning with the fire of Torah, proclaiming God's unity in love and fear. Such a "king" whose thought is to be seen also in his deeds, is the one whom you should choose. All this belongs to that Tzaddik as tradition received from those sublime holy men who were his own masters; these are the "levitical priests" of whom the verse speaks.

AUTHORITY AND COMMUNITY

CHAPTER 8
IN CHRISTIANITY

8.1 APOSTLES AND BISHOPS

Written around 96 CE by Clement, bishop of Rome and successor to Saint Peter, the First Letter of Clement of Rome is one of the oldest Christian documents and was considered part of the Sacred Scriptures by some churches during the first three centuries. Clement is writing here to the Christians of Corinth in the name of the Church of Rome. The issue at hand is fierce quarrelling among the Christians at Corinth, where disputes about authority led to the ouster of some presbyters (elders). Clement called upon the Corinthians to repent and forgive one another and reminded them of the "orderly procedures" that Jesus Christ himself ("the Master") had set up for his church, where bishops stood in the place of the apostles. This selection offers a clear example of the way in which authority was defined among early Christian communities.

8.1A THE FIRST LETTER OF CLEMENT OF ROME

Now that this is clear to us and we have peered into the depths of the divine knowledge, we are bound to do in an orderly fashion all that the Master has bidden us to do at the proper times he set. He ordered sacrifices and services to be performed; and required this to be done, not in a careless and disorderly way, but at

The First Letter of Clement of Rome, from Cyril Richardson, *Early Christian Fathers.* Reprinted with the permission of Westminster John Knox Press.

the times and seasons he fixed. Where he wants them performed, and by whom, he himself fixed by his supreme will, so that everything should be done in a holy way and with his approval, and should be acceptable to his will. Those, therefore, who make their offerings at the time set, win his approval and blessing. For they follow the Master's orders and do no wrong. The high priest is given his particular duties: the priests are assigned their special place, while on the Levites particular tasks are imposed. The layman is bound by the layman's code.

"Each of us," brothers, "in his own rank" must win God's approval and have a clear conscience. We must not transgress the rules laid down for our ministry, but must perform it reverently. Not everywhere, brothers, are the different sacrifices—the daily ones, the freewill offerings, and those for sins and trespasses—offered, but only in Jerusalem. And even there sacrifices are not made at any point, but only in front of the sanctuary, at the altar, after the high priest and the ministers mentioned have inspected the offering for blemishes. Those, therefore, who act in any way at variance with his will, suffer the penalty of death. You see, brothers, the more knowledge we are given, the greater risks we run.

The apostles received the gospel for us from the Lord Jesus Christ; Jesus, the Christ, was sent from God. Thus Christ is from God and the apostles from Christ. In both instances the orderly procedure depends on God's will. And so the apostles, after receiving their orders and being fully convinced by the resurrection of our Lord Jesus Christ and assured by God's word, went out in the confidence of the Holy Spirit to preach the good news that God's Kingdom was about to come. They preached in country and city, and appointed their first converts, after testing them by the Spirit, to be the bishops and deacons of future believers. Nor was this any novelty, for Scripture had mentioned bishops and deacons long before. . . .

Ancient Christian lists of bishops indicate that Saint Peter the Apostle was the first bishop of Antioch before moving on to become the first bishop of Rome. As Clement succeeded Peter in Rome, so did Ignatius in Antioch. Like Clement, Ignatius was convinced that the established hierarchy of the church had been set in place by Jesus Christ himself, and that obedience to the bishops was necessary for salvation. In these two letters, written in the first decade of the second century, Ignatius reminds his readers that unity and obedience under the bishops are demanded by Christ himself.

8.1B IGNATIUS OF ANTIOCH, LETTERS TO THE EPHESIANS AND TRALLIANS

United in your submission, and subject to the bishop and the presbytery, you will be real saints.

I do not give you orders as if I were somebody important. For even if I am a prisoner for the Name, I have not yet reached Christian perfection. I am only

Letters to the Ephesians and Trallians, from Cyril Richardson, *Early Christian Fathers.* Reprinted with the permission of Westminster John Knox Press.

beginning to be a disciple, so I address you as my fellow students. I need your coaching in faith, encouragement, endurance, and patience. But since love forbids me to keep silent about you, I hasten to urge you to harmonize your actions with God's mind. For Jesus Christ—that life from which we can't be torn—is the Father's mind, as the bishops too, appointed the world over, reflect the mind of Jesus Christ.

Hence you should act in accord with the bishop's mind, as you surely do. Your presbytery, indeed, which deserves its name and is a credit to God, is as closely tied to the bishop as the strings to a harp. Wherefore your accord and harmonious love is a hymn to Jesus Christ. Yes, one and all, you should form yourselves into a choir, so that, in perfect harmony and taking your pitch from God, you may sing in unison and with one voice to the Father through Jesus Christ. Thus he will heed you, and by your good deeds he will recognize you are members of his Son. Therefore you need to abide in irreproachable unity if you really want to be God's members forever.

If in so short a time I could get so close to your bishop—I do not mean in a natural way, but in a spiritual—how much more do I congratulate you on having such intimacy with him as the Church enjoys with Jesus Christ, and Jesus Christ with the Father. That is how unity and harmony come to prevail everywhere. Make no mistake about it. If anyone is not inside the sanctuary, he lacks God's bread. And if the prayer of one or two has great avail, how much more that of the bishop and the total Church. He who fails to join in your worship shows his arrogance by the very fact of becoming a schismatic. It is written, moreover, "God resists the proud." Let us, then, heartily avoid resisting the bishop so that we may be subject to God.

The more anyone sees the bishop modestly silent, the more he should revere him. For everyone the Master of the house sends on his business, we ought to receive as the One who sent him. It is clear, then, that we should regard the bishop as the Lord himself. . . .

To the Trallians

The Christians at Tralles (a town some seventeen miles east of Magnesia) had sent their bishop, Polybius, to greet Ignatius in Smyrna. His letter in response is characteristic. Its leading themes are unity and obedience to the Church officials—themes provoked by the spreading danger of the Docetic heresy. It contains, too, several flashes that reveal Ignatius' character. Particularly striking is ch. 4, where he discloses his own impetuous and fervent nature which contrasts with the calm gentleness of Polybius.

The Text

Full hearty greetings in apostolic style, and every good wish from Ignatius, the "God-inspired," to the holy church at Tralles in Asia. You are dear to God, the Father of Jesus Christ, elect and a real credit to him, being completely at peace by reason of the Passion of Jesus Christ, who is our Hope, since we shall rise in union with him.

Well do I realize what a character you have—above reproach and steady under strain. It is not just affected, but it comes naturally to you, as I gathered from

Polybius, your bishop. By God's will and that of Jesus Christ, he came to me in Smyrna, and so heartily congratulated me on being a prisoner for Jesus Christ that in him I saw your whole congregation. I welcomed, then, your godly good will, which reached me by him, and I gave thanks that I found you, as I heard, to be following God.

For when you obey the bishop as if he were Jesus Christ, you are (as I see it) living not in a merely human fashion but in Jesus Christ's way, who for our sakes suffered death that you might believe in his death and so escape dying yourselves. It is essential, therefore, to act in no way without the bishop, just as you are doing. Rather submit even to the presbytery as to the apostles of Jesus Christ. He is our Hope, and if we live in union with him now, we shall gain eternal life. Those too who are deacons of Jesus Christ's "mysteries" must give complete satisfaction to everyone. For they do not serve mere food and drink, but minister to God's Church. They must therefore avoid leaving themselves open to criticism, as they would shun fire.

Correspondingly, everyone must show the deacons respect. They represent Jesus Christ, just as the bishop has the role of the Father, and the presbyters are like God's council and an apostolic band. You cannot have a church without these. I am sure that you agree with me in this. . . .

8.2 Apostolic Succession Versus Secret Knowledge

In the second century, as gnostic Christian churches proliferated, Irenaeus, speaking as bishop of Lyons and successor to the apostles, sought to set the record straight: The churches that claimed a "secret" knowledge and held other texts as sacred revelation were not the genuine article. In the following selection, Irenaeus lays out not only the genealogy of the Christian scriptures, but also the history of apostolic succession. True and valid authority rested only on those who could clearly identify themselves in direct line of succession from Jesus and the apostles. Religious leaders such as Marcion, Basilides, Valentinus, and Cerinthus were but mere impostors and their scriptures nothing less than "shameless blasphemy." This document offers a clear glimpse into the process whereby the hierarchy of the orthodox church defined its authority over and against other popular and charismatic leaders.

8.2A Irenaeus of Lyons, *Against Heresies*

The Traditions of the Gospels

For we learned the plan of our salvation from no others than from those through whom the gospel came to us. They first preached it abroad, and then later by the

From Ignatius of Lyons, *Against Heresies*, from Cyril Richardson, *Early Christian Fathers*. Reprinted with the permission of Westminster John Knox Press.

will of God handed it down to us in Writings, to be the foundation and pillar of our faith. For it is not right to say that they preached before they had come to perfect knowledge, as some dare to say, boasting that they are the correctors of the apostles. For after our Lord had risen from the dead, and they were clothed with the power from on high when the Holy Spirit came upon them, they were filled with all things and had perfect knowledge. They went out to the ends of the earth, preaching the good things that come to us from God, and proclaiming peace from heaven to men, all and each of them equally being in possession of the gospel of God. So Matthew among the Hebrews issued a Writing of the gospel in their own tongue, while Peter and Paul were preaching the gospel at Rome and founding the Church. After their decease Mark, the disciple and interpreter of Peter, also handed down to us in writing what Peter had preached. Then Luke, the follower of Paul, recorded in a book the gospel as it was preached by him. Finally John, the disciple of the Lord, who had also lain on his breast, himself published the Gospel, while he was residing at Ephesus in Asia. All of these handed down to us that there is one God, maker of heaven and earth, proclaimed by the Law and the Prophets, and one Christ the Son of God. If anyone does not agree with them he despises the companions of the Lord, he despises Christ the Lord himself, he even despises the Father, and he is self-condemned, resisting and refusing his own salvation, as all the heretics do.

The Apostolic Tradition

But when they are refuted from the Writings they turn around and attack the Writings themselves, saying that they are not correct, or authoritative, and that the truth cannot be found from them by those who are not acquainted with the tradition. For this [they say] was not handed down in writing, but orally, which is why Paul said, "We speak wisdom among the perfect, but not the wisdom of this world." Each of them utters a wisdom which he has made up, or rather a fiction, so that according to them the truth was once to be found in Valentinus, then at another time in Marcion, at another time in Cerinthus, then later in Basilides, or was also in that opponent, who has no saving message to utter. Each one of them is wholly perverse, and is not ashamed to preach himself, corrupting the rule of faith.

But when we appeal again to that tradition which has come down from the apostles and is guarded by the successions of elders in the churches, they oppose the tradition, saying that they are wiser not only than the elders, but even than the apostles, and have found the genuine truth. For the apostles [they say] mixed matters of the Law with the words of the Saviour, and not only the apostles, but even the Lord himself, spoke sometimes from the Demiurge, sometimes from the middle power, sometimes from the highest, while they know the hidden mystery without doubt or corruption, and in its purity. This is in nothing less than shameless blasphemy against their Maker. What it comes to is that they will not agree with either Scripture or tradition. It is such people, my dear friend, that we have to fight with, who like slippery snakes are always trying to escape us. Therefore we must resist them on all sides, hoping that by cutting off their escape we may be able to bring them to turn to the truth. For although it is not easy for a soul which has been seized by error to turn back, still it is not absolutely impossible to put error to flight by putting the truth beside it.

The tradition of the apostles, made clear in all the world, can be clearly seen in every church by those who wish to behold the truth. We can enumerate those who were established by the apostles as bishops in the churches, and their successors down to our time, none of whom taught or thought of anything like their mad ideas. Even if the apostles had known of hidden mysteries, which they taught to the perfect secretly and apart from others, they would have handed them down especially to those to whom they were entrusting the churches themselves. For they certainly wished those whom they were leaving as their successors, handing over to them their own teaching position, to be perfect and irreproachable, since their sound conduct would be a great benefit [to the Church], and failure on their part the greatest calamity. But since it would be very long in such a volume as this to enumerate the successions of all the churches, I can by pointing out the tradition which that very great, oldest, and well-known Church, founded and established at Rome by those two most glorious apostles Peter and Paul, received from the apostles, and its faith known among men, which comes down to us through the successions of bishops, put to shame all of those who in any way, either through wicked self-conceit, or through vainglory, or through blind and evil opinion, gather as they should not. For every church must be in harmony with this Church because of its outstanding pre-eminence, that is, the faithful from everywhere, since the apostolic tradition is preserved in it by those from everywhere.

When the blessed apostles had founded and built up the Church, they handed over the ministry of the episcopate to Linus. Paul mentions this Linus in his Epistles to Timothy. Anencletus succeeded him. After him Clement received the lot of the episcopate in the third place from the apostles. He had seen the apostles and associated with them, and still had their preaching sounding in his ears and their tradition before his eyes—and not he alone, for there were many still left in his time who had been taught by the apostles. In this Clement's time no small discord arose among the brethren in Corinth, and the Church in Rome sent a very powerful letter to the Corinthians, leading them to peace, renewing their faith, and declaring the tradition which they had recently received from the apostles, which declared one almighty God, maker of heaven and earth and fashioner of man, who brought about the Deluge, and called Abraham; who brought out the people from the land of Egypt; who spoke with Moses; who ordained the Law and sent the Prophets; and who has prepared fire for the devil and his angels. Those who care to can learn from this Writing that he was proclaimed by the churches as the Father of our Lord Jesus Christ, and so understand the apostolic tradition of the Church, since this Epistle is older than those present false teachers who make up lies about another God above the Demiurge and maker of all these things that are. Evarestus succeeded to this Clement, and Alexander to Evarestus;

then Xystus was installed as the sixth from the apostles, and after him Telesphorus, who met a glorious martyrdom; then Hyginus, then Pius, and after him Anicetus. Soter followed Anicetus, and Eleutherus now in the twelfth place from the apostles holds the lot of the episcopate. In this very order and succession the apostolic tradition in the Church and the preaching of the truth has come down even to us. This is a full demonstration that it is one and the same life-giving faith which has been preserved in the Church from the apostles to the present, and is handed on in truth.

Similarly Polycarp, who not only was taught by apostles, and associated with many who had seen Christ, but was installed by apostles for Asia, as bishop in the church in Smyrna—I saw him myself in my early youth—survived for a long time, and departed this life in a ripe old age by a glorious and magnificent martyrdom. He always taught what he learned from the apostles, which the Church continues to hand on, and which are the only truths. The churches in Asia all bear witness to this, as do those who have succeeded Polycarp down to the present time; he is certainly a much more trustworthy and dependable witness than Valentinus and Marcion and the other false thinkers. When he visited Rome under Anicetus, he converted many of the above-mentioned heretics to the Church of God, proclaiming that he had received from the apostles the one and only truth, the same which is handed on by the Church. There are those who have heard him tell how when John the disciple of the Lord went to bathe at Ephesus, and saw Cerinthus inside, he rushed out of the bath without washing, but crying out, "Let us escape, lest the bath should fall while Cerinthus the enemy of the truth is in it." Polycarp himself, when Marcion once met him and said, "Do you know us?" answered, "I know you, the first-born of Satan." The apostles and their disciples took such great care not even to engage in conversations with the corrupters of the truth, as Paul also said, "A heretical man after a first and second warning avoid, knowing that such a man has fallen away and is a sinner, being self-condemned." There is also a very powerful letter of Polycarp addressed to the Philippians, from which those who care to, and are concerned for their own salvation, can learn the character of his faith and [his] preaching of the truth. The church in Ephesus also, which was founded by Paul, and where John survived until the time of Trajan, is a true witness of the tradition of the apostles.

Since there are so many clear testimonies, we should not seek from others for the truth which can easily be received from the Church. There the apostles, like a rich man making a deposit, fully bestowed upon her all that belongs to the truth, so that whoever wishes may receive from her the water of life. She is the entrance to life; all the others are thieves and robbers. Therefore we ought to avoid them, but to love with the greatest zeal the things of the Church, and so to lay hold of the tradition of the truth. What if there should be a dispute about some matter of moderate importance? Should we not turn to the oldest churches, where the apostles themselves were known, and find out from them the clear and certain answer to the problem now being raised? Even if the apostles had not left their Writings to us, ought we not to follow the rule of the tradition which they handed down to those to whom they committed the churches?

8.3 Papal and Scriptural Authority

In a society such as medieval Western Europe, in which everyone belonged to the same church, who was the ultimate authority: the popes or the secular rulers (whether princes, kings, or emperors)? This is the question addressed by Pope Boniface VIII in 1302. Pope Boniface was involved in a fierce power struggle with King Philip IV of France. At issue was the control of the French clergy. Did King Philip have any authority over the priests and bishops of his realm, or were they completely immune from his power to command, tax, discipline, and punish? Pope Boniface was a proponent of supreme papal authority. In his thinking, all secular rulers were ultimately subject to him. This document is the strongest such claim ever made by a pope against a monarch. If Boniface's claims in this bull had been accepted by the reigning monarchs of Christendom, the pope would have become the supreme ruler of Europe.

Note: Important papal pronouncements of this sort are known as *bulls* because of the special seal that confirmed their authenticity (Latin; *bulla* = "seal"). Their titles are derived from the opening words (in this case, "One Holy . . .").

8.3a Pope Boniface VIII, *Unam Sanctam*

That there is one holy, Catholic and apostolic church we are bound to believe and to hold, our faith urging us, and this we do firmly believe and simply confess; and that outside this church there is no salvation or remission of sins, as her spouse proclaims in the Canticles, "One is my dove, my perfect one. She is the only one of her mother, the chosen of her that bore her" (Canticles 6:8); which represents one mystical body whose head is Christ, while the head of Christ is God. In this church there is one Lord, one faith, one baptism. At the time of the Flood there was one ark, symbolizing the one church. It was finished in one cubit and had one helmsman and captain, namely Noah, and we read that all things on earth outside of it were destroyed. This church we venerate and this alone, the Lord saying through his prophet, "Deliver, O God, my soul from the sword, my only one from the power of the dog" (Psalm 21:21). He prayed for the soul, that is himself, the head, and at the same time for the body, which he called the one church on account of the promised unity of faith, sacraments and charity of the church. This is that seamless garment of the Lord which was not cut but fell by lot. Therefore there is one body and one head of this one and only church, not two heads as though it were a monster, namely Christ and Christ's vicar, Peter and Peter's successor, for the Lord said to this Peter, "Feed my sheep" (John 21:17). He said "My sheep" in general, not these or those, whence he is understood to have committed them all to Peter. Hence, if the Greeks or any others say that they were

From Brian Tierney, *The Crisis of Church and State, 1050–1300.* Copyright © 1964 by Prentice-Hall, Inc., renewed 1992 by Brian Tierney. Reprinted with the permission of Simon & Schuster, Inc.

not committed to Peter and his successors, they necessarily admit that they are not of Christ's flock, for the Lord says in John that there is one sheepfold and one shepherd.

We are taught by the words of the Gospel that in this church and in her power there are two swords, a spiritual one and a temporal one. For when the apostles said "Here are two swords" (Luke 22:38), meaning in the church since it was the apostles who spoke, the Lord did not reply that it was too many but enough. Certainly anyone who denies that the temporal sword is in the power of Peter has not paid heed to the words of the Lord when he said, "Put up thy sword into its sheath" (Matthew 26:52). Both then are in the power of the church, the material sword and the spiritual. But the one is exercised for the church, the other by the church, the one by the hand of the priest, the other by the hand of kings and soldiers, though at the will and suffrance of the priest. One sword ought to be under the other and the temporal authority subject to the spiritual power. For, while the apostle says, "There is no power but from God and those that are ordained of God" (Romans 13:1), they would not be ordained unless one sword was under the other and, being inferior, was led by the other to the highest things. For, according to the blessed Dionysius, it is the law of divinity for the lowest to be led to the highest through intermediaries. In the order of the universe all things are not kept in order in the same fashion and immediately but the lowest are ordered by the intermediate and inferiors by superiors. But that the spiritual power excels any earthly one in dignity and nobility we ought the more openly to confess in proportion as spiritual things excel temporal ones. Moreover we clearly perceive this from the giving of tithes, from benediction and sanctification, from the acceptance of this power and from the very government of things. For, the truth bearing witness, the spiritual power has to institute the earthly power and to judge it if it has not been good. So is verified the prophecy of Jeremias [1:10] concerning the church and the power of the church, "Lo, I have set thee this day over the nations and over kingdoms" etc.

Therefore, if the earthly power errs, it shall be judged by the spiritual power, if a lesser spiritual power errs it shall be judged by its superior, but if the supreme spiritual power errs it can be judged only by God not by man, as the apostle witnesses, "The spiritual man judgeth all things and he himself is judged of no man" (I Corinthians 2:15). Although this authority was given to a man and is exercised by a man it is not human but rather divine, being given to Peter at God's mouth, and confirmed to him and to his successors in him, the rock whom the Lord acknowledged when he said to Peter himself "Whatsoever thou shalt bind" etc. (Matthew 16:19). Whoever therefore resists this power so ordained by God resists the ordinance of God unless, like the Manicheans, he imagines that there are two beginnings, which we judge to be false and heretical, as Moses witnesses, for not "in the beginnings" but "in the beginning" God created heaven and earth (Genesis 1:1). Therefore we declare, state, define and pronounce that it is altogether necessary to salvation for every human creature to be subject to the Roman Pontiff.

8.4 Dethroning the Pope, Enthroning Scripture

In order to reject the authority of the pope, Martin Luther had to be convinced not only of the falsehood of the pope's claims, but also of the existence of some other supreme authority. For Luther, the ultimate authority was the Word of God, not the bishop of Rome. This meant, of course, that the Roman Catholic Church was not the genuine church instituted by Christ, but rather some corruption of it. As far as Luther was concerned, the ultimate proof of the "falsehood" of the papal church was its deviation from the Word of God. In the following sermon preached in 1539, two decades after his break with Rome, Luther lays out the difference between the "genuine" Word-faithful church that now existed in parts of Germany and the papal church.

8.4a Martin Luther, "Sermon in Castle Pleissenburg, Leipzig"

But what is the dissension about between the papists and us? The answer is: about the true Christian church. Should one then be obedient to the Christian church? Yes, certainly, all believers owe this obedience; for St. Peter commands in the fourth chapter of his first Epistle: "Whoever speaks" should speak "as one who utters oracles of God" [I Pet. 4:11]. If anybody wants to preach, let him suppress his own words and let them prevail in worldly and domestic affairs; here in the church he should speak nothing but the Word of this rich Householder; otherwise it is not the true church. This is why it must always be said that it is God who is speaking. After all, this is the way it must be in this world; if a prince wants to rule, his voice must be heard in his country and his house. And if this happens in this miserable life, so much the more must we let God's Word resound in the church and in eternal life. All subjects and governments must be obedient to the Word of their Lord. This is called administration. Therefore a preacher conducts the household of God by virtue and on the strength of his commission and office, and he dare not say anything different from what God says and commands. And even though there may be a lot of talk which is not the Word of God, the church is not in all this talk, even though they begin to yell like mad. All they do is to shriek: church, church! Listen to the pope and the bishops!

But when they are asked: What is the Christian church? What does it say and do? they reply: The church looks to the pope, cardinals, and bishops. This is not true! Therefore we must look to Christ and listen to him as he describes the true Christian church in contrast to their phony shrieking. For one should and one must rather believe Christ, and the apostles, that one must speak God's Word and do as St. Peter and here the Lord Christ says: He who keeps my Word, there is my

From Helmut T. Lehman and John W. Doberstein, eds. and trans., *Luther's Work, Volume 51,* Sermons 1, pp. 303–312. Copyright © 1959 by Fortress Press. Reprinted with the permission of Augsburg Fortress.

dwelling, there is the Builder, my Word must remain in it; otherwise it shall not be my house. Our papists want to improve on this, and therefore they may be in peril. Christ says: "We will make our home with him"; there the Holy Spirit will be at work. There must be a people that loves me and keeps my commandments. Quite bluntly, this is what he wants.

Here Christ is not speaking of how the church is built, as he spoke above concerning the dwelling. But when it has been built, then the Word must certainly be there, and a Christian should listen to nothing but God's Word. Elsewhere, in worldly affairs, he hears other things, how the wicked should be punished and the good protected, and about the economy. But here in the Christian church it should be a house in which only the Word of God resounds. Therefore let them shriek themselves crazy with their cry: church, church! Without the Word of God it is nothing. My dear Christians are steadfast confessors of the Word, in life and in death. They will not forsake this dwelling, so dearly do they love this Prince. Whether in favor or not, for this they will leave country and people, body and life. Thus we read of a Roman centurion, a martyr, who, when he was stripped of everything, said, "This I know; they cannot take away from me my Lord Christ." Therefore a Christian says: This Christ I must have, though it cost me everything else; what I cannot take with me can go; Christ alone is enough for me. Therefore all Christians should stand strong and steadfast upon the Word alone, as St. Peter says, "by the strength which God supplies" [I Pet. 4:11].

Behold, how it all happens in weakness. Look at baptism, it is water; where does the hallowing and the power come from? From the pope? No, it comes from God, who says, "He who believes and is baptized" [Mark 16:16]. For the pope puts trust in the consecrated water. Why, pope? Who gave you the power? The *ecclesia,* the church? Yes, indeed, where is it written? Nowhere! Therefore the consecrated water is Satan's goblin bath [*Kobelbad*], which cripples, blinds, and consecrates the people without the Word. But in the church one should teach and preach nothing besides or apart from the Word of God. For the pastor who does the baptizing says: It is not I who baptize you; I am only the instrument of the Father, Son, and Holy Spirit; this is not my work.

Likewise, the blessed sacrament is not administered by men, but rather by God's command; we only lend our hands to it. Do you think this is an insignificant meal, which feeds not only the soul but also the mortal body of a poor, condemned sinner for the forgiveness of sins in order that the body too may live? This is God's power, this Householder's power, not men's.

So also in the absolution, when a distressed sinner is pardoned. By what authority and command is he pardoned? Not by human command, but by God's command. Behold, here by God's power I deliver you from the kingdom of the devil and transfer you to the kingdom of God [Col. 1:13]. So it is too with our prayer, which gains all things from God, not through its own power, or because it is able to do this, but because it trusts in God's promise. In the world you see how hard it is to approach the Roman emperor and gain help; but a devout Christian can always come to God with a humble, believing prayer and be heard.

In short, the Word and the Holy Spirit, who prepares us for prayer, are in God's power. It is the Word which we believe—this is what makes our hearts so bold that we dare to call ourselves the children of the Father. Where does this come from? The answer is: From God, who teaches us to pray in the Lord's Prayer and puts into our hands the book of Psalms. For if we prayed without faith, this would be to curse twice over, as we learned in our nasty papistical holiness. But where there is a believing heart and that heart has before it the promise of God it quite simply and artlessly prays its "Our Father" and is heard. Outside of this church of God you may present your prayers and supplications to great lords and potentates to the best of your ability, but here you have no ability to pray except in Christ Jesus, in order that we may not boast that we are holy as they do in the papacy, who protest, of course, and say: Oh, it would be a presumption for anybody to call himself holy and fit; and yet they teach that man of himself has a "certain preparation" for prayer. . . .

Concerning penitence or penance we teach that it consists in the acknowledgment of sins and genuine trust in God, who forgives them all for Christ's sake. The pope, on the contrary, does nothing but scold and devise intolerable burdens; and besides he knows nothing of grace and faith, much less does he teach what the Christian church really is.

But don't you forget the main point here, namely, that God wants to make his dwelling here. Therefore, when the hand is laid upon your head and the forgiveness of sins is proclaimed to you in the words: "I absolve you from all your sins in the name of Christ," you should take hold of this Word with a sure faith and be strengthened out of the mouth of the preacher. And this is what Christ and St. Peter are saying: He, the Lord, wants to dwell in this church; the Word alone must resound in it.

In short, the church is a dwelling, in order that God may be loved and heard. Not wood or stones, not dumb animals, it should be people, who know, love, and praise God. And that you may be able to trust God with certainty in all things, including cross and suffering, you should know that it is the true church, even though it be made up of scarcely two believing persons. That's why Christ says: He who loves me keeps my Word; there I will dwell, there you have my church.

So now you must guard yourselves against the pope's church, bedaubed and bedizened with gold and pearls; for here Christ teaches us the opposite. To love God and keep his Word is not the pope's long robe and crown, nor even his decretals. There is a great difference between what God commands and what men command. Look how the pope brazenly announces—we should invoke the saints and conduct ourselves according to his human precepts. Does God's Word command this too? I still do not see it. But this I know very well, that God's Word says: I, Christ, go to the Father, and he who believes in me will be saved. For I, I have suffered for him and I also give him the Holy Spirit from on high.

So the Lord Christ and the pope each have their own church, but with this mighty difference, which Christ himself . . . here describes, telling us what it is and where it is, namely, where his Word is purely preached. So where you hear this, there you may know that this is the true church. For where the Word of God is not present, there also are no true-believing confessors and martyrs. And if the Word of God were lacking, then we would have been deceived by Christ; then he really would have betrayed us! . . .

From this then you can answer the screamers and spitters who have nothing in their gabs but "church! church!": Tell me, dear pope, what is the church? Answer: the pope and his cardinals. Oh, listen to that; you dunce, where is it written in God's Word that Father Pope and Brother Cardinal are the true church? Was it because that was what the fine parrot bird said to the black jackdaw?

But Christ tells you and me something far different. He says: My church is where my Word is preached purely and is unadulterated and kept. Therefore St. Paul warns that we should flee and avoid those who would lead us away from God's Word, for if anyone defiles God's temple, which we are, God will destroy him [I Cor. 3:17]. And St. Peter also says: Take heed, if you are going to preach, then you should preach nothing but God's Word [I Pet. 4:11], otherwise you will defile God's church.

Hence it is again to be diligently noted how Christ described his church for us; for this description is a strong thunderbolt against the miserable pope and his decretals by which he has made of the church of God a filthy privy.

If anybody wants to teach human precepts, let him do so in secular and domestic affairs and leave the church alone. After all, the papists are really empty spewers and talkers, since Christ himself here says: He who hears my Word and keeps it, to him will I and my Father come and make our home with him. This is the end of Jerusalem and Moses; here there is to be a little band of Christ, [*Heufflein Christi*], who hear God's Word and keep the same and rely upon it in every misfortune. This is my church. This Lord we shall believe, even though the pope blow his top over it.

But in these words Christ was also answering the apostle Judas, who also allowed himself to imagine that Christ would become a great secular emperor and that they, the apostles, would become great lords in the nations when he should manifest himself. But how wrong he was! Here Christ tells them straight out that his kingdom is not of this world, but that they and all believers should be that kingdom of heaven in which God the Father, Son, and Holy Spirit himself dwells. He does not install angels, emperors, kings, princes, and lords in that church. He himself wants to be the householder and be the only one to speak and act; there I will dwell, he says, and with me all believers from everlasting to everlasting.

But Judas, the good man, still cannot understand this and therefore the Holy Spirit must come and teach it to him. Of this future and this ministry, dear Christians, you will hear tomorrow, God willing. If I cannot do it, then it will be done by others who can do it better than I, though they will not admit it. Let this today serve as an introduction or the morning sermon. May the Lord help us, I cannot go on further now.

8.5 WOMEN AND RELIGIOUS AUTHORITY

Amanda Berry Smith (1837–1915) was an African American missionary to India and Africa, an evangelist of wide repute, and the founder and administrator of a children's home outside Chicago. At the time that she determined to become an evangelist—her experience of a "call to preach"—there was little support in the male Protestant ministry for women preachers. In this excerpt from her *Autobiography*, she describes the process by which she became certain that she was called by God to a position of leadership in the community.

8.5A AMANDA BERRY SMITH, *AN AUTOBIOGRAPHY*

It was in November, 1869. God had led me clearly up to this time confirming His work through me as I went all about—sometimes to Brooklyn, then to Harlem, then to Jersey City. All this was among my own people, and our own colored churches, though I often went beside to old Second Street, Norfolk Street, Willett Street, Bedford Street, and to different white Methodist churches, to class meetings and prayer meetings; but very little with white people, comparatively. The most I did was among my own people. There were then but few of our ministers that were favorable to women's preaching or taking any part, I mean in a public way; but, thank God, there always were a few men that dared to stand by woman's liberty in this, if God called her. Among these, I remember, was Henry Davis, Rev. James Holland, Rev. Joshua Woodland, Rev. Joseph H. Smith, and Rev. Leonard Patterson, and others—but it is different now. We have women deaconesses, and leaders, and women in all departments of church work. May God in mercy save us from the formalism of the day, and bring us back to the old time spirituality and power of the fathers and mothers. I often feel as I look over the past and compare it with the present, to say: "Lord, save, or we perish."

As the Lord led, I followed, and one day as I was praying and asking Him to teach me what to do I was impressed that I was to leave New York and go out. I did not know where, so it troubled me, and I asked the Lord for light, and He gave me these words: "Go, and I will go with you." The very words He gave to Moses, so many years ago.

I said, "Lord, I am willing to go, but tell me where to go and I will obey Thee;" and clear and plain the word came, "Salem!" I said, "Salem! why, Lord, I don't know anybody in Salem. O, Lord, do help me, and if this is Thy voice speaking to me, make it plain where I shall go." And again it came, "Salem."

"O, Lord, Thou knowest I have never been to Salem, and only have heard there is such a place."

I remembered that five years before while living in Philadelphia, I was at Bethel Church one morning, and the minister gave out that their quarterly meeting was to be held at Salem the next Sunday. I could not go—I was at service—this was all that I had heard about Salem, or knew. I said: "O, Lord, don't let Satan deceive me, make it very plain to me, and if this is Thy voice, speak again to me, do Lord, make it clear, so as to make me understand it, and I will obey Thee. Now, Lord, I wait to hear Thee speak to me, and tell me where to go," and I heard the word coming, I was afraid, it seemed as though the Lord would strike me down, and I drew down as though to hide, and the word came with power, "Salem," and I said, "Lord, that is enough, I will go."

A few weeks passed. O, how I was tested to the very core in every way. My rent was five dollars a month, and I wanted to pay two months before I went. I prayed and asked the Lord to help me to do this. It was wonderful how He did. I needed a pair of shoes. I told the Lord I was willing to go with the shoes I had if He

From *An Autobiography: The Story of the Lord's Dealings with Mrs. Amanda Smith, The Colored Evangelist* (New York, 1987), pp. 132–133. Originally published 1893.

wanted me to, but they were broken in the sole, and I said: "Lord, Thou knowest if I get my feet wet I will be sick; now, if it is Thy will to get the shoes, either give me some work to do or put it in the heart of somebody to give me the money to get the shoes." And these words came from God to my heart: "If thou canst believe; all things are possible to him that believeth." And I said, "Lord, the shoes are mine," and I put them on as really as ever I put on a pair of shoes in my life! O, how real it was. I claimed them by faith. When I got up I walked about and felt I really had the very shoes I had asked for on my feet. O, how very true that blessed promise— "What things so ever ye desire, when ye pray, believe that ye receive them and ye shall have them." I know that truth. Hallelujah!

Like Amanda Berry Smith, Lydia Sexton, who was born in New Jersey in 1799, received a "call" to preach. Noting her "manfearing spirit," Sexton nevertheless determined to act upon her sense of obligation to preach. In this excerpt from her *Autobiography* (1882), she recounts her efforts in the early 1840's to break into a circle of church authority dominated by men.

8.5B *AUTOBIOGRAPHY OF LYDIA SEXTON*

There was all this time a secret monitor within telling me I should be calling sinners to repentance. I could not get clear of that reflection by day nor by night. All the day long and during the silent watches of the night, waking or dreaming, I seemed to have a large congregation before me, all in tears, as I told them the story of the cross. Thus for ten long years did I debate and falter and hesitate, and, like Jonah, trim my sails for Tarshish.

I thought, if I were only a man it would be no hardship to me, nor even a cross, to preach, but rather a pleasure. But for me, a woman, to preach, even if I could; to make myself a subject of ridicule and comment among my friends and kindred, and thus also bring reproach upon our glorious cause! Always before when I had trouble I would flee to the stronghold of my faith and grace and prayer; but somehow when I went in secret to pray the words seemed to come to me, "You deny me before men, I will deny you before my Father and the holy angels." I found no relief in secret prayer. Ah, me, the awful reflection. I would say to myself, "How would it look for me, a woman, to preach? Surely it would bring shame and disgrace on the cause of my Savior and my dear church." Then I would go to my dear Bible for comfort and guidance, and search for Bible-teachings and examples. Yes, yes; who made sport of Miriam when the poet said,—

> "An elder sister led the band,
> With sounding timbrels in her hand;
> And virgins moved in order grand,
> And after her they shouting danced!"

From *Autobiography of Lydia Sexton* (New York, 1987), pp. 213–217. Originally published 1882.

Again the Lord put his erring people in remembrance of His great blessings to Israel. "Did I not send thee Moses and Aaron and Miriam to be your leaders?" Again the prophetess was ordained of God,—or at least God ordained her a prophetess,—there was trouble on hand. Barak dare not meet the enemy unless Deborah led the van. The noble woman, always ready to work for God and His cause, said, "I will surely go. God's people must not be a 'prey to his enemies.'" Oh, no. "Call out the men of Israel, Sisera's mighty hosts are gathering. We must away."

As I perused my blessed Bible I saw that in all ages of the world the good Lord raised up of his own choosing, men, women, and children, Miriam, Deborah, Hannah, Huldah, Auna, Phebe, Narcissus, Tryphena, Tryphosa, Persis, Julia, the Marys, and the sisters who were co-workers with Paul in the gospel, whose names were in the book of life, and many other women whose labors are mentioned with praise. Even children were made the instrument of His praise and glory. See Romans xvi; I. Samuel iii. and iv.; Jeremiah i. 6; Numbers xxii. 28. While reading these examples, I could only think of my want of courage and heroism in so noble a cause. I was hoping that by the search of the Scriptures I might find something that would justify my conduct. But all would not do. The more I investigated, the more I found to condemn me. There was the master giving one, two, and five talents, and the moral obligation of each person receiving them and their several rewards. I was the one having the one talent which was hidden.

> The way of the cross to the transgressor is hard,
> No peace in the gospel they find;
> But those who are faithful shall have a reward
> Of heavenly peace in the mind.

How true. How very true.

With all this grief and burden on my mind day after day,—and I write in sorrow,—year after year I struggled on with all the diffidence and evasions so common to professors, amounting almost to downright cowardice, like Jonah above mentioned, or like Elijah who fled to the caves in Sinai. The Lord through the Apostle Paul commanded, "Not forsaking the assembling of ourselves together, as the manner of some is; but exhorting one another: and so much the more, as ye see the day approaching." And again: "They that feared the Lord spake often one to another: and the Lord hearkened and heard it, and a book of remembrance was written before them that feared the Lord, and that thought upon his name. And they shall be mine, saith the Lord of hosts, in that day when I make up my jewels."

The encouraging words of Brother Shingledecker rather embarrassed than helped me. The warm expression of his opinion of my ability to do work in the vineyard of the Lord intensified my sense of my obligations to preach; and his opinions were freely expressed, and had great weight with others as well as myself. We have many very excellent and able ministers in our church, such as the Kumlers, the Kenoyers, Father Griffith, Bishop Edwards, Bishop Davis, Professor Shuck, Bishop Shuck, Thomas Hamilton, the Terrills, Brother A. N. Walker, and scores besides that I have heard; and there are many others whose praise is in all the churches. With all these before me as a standard of comparison Brother Shingledecker stands well along in the front rank, in point of natural ability. It would be very difficult to describe him, either personally or in manner of address. He was very tall, and straight as an arrow. His style of preaching was, to say the least, sometimes very eccentric. On one occasion he was addressing an imaginary man of *straw* (people of the world); and in a conversational tone he carried on a dialogue with the man of straw, who appeared to have a treble, squeaking voice. He went on telling the straw man all the faults of his people—of the scandalous pride of his people, some of them poor as beggars, who, like the turtle or snail, carried all they were worth on their backs, and if they could only by dint of a hard scuffle with poverty and the tailors succeed in getting a satin vest and top out with a silk stove-pipe hat and sport a pair of shining boots they were all right.

"As for that," said the man of straw, "the less you say about it the better. Just look behind you in the pulpit." He whirled around and looked at the preachers sitting there. After eyeing them well he turned to his man of straw, exclaiming, "See here, Straw, if you will quit I will."

The elder and class had offered to license me to preach; and I did believe firmly that it was my bounden duty to preach. But oh! that man-fearing spirit. Why, I fairly shudder at the thought. But at the same time, I resolved that "let others do as they may, as for me and my house, I will serve the Lord, at least all of them that I can influence."

AUTHORITY AND COMMUNITY

CHAPTER 9
IN ISLAM

9.1 THE OFFICE OF CALIPH-IMAM

The institution of the caliphate was established after the death of Muhammad. Over the years the office grew in authority until it came to resemble, in some respects, royal authority as found in the mighty civilizations that preceded it in the Near East. In the following excerpt, Ibn Khaldūn, the great Muslim cultural historian (d. 1406) reviews the main elements of the caliphal office, both real and ideal.

9.1A THE CALIPHATE

Royal authority implies a form of organization necessary to mankind. It requires superiority and force, which express the wrathfulness and animality (of human nature). The decisions of the ruler will therefore, as a rule, deviate from what is right. They will be ruinous to the worldly affairs of the people under his control, since, as a rule, he forces them to execute his intentions and desires, and this may be beyond their ability. This situation will differ according to the intentions to be

From Ibn Khaldun, *The Muqaddimah: An Introduction to History,* translated from the Arabic by Franz Rosenthal, abridged and edited by N. J. Dawood. Copyright © 1967 by Princeton University Press. Reprinted with the permission of the publishers.

found in different generations. It is for this reason difficult to be obedient to the ruler. Disobedience makes itself noticeable and leads to trouble and bloodshed.

Therefore, it is necessary to have reference to ordained political norms, which are accepted by the mass and to whose laws it submits. The Persians and other nations had such norms. The dynasty that does not have a policy based on such (norms) cannot fully succeed in establishing the supremacy of its rule.

If these norms are ordained by the intelligent and leading personalities and minds of the dynasty, the result will be a political (institution) with an intellectual (rational) basis. If they are ordained by God through a lawgiver who establishes them as (religious) laws, the result will be a political (institution) with a religious basis, which will be useful for life in both this and the other world.

This is because the purpose of human beings is not only their worldly welfare. This entire world is trifling and futile. It ends in death and annihilation. The purpose (of human beings) is their religion, which leads them to happiness in the other world. Therefore, religious laws have as their purpose to cause (them) to follow such a course in all their dealings with God and their fellow men. This (situation) also applies to royal authority, which is natural in human social organization. (The religious laws) guide it along the path of religion, so that everything will be under the supervision of the religious law. Anything (done by royal authority) that is dictated by force, superiority, or the free play of the power of wrathfulness, is tyranny and injustice and considered reprehensible by (the religious law), as it is also considered reprehensible by the requirements of political wisdom. Likewise, anything (done by royal authority) that is dictated by considerations of policy or political decisions without supervision of the religious law, is also reprehensible, because it is vision lacking the divine light. At the Resurrection, the actions of human beings, whether they had to do with royal authority or anything else, will all come back to them.

Political laws consider only worldly interests. On the other hand, the intention the Lawgiver has concerning mankind is their welfare in the other world. Therefore, it is necessary, as required by the religious law, to cause the mass to act in accordance with the religious laws in all their affairs touching both this world and the other world. The authority to do so was possessed by the representatives of the religious law, the prophets; then by those who took their place, the caliphs.

This makes it clear what the caliphate means. (To exercise) natural royal authority means to cause the masses to act as required by purpose and desire. (To exercise) political (royal authority) means to cause the masses to act as required by intellectual (rational) insight into the means of furthering their worldly interests and avoiding anything that is harmful in that respect. (To exercise) the caliphate means to cause the masses to act as required by religious insight into their interests in the other world as well as in this world. (Worldly interests) have bearing upon (the interests in the other world), since according to Muḥammad all worldly conditions are to be considered in their relation to their value for the other world. Thus, (the caliphate) in reality is a substitute for Muḥammad inasmuch as it serves, like him, to protect the religion and to exercise leadership of the world.

The Differences of Muslim Opinion Concerning the Laws and Conditions Governing the Caliphate

We have explained the real meaning of the (caliphate). It is a substitute for Muḥammad inasmuch as it serves, like him, to preserve the religion and to exercise (political) leadership of the world. (The institution) is called 'the caliphate' or 'the imamate.' The person in charge of it is called 'the caliph' or 'the imam.'

In later times, he has been called 'the sultan,' when there were numerous (claimants to the position) or when, in view of the distances (separating the different regions) and in disregard of the conditions governing the institution, people were forced to render the oath of allegiance to anybody who seized power. . . .

The position of imam is a necessary one. The consensus of the men around Muḥammad and the men of the second generation shows that (the imamate) is necessary according to the religious law. At the death of the Prophet, the men around him proceeded to render the oath of allegiance to Abû Bakr and to entrust him with the supervision of their affairs. And so it was at all subsequent periods. In no period were the people left in a state of anarchy. This was so by general consensus, which proves that the position of imam is a necessary one.

Some people have expressed the opinion that the necessity of the imamate is apparent for rational reasons, and that the consensus which happens to exist merely confirms the authority of the intellect in this respect. As they say, what makes (the imam rationally) necessary is the need of human beings for social organization and the impossibility of their living and existing by themselves. One of the necessary consequences of social organization is disagreement, because of the pressure of cross-purposes. As long as there is no ruler who exercises a restraining influence, this leads to trouble which, in turn, may lead to the destruction and uprooting of mankind. Now, the preservation of the species is one of the necessary intentions of the religious law.

This very idea is the one the philosophers had in mind when they considered prophethood as something (intellectually) necessary for mankind. We have already shown the incorrectness of their reasoning. One of its premises is that the restraining influence comes into being only through a religious law from God, to which the mass submits as a matter of belief and religious creed. This premise is not acceptable. The restraining influence comes into being as the result of the impetus of royal authority and the forcefulness of the mighty, even if there is no religious law. This was the case among heathens and other nations who had no scriptures and had not been reached by a prophetic mission.

Or, we might say: In order to remove disagreement, it is sufficient that every individual should know that injustice is forbidden him by the authority of the intellect. Then, their claim that the removal of disagreement takes place only through the existence of the religious law in one case, and the position of the imam in another case, is not correct. It may (be removed) as well through the existence of powerful leaders, or through the people refraining from disagreement and mutual injustice, as through the position of the imam. Thus, the intellectual proof based upon that premise does not stand up. This shows that the necessity of (an imam) is indicated by the religious law, that is, by the consensus, as we have stated before.

Some people have taken the exceptional position of stating that the position of imam is not necessary at all, neither according to the intellect nor according to the religious law. People who have held that opinion include the Mu'tazilah al-Aṣamm and certain Khârijites, among others. They think that it is necessary only to observe the religious laws. When Muslims agree upon (the practice of) justice and observance of the divine laws, no imam is needed, and the imamate is not necessary. Those (who so argue) are refuted by the consensus. They adopted such an opinion because they were (attempting to) escape the royal authority and its overbearing, domineering, and worldly ways. They had seen that the religious law was full of censure and blame for such things and for the people who practised them, and that it encouraged the desire to abolish them.

The religious law does not censure royal authority as such and does not forbid its exercise. It merely censures the evils resulting from it, such as tyranny, injustice, and pleasure-seeking. Here, no doubt, we have forbidden evils. They are the concomitants of royal authority. The religious law praises justice, fairness, the fulfilment of religious duties, and the defence of religion. It states that these things will of necessity find their reward (in the other world). Now, all these things are concomitants of royal authority, too. Thus, censure attaches to royal authority only on account of some of its qualities and conditions, not others. (The religious law) does not censure royal authority as such, nor does it seek to suppress it entirely. It also censures concupiscence and wrathfulness in responsible persons, but it does not want to see either of these qualities relinquished altogether, because necessity calls for their existence. It merely wants to see that proper use is made of them. David and Solomon possessed royal authority such as no one else ever possessed, yet they were divine prophets and belonged, in God's eyes, among the noblest human beings that ever existed.

Furthermore, we say to them: The (attempt to) dispense with royal authority by (assuming) that the institution (of the imamate) is not necessary does not help you at all. You agree that observance of the religious laws is a necessary thing. Now, that is achieved only through group feeling and power, and group feeling, by its very nature, requires royal authority. Thus, there will be royal authority, even if no imam is set up. Now, that is just what you (wanted to) dispense with.

If it has been established that the institution (of the imamate) is necessary by the consensus, (it must be added that this institution) is a community duty and is left to the discretion of all competent Muslims. It is their obligation to see to it that (the imamate) is set up, and everybody has to obey (the imam) in accordance with the verse of the Qur'ân, 'Obey God, and obey the apostle and the people in authority among you' [4:59].

It is not possible to appoint two men to the position (of imam) at the same time. Religious scholars generally are of this opinion, on the basis of certain traditions.

Others hold that (the prohibition against two imams) applies only to two imams in one locality, or where they would be close to each other. When there are great distances and the imam is unable to control the farther region, it is permissible to set up another imam there to take care of public interests. . . .

The pre-requisites governing the institution of (the imamate) are four: (1) knowledge, (2) probity, (3) competence, and (4) freedom of the senses and limbs from any defect that might affect judgment and action. There is a difference of opinion concerning a fifth pre-requisite, that is, (5) Qurashite descent.

1. The necessity of knowledge as a pre-requisite is obvious. The imam can execute the divine laws only if he knows them. Those he does not know, he cannot properly present. His knowledge is satisfactory only if he is able to make independent decisions. Blind acceptance of tradition is a shortcoming, and the imamate requires perfection in all qualities and conditions.

2. Probity is required because (the imamate) is a religious institution and supervises all the other institutions that require (this quality). There is no difference of opinion as to the fact that his probity is nullified by the actual commission of forbidden acts and the like. But there is a difference of opinion on the question of whether it is nullified by innovations in dogma.

3. Competence means that he is willing to carry out the punishments fixed by law and to go to war. He must understand warfare and be able to assume responsibility for getting the people to fight. He also must know about group feeling and the fine points (of diplomacy). He must be strong enough to take care of political duties. All of which is to enable him to fulfil his functions of protecting religion, leading in the holy war against the enemy, maintaining the (religious) laws, and administering the (public) interests.

4. Freedom of the senses and limbs from defects or disabilities such as insanity, blindness, muteness, or deafness, and from any loss of limbs affecting (the imam's) ability to act, such as missing hands, feet, or testicles, is a pre-requisite of the imamate, because all such defects affect his full ability to act and to fulfil his duties. Even in the case of a defect that merely disfigures the appearance, as, for instance, loss of one limb, the condition of freedom from defects (remains in force as a condition in the sense that it) aims at his perfection.

Lack of freedom of action is connected with loss of limbs. Such a lack may be of two kinds. One is forced (inaction) and complete inability to act through imprisonment or the like. (Absence of any restriction upon freedom of action) is as necessary a condition (of the imamate) as freedom from bodily defects. The other kind is in a different category. (This lack of freedom of action implies that) some of (the imam's) men may gain power over him, although no disobedience or disagreement may be involved, and keep him in seclusion. Then, the problem is shifted to the person who has gained power. If he acts in accordance with Islam and justice and praiseworthy policies, it is permissible to acknowledge (him). If not, Muslims must look for help from persons who will restrain him and eliminate the unhealthy situation created by him, until the caliph's power of action is re-established.

5. The pre-requisite of a Qurashite origin is based upon the consensus on this point that obtained in the men around Muhammad on the day of Abû Bakr's elevation to the caliphate. . . .

Among those who deny that Qurashite descent is a condition of the imamate is Judge Abû Bakr al-Bâqillânî. The Qurashite group feeling had come to disappear and dissolve (in his day), and non-Arab rulers controlled the caliphs. Therefore, when he saw what the condition of the caliphs was in his day, he dropped the pre-requisite of a Qurashite origin.

Scholars in general, however, retain Qurashite descent as a condition (of the imamate). (They maintain that) the imamate rightly belongs to a Qurashite, even if he is too weak to handle the affairs of the Muslims. Against them is the fact that this involves dropping the pre-requisite of competence, which requires that he have the power to discharge his duties. If his strength has gone with the disappearance of group feeling, his competence, too, is gone. And if the condition of competence be eliminated, that will reflect further upon knowledge and religion. (In this case, then, all) the conditions governing the institution would no longer be considered, and this would be contrary to the consensus. . . .

When one considers what God meant the caliphate to be, nothing more needs (to be said) about it. God made the caliph his substitute to handle the affairs of His servants. He is to make them do the things that are good for them and forbid them to do those that are harmful. He has been directly told so. A person who lacks the power to do a thing is never told directly to do it. The religious leader, Ibn al-Khaṭîb, said that most religious laws apply to women as they do to men. However, women are not directly told (to follow the religious laws) by express reference to them in the text, but, in (Ibn al-Khaṭîb's) opinion, they are included only by way of analogical reasoning. That is because women have no power whatever. Men control their (actions), except in as far as the duties of divine worship are concerned, where everyone controls his own. Therefore, women are directly told (to fulfil the duties of divine worship) by express reference to them in the text, and not (merely) by way of analogical reasoning.

Furthermore, (the world of) existence attests to (the necessity of group feeling for the caliphate). Only he who has gained superiority over a nation or a race is able to handle its affairs. The religious law would hardly ever make a requirement in contradiction to the requirements of existence. . . .

9.2 The Authority of the Prophet Muhammad's Sunna

It goes without saying that the chief authorities for Islamic faith and order are the Qur'an and Muhammad's Sunna, with special prestige attached to the early generations—known as the Salaf—that interpreted and applied them. But even the decision to rely on the Prophetic Hadith above all others, for purposes of law, did not come about overnight. The definitive impetus came from one of the most influential thinkers of early Islamic history, the jurist Abu ʿAbd Allah Muḥammad b. Idrīs al-Shāfiʿī, the inspirer of the Sunnī legal school that bears his name. Al-Shāfiʿī, distantly related to the Prophet, was born in Palestine. Raised in Mecca, he lived and worked in Baghdad and Fustat (the future site of Cairo) for varying periods, dying in the latter city in 820. Al-Shāfiʿī effectively created the science of Islamic jurisprudence and systematically defined its "roots" (*uṣūl*), in their proper descending order, as Qurʾan, the Hadith-Sunna of Muhammad, community consensus (*ijmāʿ*) and analogical reasoning (*qīyās*). The following excerpt is from his *Kitāb al-risāla fī uṣūl al-fiqh* ("The Treatise on the Roots of Jurisprudence"), known universally simply as Shāfiʿī's *Risāla*. The subject of the following excerpt is the obligation to follow the Prophet's Sunna.

9.2A Shāfiʿī's *Risāla*

A Declaration Concerning the Duty Imposed by God, as Laid Down in His Book, [Ordering Men] To Follow the Prophet's Sunna

86. Shāfiʿī said: God has placed His Apostle—[in relation to] His religion, His commands and His Book—in the position made clear by Him as a distinguishing standard of His religion by imposing the duty of obedience to Him as well as prohibiting disobedience to Him. He has made His merits evident by associating belief in His Apostle with the belief in Him. For God, Blessed and Most High, said:

> So believe in God and His Apostles, and do not say: "Three." Refrain; [it will be] better for you. God is only one God. Glory be to Him. His having a son is something alien to him [Q. IV, 169].

And He said:

> The believers are only those who have believed in God and His Apostle, and who when they are with him on some common affair do not go away until they ask his permission [Q. XXIV, 62].

Thus [God] prescribed that the perfect beginning of the faith, to which all other things are subordinate, shall be the belief in Him and then in His Apostle. For if a person believes only in Him, not in His Apostle, the name of the perfect faith will never apply to him until he believes in His Apostle together with Him.

So the Apostle laid down the sunna [of reciting the Prophet's name together with that of God] for testing the faith of every man [as the following tradition indicates]:

Mālik b. Anas told us from Hilāl b. Usāma from 'Aṭā' b. Yasār from 'Umar b. al-Ḥakam, who said:

> I went to the Apostle of God with a slave-girl and I asked him: 'I have taken an oath [to free a slave]; may I free her?' 'Where is God?' the Apostle asked her. 'In heaven,' she answered. 'And who am I?' asked he. 'You are the Apostle of God,' she answered. 'You may free her,' [the Prophet] said.

[The transmitter's name, 'Umar b. al-Ḥakam]—Shāfi'ī says—should read Mu'āwiya b. al-Ḥakam, for Mālik, I believe, has not correctly reported the name, as others did.

87. Shāfi'ī said: God has imposed the duty on men to obey His divine communications as well as the sunna of His Apostle. For He said in His Book:

> O our Lord, raise up amongst them an Apostle, one of themselves, to recite to them Thy signs and to teach them the Book and Wisdom and to purify them. Verily Thou art All-mighty, All-wise [Q. II, 123].

And He, glorious be His praise, said:

> And also we have sent among you an Apostle, one of yourselves, to recite to you our signs, and purify you, to teach you the Book and the Wisdom, and to teach you what you did not know [Q. II, 146].

And He said:

> God bestowed a favor upon the believers when He raised up amongst them an Apostle, one of themselves, to recite His signs to them, to purify them and to teach them the Book, although they had formerly been in manifest error [Q. III, 158].

And He, glorious be His praise, said:

> It is He who has raised up an Apostle among the untutored people, one of their number to recite to them His signs, to purify them, and to teach them the Book and the Wisdom, though formerly they had been in manifest error [Q. LXII, 2].

And He said:

> But remember the goodness which God has shown you and how much of the Book and the Wisdom He has sent down to you to admonish you thereby [Q. II, 231].

And He said:

> God has sent down to thee the Book and the Wisdom, and has taught thee what thou did not know before; the bounty of God towards thee is ever great [Q. IV, 113].

And He said:

And call to mind the signs of God and the Wisdom which are recited in your houses; verily God is gentle, well-informed [Q. XXXIII, 34].

So God mentioned His Book—which is the Qur'ān—and Wisdom, and I have heard that those who are learned in the Qur'ān—whom I approve—hold that Wisdom is the sunna of the Apostle of God. This is like what [God Himself] said; but God knows best! For the Qur'ān is mentioned [first], followed by Wisdom; [then] God mentioned His favor to mankind by teaching them the Qur'ān and Wisdom. So it is not permissible for Wisdom to be called here [anything] save the sunna of the Apostle of God. For [Wisdom] is closely linked to the Book of God, and God has imposed the duty of obedience to His Apostle, and imposed on men the obligation to obey his orders. So it is not permissible to regard anything as a duty save that set forth in the Qur'ān and the sunna of His Apostle. For [God], as we have [just] stated, prescribed that the belief in His Apostle shall be associated with the belief in Him.

The sunna of the Apostle makes evident what God meant [in the text of His Book], indicating His general and particular [commands]. He associated the Wisdom [embodied] in the sunna with his Book, but made it subordinate [to the Book]. Never has God done this for any of His creatures save His Apostle.

God's Command Ordering Obedience to the Apostle Is Both Associated with Obedience to Him and Ordered Independently

88. [Shāfi'ī said]: God said:

When God and His Apostle have decreed a matter, it is not for a believing man or a woman to exercise a choice in a matter affecting him; whoever opposes God and His Apostle has deviated into manifest error [Q. XXXIII, 36].

And He said:

O you who believe, obey God and obey the Apostle and those in authority among you. If you should quarrel about anything, refer it to God and the Apostle, if you believe in God and the Last Day. That is better and fairer in the issue [Q. IV, 62].

Some scholars have held that "those in authority" [means] the commanders of the Apostle's army. That is what more than one commentator has told us. But God knows best.

This is in accord with what [God] said, for the Arabs who had been around Makka knew nothing about command, and [the idea of] some submitting to the command of others was repugnant to them.

When, however, they submitted to [the authority of] the Apostle, they did not think that [such an authority] was fit to reside in any hands other than the Apostle's.

So they were commanded to obey "those in authority"—the ones whom the Apostle appointed, with conditional but not absolute obedience, concerning their rights and duties. However, [God] said: "If you should quarrel about anything, refer it to God," that is, in the event of disagreement.

89. Shāfiʿī said: This [i.e., the meaning implied in the latter command] is, if God will, as He said about "those in authority," namely, that "If you should quarrel" (but God knows best), they [the people] and the commander whom they were ordered to obey—should "refer it to God and the Apostle" for a settlement on the basis of what God and His Apostle said, if they know it. If you do not know what God's commands are, you should ask the Apostle, if you are able to reach him, or any one of you who is able to do so. For this is an obligation concerning which there should be no disagreement, in accordance with God's saying:

> When God and His Apostle have decreed a certain matter, it is not for a believing man or a woman to have a choice in a matter affecting him [Q. XXXIII, 36].

As to the disputes that happened after the Apostle's [death], the matter was decided in accordance with God's judgment [as laid down in the Qurʾān] and then that of His Apostle [as laid down in the sunna]. But if a text were not applicable, the matter was decided by analogy on the strength of a precedent sought [either in the Qurʾān or the sunna] in the same manner as I have [already] explained concerning the qibla, [witnesses of] just character, equal compensation, and whatever God has prescribed in parallel cases. For He said:

> Those who obey God and the Apostle are with the prophets and the veracious and the martyrs and the upright upon whom God has bestowed favor. Good company are these [Q. IV, 71].

And He said:

> O you who have believed, obey God and His Apostle [Q. VIII, 20].

God's Command Ordering Obedience to His Apostle

90. [Shāfiʿī said]: God, glorious be His praise, said:

> Verily, those who swear allegiance to thee swear allegiance really to God; the hand of God is above their hands. So whoever breaks his oath, breaks it only to his own hurt, and to him who fulfils what he has pledged to God, He will grant a great reward [Q. XLVIII, 10].

And He said:

> Whoever obeys the Apostle has obeyed God [Q. IV, 82].

So God instructed [men] that their homage to the Apostle is homage to Him, and their obedience [to him] is obedience to Him.

And He said:

> But no! by thy Lord, they will not become believers until they make thee judge in their disputes and do not afterwards find difficulty in Thy decisions, but surrender in full submission [Q. IV, 68].

This verse, we have been told, was revealed in connection with a land dispute between al-Zubayr and another man in which the Prophet gave a decision in favor of al-Zubayr. This decision is a sunna laid down by the Apostle, not a command in the text of the Qur'ān.

The Qur'ān indicates what I have just stated; for if this decision were a Quranic decision, it should have been prescribed in the text of the Book of God.

But if men fail to accept a decision based on a clear text of the Book of God, they undoubtedly cease to be believers, for they are rejecting a decision based on divine legislation. For God, Blessed and Most High, said:

> Do not put the Apostle's calling on you for aid on the same footing amongst you as your calling on each other. God knows those of you who slip away secretly, so let those who go against His command beware lest a trial befall them, or a painful punishment [Q. XXIV, 63].

And He said:

> When they are called to God and to His Apostle that he may judge between them, lo, a party of them avert themselves. But if they are in the right, they will come to him in submission.
>
> Is there sickness in their hearts, or are they in doubt, or do they fear that God and His Apostle may act unjustly towards them. Nay, but they are the evildoers.
>
> All that the believers said when they were called to God and His Apostle that he might judge between them was: 'We hear and obey.' These are the ones who prosper.
>
> Whoever obeys God and His Apostle, and fears God and shows piety—these are the ones who attain felicity [Q. XXIV, 47–51].

Through this communication, God instructed men that their recourse to the Apostle to judge among them is a recourse to God's judgment, for the Apostle is the judge among them, and when they accept his judgment they do so only because of an obligation imposed by God.

And He instructed them that the [Prophet's] judgment is His judgment, for his judgment is imposed by Him and by His established knowledge—rendering him a man of destiny and assisting him by preserving him from error and [worldly] success—and by testifying that He guides him and causes him to obey His order.

So God imposed the obligation upon His creatures to obey His Apostle, and He instructed them that [obedience] to him is obedience to Him.

The sum-total of what He instructed them is the duty to obey Him and His Apostle, and that obedience to the Apostle is obedience to Him. He [also] instructed them that He imposed the duty on His Apostle to obey His order, Glorious be His praise.

9.3 SHI'ITES AND SUNNIS: PARALLEL ORTHODOXIES SHARING ONE ORTHOPRAXY

Shi'ism and Sunnism differed early on the political question of who was to lead the Muslim community. The Shi'ites recognized Imams descended from Muhammad through Ali and Fatima. The Sunnis (as they later came to be known) preferred to select their leaders from a representative range of Muslims, based on certain agreed-upon qualifications having nothing essentially to do with lineage. But the two orientations, as Muslims often point out, at least share a common *dīn*—the central structure of religious beliefs (*īmān*) and rites (the Pillars of Islam)—although there are other matters of doctrine and ritual over which they differ. The following discussion on the differences between Sunnis and Shi'ites is by the contemporary Muslim scholar Hamid Enayet.

9.3A THE NATURE AND SCOPE OF SHI'ITE ISLAM

The distinguishing features of Shi'ism in relation to Sunnism should be sought not only in its fundamental principles, but perhaps more importantly in its ethos, in the tone of historically developed attitudes which have informed and infused the Shi'i stance on the controversial issues of Islamic history, society and dogma. The actual disagreements between the Sunnis and Shi'is in certain details of theology and legal practices have not been as important as this ethos, or in the words of the modern Shi'i scholar S. Husain M. Jafri, 'as the "spirit" working behind these rather minor divergences'. In trying to understand this ethos, one has to deal with 'Historical Shi'ism,' namely, a Shi'ism which has taken shape in the actual, living experience of specific groups of Muslims, through attitudes which stemmed sometimes clearly from Shi'i tenets, and sometimes from individual interpretations and a slowly emerging consensus, without necessarily being recognised as fundamental principles in the Shi'i sources.

Considered in this light, perhaps the most outstanding feature of Shi'ism is an attitude of mind which refuses to admit that majority opinion is necessarily true or right, and—which is its converse—a rationalised defence of the moral excellence of an embattled minority. One can find numerous examples of this attitude in classical Shi'i sources. An anecdote, for instance, in the *Amali* of Shaykh Tusi (d. 461/1068), unquestionably the prime founder of Shiʿi jurisprudence, typifies it vividly: Kumayl ibn Ziyad al-Nakhaʿi, a close disciple of the first Imam, ʿAli, relates:

> I was with the Prince of the Faithful at the Kufah Mosque. When we finished the last evening prayer, he [ʿAli] took me by my hand, until we left the Mosque, until we left Kufah, and reached the suburb of the town. And all that time he had not uttered a word to me. Then he said: "O Kumayl, the hearts of men are like vessels, the best of them is the most retentive of them. So keep with yourself what you hear from me. The people are of three kinds: the divine scholar, those who seek knowledge and tread the path of salvation, and the rabble [*hamaj raʿa*] who follow every crowing creature, never partaking of the light of knowledge, never relying on a solid base."

This anecdote is significant in several respects: first, its adage is attributed to ʿAli, namely the only Imam among the twelve who became ruler of all Muslims. Secondly, the incident reported takes place in the Kufan period of ʿAli's career when after years of overt or covert opposition to 'usurping' Caliphs, he achieved political power: the reader is thus warned to take ʿAli's censure of popular fickleness not as the fulmination of an impractical, anti-social visionary but as the considered judgement of an experienced statesman. Thirdly, the extreme caution and discretion exercised by ʿAli in making his remark makes the bigotry, ignorance and unreliability of the 'rabble' to appear all the more reprehensible.

In his treatise *al-Idah*, to mention another example from a less important but earlier source, the third century jurisconsult and theologian Fadl ibn Shazan Nayshaburi (d. 290/902) is at pains to discredit the Sunnis' constant boasting of majority support as evidence of their righteousness, by arguing that the Qurʾan, in an overwhelming number of verses, takes a sinister view of the majority, and only rarely accepts it as a factor of legitimacy; it deprecates the majority for following its whims and conjectures (VI, 116), lacking knowledge and understanding (VII, 187; XLIX, 4; V, 103), being polytheists at heart (XII, 106), ungrateful (VII, 17; XII, 38) and transgressors to one another (XXXVIII, 24). That is why, in the history of the conflict of ideas 'many a small party has triumphed over a large party' (II, 249).

The reverse of the same attitude—the inherent virtue of belonging to a militant minority—is illustrated by Sayyid al-Murtada (d. 436/1043), the teacher of Shaykh Tusi. In his *Kitab al-Intisar*, enumerating in minute detail the legal and ritual points of difference between Shiʿism and other Muslim sects, he defiantly insists on the 'isolationist' character of Shiʿism (*maʾnfarad bihiʾl-imamiyyah*) by arguing that the paucity of the following of an idea does not affect its validity, just as the immense popularity of another cannot be proof of its truth. But more relevant to the spirit of present-day Shiʿism is the expression of this defiance in the revolt of the third Imam, Husayn ibn ʿAli, and his seventy-two companions, in 61/680. The memory of Husayn's martyrdom serves as an everlasting exhortation to the Shiʿis of all times to brave their numerical inferiority in the face of firmly established majorities.

In sustaining both aspects of their cautious attitudes towards majority amidst the global Muslim community, the Shiʿis have had to contend with powerful shibboleths. This has been partly due to the collective slant of Islamic political doctrines, greatly accentuated in the case of Sunnism because of its belief in the sanctity of the consensus (*ijma'*) of the community. 'My community will never agree in error': the Prophet is thus claimed by the Sunnis to have conferred on his community the very infallibility that the Shi'is ascribe to their Imams. The Shi'is have tried to prove the Sunnis' unfitness to qualify as the community envisaged in the Prophet's prediction by pointing to their connivance in the misdeeds of their rulers during the greater part of Islamic history. An outcome of the Shi'is' refusal to be intimidated, let alone bound, by false 'public opinion' is the restricted permissibility of consensus among them as a source of jurisprudential rules. Whereas the Sunnis have defined consensus as 'the agreement among the "people who loose and bind"' (namely, the holders of power and position, according to Imam Fakhr al-Din al-Razi), and even as the agreement of the community in general (according to Ghazzali), the Shi'is hold consensus to be valid only when it includes the opinion of 'the infallible and the impeccable' (*ma'sum*), namely the Imam. This doctrine has not caused the Shi'is to abandon consensus as an element of their legal system, since they always justify it by invoking the convenient maxim that 'the earth is never empty of the *ma'sum*,' which means that whenever a consensus is formed, one has to presume that the community of concurring scholars must have included a *ma'sum* in their midst. But the doctrine has been a perfect safeguard against majority impositions.

The Shi'i view on majority seems to be primarily a result of its legitimist theory of succession to the Prophet, confining rightful government in the first instance to members of his House. Any political theory so exclusive in its outlook tends to breed exponents who jealously guard its purity from diffuse notions of authority. But as time went on, Shi'i authors resorted to diverse philosophical, theological and mystical vehicles to elaborate their principal beliefs. By their very nature, these vehicles too were elitist, capable of being developed and appreciated by only tiny literate groups. Significantly, of all these components in the Iranian Shi'i culture, literature which is alone suitable for popular appreciation has fared the worst, since it has been allocated mainly to recounting the lives of the Imams, often in stilted and morose style, and aimed merely at eliciting maximum grief over their sufferings.

Further explanations of the same attitude comes from the imperative of survival in hostile environments. Any minority constantly harassed and persecuted inevitably turns inward and, distancing itself increasingly from the majority, gradually develops its own mental habits and attitudes. In this capacity, the Shi'i attitude towards majority was supplemented by two other idiosyncratic practices: the esoteric style of teaching religious truths, which is mainly cherished by the Isma'ili school, and *taqiyyah*, which can temporarily be translated as expedient dissimulation. . . .

The Shi'is agree with the Sunnis that Muslim history since the era of the four Rightly-Guided Caliphs (11–40/632–61) has been for the most part a tale of woe. But whereas for the Sunnis the course of history since then has been a movement *away* from the ideal state, for the Shi'is it is a movement *towards* it:

'The incidence of fortune,' say the Brethren of Purity, 'among certain peoples and nations, the increase in the power of some rulers, the outbreak of rebellions, the renewal of governorship in the kingdom, and other similar events [are aimed at] the betterment of the conditions of the world, and its elevation towards progress and wholeness. But often the factors of destruction prevail, such as wars, seditions and ravages, resulting in the ruin of the cities, the loss of the fortunes of a good people, and the demise of their prosperity, but *ultimately they all conduce to the good.*

True, the Sunnis too, in their fighting moments, like the militants of all times, produce rhetoric replete with expressions of faith in the final triumph of their cause—whether it is the fight against the infidels, or struggle for national independence, or confrontation with Israel. But there is nothing in their creed or theology which would make this triumph an inevitable occurrence in the divine scheme of things. Hence their general reluctance to indulge in philosophising about history. The few historians who have overcome this reluctance among them have usually come up with cyclical theories, expounding the notion that history consists of alternating patterns of the rise and fall of nations, or even of tedious repetitions of past events. Thus Ibn Khaldun explains the gradual decline and collapse of powerful dynasties and polities as an inexorable, and almost mechanical, transition from the virtuous ways of the desert life to the corrupting prosperity of urban settlement. And Maqrizi (d. 841/1437) sees the internecine conflicts between the Umayyads and Hashimites, and indeed the whole history of the Muslim Caliphate after the death of Muhammad, as a complete replica of the history of the Israelites.

By contrast, what lends an historicist thrust to the Shi'is' confidence in the ultimate victory over the 'forces of injustice' is their millenarian anticipation of the Return of the hidden Imam. The Qur'anic verses usually invoked by Shi'i commentators as evidence of the doctrine of the Return, although making no apparent mention of a future Mahdi, promise the sovereignty of the earth to the righteous and the oppressed:

1. 'God hath promised to those of you who believe and do the things that are right, that He will cause them to succeed others in the land as He gave succession to those who were before them, and that He will establish for them that religion which they delight in, and that after their fear He will give them security in exchange. They shall worship Me: nought shall they join me' (XXIV, 55).
2. 'And we were minded to show favour to those who were brought low in the land, and to make them spiritual chiefs [*Imams*], and to make them *Pharaoh's*[1] heirs' (XXVIII, 5).
3. 'My servants, the righteous shall inherit the earth' (XXI, 105).
4. 'The earth is God's: to such of His servants as He pleaseth doth He give it as a heritage' (VII, 128).

Sunni commentators interpret the promise contained in the first verse as addressed to Prophet Muhammad's followers in his own time, that in the second to

---

[1]Italics indicate addition by the translator (Rodwell).

the Israelites, and that in the third and fourth to the entire community of the faithful. Shi'i commentators, however, maintain all of them to be referring to the Mahdi's followers at the end of time; they particularly substantiate their reading on the basis of a saying attributed to Muhammad to the effect that: 'Even if there remains but one single day of the world, God will lengthen that day until He has designated a righteous man from my House to fill it with justice and equity, just as it was filled with injustice and oppression.' This link between the Return and the ultimate, global sovereignty of the righteous and the oppressed makes Shi'i historicism a *potential* tool of radical activism. But throughout the greater part of Shi'i history, it never went beyond the potential state, remaining in practice merely a sanctifying tenet for the submissive acceptance of the *status quo*. This is apparent from the semantic structure of the term for the millenarian anticipation of the Return: *intizar*, which denotes an essentially submissive expectation of things to come. Hence a tendency grew among the Shi'is to consider just government in the strict sense as an ideal which is impossible to achieve before the age of the Return. This eventually made the ideal state in Shi'ism to appear as a regime beyond the reach of ordinary human beings, and pushed it into the realm of meta-history:

'It is well established by the Tradition,' says Qadi Sa'id Qumi (d. 1103/1691), a theosophist of the Safavid period, 'that the Apostle of God, having been offered the choice between the status of servant and that of kingship, chose to be a Prophet Servant (*'abd nabi*) rather than a Prophet King (*malik nabi*). Thus, there cannot be an exoteric kingship (*saltanah zahirah*) to succeed him, much less the kind of sovereignty exercised by the tyrants (*imamah al-jababirah*). Because, when such sovereignty did not belong to the Prophet himself, how could it belong to his successor? So if the Prophet is to have a successor, it is imperative that this succession should be of a religious nature (*khilafah diniyyah*), guaranteeing to the faithful the best conditions of viaticum and the Return, and that this spiritual kingship (*saltanah ruhaniyyah*) should fall on him who is of unshakeable devotion, he of whom it can be said that he is the very soul of the Prophet, just as the Prophet has declared it in the case of 'Ali, Hasan and Husayn.'. . .

PART IV
WORSHIP AND RITUAL

CHAPTER 10
IN JUDAISM

10.1 TEXTS FROM THE RABBINIC LITURGY

The Shemoneh Esreh, also known as the Amidah, is the main prayer of rabbinic public worship, recited three times a day. The rhetorical structure of the Amidah is simple: benedictions 1–3 praise God, benedictions 4–16 petition Him, and benedictions 17–19 thank Him for hearing the prayer. Special versions are also recited on Sabbaths and holidays. These omit the petitionary benedictions and substitute a special benediction appropriate to the theme of the Sabbath or Festival. The full text of the daily morning Amidah, as transmitted in most European Jewish traditions follows. The name Adonai (Lord) is recited in place of the unpronounceable divine name, YHWH.

10.1A THE MORNING AMIDAH

1. Blessed are you, Adonai, our God and God of our fathers, God of Abraham, God of Isaac, God of Jacob. The great, mighty and awesome God, the Supernal God, who bestows profound kindness, creates all and recalls the righteous acts of the fathers, and shall bring a redeemer to their children's children in love, for the sake of His name—King, Helper, Redeemer and Shield. Blessed are you, Adonai, Shield of Abraham.

   2. You are eternally mighty, Adonai—reviving the dead. You redeem magnificently, sending round the winds and bringing down the rains. He sustains life

with kindness, revives the dead in profound mercy, supports the fallen, heals the sick, frees the imprisoned and keeps his trust with those who sleep in the dust. Who is like you, Marvel Worker, and who is comparable to you? A King who kills and gives life, who brings forth redemption—you are certain to revive the dead. Blessed are you, Adonai, who revives the dead.

3. You are holy and your name is holy, and the Holy Ones praise you each day! Blessed are you, Adonai, the holy God.

4. You favor people with knowledge and teach understanding to humanity. So may you extend to us your own knowledge, discernment and intelligence. Blessed are you, Adonai, who grants knowledge.

5. Return us, our Father, to your Torah, and bring us near, our King, to your service, and restore us in full repentance before you. Blessed are you, Adonai, who is gratified by repentance.

6. Forgive us, our Father, for we have sinned. Absolve us, our King, for we have transgressed, for you forgive and absolve. Blessed are you, Adonai, merciful and ready to forgive.

7. Notice now our affliction! Wage our battles! And redeem us speedily for your name's sake, powerful redeemer that you are. Blessed are you, Adonai, Redeemer of Israel.

8. Heal us, Adonai, that we may be healed, save us that we may be saved, for you are our praise. And cause speedy healing for all our diseases—for you, O royal God, are a trusted and merciful healer. Blessed are you, Adonai, Healer of the sick of your people Israel.

9. Bless for us, Adonai our God, this year and all of its produce for a blessing. And send blessing upon the earth, and satisfy us with its plenty, and bless our years as years of plenty. Blessed are you, Adonai, Blesser of the years.

10. Blow a great blast of the trumpet for our liberation, and lift up the banner to gather in our Exiles, and gather us together from the four corners of the earth. Blessed are you, Adonai, Gatherer of the dispersed of his people Israel.

11. Restore our judges as of old and our counselors as in the beginning, and remove from us suffering and oppression and reign over us—you alone, Adonai—in kindness and compassion, and declare us innocent with justice. Blessed are you, Adonai, a King loving righteousness and justice.

12. As for the informers against us—let them have no hope! And let all wickedness disappear in a flash. And may all your people's enemies be speedily cut off. And may you speedily and in our day uproot, crush, destroy and humiliate the arrogant! Blessed are you, Adonai, who crushes enemies and humiliates the arrogant.

13. May your mercies be aroused, Adonai our God, for your righteous, your adoring ones, the elders of your people Israel, the remnants of your scholars, for the righteous converts and for us. And offer a rich reward to all who truly trust in your name. And place our portion with theirs forever, and let us not be shamed, for in you we place our trust. Blessed are you, Adonai, Staff and Support of the righteous.

14. And to Jerusalem your city return in compassion. And dwell within her as you promised, and rebuild her eternally soon in our day. And speedily set up with her the throne of David. Blessed are you, Adonai, Rebuilder of Jerusalem.

15. Cause the shoot of David, your servant, to flower, and raise up his horn in salvation, for each day we expect your salvation. Blessed are you, Adonai, who causes the horn of salvation to flower.

16. Hear our voice, Adonai our God—have compassion upon us, and accept with compassion and favor our prayer. For you are a God who hears prayers and supplications. And please do not send us away empty handed, for in compassion you hear the prayer of your people Israel. Blessed are you, Adonai, Hearer of prayer.

17. Adonai our God, accept your people Israel and their prayer. And restore the sacrificial service to the sanctuary of your house. And accept with love their prayer, and may the service of Israel your people be always acceptable to you. And may our eyes witness your compassionate return to Zion. Blessed are you, Adonai, who restores his presence to Zion.

18. We thank you! For you are Adonai—our God and the God of our fathers for ever and ever. Foundation of our life, shield of our salvation—this you are in all generations! We are grateful to you and recount your praises for our lives which are in your hands, and for our souls which are entrusted to you, and for your miracles which support us every day, and for your wonders, and your kindnesses which we receive each moment—evening, morning and noon. You are a source of goodness whose mercy never fails, a source of mercy whose kindness is never exhausted. Eternally do we place our hope in you. And for all this by your name, our king, be blessed and exalted forever. And all life is grateful to you and praises your name in truth—the God of our salvation and our help. Blessed are you, Adonai—your name is good and to you is all thanks due.

19. Grant peace, plenty, blessing, grace, kindness and compassion to us and all your people Israel. Bless all of us as one, our father, with the presence of your face. For through the presence of your face have you given us, Adonai our God, a Torah of life, and loving mercy, and righteousness, and blessing and compassion, and life and peace. And you deem it good to bless your people Israel at every moment and hour with your peace. Blessed are you, Adonai, Blesser of his people Israel with peace.

In addition to the Amidah, a second focal point of the morning and evening liturgy throughout the year is the recitation of the Shma, a series of biblical passages (Deut. 6:4–9, 11:13–21; Num. 15:37–41) that focus upon the covenantal promises and redemptive acts of God. Recitation of these passages is preceded and followed by benedictions that anticipate and summarize the themes of the Shma. Following is a translation of the first benediction recited on weekday mornings in the European tradition. It contains, in a nutshell, the rabbinic theology of creation as a covenantal gift to humanity in general and to Israel in particular. Note how Isaiah 6:3 ("holy, holy, holy") is contextualized as a liturgical performance of various angelic beings in the heavenly world.

10.1B FIRST BENEDICTION OF THE SHMA

Blessed are you, Adonai, our God and King of the universe, Shaper of Light and Creator of Darkness, Maker of Peace and Creator of All. The one who in mercy illumines the earth and all who dwell upon it, and who, in his goodness, renews perpetually each day the primordial creative act. How great are your deeds, Adonai! You have done all of them in wisdom, the earth is filled with your creations!

You are the exalted King, alone from the very beginning of things, who has been praised, adored and exalted since ancient days. Eternal God, have compassion upon us in your great compassion! Lord of our Strength, Fortress of our Protection, Shield of our Salvation, our Protector!

The blessed God, great in knowledge, prepared and enlivened the rays of the sun; he formed the fullness of things for the glory of his name; he arranged heavenly lights surrounding his power. Leaders of his heavenly, holy forces—the Exalters of the Almighty—perpetually recount the glory of God and his sanctity. Be blessed, Adonai our God, for the excellence of the work of your hands, and for the luminous lights which you made—may they glorify you!

Be blessed, our Former, our King, our Redeemer, Creator of holy beings! May your name be praised forever, our King, Creator of his servants; indeed, his angelic servants all stand in the heights of the universe and, in awe, call out together the words of the Living God, King of the universe. All of them are beloved; all of them are purified; all of them are mighty; and all perform in trembling and awe the will of their Creator. And all open their mouths in holiness and in purity, in song and chant, and bless, praise, glorify, revere, sanctify and enthrone the name of God, the great King, the mighty and awesome, the Holy. And all accept upon themselves the kingdom of heaven from each other, and receive permission from each other to sanctify their Creator.

In tranquility of spirit, with articulate and tuneful lips they all recite the sanctification, proclaiming in awe: "Holy, holy, holy is Adonai of Hosts, the whole earth is full of His glory!" Then the Supernal Beings and the Holy Creatures raise themselves upwards opposite the Fire Beings in praise, proclaiming: "Blessed is the glory of Adonai from His place!"

To the blessed God they offer sweet tunes; to the King, the Living and Abiding God, they recite songs and utter praises. For he alone is the Mighty One, Maker of the New, Warrior, Sower of Righteousness, Sprouter of Salvation, Creator of Cures, Awesome Beyond Song, Lord of Wonders, who perpetually each day renews through his goodness the primoridal creative act, as it is said: "Give thanks to the Creator of the great lights, for his kindness endures forever." Cause a new light to shine upon Zion, that all of us may speedily merit its illumination! Blessed are you, Adonai, Former of the lights.

On the Sabbath, the following benediction replaces the middle benedictions of the weekday Amidah. This text conforms to the rite of most communities of Spanish origin.

10.1c Sabbath Benediction of the Amidah

Let Moses rejoice in his portion, for you have deemed him a faithful servant. A crown of splendor did you place upon his head as he stood before you on Mt. Sinai; two slabs of stone he brought down in his hand, upon them written the laws of the Sabbath. And so is it written in your Torah: And Israel shall preserve the Sabbath, to create the Sabbath for all their generations as an eternal covenant. Between me and the children of Israel it is an eternal sign. For in six days did Adonai create the heavens and the earth, but on the seventh day he ceased and rested.

Yet, Adonai our God, you did not bestow it upon the nations of the lands, nor did our King bequeath it to those who serve idols. Further, into his sheltering rest the uncircumcised are not invited. Rather, to your people Israel have you given it in love, to the descendants of Jacob whom you have chosen.

Let the preservers of the Sabbath rejoice in your kingdom—those who celebrate it as a delight! The people who sanctify the seventh day—let all of them be filled with your plenty and delight in it! For you delight in the seventh day and have sanctified it. You named it the Delight of Days.

Our God and God of our fathers—take delight in our rest, sanctify us with your commandments, place our portion with your Torah, fill us with your plenty, rejoice our souls with your salvation, and purify our hearts so we may serve you in truth. Adonai our God, give us in love and acceptance the heritage of your holy Sabbath, that all Israel, who sanctify your name, may rest upon it. Blessed are you, Adonai, Sanctifier of the Sabbath.

On Sabbaths, Festivals, and New Moons an additional Amidah (*Musaf*) is offered to commemorate the additional sacrifice offered on those days in Temple times. This Amidah refers back to the Temple period and anticipates the renewal of the sacrificial service in messianic times. Like the Sabbath Amidah, the *Musaf* uses the structure of the three introductory and concluding benedictions as a framework to insert a special benediction appropriate to the day at hand. Following is the New Moon benediction in the Spanish tradition.

10.1d Musaf Amidah

You gave your people New Moons, a time for atonement through all their generations, as they offered before you acceptable sacrifices and the goat of purification to make atonement for them. It was a memorial for all of them, redeeming their souls from the hands of the Enemy. May you establish a new altar in Zion, and may we bring up the burnt offering of the New Moon, and may we prepare the goat with your favor, and may all of us rejoice in the service of your Temple, and may we hear again the songs of your servant, David, formerly recited before your Altar—eternal love may you bring to them, and may you remember for the children the covenant of the fathers.

May it be your will, Adonai our God and God of our fathers, that you may bring us up in joy to our land and root us in our borders. And there shall we perform in your presence the obligatory offerings, the Perpetual Offerings in their sequence and the Additional Offerings in accord with their procedures. May we prepare and offer the Additional Offering of the New Moon in your presence, in love, in accord with your explicit will, as you wrote for us in your Torah by means of Moses your servant, from the very mouth of your glory, as is said: "And on your New Moons shall you offer a burnt offering to Adonai, two bulls of the herd and one ram, seven perfect yearling lambs." And their grain and wine offerings, as is stated: "Three measures for each bull, and two measures for the ram, and a measure to each lamb, and wine to be poured out, and a goat for atonement, and two Perpetual Offerings in accord with their procedure."

Our God and God of our fathers, renew for us this month for plenty and for blessing, for exaltation and joy, for salvation and consolation, for financial security and support, for a good life and for peace, for forgiveness of sin and pardon of transgression. And may this New Moon witness an end and conclusion to all our miseries, an inauguration and advent of the redemption of our souls. For you have chosen your people Israel from among all the nations, and the laws of the New Moons you established among them. Blessed are you, Adonai, Sanctifier of Israel and the New Moons.

Of all the various Festival rituals of Judaism, none is more effective than the Passover Seder in drawing Scripture, the remembered Jewish past, and the experienced present into communication. The ritual core of the Seder is the recitation of a midrashic account of the liberation of Israel from Egypt. The book containing this account, as well as other blessings, recitations, and songs, is called the Haggadah ("Retelling"). The earliest versions of the Haggadah were edited in Gaonic times on the bases of post-Temple rabbinic traditions. The following passage from the Haggadah explains the significance of certain symbolic foods that are placed prominently at the center of the Seder table.

10.1E THE HAGGADAH

Rabban Gamaliel would say: Whoever hasn't explained these three items on Passover has not satisfied his obligation. And these are: the Passover sacrifice, the matzah and the bitter herb.

This Passover sacrifice that our fathers ate while the Temple stood—what for? Because the Holy One Blessed be He passed over the houses of our fathers in Egypt, as it is said: "Now you shall say, it is a Passover sacrifice to Adonai, who passed over the houses of the children of Israel in Egypt while he attacked the Egyptians; but our houses he spared. And the people bowed and worshipped."

This matzah which we eat—what for? Because the dough of our fathers had no time to rise before the King, King of Kings, the Holy One Blessed be He, appeared to them and redeemed them, as it is said: "And they baked the dough which they brought from Egypt unto unleavened matzah-loaves; for they were expelled from Egypt, and were unable to tarry. They were unable even to bring provisions."

This bitter herb which we eat—what for? Because the Egyptians embittered the lives of our fathers in Egypt, as it is said: "And they embittered their lives with hard labor, with mortar and brick, and all types of field work. And all the labor they imposed upon them was cruel."

In each generation a person is obliged to regard himself as if he too escaped Egypt, as it is said: "And you shall tell this to your son on that day, saying: Because of this, which Adonai did for me when I left Egypt." And not our fathers alone did the Holy One Blessed be He redeem! Rather, he redeemed us with them, as it is said: "And he brought us out of there so that he could bring us to and give us the land he swore to our fathers."

10.2 MODERN TRANSFORMATIONS OF RABBINIC LITURGICAL TEXTS

The earliest efforts to shape Judaism into a religion suitable to the needs of modern western and central Europeans focused on the synagogue and its service. Reform, Conservative, and Orthodox parties each took important steps to bring synagogue worship into greater harmony with prevailing European tastes. But no party went so far as the Reform party in reconstructing elements of the received tradition into new constellations or abandoning elements deemed inappropriate in the new circumstances. The following explanation of the rationale for such reforms was penned in the early nineteenth century by Rabbi Aaron Chorin, a traditional Hungarian rabbi who became an avid proponent of the Reform movement. Note Rabbi Chorin's argument well: The point of change is not simply to modernize; it is to purify the service from medieval accretions that bar the access of modern people to the genuine religious experience contained in the liturgy.

10.2A THE RATIONALE OF REFORM

The permanent elements of religion must be expressed in terms that appeal to the people and are consonant with the needs of life. If our religion and life appear to conflict with one another this is due either to the defacement of the sanctuary by foreign additions or to the license of the sinning will which desires to make its unbridled greed and its false tendency authoritative guides for life. If we show ourselves as ready to strip off these unessential additions which often forced themselves upon our noble faith as the spawn of obscure and dark ages, as we are determined to sacrifice our very lives for the upholding of the essential, we will be able to resist successfully with the help of God all wanton, thoughtless and presumptuous attacks which license or arrogance may direct against our sacred

Paul Mendes-Flohr and Judah Reinharz, eds., *The Jew in the Modern World,* 2nd ed. (New York: Oxford University Press, 1995), pp. 187–188. Originally published 1844.

cause; the seeming conflict will then disappear and we will have accomplished something lasting for God.

I need not tell you that of all the external institutions the public service demands our immediate and undivided attention. He who is faithful to his God, and is earnestly concerned for the welfare of his religion, must exert himself to rescue our service from the ruin into which it has fallen and to give it once again that inspiring form which is worthy of a pious and devout worship of the one true God. For it is not only the excrescences of dark ages which cover it with disgrace, but thoughtlessness, lack of taste, absence of devotion, and caprice that have disfigured its noble outlines.

In the Reform tradition, the tendency of prayer-book reform has been to streamline the inherited rabbinic service, to universalize its ethnocentric messianism, and to rephrase explicitly otherworldly or miraculous ideas into more this-worldly terms. The reworkings of the Amidah benedictions in the Reform tradition are excellent examples. Reform liturgical scholars quickly removed the twelfth benediction (against informers) from the liturgy, returning the Amidah to its original eighteen benedictions. They also reframed the second benediction (resurrection of the dead), the tenth (end of exile), the eleventh (return of Israel's judges), the thirteenth (for the righteous scholars of Israel), the fourteenth (for the restoration of Jerusalem), the fifteenth (for the reestablishment of Davidic rule), and the seventeenth (acceptance of prayer and sacrifice). Compare the following versions with those of the rabbinic liturgy you studied earlier.

10.2B Benedictions from the *Gates of the House*

2. Eternal is Your might, O Lord; all life is your gift; great is Your power to save! With love You sustain the living, with great compassion you give life to all. You send help to the falling and healing to the sick; You bring freedom to the captive and keep faith with those who sleep in the dust. Who is like You, Master of Might? Who is Your equal, O Lord of life and death, Source of salvation? Blessed is the Lord, the Source of life.

10. Sound the great horn to proclaim freedom, inspire us to strive for the liberation of the oppressed, and let the song of liberty be heard in the four corners of the earth. Blessed is the Lord, Redeemer of the oppressed.

11. Pour your spirit upon the rulers of all lands; guide them, that they may govern justly. O may You alone reign over us in steadfast love and compassion! Blessed is the Sovereign Lord, who loves righteousness and justice.

From Reform prayers, from *Gates of the House: The New Union Home Prayerbook,* pp. 161–167. Reprinted with the permission of Central Conference of American Rabbis.

13. Have mercy, O Lord our God, upon the righteous and faithful of all peoples, and upon all of us. Uphold all who faithfully put their trust in You, and grant that we may always be numbered among them. Blessed is the Lord, the Staff and Support of the righteous.

14. And turn in compassion to Jerusalem, Your city. Let there be peace in her gates, quietness in the hearts of her inhabitants. Let Your Torah go forth from Zion and Your word from Jerusalem. Blessed is the Lord, who gives peace to Jerusalem.

15. Cause the plant of justice to spring up soon. Let the light of deliverance shine forth according to Your word, for we await Your deliverance all the day. Blessed is the Lord, who will cause the light of deliverance to dawn for all the world.

17. Be gracious, O Lord our God, to Your people Israel, and receive our prayers with love. O may our worship always be acceptable to You. Fill us with the knowledge that You are near to all who seek You in truth. Let our eyes behold Your presence in our midst and in the midst of our people in Zion. Blessed is the Lord, whose presence gives life to Zion and all Israel.

In the late twentieth century, especially in North America, feminism has begun to have a profound impact upon the religious lives of Jews. In addition to the integration of women into the authoritative synagogue roles once reserved for men, new liturgies reflecting explicitly feminist religious sensibilities are continually being constructed and reformulated. Rabbi Marcia Falk is one of the more prolific interpreters of feminist Jewish liturgical needs. In the following passage, Rabbi Falk explains the experiential foundations of her attempts to create new Jewish liturgical texts.

10.2c *Four Centuries of Jewish Women's Spirituality*

For a long time before I began to write my own blessings, I struggled with the traditional Hebrew prayers, attempting to make them work for me, wanting to have them articulate what I believe as a practicing feminist Jew. I finally had to acknowledge that, unlike Humpty Dumpty, I could not make words mean whatever I wanted them to. Although my private . . . meditations could help me focus to pray, they could not stretch the meanings of the liturgy beyond certain limits: I simply could not trick myself into believing that the traditional Hebrew prayers expressed the theology out of which I live. Nor did they express the values of the Jewish communities with which I identify, especially those of the Jewish feminist community.

Nonetheless, I felt . . . strongly connected to my history as a Jew and, in particular, to the Hebrew poetic tradition—the tradition that produced the liturgy that appears in our prayer books today. But tradition implies process and change, the movement of the past into the future, the continual forging of links on an unending chain. The liturgy was not always "fixed"; the old prayers were once new creations of individuals living in particular cultures and times. Prayers changed as communities changed; they evolved as Judaism itself evolved. I believe that the challenge for heterodox Jewish communities today. . . is not just to study and preserve the classic texts but to create new ones, just as we create new practices and customs, to keep Jewish tradition moving forward into the future.

My *berakhot* (blessings) do not bless a "Lord God King of the Universe" or, indeed, any "sovereign" at all. Instead, they point toward a divinity that is immanent, that inheres in all creation and nurtures all creativity. Because I believe in a monotheism that does not deny diversity but instead celebrates differences, I use a multiplicity of images to point toward an underlying unity—the unity that embraces all creation. Thus, no single formula replaces "Lord God King" in my *berakhot;* rather, I vary my metaphors for divinity to reflect the particular moment being marked by the blessing. All my images have their roots in classical Jewish sources—Bible, *midrash, piyyut* (synagogue hymns)—although, of course, most are turned and shaped to reflect my own poetic sensibility.

In some instances Jewish worship groups—many of them committed to egalitarian approaches to gender roles in worship—form outside the boundaries of institutionalized synagogue communities. One such group is Seattle, Washington's Congregation Eitz Or ("Tree of Light"), founded by Rabbi Vicki Hollander. Rabbi Hollander has composed a number of prayer texts, among them a Sabbath (*Shabbat*) Amidah and a special meditation for the New Moon of the Month of Av, the month that commemorates the destruction of the Solomonic and Herodian Temples. The Sabbath Amidah closely follows the rabbinic text, but it continually expands the metaphorical resonances of the male rabbinic images. Where the traditional text would refer to God's unpronounceable name as "Adonai," Rabbi Hollander uses "G." The meditation for the New Moon of Av interweaves traditional themes of loss with sensuous images of embodied experience characteristic of much feminist religious literature. The name for God in this meditation—"El Ro-ei, One of Vision"—is the name for God associated in biblical tradition with Abraham.

10.2D SABBATH MORNING AMIDAH

Blessed are You
our G and our ancestor's G:
G of Abraham, G of Isaac, G of Jacob,
G of Sarah, G of Rebecca, G of Leah, G of Rachel.
Great One, Warrior, Awesome One
Dweller of High Places

From Rabbi Vicki Hollander, Sabbath Morning Amidah and Rosh Chodesh Av. Reprinted with the permission of Rabbi Vicki Hollander.

Doer of kindnesses
Source of All.
From the depths of love,
remember the compassionate deeds of our ancestors and
for us their children's children.
Help us.
Powerful One, Nurturer, Protector, Defender,
Blessed are You,
who shielded Sarah and Abraham.

You continually go, a Warrior,
breathing life into the dead.
Great Reviver,
Compassionately nourishing life.
With overflowing tenderness You infuse the dead with life,
supporting those who have fallen
healing those who are ill
untying those bound
implanting faith in those who sleep in dust.
Who is like You, One who transcends strength itself?
Who can even come close to You, Powerful One,
who removes and encourages life,
who causes unseen sources of help to spring up,
who faithfully folds life into the dead?
Blessed are You, who causes life to well up in those dead.

We on earth, with and through Your name,
desire to know and
strive to experience and shape holiness.
We, together with those in realms above,
join voice singing:
As it is written by the prophet's hand,

> So Holy, So Sacred, So Set Apart, are You, Our Core, the entire
> earth glows from Your Presence

Then with one voice,
great rushing, splendid and strong,
we made our voices heard and
rising upwards towards the Seraphim
filled with blessings we said:

> May Blessings Surround You, HaMakom

Oh Powerful One, appear to us from Your place,
shine out and guide us
for we need and wait for You.

When shall you come and dwell among us?
May it be soon, soon in our days.

Throughout all times and throughout all generations,
may Jerusalem, Your city,
be infused with Your presence and be
filled with light, with the sacred.
Do open your eyes that we may see You.
For David, Just One, Guide,
sung sweetly of You from the very depths of his soul:

> Throughout all time and the generations
> You are with us.
> Our praises rise to You.

For generations we will speak of Your wonders,
for time beyond time we will tell of Your Holiness,
Our mouths shall never cease praising You, Our G,
for You are Powerful, Wondrous, Set Apart,
Blessed are You, One of Holiness.

May we know the joy of Moses,
who was content with his portion,
knowing inner faith.
May we know the inner connectedness with You
that he had
when standing before You on Mount Sinai,
and when descending, he held in his arms
two tablets of stone,
engraved with the letters: be guardians of Shabbat,
as it is written:

> Treasure Shabbat,
> that throughout time, throughout all generations
> it marks our connection.
> Between Israel and Me.
> Shabbat forever is a sign.
> For in six days G made heaven and earth
> and on the seventh G rested and
> renewed.

Out of loving
You gave Israel Shabbat.
You mindfully planted it within Jacob's seed.
Those who seek the sacred within the seventh day,
Your goodness will fill them,
and they'll know celebration.
You who so desired the seventh day,
making it sacred time,
calling it sweetest of days,
Reminding us,
taking us back to the beginning
to feel the birth of all Creation.

Our G and G of our ancestors,
who desires that we rest,
May Your mitzvot touch us with holiness
May Your Torah be our portion,
May Your goodness fill us up,
May Your visions bring us joy.
With fire and water transform our hearts
so through our core of inner knowing
wells up longing to serve You.
Through loving and desire,
G, our G, enable us to embrace
Shabbat, sacred time.
From deep within it,
may Israel,
who through Your name weaves sacredness,
know deep tranquility.
Blessed are You, who fills Shabbat with holiness.

10.2ᴇ Rosh Chodesh Av

El Ro-ei,
One of Vision,
aid us unveil,
that we might weep, weep,
for that which lies broken,
for that which remains incomplete,
for dreams lost, and hope shattered,
for houses burned, and souls extinguished
before their time.
El Ro-ei,
One of Vision,
uncover our eyes
that we might weep, weep
for that which once birthed healing,
no lying in ashes,
for that which once inspired souls,
now destroyed and in ruins,
that within the world of time
for that within ourselves that now lies dead.

The month of Av
bids us mourn for that gone by.
She enjoins us to feel the empty spot
long covered with desert brush and thistles,
to walk and let the horns scratch our legs,
drawing rivulets of blood
reminding us that despite the deadness
we yet live.

The month of Av
instructs us to grieve,
while in the fields the grapes ripen and are harvested.
She summons us to wail
while scents of maturing fruits waft into our homes.
Av teaches
how we need to receive the earth's messages of comfort:
the fragrance of sand lily borne in the evening's breeze,
the gentle bleating of newborn lambs,
the ever increasing coolness of air and goldening of sun
softly caressing our bodies
as we walk the hills at sunset
seeking solace from the land,
as sorrow rises like a tide within
thrusting lustily to the surface
in ever increasing waves.

They say
one day in Av
Mashiach will come.
That in this time,
when pain and life commingle with sweet bitterness of wine,
sorrow will transform to joy and
wounds will be healed.

We wait El Ro-ei,
One who Sees.
We wait and prune our vines, and
stride the hills, and
smell the earth's fragrances, and
weep our tears into fertile ground, and
feel our hurts.
And we look into the sun's face
for strength to step forward each day
to cut our grapes
to crush our wine.

Comfort us.
Let tears cloud our eyes,
that we might sleep well and
dream our dreams,
so on awakening we will see yet more keenly than before.
Wipe our brow, and
sing hope into our bones.
Stir the winds to dance round us and
weave a cloak replete with healing visions.

El Ro-ei,
Stand with us as we walk.
Stand with us as we walk.

WORSHIP AND RITUAL

CHAPTER 11
IN CHRISTIANITY

11.1 CHRISTIAN RITUAL AGAINST
A JEWISH BACKGROUND

Written between 56 CE and 60 CE to quell dissent and establish order among the Christians of Corinth, Paul's First Letter to the Corinthians contains a brief section on the celebration of the eucharist. Paul does more than simply relate the story of Jesus' climactic passover meal; he also instructs the Corinthians on how to properly celebrate this ritual. Paul's instructions and admonitions reveal that confusion and disorder did indeed exist among early Christian communities and also disclose to us how authority figures could intervene in local affairs, gradually imposing a more homogeneous ritual across different cultures.

11.1A PAUL'S FIRST LETTER TO THE CORINTHIANS

The Lord's Supper

Now that I am on the subject of instructions, I cannot say that you have done well in holding meetings that do you more harm than good. In the first place, I hear that when you all come together as a community, there are separate factions among you, and I half believe it—since there must no doubt be separate groups among you, to distinguish those who are to be trusted. The point is, when you hold these meetings, it is not the Lord's Supper that you are eating, since when the time comes to eat, everyone is in such a hurry to start his own supper that one person goes hungry while another is getting drunk. Surely you have homes for eating and drinking in? . . .

For this is what I received from the Lord, and in turn passed on to you: that on the same night that he was betrayed, the Lord Jesus took some bread, and thanked God for it and broke it, and he said, "This is my body, which is for you; do this as a memorial of me." In the same way he took the cup after supper, and said, "This cup is the new covenant in my blood. Whenever you drink it, do this as a memorial of me." Until the Lord comes, therefore, every time you eat this bread and drink this cup, you are proclaiming his death, and so anyone who eats the bread or drinks the cup of the Lord unworthily will be behaving unworthily toward the body and blood of the Lord.

Everyone is to recollect himself before eating this bread and drinking this cup; because a person who eats and drinks without recognizing the Body is eating and drinking his own condemnation. In fact that is why many of you are weak and ill and some of you have died. If only we recollected ourselves, we should not be punished like that. But when the Lord does punish us like that, it is to correct us and stop us from being condemned with the world.

So to sum up, my dear brothers, when you meet for the Meal, wait for one another. Anyone who is hungry should eat at home, and then your meeting will not bring your condemnation.

The Letter to the Hebrews contains the most systematic theological explanation of the Christian eucharistic ritual found in the New Testament. Written for a Jewish community around 60 CE, this letter focuses on how the Old Covenant is fulfilled and transformed into the New Covenant by Jesus Christ. In this selection, the author contrasts the sacrificial rituals of the Temple and the sacrifice of Christ on the cross. Later Christian writers would link this sacrificial theology to the ritual of the eucharist itself.

11.1B THE LETTER TO THE HEBREWS

Christ Enters the Heavenly Sanctuary

The first covenant also had its laws governing worship, and its sanctuary, a sanctuary on this earth. There was a tent which comprised two compartments: the first, in which the lampstand, the table and the presentation loaves were kept, was called the Holy Place; then beyond the second veil, an innermost part which was called the Holy of Holies to which belonged the gold altar of incense, and the ark of the covenant, plated all over with gold. In this were kept the gold jar containing the manna, Aaron's branch that grew the buds, and the stone tablets of the covenant. On top of it was the throne of mercy, and outspread over it were the glorious cherubs. This is not the time to go into greater detail about this.

Under these provisions, priests are constantly going into the outer tent to carry out their acts of worship, but the second tent is entered only once a year, and then only by the high priest who must go in by himself and take the blood to offer for his own faults and the people's. By this, the Holy Spirit is showing that no one has the right to go into the sanctuary as long as the outer tent remains standing; it is a symbol for this present time. None of the gifts and sacrifices offered under these regulations can possibly bring any worshiper to perfection in his inner self; they are rules about the outward life, connected with foods and drinks and washing at various times, intended to be in force only until it should be time to reform them.

But now Christ has come, as the high priest of all the blessings which were to come. He has passed through the greater, the more perfect tent, which is better than the one made by men's hands because it is not of this created order; and he has entered the sanctuary once and for all, taking with him not the blood of goats and bull calves, but his own blood, having won an eternal redemption for us. The blood of goats and bulls and the ashes of a heifer are sprinkled on those who have incurred defilement and they restore the holiness of their outward lives; how much more effectively the blood of Christ, who offered himself as the perfect sacrifice to God through the eternal Spirit, can purify our inner self from dead actions so that we do our service to the living God.

Christ Seals the New Covenant with His Blood

He brings a new covenant, as the mediator, only so that the people who were called to an eternal inheritance may actually receive what was promised: his death took place to cancel the sins that infringed the earlier covenant. . . . It is not as though Christ had entered a man-made sanctuary which was only modeled on the real one; but it was heaven itself, so that he could appear in the actual presence of God on our behalf. And he does not have to offer himself again and again, like the high priest going into the sanctuary year after year with the blood that is not his own, or else he would have had to suffer over and over again since the world began. Instead of that, he has made his appearance once and for all, now at the end of the last age, to do away with sin by sacrificing himself. Since men only die once, and after that comes judgment, so Christ, too, offers himself only once *to take the faults of many on himself,* and when he appears a second time, it will not be to deal with sin but to reward with salvation those who are waiting for him.

Summary: Christ's Sacrifice Superior to the Sacrifices of the Mosaic Law

The Old Sacrifices Ineffective

So, since the Law has no more than a *reflection* of these realities, and no finished picture of them, it is quite incapable of bringing the worshipers to perfection, with the same sacrifices repeatedly offered year after year. Otherwise, the offering of them would have stopped, because the worshipers, when they had been purified once, would have no awareness of sins. Instead of that, the sins are recalled year after year in the sacrifices. Bulls' blood and goats' blood are useless for taking away sins, and this is what he said, on coming into the world:

> You who wanted no sacrifice or oblation,
> prepared a body for me.
> You took no pleasure in holocausts or sacrifices for sin;
> then I said,
> just as I was commanded in the scroll of the book,
> "God, here I am! I am coming to obey your will." (Ps. 40:6–8)

Notice that he says first: *You did not want* what the Law lays down as the things to be offered, that is: *the sacrifices, the oblations, the holocausts and the sacrifices for sin,* and *you took no pleasure* in them; and then he says: *Here I am! I am coming to obey your will.* He is abolishing the first sort to replace it with the second. And this *will* was for us to be made holy by the *offering* of his *body* made once and for all by Jesus Christ.

The Efficacy of Christ's Sacrifice

All the priests stand at their duties every day, offering over and over again the same sacrifices which are quite incapable of taking sins away. He, on the other hand, has offered one single sacrifice for sins, and then taken his place for ever, *at the right hand of God*, where he is now waiting *until his enemies are made into a footstool for him.* By virtue of that one single offering, he has achieved the eternal perfection of all whom he is sanctifying. The Holy Spirit assures us of this; for he says, first:

> This is the covenant I will make with them
> when those days arrive;

and the Lord then goes on to say:

> I will put my laws into their hearts
> and write them on their minds.
> I will never call their sins to mind,
> or their offenses. (Jer. 31:31–34)

When all sins have been forgiven, there can be no more sin offerings.

IV. Persevering Faith

The Christian Opportunity

In other words, brothers, through the blood of Jesus we have the right to enter the sanctuary, by a new way which has opened for us, a living opening through the curtain, that is to say, his body. And we have the *supreme high priest* over all *the house of God.* So as we go in, let us be sincere in heart and filled with faith, our minds sprinkled and free from any trace of bad conscience and our bodies washed with pure water. Let us keep firm in the hope we profess, because the one who made the promise is faithful. Let us be concerned for each other, to stir a response in love and good works. Do not stay away from the meetings of the community, as some do, but encourage each other to go; the more so as you see the Day drawing near.

As more and more Gentile converts joined the Jewish Christian community, many adjustments had to be made. For instance, were the dietary laws of Judaism still to be observed? Did male Christians need to be circumcised? This selection from *The Acts of the Apostles* chronicles some of the key turning points in the evolution of the early church, especially the momentous decision to abandon much of Jewish ritual. Notice that the changes are ascribed to a new revelation from God rather than to a humanly reasoned decision. Notice also that the changes were not accepted without controversy.

11.1c THE ACTS OF THE APOSTLES

Controversy at Antioch

Then some men came down from Judaea and taught the brothers, "Unless you have yourselves circumcised in the tradition of Moses you cannot be saved." This led to disagreement, and after Paul and Barnabas had had a long argument with these men it was arranged that Paul and Barnabas and others of the church should go up to Jerusalem and discuss the problem with the apostles and elders.

All the members of the church saw them off, and as they passed through Phoenicia and Samaria they told how the pagans had been converted, and this news was received with the greatest satisfaction by the brothers. When they arrived in Jerusalem they were welcomed by the church and by the apostles and elders, and gave an account of all that God had done with them.

Controversy at Jerusalem

But certain members of the Pharisees' party who had become believers objected, insisting that the pagans should be circumcised and instructed to keep the Law of Moses. The apostles and elders met to look into the matter, and after the discussion had gone on a long time, Peter stood up and addressed them.

Peter's Speech

"My brothers," he said, "you know perfectly well that in the early days God made his choice among you: the pagans were to learn the Good News from me and so become believers. In fact God, who can read everyone's heart, showed his approval of them by giving the Holy Spirit to them just as he had to us. God made no distinction between them and us, since he purified their hearts by faith. It would only provoke God's anger now, surely, if you imposed on the disciples the very burden that neither we nor our ancestors were strong enough to support?

11.2 RITUAL ASPECTS OF MARTYRDOM AND SELF-DENIAL

The persecution of Christians within the Roman Empire, which lasted for nearly three centuries, had a profound impact on the development of Christian ritual. Because Christians were not usually executed without first being given the opportunity to renounce their faith, usually by being asked to take part in non-Christian rituals, martyrdom quickly assumed a ritual dimension within the Christian community: it was the ultimate confirmation of the faith and a participation in the sacrificial death of Christ himself. Polycarp of Smyrna (ca. 65–155), one of the leading bishops of Asia Minor, was more than willing to die for his beliefs. This account of his martyrdom is one of the earliest testimonies we have of the dynamics of persecution. Notice that Polycarp and the Christians are accused of destroying the pagan gods and of "teaching many not to sacrifice or worship." In other words, in the eyes of the Roman authorities, Christian ritual was not valid, and hence dangerous. Notice also how the Christians approach Polycarp's remains after he is burnt to cinders—how they reverently collect his relics and look forward to a ritual commemoration of his martyrdom. Here, in midsecond century, we can already see the cult of the saints in full bloom.

11.2A THE MARTYRDOM OF POLYCARP

And when finally he was brought up, there was a great tumult on hearing that Polycarp had been arrested. Therefore, when he was brought before him, the proconsul asked him if he were Polycarp. And when he confessed that he was, he tried to persuade him to deny [the faith], saying, "Have respect to your age"—and other things that customarily follow this, such as, "Swear by the fortune of Caesar; change your mind; say, 'Away with the atheists!'"

But Polycarp looked with earnest face at the whole crowd of lawless heathen in the arena, and motioned to them with his hand. Then, groaning and looking up to heaven, he said, "Away with the atheists!"

But the proconsul was insistent and said: "Take the oath, and I shall release you. Curse Christ."

Polycarp said: "Eighty-six years I have served him, and he never did me any wrong. How can I blaspheme my King who saved me?"

And upon his persisting still and saying, "Swear by the fortune of Caesar,"

The Martyrdom of Polycarp from Cyril Richardson, *Early Christian Fathers.* Reprinted with the permission of Westminster John Knox Press.

he answered, "If you vainly suppose that I shall swear by the fortune of Caesar, as you say, and pretend that you do not know who I am, listen plainly: I am a Christian. But if you desire to learn the teaching of Christianity, appoint a day and give me a hearing."

The proconsul said, "Try to persuade the people."

But Polycarp said, "You, I should deem worthy of an account; for we have been taught to render honor, as is befitting, to rulers and authorities appointed by God so far as it does us no harm; but as for these, I do not consider them worthy that I should make defense to them."

But the proconsul said: "I have wild beasts. I shall throw you to them, if you do not change your mind."

But he said: "Call them. For repentance from the better to the worse is not permitted us; but it is noble to change from what is evil to what is righteous."

And again [he said] to him, "I shall have you consumed with fire, if you despise the wild beasts, unless you change your mind."

But Polycarp said: "The fire you threaten burns but an hour and is quenched after a little; for you do not know the fire of the coming judgment and everlasting punishment that is laid up for the impious. But why do you delay? Come, do what you will."

And when he had said these things and many more besides he was inspired with courage and joy, and his face was full of grace, so that not only did it not fall with dismay at the things said to him, but on the contrary, the proconsul was astonished, and sent his own herald into the midst of the arena to proclaim three times: "Polycarp has confessed himself to be a Christian."

When this was said by the herald, the entire crowd of heathen and Jews who lived in Smyrna shouted with uncontrollable anger and a great cry: "This one is the teacher of Asia, the father of the Christians, the destroyer of our gods, who teaches many not to sacrifice nor to worship."

Then these things happened with such dispatch, quicker than can be told— the crowds in so great a hurry to gather wood and faggots from the workshops and the baths, the Jews being especially zealous, as usual, to assist with this. When the fire was ready, and he had divested himself of all his clothes and unfastened his belt, he tried to take off his shoes, though he was not heretofore in the habit of doing this because [each of] the faithful always vied with one another as to which of them would be first to touch his body. For he had always been honored, even before his martyrdom, for his holy life. Straightway then, they set about him the material prepared for the pyre. And when they were about to nail him also, he said: "Leave me as I am. For he who grants me to endure the fire will enable me also to remain on the pyre unmoved, without the security you desire from the nails."

So they did not nail him, but tied him. And with his hands put behind him and tied, like a noble ram out of a great flock ready for sacrifice, a burnt offering ready and acceptable to God, he looked up to heaven and said:

"Lord God Almighty, Father of thy beloved and blessed Servant Jesus Christ, through whom we have received full knowledge of thee, 'the God of angels and powers and all creation' and of the whole race of the righteous who live in thy presence: I bless thee, because thou hast deemed me worthy of this day and hour, to take my part in the number of the martyrs, in the cup of thy Christ, for 'resurrection to eternal life' of soul and body in the immortality of the Holy Spirit; among whom may I be received in thy presence this day as a rich and acceptable sacrifice just as thou hast prepared and revealed beforehand and fulfilled, thou that art the true God without any falsehood. For this and for everything I praise thee, I bless thee, I glorify thee, through the eternal and heavenly High Priest, Jesus Christ, thy beloved Servant, through whom be glory to thee with him and Holy Spirit both now and unto the ages to come. Amen."

And when he had concluded the Amen and finished his prayer, the men attending to the fire lighted it. And when the flame flashed forth, we saw a miracle, we to whom it was given to see. And we are preserved in order to relate to the rest what happened. For the fire made the shape of a vaulted chamber, like a ship's sail filled by the wind, and made a wall around the body of the martyr. And he was in the midst, not as burning flesh, but as bread baking or as gold and silver refined in a furnace. And we perceived such a sweet aroma as the breath of incense or some other precious spice.

At length, when the lawless men saw that his body could not be consumed by the fire, they commanded an executioner to go to him and stab him with a dagger. And when he did this [a dove and] a great quantity of blood came forth, so that the fire was quenched and the whole crowd marveled that there should be such a difference between the unbelievers and the elect. And certainly the most admirable Polycarp was one of these [elect], in whose times among us he showed himself an apostolic and prophetic teacher and bishop of the Catholic Church in Smyrna. Indeed, every utterance that came from his mouth was accomplished and will be accomplished.

But the jealous and malicious evil one, the adversary of the race of the righteous, seeing the greatness of his martyrdom and his blameless life from the beginning, and how he was crowned with the wreath of immortality and had borne away an incontestable reward, so contrived it that his corpse should not be taken away by us, although many desired to do this and to have fellowship with his holy flesh. He instigated Nicetas, the father of Herod and brother of Alce, to plead with the magistrate not to give up his body, "else," said he, "they will abandon the Crucified and begin worshiping this one." This was done at the instigation and insistence of the Jews, who also watched when we were going to take him from the fire, being ignorant that we can never forsake Christ, who suffered for the salvation of the whole world of those who are saved, the faultless for the sinners, nor can we ever worship any other. For we worship this One as Son of God, but we love the martyrs as disciples and imitators of the Lord, deservedly so, because of their unsurpassable devotion to their own King and Teacher. May it be also our lot to be their companions and fellow disciples!

The captain of the Jews, when he saw their contentiousness, set it [i.e., his body] in the midst and burned it, as was their custom. So we later took up his bones, more precious than costly stones and more valuable than gold, and laid them away in a suitable place. There the Lord will permit us, so far as possible, to gather together in joy and gladness to celebrate the day of his martyrdom as a birthday, in memory of those athletes who have gone before, and to train and make ready those who are to come hereafter. . . .

11.3 MONASTIC SELF-DENIAL

Even as they were being hunted down and executed, Christians also began to exalt and ritualize other types of suffering, including that which was self-inflicted. When persecution ceased, Christians increasingly internalized the sacrificial ritual of martyrdom. A life of ceaseless prayer accompanied by fasting and sexual abstinence came to be viewed as a prolonged martyrdom and as the most perfect way to imitate Christ's own sacrificial self-denial. In third-century Egypt, many Christians fled to the desert, where they lived as hermits, praying and heroically battling temptation. Many of these hermits met with one another for mutual encouragement and instruction. Gradually, the wisdom of the older, more experienced hermits began to be collected in written form. This fourth-century selection from the *Sayings of the Desert Fathers* reveals the passionate intensity with which these ascetics approached their own natural inclinations. It bears keeping in mind that this kind of life came to be considered as the most holy and sanctified by the Christian community at large.

11.3A *SAYINGS OF THE DESERT FATHERS*

He also said: "Fasting is the monk's rein over sin. The man who stops fasting is like a stallion who lusts the moment he sees a mare."

He also said: "When the monk's body is dried up with fasting, it lifts his soul from the depths. Fasting dries up the channels down which worldly pleasures flow.". . .

Once there was a feast in Scete, and they gave a cup of wine to an old man. He threw it down, saying: "Take that death away from me." When the others who were eating with him saw this, they also did not drink. . . .

A brother felt hungry at dawn, and struggled with his soul not to eat till 9 o'clock. And when 9 o'clock came, he extracted from himself a resolution to wait till noon. At noon he dipped his bread and sat down to eat—but then rose up again, saying: "I will wait till three." And at 3 o'clock he prayed, and saw the devil's work going out of him like smoke; and his hunger ceased. . . .

They said of one old man that he sometimes longed to eat cucumber. So he took it and hung it in front of him where he could see it. And he was not conquered by his longing, and did not eat it, but tamed himself, and did penitence that he wanted it at all.

Once a brother went to visit his sister who was ill in a nunnery. She was a person full of faith. She herself did not consent to see a man: nor did she want to

From *Sayings of the Desert Fathers,* Chadwick, ed., *Western Asceticism.* Reprinted with the permission of Westminster John Knox Press.

give her brother occasion to come into the midst of women. So she commanded him thus: "Go, my brother, pray for me. For by Christ's grace I shall see you in the kingdom of heaven."

On a journey a monk met some nuns and when he saw them he turned aside off the road. The abbess said to him: "If you had been a perfect monk, you would not have looked so closely as to see that we were women.". . .

An old man made a resolution not to drink for forty days. And if ever he thirsted he washed a vessel and filled it with water and hung it in front of his eyes. And when the brothers asked him why he was doing this, he replied: "So that if I do not taste what I long for and can see, my devotion will be greater and I shall be granted a greater reward by the Lord."

On a journey, one brother had with him his mother, who had now grown old. They came to a river, and the old woman could not get across. Her son took off his cloak, and wrapt it round his hands, so as not to touch his mother's body, and carried her across the river. His mother said to him: "Why did you wrap your hands like that, my son?" He said: "Because a woman's body is fire. Simply because I was touching you, the memory of other women came into my soul.". . .

At a meeting of the brothers in Scete, they were eating dates. And one of them, who was ill from excessive fasting, brought up some phlegm in a fit of coughing, and unintentionally it fell on another of the brothers. This brother was tempted by an evil thought and driven to say: "Be quiet, and do not spit on me." So to tame himself and restrain his own angry thought he picked up what had been spat and put it in his mouth and swallowed it. And then he began to say to himself: "If you say to your brother what will sadden him, you will have to eat what nauseates you."

11.4 POPULAR PIETY

By the late fifteenth century, the ritual life of Western Christendom had developed into a complex system of worship and devotion. Though much of Christian ritual focused on Jesus Christ as savior, much attention was also paid to the Virgin Mary and to the saints of the church. In the hierarchical societies of the Byzantine Empire and of feudal Western Europe, Christians conceived of heaven very much as a court, and of God as a ruler and judge who was best approached through intermediaries. In the case of the heavenly court, those advocates were the holy men and women who now dwelt there, near God's throne. Furthermore, popular piety focused a great deal of attention on the relics and images of the saints, and on the holy places where their relics were venerated. Erasmus of Rotterdam (1469–1536), a learned humanist scholar, wished to redirect the focus of Christian piety toward Christ and toward a more interior sort of devotion. Erasmus's critique of late medieval piety gained a following among many of the educated elite throughout Europe, and there is no doubt that he influenced many Protestant reformers. In this selection from Erasmus's *Colloquies*, we see him poking fun at the piety of his contemporaries with a reforming goal in mind. It was precisely this kind of acid-tongued satire that led many to believe that Erasmus laid the egg that Luther hatched.

11.4A ERASMUS OF ROTTERDAM, *A PILGRIMAGE FOR RELIGION'S SAKE*

Menedemus. What fortune brought you back to England?

Ogygius. An unexpectedly favorable breeze carried me there, and I had virtually promised the saint-by-the-sea that I would pay her another visit in two years.

Menedemus. What were you going to ask of her?

Ogygius. Nothing new, just the usual things: family safe and sound, a larger fortune, a long and happy life in this world, and eternal bliss in the next.

Menedemus. Couldn't the Virgin Mother here at home see to those matters? At Antwerp she has a church much grander than the one by the sea.

Ogygius. I can't deny that, but different things are bestowed in different places, either because she prefers this or (since she is obliging) because she accommodates herself in this respect to our feelings.

Menedemus. I've often heard about James, but I beg you to describe for me the domain of the Virgin-by-the-Sea.

Ogygius. Well, I'll do the best I can in brief. She has the greatest fame throughout England, nor would you readily find anyone in that island who hoped for prosperity unless he greeted her annually with a small gift, according to his means.

Menedemus. Where does she live?

Ogygius. By the northwest[1] coast of England, only about three miles from the sea. The village has scarcely any means of support apart from the tourist trade. . . .

Ogygius. To the east is a small chapel, filled with marvels. I betake myself to it. Another custodian receives us. After we've prayed briefly, we're immediately shown the joint of a human finger (the largest of three). I kiss it and then ask whose relics these are. "Saint Peter's," he says. "Not the Apostle Peter's?" "Yes." Then, looking at the great size of the joint, which might have been a giant's, I said, "Peter must have been an extremely big man." At this one of my companions burst into a loud laugh, which annoyed me no end, for if he had been quiet the attendant would have kept none of the relics from our inspection. However, we appeased him with some coins.

In front of the little building was a structure that during the wintertime (he said), when everything was covered by snow, had been brought there suddenly from far away.[2] Under this were two wells, filled to the top. They say the stream of

---

[1]A slip; Walsingham is in northern Norfolk.
[2]The "little building" must be the chapel mentioned in the preceding paragraph (i.e., the chapel of St. Laurence, east of the church). The "structure . . . brought there suddenly from far away" seems to be a reference to another chapel, the Holy House, which contained the famous statue of Our Lady. This chapel was supposedly a copy of the house in Nazareth in which Mary received the Annunciation. (The original house at Nazareth, according to a late medieval legend, was miraculously transported to Loretto, in Italy, where it became a favorite resort of pilgrims.) There was a story that while the Holy House was being built east of the church, angels moved it 200 feet to the north side. Erasmus perhaps confuses this story with the wilder one about the Santa Casa of Loretto.

From Erasmus, *Ten Colloquies,* translated by Craig R. Thompson (Indianapolis: Library of Liberal Arts/The Bobbs-Merrill Company, 1957). Copyright © 1957. Reprinted with the permission of Prentice-Hall, Inc., Upper Saddle River, NJ.

water is sacred to the Holy Virgin. It's a wonderfully cold fluid, good for headache and stomach troubles.

Menedemus. If cold water cures headache and stomach troubles, oil will put out fire next.

Ogygius. You're hearing about a miracle, my good friend—besides, what would be miraculous about cold water quenching thirst?

Menedemus. Clearly this is only one part of the story.

Ogygius. That stream of water, they declared, suddenly shot up from the ground at the command of the Most Holy Virgin. Inspecting everything carefully, I inquired how many years it was since the little house had been brought there. "Some ages," he replied. "In any event," I said, "the walls don't look very old." He didn't dissent. "Even these wooden posts don't look old." He didn't deny they had been placed there recently, and the fact was self-evident. "Then," I said, "the roof and thatch of the house seem rather recent." He agreed. "Not even these cross-beams, nor the very rafters supporting the roof, appear to have been put here many years ago." He nodded. "But since no part of the building has survived, how is it known for certain," I asked, "that this *is* the cottage brought here from so far away?"

Menedemus. How did the attendant get out of that tangle, if you please?

Ogygius. Why, he hurriedly showed us an old, worn-out bearskin fastened to posts, and almost laughed at us for our dullness in being slow to see such a clear proof. So, being persuaded, and excusing our stupidity, we turned to the heavenly milk of the Blessed Virgin.

Menedemus. O Mother most like her Son! He left us so much of his blood on earth; she left so much of her milk that it's scarcely credible a woman with only one child could have so much, even if the child had drunk none of it.

Ogygius. The same thing is said about the Lord's Cross, which is exhibited publicly and privately in so many places that if the fragments were joined together they'd seem a full load for a freighter. And yet the Lord carried his whole cross.

Menedemus. Doesn't it seem amazing to you, too?

Ogygius. It could be called unusual, perhaps, but "amazing"—no, since the Lord, who multiplies these things as he wills, is omnipotent.

Menedemus. You explain it reverently, but for my part I'm afraid many such affairs are contrived for profit.

Ogygius. I don't think God will stand for anybody mocking him in that way.

Menedemus. On the contrary, although Mother and Son and Father and Spirit are robbed by the sacrilegious, sometimes they don't even bestir themselves slightly enough to frighten off the criminals by a nod or a noise. So great is the mildness of divinity.

Ogygius. That's true. But hear the rest. This milk is kept on the high altar, in the midst of which is Christ; on the right, for the sake of honor, is his mother. For the milk represents his Mother.

Menedemus. So it's in plain sight.

Ogygius. Enclosed in crystal, that is.

Menedemus. Therefore liquid.

Ogygius. What do you mean, liquid, when it flowed fifteen hundred years ago? It's hard: you'd say powdered chalk, tempered with white of egg.

Menedemus. Why don't they display it exposed?

Ogygius. To save the virginal milk from being defiled by the kisses of men.

Menedemus. Well said, for in my opinion there are those who would bring neither clean nor chaste mouths to it.

Ogygius. When the custodian saw us, he rushed up to it, donned a linen vestment, threw a sacred stole round his neck, prostrated himself devoutly, and adored. Soon afterward he held out the sacred milk for us to kiss. We prostrated ourselves devoutly on the lowest step of the altar and, after first saluting Christ, uttered to the Virgin a short prayer I had prepared for this occasion: "Virgin Mother, who hast had the honor of suckling at thy maidenly breast the Lord of heaven and earth, thy Son Jesus, we pray that, cleansed by his blood, we may gain that blessed infancy of dovelike simplicity which, innocent of all malice, deceit, and guile, longs without ceasing for the milk of gospel doctrine until it attains to the perfect man, to the measure of the fullness of Christ, whose blessed company thou enjoyest forever, with the Father and Holy Spirit. Amen."

Menedemus. Certainly a devout intercession. What effect did it have?

Ogygius. Mother and Son both seemed to nod approval, unless my eyes deceived me. For the sacred milk appeared to leap up, and the Eucharistic elements gleamed somewhat more brightly. Meanwhile the custodian approached us, quite silent, but holding out a board[3] like those used in Germany by toll collectors on bridges.

Menedemus. Yes, I've often cursed those greedy boards when traveling through Germany.

Ogygius. We gave him some coins, which he offered to the Virgin. Next, through an interpreter who understands the language well, I tried as civilly as I could to find out what proof he had that this *was* the Virgin's milk. I wanted to know this clearly for the pious purpose of stopping the mouths of certain unbelievers who are accustomed to laugh at all these matters. At first the custodian frowned and said nothing. I told the interpreter to press him, but even more politely. He did so with the utmost grace, such that if with words of that sort he had entreated the Mother herself, recently out of childbed, she would not have taken offense. But the custodian, as if possessed, gazed at us in astonishment, and as though horrified by such a blasphemous speech, said, "What need is there to inquire into that when you have an authentic record?" And it looked very much as if he would throw us out for heretics, had we not calmed the fellow's wrath with money.

Menedemus. What did you do then?

Ogygius. What do you suppose we did? As though beaten with a club, or struck by a thunderbolt, we took ourselves out of there, humbly begging pardon (as one should in sacred matters) for such outrageous presumption. Then on to the little chapel, the shrine of the Holy Virgin. At our approach a custodian turns up,

---

[3]Or "box."

a Minorite, and gazes at us, as though studying us; after we go a little farther a second one turns up, likewise staring at us; then a third.

Menedemus. Perhaps they wanted to draw you.

Ogygius. But I suspected something very different.

Menedemus. What was that?

Ogygius. That a sacrilegious person had filched something from the Holy Virgin's ornaments, and that their suspicion was directed against me. So when I entered the chapel I greeted the Virgin Mother with a short prayer, like this: "O thou alone of all womankind Mother and Virgin, Mother most blessed, purest of maidens, we who are unclean come unto thee who art pure. We bless thee, we worship thee as best we can with our poor gifts. May thy Son grant us that, by emulating thy most blessed life, we too, through the grace of the Holy Spirit, may be made worthy to conceive the Lord Jesus spiritually in our inmost hearts, and never lose him once conceived. Amen." Kissing the altar at the same time, I laid some coins upon it and went way.

Menedemus. What did the Virgin do at this? Didn't she indicate by the slightest nod that your short prayer was heard?

Ogygius. As I told you, there was a dim religious light, and she stood in the shadows, to the right of the altar. Finally, the first custodian's harangue had so squelched me that I didn't dare lift my eyes.

Menedemus. So this expedition didn't end very happily.

Ogygius. On the contrary, quite happily.

Johann Arndt (1555–1621) was a German Lutheran pastor and editor of some of the writings of Martin Luther. In 1605 he published *True Christianity*, his reflections of the practice of the Christian life. The book was reprinted over 125 times before the close of the eighteenth century and was translated into many languages. *True Christianity* is of the same genre as *The Imitation of Christ*, a fifteenth-century classic of Christian devotional literature, though in its writing it resembles a collection of sermons more so than does the earlier work. Each chapter takes as its point of departure a passage from the Bible, and moves from there to meditations on images of love, forgiveness, holiness, and community life contained in that passage. This excerpt from *True Christianity* begins—as did many devotional manuals before and since—with an assertion of the obligation to follow the example of Christ, and in the course of its argument it juxtaposes spiritual pleasures to carnal indulgences.

11.4B *TRUE CHRISTIANITY*

He Who Does Not Follow Christ in His Life Is Not Truly Repentant, Is No Christian, and Is Not the Child of God. What the New Birth Is, and What the Yoke of Christ Is

Christ has left us an example that we should follow in his footsteps (1 Pet. 2:21).

God gave us his beloved Son as a prophet, doctor, and teacher, affirmed his calling through a voice from heaven, and ordered us to hear him. The Son of God fulfilled his teaching capacity not only with words but also with actions and with the beautiful examples of his most holy life as was fitting for a righteous teacher. Saint Luke speaks of this in Acts 1:1. *In the first book, O Theophilus, I have dealt with all that Jesus began to do and teach until the day when he was taken up.* In this verse, the evangelist puts the word "do" before the word "teach" to point out that doing and teaching belong together. Indeed a perfect teacher must first do and then teach. Thus, Christ's life is the true teaching and the true Book of Life.

God's Son became man and walked among men upon this earth so that he might give us a clear, living example of a godly, innocent, perfect, holy life, so that we might follow him as a light in the darkness. Therefore, he is called the light of the world and he who follows him walks not in darkness (John 8:12).

From this it is clear that a person must remain in darkness who does not follow Christ in faith and holy life, and that such a person can nevermore have the light of life. What is darkness, however? It is nothing other than an unrepentant life, which Paul calls "the works of darkness," which we must cast off and we must put on the armor of light (Rom. 13:12). In a word this means to be repentant.

It was earlier said fully enough that godly sorrow and true faith changes the whole man, crucifies the flesh, and brings about a new life through the Holy Spirit, so that there are not only words that tell us of this. So that we might have a living, visual example of the Spirit that makes one alive or makes a new man, God placed before us his beloved Son, not only as a Savior but as a mirror of godliness, with his holy life, as the true new man in whom nothing of the Adamic, sinful flesh rules and lives except God himself, to the end that we also might be daily renewed according to his image. Concerning this, we must note the following account:

We know and experience, unfortunately daily, how our sinful nature, flesh and blood, body and soul, is wrapped around with so many impurities, evils, sins, and vices. These are all the works, qualities, and characteristics of the Devil in the fleshly, natural man. Above all there is the evil will of man. Out of an evil will all sin arises. If there were no evil will, sin would nevermore occur. An evil will turns itself from God. Everything that turns itself from God as from the eternal good is and must necessarily be evil. This turning away is the fall of man and of the Devil and for this reason sin came, which is inherited by all men and continued through man.

From this it is clear that our flesh and blood are poisoned in nature by the Devil's quality and our fleshly will is poisoned by Satan's evil, as by lies, pride, evil desire, and all kinds of vice that stand against God. Because of such evil qualities, the Lord Christ named the Pharisees "children of the Devil" (John 8:44) and gave one of his apostles over to the Devil (John 13:2). He gave him over to the Devil as if he were covetousness, lies, pride, and all the evil lusts of the Devil himself by which the natural, carnal man is ensnared.

From this it follows that all those who live in unrepentance, in pride, covetousness, lust, and envy, live in the Devil and are ensnared with the Devil's lifestyle. They may adorn themselves externally as beautifully as they please; they still remain devils in their hearts, as our Lord said to the Jews. Although this is very frightful, it is nevertheless the truth.

Although our miserable, greatly corrupted human nature is ensnared in so unspeakable and frightful a sorrow, it may be made better and renewed. How? Since it is corrupted with the most abominable evil, it must be made better and renewed by the highest good, namely, by God himself and, therefore, God had to become man.

God's Son did not become man for his own sake but for ours, so that he might unite us once again with God through himself, and make up participants of the highest good, and purify and make us holy once again. That which is to be made holy must be made holy through God and with God. As God is personally in Christ, so God must be united with us through faith and man must live in God and God in him; man must live in Christ and Christ in him. God's will must be in man and man must live in God's will. Christ Jesus must be the medicine for our corrupted nature. The more Christ lives in man, the more is human nature made better.

Would not that man be more noble in whom Christ brings about all things, whose will is Christ's will, whose thoughts are Christ's thoughts, whose mind is Christ's mind (as Saint Paul said, *"We have the mind of Christ"* [in 1 Cor. 2:16]) and whose speech and word is Christ's word? Indeed, we must thus be free. Christ's life is the new life in man and the new man is the man in whom Christ lives in the spirit. Christ's meekness must be the meekness of the new man; Christ's humility, the humility of the new man; Christ's patience is the patience of the new man, and so forth. The whole life of Christ must be in the life of the new man. This is a new creature and the noble life of Christ in us as Saint Paul says: *"It is no longer I who live, but Christ who lives in me"* (Gal. 2:20). To repent properly is to properly follow Christ. By this, the old man dies and the carnal life dies and the new spiritual life begins. There is then a true Christian not only according to title and name, but according to act and truth. Indeed, he is a true child of God, born out of God and Christ, renewed in Christ and made living through faith.

Although we are not able in our present weakness to come to perfection, yet we must strive after it. We must weep and hope in our hearts that Christ and not Satan will live in us and have his reign in us. Indeed, we are to strive for this and, through daily sorrow, mortify the old man. Insofar as the old man dies, Christ will live in us. Insofar as the evil nature through the Spirit of God is taken off, grace is placed in man. Insofar as the flesh is crucified, the spirit is made living. Insofar as the work of darkness is extinguished in man, man is more and more enlightened. Insofar as the external man is cast off and mortified, the internal man is renewed (2 Cor. 4:16). Insofar as one's own affectations and the whole carnal life in man dies—such as self-love, self-honor, wrath, covetousness, lust—insofar Christ lives in him. The more the world leaves man in the lust of the eyes, the lust of the flesh, and the pride of life, the more do God, Christ, and the Holy Spirit enter man and possess him. Thus, the more nature, flesh, darkness, and the world rule in man, the less grace, spirit, light, God, and Christ exist in man.

If this is to happen it will be a bitter cross for the flesh, for by it the flesh will be extinguished, crucified with its lusts and desires, and this is the true power and fruit of repentance. Flesh and blood wish for themselves a free, dissolute, certain life, according to their own lusts and wills. That is, for the flesh, the sweetest and most pleasant life. Christ's life is for the flesh and the old man a bitter cross, however. For the new, spiritual man, nevertheless, it is an easy yoke and a light burden and a lovely rest. In what does loving peace consist other than in faith in Christ in his meekness, humility, patience, and in the love of Christ (Matt. 11:29)? Thus you will find peace for your soul. Indeed, for the person who properly loves Christ, death for Christ's sake is the highest joy. This is the easy yoke of Christ, which we are to take upon ourselves and in which the true peace of the soul consists.

If we are to take the yoke of Christ upon ourselves as it is, that is, his holy, noble life, we must cast off the Devil's yoke, that is, the carnal, seeking, dissolute life, and we must not allow the flesh to rule over the spirit but everything that is in man, the will, understanding, reason, desires, and all Adamic fleshly lusts must come under the yoke of Christ and under his obedience.

The flesh is pleased to be honored, highly considered, and praised. It wishes to gain wealth, good days, and pleasure, but all this must be brought under the yoke of Christ, that is, under Christ's rejection, poverty, and shame. One is to consider pleasures as worthless, to draw oneself away from all that is high, glorious, pompous, powerful, and beautiful in the world. This is the true humility of Christ and his noble life and his easy yoke, which is a light burden. He did not come to be served but to serve us and he gave his life as a payment for our sins (Matt. 20:28). What is Christ's life other than holy poverty, external rejection, and the highest pain?

WORSHIP AND RITUAL

CHAPTER 12
IN ISLAM

12.1 ISLAMIC WORSHIP AND DEVOTIONAL PRACTICES

Here we take a closer look at selected aspects of the Islamic religious life, as prescribed in the Qur'an, as interpreted by the great classical thinker and teacher al-Ghazālī, as viewed by a contemporary Muslim therapist and psychoethicist, and as discussed by a twentieth-century Western scholar-traveler who collected many valuable prayer manuals in her sojourns in Muslim countries.

Most of the detail concerning the observance of Islamic devotional duties is found in the Hadith literature. But the original commandments and regulations are contained in the Qur'anic revelation itself. Before performing the prayer, it is necessary for Muslims to purify themselves by means of ablutions. The minor ablution, known as *wuḍū'*, is described in sura 5:6.

12.1A QUR'ANIC PASSAGES COMMANDING DEVOTIONAL DUTIES

5:6. O ye who believe! When ye rise up for prayer, wash your faces, and your hands up to the elbows, and lightly rub your heads and (wash) your feet up to the ankles. And if ye are unclean, purify yourselves. And if ye are sick or on a journey, or one of you cometh from the closet, or ye have had contact with women, and ye find not water, then go to clean, high ground and rub your faces and your hands with some of it. Allah would not place a burden on you, but He would purify you and would perfect His grace upon you, that ye may give thanks.

The Qur'an often speaks of rising up for the salat (prayer) and giving the zakat (alms). The following passage tells who the recipients of alms should be.

9:60. The alms are only for the poor and the needy, and those who collect them, and those whose hearts are to be reconciled, and to free the captives and the debtors, and for the cause of Allah, and (for) the wayfarers; a duty imposed by Allah. Allah is Knower, Wise.

Fasting (*ṣaum*) during the holy month of Ramadan is commanded in sura 2:183–187.

183. O ye who believe! Fasting is prescribed for you, even as it was prescribed for those before you, that ye may ward off (evil);

184. (Fast) a certain number of days; and (for) him who is sick among you, or on a journey, (the same) number of other days; and for those who can afford it there is a ransom: the feeding of a man in need—But whoso doeth good of his own accord, it is better for him: and that ye fast is better for you if ye did but know—

185. The month of Ramadân in which was revealed the Qur'ân, a guidance for mankind, and clear proofs of the guidance, and the Criterion (of right and wrong). And whosoever of you is present, let him fast the month, and whosoever of you is sick or on a journey, (let him fast the same) number of other days. Allah desireth for you ease; He desireth not hardship for you; and (He desireth) that ye should complete the period, and that ye should magnify Allah for having guided you, and that peradventure ye may be thankful.

186. And when My servants question thee concerning Me, then surely I am nigh. I answer the prayer of the suppliant when he crieth unto Me. So let them hear My call and let them trust in Me, in order that they may be led aright.

187. It is made lawful for you to go unto your wives on the night of the fast. They are raiment for you and ye are raiment for them. Allah is aware that ye were deceiving yourselves in this respect and He hath turned in mercy toward you and relieved you. So hold intercourse with them and seek that which Allah hath ordained for you, and eat and drink until the white thread becometh distinct to you from the black thread of the dawn. Then strictly observe the fast till nightfall and touch them not, but be at your devotions in the mosques. These are the limits imposed by Allah, so approach them not. Thus Allah expoundeth His revelations to mankind that they may ward off (evil).

The pre-Islamic Arabs observed an annual pilgrimage to Mecca. Muhammad's prophetic career was, in part, dedicated to restoring what the Qur'an teaches to be the primordial monotheism of Abraham, who rebuilt the Ka'aba at Mecca, according to tradition (which held that Adam had built the original structure). Afterwards, the cult deteriorated into idolatrous worship practices, so that by Muhammad's time some 360 different deities were worshipped at the Meccan sanctuary. Muhammad's first task, upon entering victoriously into Mecca in 630, was the destruction of the idols and the purification of the Ka'aba as Islam's most sacred place.

12.1B PILGRIMAGE (HAJJ) TO MECCA (2:196–203; 22:26–38)

Sura 2:196–203

196. Perform the pilgrimage and the visit (to Mecca) for Allah. And if ye are prevented, then send such gifts as can be obtained with ease, and shave not your heads until the gifts have reached their destination. And whoever among you is sick or hath an ailment of the head must pay a ransom of fasting or almsgiving or offering. And if ye are in safety, then whosoever contenteth himself with the Visit for the Pilgrimage (shall give) such gifts as can be had with ease. And whosoever cannot find (such gifts), then a fast of three days while on the pilgrimage, and of seven when ye have returned; that is, ten in all. That is for him whose folk are not present at the Inviolable Place of Worship. Observe your duty to Allah, and know that Allah is severe in punishment.

197. The pilgrimage is (in) the well-known months, and whoever is minded to perform the pilgrimage therein (let him remember that) there is (to be) no lewdness nor abuse nor angry conversation on the pilgrimage. And whatsoever good ye do Allah knoweth it. So make provision for yourselves (hereafter); for the best provision is to ward off evil. Therefore keep your duty unto Me, O men of understanding.

198. It is no sin for you that ye seek the bounty of your Lord (by trading). But, when ye press on in the multitude from 'Arafât, remember Allah by the sacred monument. Remember Him as He hath guided you, although before ye were of those astray.

199. Then hasten onward from the place whence the multitude hasteneth onward, and ask forgiveness of Allah. Lo! Allah is Forgiving, Merciful.

200. And when ye have completed your devotions, then remember Allah as ye remember your fathers or with a more lively remembrance. But of mankind is he who saith: "Our Lord! Give unto us in the world," and he hath no portion in the Hereafter.

201. And of them (also) is he who saith: "Our Lord! Give unto us in the world that which is good and in the Hereafter that which is good, and guard us from the doom of Fire."

202. For them there is in store a goodly portion out of that which they have earned. Allah is swift at reckoning.

203. Remember Allah through the appointed days. Then whoso hasteneth (his departure) by two days, it is no sin for him, and whoso delayeth, it is no sin for him; that is for him who wardeth off (evil). Be careful of your duty to Allah, and know that unto Him ye will be gathered.

Sura 22:26–38

26. And (remember) when We prepared for Abraham the place of the (holy) House, saying: Ascribe thou no thing as partner unto Me, and purify My House for those who make the round (thereof) and those who stand and those who bow and make prostration.

27. And proclaim unto mankind the Pilgrimage. They will come unto thee on foot and on every lean camel; they will come from every deep ravine.

28. That they may witness things that are of benefit to them, and mention the name of Allah on appointed days over the beast of cattle that He hath bestowed upon them. Then eat thereof and feed therewith the poor unfortunate.

29. Then let them make an end of their unkemptness and pay their vows and go around the ancient House.

30. That (is the command). And whoso magnifieth the sacred things of Allah, it will be well for him in the sight of his Lord. The cattle are lawful unto you save that which hath been told you. So shun the filth of idols, and shun lying speech.

31. Turning unto Allah (only), not ascribing partners unto Him; for whoso ascribeth partners unto Allah, it is as if he had fallen from the sky and the birds had snatched him or the wind had blown him to a far-off place.

32. That (is the command). And whoso magnifieth the offerings consecrated to Allah, it surely is from devotion of the hearts.

33. Therein are benefits for you for an appointed term; and afterward they are brought for sacrifice unto the ancient House.

34. And for every nation have We appointed a ritual, that they may mention the name of Allah over the beast of cattle that He hath given them for food; and your God is One God, therefor surrender unto Him. And give good tidings (O Muhammad) to the humble.

35. Whose hearts fear when Allah is mentioned, and the patient of whatever may befall them, and those who establish worship and who spend of that We have bestowed on them.

36. And the camels! We have appointed them among the ceremonies of Allah. Therein ye have much good. So mention the name of Allah over them when they are drawn up in lines. Then when their flanks fall (dead), eat thereof and feed the beggar and the suppliant. Thus have We made them subject unto you, that haply ye may give thanks.

37. Their flesh and their blood reach not Allah, but the devotion from you reacheth Him. Thus have We made them subject unto you that ye may magnify Allah that He hath guided you. And give good tidings (O Muhammad) to the good.

38. Lo! Allah defendeth those who are true. Lo! Allah loveth not each treacherous ingrate.

12.2 HOW A MUSLIM SHOULD GO TO BED (AND IN THE PROCESS PREPARE FOR DEATH)

Abū Ḥāmid Muḥammad al-Ghazālī (d. 1111) was from Persia. He and his brother, who also became a famous Sufi, were orphaned as boys but given a good education by their guardian. Al-Ghazālī became a famous teacher of Islamic sciences at a new university in Baghdad. But he came to have spiritual conflicts about his success, suspecting inwardly that he was actually in danger of hellfire. He had thoroughly studied philosophy, theology, and law and wrote important treatises on those subjects. But during his period of self-doubt, he became paralyzed and incapable even of eating. Then he totally surrendered to God and found a profound peace. Having become a sort of "born again" Muslim, he gave up his important academic position and took to the road, pursuing a life of renunciation and spiritual contemplation. During this period, he wrote his greatest treatise, "The Revival of the Sciences of Religion," which fills four large volumes in a modern Arabic edition.

In his *Iḥyā'* ("Revival"), al-Ghazālī treats virtually every aspect of Islam and of human life. The goal throughout is reformation and revitalization of Muslim life. Al-Ghazālī believed himself—and this belief was shared by many—to have been designated by God as the "Renewer" (*mujaddid*) of Islam for his age. His cogent attacks on Greek philosophy (as it had affected Islamic discourse) had a definitive influence on subsequent Islamic intellectual activity, and his accommodation of systematic theology and law with mysticism at least enabled each side to be less suspicious and condemning of the other (although the later Jalāl al-Dīn Rūmī still detested theological hairsplitting, as we saw earlier). Al-Ghazālī was saved by Sufism, although his Sufi beliefs never reached the daring levels of both earlier and later exponents such as al-Ḥallāj, Ibn 'Arabī, or Rūmī.

The old children's bedtime prayer, "Now I lay me down to sleep," dating at least to the twelfth century and appearing in the New England Primer of 1737, would have been conceptually acceptable to al-Ghazālī. But he adds considerably more detail about how one should prepare for bedtime in his chapter "Going to Sleep" from "The Beginning of Guidance."

12.2A GOING TO SLEEP

When you want to go to sleep, lay out your bed pointing to Mecca, and sleep on your right side, the side on which the corpse reclines in the tomb. Sleep is the similitude of death and waking of the resurrection. Perhaps God most high will take your spirit this night; so be prepared to meet Him by being in a condition of purity when you sleep. Have your will written and beneath your head. Repent of your faults, seek pardon, resolve not to return to your sin, and so sleep. Resolve to do good to all Muslims if God most high raises you up again. Remember that in like manner you will lie in the tomb, completely alone; only your works will be with you, only the effort you have made will be rewarded.

Do not try to induce sleep by laboriously seeing that your bed is soft and smooth; for sleep is the rejection of life, except when to be awake is unwholesome for you; in that case sleep preserves your religion. Night and day are twenty-four hours; the amount of sleep you take altogether, by night or day, should not be more than eight hours. It is enough, supposing you live for sixty years, that you lose twenty of these years or a third of your life. As you go to bed make ready your tooth-stick and washing things, and resolve to get up during the night (*sc.* for prayer) or else to get up before dawn. Two *rak'ahs* [prayer units] in the middle of the night is one of the treasures of the righteous man. Try to multiply your treasures against the day of your poverty. The treasures of this world will be of no use to you when you are dead.

As you go to sleep say: 'In Thy name, Lord, I lay me down and in Thy name will I rise up; forgive my sins; O God, keep me from Thy punishment in the day when Thou raisest Thy servants. O God, in Thy name do I live and die; and with Thee, O God, do I take refuge from the evil wrought by evil things and from the evil of every beast Thou takest by the forelock; verily my Lord is upon a straight path (cp. Q. II, 59). O God, Thou art the first and before Thee there is nothing; Thou art the last and after Thee there is nothing; Thou art the outmost and above Thee there is nothing; Thou art the inmost and below Thee there is nothing. O God, Thou didst create my soul, and Thou wilt bring it to death. In Thy hand is its dying and its living. If Thou makest it die, pardon it, and if Thou makest it live, preserve it from sin, as Thou preservest Thy righteous servants. O God, I beseech Thee for pardon and health. Waken me, O God, in the hour most pleasing to Thee and use me in the works most pleasing to Thee, that Thou mayest bring me ever nearer to Thyself and remove me ever farther from Thy anger. I beseech Thee and do Thou grant, I seek forgiveness and do Thou forgive, I pray to Thee and do Thou answer.'

Then repeat the Throne Verse (Q. 2, 256) and from 'The Messenger has believed' (Q. 2, 285) to the end of the Surah, the Surah of Purity (112), the two Surahs of Taking Refuge (113, 114) and the Surah 'Blessed be He in Whose hand is the kingship' (67). Let sleep come upon you while you are recollecting the name of God and are in purity. Whoever does this, lifts up his spirit to the Throne and he is written down as praying until he wakes up.

When you wake up, return to what I told you first of all, and continue in this routine for the rest of your life. If continuing thus is burdensome to you, be patient in the same way as a sick man is patient at the bitterness of sickness since he looks forward to being well again. Reflect upon the shortness of your life. If you were to live, for example to be a hundred, even that would be little compared with your residence in the mansion of the world to come, which is to all eternity. Consider how in the quest for this-world you endure hardship and humiliation for a month or a year since you hope that thereby you will have rest for twenty years, for example. How, then, do you not endure these things for a few days in the hope of having rest to all eternity?

Do not cherish long hopes which lay heavy labour upon you, but suppose that death is near and say to yourself, 'I shall endure the hardship today; perhaps I shall die tonight,' and 'I shall be patient tonight; perhaps I shall die tomorrow,' For death does not come upon us at a specified time or in a specified way or at a specified age; but come upon us he does, and so preparation for death is better than preparation for this world. You know that you remain here for only a brief space—perhaps there remains but a single day of your allotted span, perhaps but a single breath. Imagine this in your heart every day and impose upon yourself patience in obeying God daily. If with the supposition that you have fifty years to live you lay upon your soul the obligation of patience in obeying God most high, your soul will break away and be difficult to handle. If you do what I suggest, you will rejoice at death unceasingly; but if you put off and are easy-going, death will come to you when you do not reckon on it and you will sigh unceasingly. When morning comes and the night-journey is over, people praise night-travel; when death comes, you learn the outcome; 'ye shall surely know the report of it after a while' (Q. 38, 88).

12.3 How to Perform the Salat Worship: Daily and Friday

The following extract from "The Beginning of Guidance" provides clear instructions with sufficient detail on the performance of the daily worship. Al-Ghazālī was likely writing his treatise as a guide for Muslims devoted to cultivating Islam as a complete way of life. Although we do not have specific evidence, it seems that al-Ghazālī was leader of a religious community. And it is true that after his time, the Sufi orders, in the sense of specific orders with property, communities, regulations, and so forth began to develop and spread across the Muslim world. In some respects they were parallel to Christian orders, although not monastic in the sense of requiring celibacy. But poverty, both spiritual and material, was enjoined, as was absolute obedience to one's spiritual master, or shaykh.

12.3A HOW TO PERFORM THE ISLAMIC PRAYER SERVICE

When you have completed the purification of the body, clothing and place of Worship from all ritual and physical impurity, and have covered your privy parts from navel to knee, set your face to the Qiblah standing upright with feet apart, not touching one another.

Then recite 'Say, I take refuge with the Lord of men' (Q. 114) as a protection against the accursed Devil. Make your heart attentive, emptying it of evil suggestions. Consider in front of Whom you stand and speak, and shrink from addressing your Patron with negligent heart and breast laden with worldly suggestions and evil passions. God most high is aware of your inmost thoughts and sees your heart. God accepts your Worship only according to the measure of your humility, submissiveness, modesty and lowliness. Serve Him in your Worship as if you see Him, for, even if you do not see Him, yet He sees you.

If your heart is not attentive and your members not at rest, this is because of your defective knowledge of the majesty of God most high. Imagine, then, that an upright man, one of the leading members of your family is watching you to learn the quality of your Worship; at that your heart will be attentive and your members at rest. Next, turn back to your soul and say: 'O evil soul, are you not ashamed before your Creator and Patron? When you imagined that you were observed by a humble servant of His, who was able neither to benefit nor to harm you, your members were submissive and your Worship was good. Yet, though you know He observes you, you do not humble yourself before His greatness. Is He, the Most High, less in your eyes than one of His servants? How presumptuous and ignorant you are!'

Use such devices in the treatment of your heart, and perhaps it will accompany you attentively in your Worship. You are credited only with that part of your Worship which you perform intelligently. In the case of what is done negligently and inattentively you require rather to seek pardon and make atonement.

When your heart is attentive, do not omit the Institution even if you are alone; if you expect other people to take part, make the Call to Worship, then say the Institution. When you have instituted, make the Intention, saying 'I perform for God most high the obligation of Noon Worship.' Let that be present in your heart at your *takbīr*, (*sc.* saying of *Allah akbar*, 'God is very great') and do not let the intention pass from you before you complete the *takbīr*.

At the *takbīr* raise your hands, which up till now have been hanging loosely, to the level of your shoulders. The hands should be open and the fingers stretched out, but without any effort on your part either to keep the fingers together or to keep them apart. Raise your hands so that your thumbs are opposite the lobes of your ears, the tips of your fingers opposite the tops of your ears, and your palms opposite your shoulders. When they are at rest in their place, say 'God is very great.' Then let them drop gently. In raising and dropping the hands do not push them forward nor draw them back, and do not move them sideways to right or left.

When you have dropped them, raise them afresh to your chest. Give honour to the right hand by placing it over the left. Stretch the fingers of the right hand along the left forearm so that they grasp the left wrist. Then, following the *takbīr*, say: 'Truly God is very great; His praises celebrate; magnify Him early and late.' Next recite 'I have set my face towards Him Who opened up the heavens and the earth, as a Hanīf, not one of [the] polytheists'. . . to the end of the following verse (*i.e.* Q. 6, 79–80). Then say, 'I take refuge with God from Satan the accursed.' Then recite the Fātiḥah (Q. 1) with special attention to its doubled letters, trying to make a difference between your enunciation of the letters *ḍād* and *ẓā'* in your Worship. Say 'Amen,' but do not make it continuous with the concluding words of the Fāti-ḥah. Let your recitation be audible at the Morning, Sunset and Evening Wor-ships—that is, at the first two *rak'ahs*—unless you are following a leader. Let the 'Amen' be audible.

After the Fātiḥah at Morning Worship recite one from the long surahs of the division of the Qur'an called the Mufassal, at the Sunset Worship one from the short surahs of that division, and at the Noon, Afternoon and Evening Worships one from the medium surahs of it, as, for example, 'By the heaven decked with constellations' (85) and those adjacent to it.

When travelling, use at the Morning Worship 'Say, O ye unbelievers' (109) and 'Say, He is God, one' (112). Do not go straight on from the surah to the *takbīr* of the bowing, but make a break between them long enough to say 'Glory to God.' As long as you are standing keep your eyes down and restrict your gaze to the place of Worship (? prayer-mat); that helps to collect your thoughts and encourages at-tentiveness of heart. Be careful not to turn to right or left in your Worship.

Next say the *takbīr* of the Bowing, raise your hands as before, and prolong the *takbīr* to the end of the Bowing. Next place your palms on your knees, with your fingers stretched out; make your knees straight; set your back and neck and head all in one line; keep your elbows away from your sides—a woman, however, does not do this but keeps them close to her sides; and say, 'Glory to my great Lord and praise!' If you are alone, to repeat this up to seven or ten times is good.

Then raise your head until you are standing upright, and raise your hands while saying, 'May God hear him who praises Him!' When you are standing steadily, say, 'O our Lord, Thine is the praise filling the heavens and the earth and whatever else Thou wilt.' If you are at the obligatory Morning Worship, recite the *Qunūt* in the second *rak'ah* when you have stood upright after the Bowing.

Next prostrate yourself saying the *takbīr* but not raising the hands. First place your knees on the ground, then your hands, then your forehead, uncovered; place your nose on the ground along with your forehead. Keep your elbows away from your sides and your stomach from your thighs—a woman, however, does not do this. Place your hands on the ground opposite your shoulders, but do not lay your forearms on the ground. Say 'Glory to my Lord, the Most High!' three times, or, if you are alone, seven or ten times.

Then rise from the Prostration saying the *takbīr* until you are sitting upright with your left foot under you, while your right foot is erect. Place your hands on your thighs with the fingers outstretched, and say: 'Lord, forgive me, have mercy on me, provide for me, guide me, restore me, preserve me, pardon me!' Then prostrate yourself a second time in the same way, and sit upright to rest in every *rakʿah* not followed by Witnessing.

Next stand, placing your hands on the ground but not moving one foot forward as you rise. Begin the *takbīr* of rising towards the end of the Sitting for Rest, and prolong it until you are half-way up to standing position. This Sitting should be short and as it were snatched.

Perform the second *rakʿah* of the Worship like the first, repeating the Seeking for Refuge at the beginning. At the end of the second *rakʿah* sit for the first Witnessing. As you do so, place the right hand on the right thigh with the fingers closed except the forefinger and thumb, which are left free. At the words 'save God,' not at the words 'There is no god,' point with your right forefinger. Place your left hand on your left thigh with fingers outstretched. In this Witnessing sit on your left foot, as between the two Prostrations. In the last Witnessing, however, sit on your hip.

After the Blessing on the Prophet (God bless and preserve him) make the well-known Traditional Supplication; during this sit on your left hip, with your left foot going out from beneath you and your right leg erect. Then, when you have finished, say twice, once to each side, 'Peace be upon you and the mercy of God,' turning so that your neighbour may see your cheek. Make the intention of withdrawing from the Worship and the intention of peace for the angels and Muslims on either side of you. This is the form taken by the Worship of a person by himself.

The pillars of the Worship are humility and recollectedness of heart, together with the recital of the Qur'an with understanding and the making of acts of adoration with understanding. Al-Ḥasan al-Baṣrī (God most high have mercy on him) said, 'Every Worship at which the heart is not present is more likely to bring punishment than reward.' Muhammad (God bless and preserve him) said, 'A man may perform the Worship so that he is given credit for only a sixth or a tenth of it'; and 'a man receives credit only for that amount of his Worship which he understands.'

Leading and Following in the Prayer Service

The leader must make the Worship light, or quick, not burdensome. Anas (may God be pleased with him) said, 'Never behind anyone did I perform a Worship that was so light and yet so complete as the Worship led by the Messenger of God (God bless and preserve him).'

The leader should not say the *takbīr* until the muezzin has completed the Institution and until the rows of worshippers are even. At each *takbīr* the leader ought to raise his voice, but those who follow him raise the voice only enough for each to hear himself. The leader makes the intention of leading in order to gain credit for this act of leading; but, even if he does not make the intention, the Worship of the congregation is still valid, provided they make the intention of following him, and they gain credit for worshipping as followers.

The leader should say secretly the Opening Supplication and the Seeking for Refuge, in the same way as the man by himself, but he should say the Fātiḥah and the Surah aloud on every occasion in the Morning Worship, and in the first two (*rak'ahs*) of the Sunset and Evening Worships. The individual does the same. He (*sc.* the leader) says aloud the word 'Amen' in the audible part of the Worship, and likewise the follower, making his saying of 'Amen' coincide with that of the leader, not come after it. The leader is silent a little at the end of the Fātiḥah in order to recollect himself. The follower recites the Fātiḥah audibly in this silence so that he may be able to listen to the leader's Recital of the Qur'an. The follower recites the Surah audibly only if he does not hear the voice of the leader. At the Bowing and the Prostration the leader does not say 'Glory be to God' more than three times; and at the first Witnessing he adds nothing after the words 'O God, bless Muhammad.' In the last two *rak'ahs* he limits himself to the Fātiḥah and does not make the Worship long for the congregation. His Supplication at the last Witnessing is of the length of his Witnessing and his Blessing of the Messenger of God (God bless and preserve him).

At the Salutation the leader makes the intention of peace for the congregation, and the congregation in saluting makes the intention of responding to him. After completing the Salutation the leader waits a little and faces the people. He does not turn, however, if there are women behind him, so that they may depart first. No one of the congregation stands up until the leader stands. The leader goes off either to right or left, as he pleases, but to the right is preferable. The leader does not specify himself (*sc.* say 'guide *me*') in the Supplication at the Qunūt of the Morning Worship, but, speaking aloud, says, 'O God, guide us,' and the congregation says 'Amen.' He does not raise his hands here, since that is not established in Tradition. The follower recites the remainder of the Qunūt, consisting of the words 'Thou passest judgement, but no judgement is passed upon Thee.'

The follower does not stand alone, but enters the row of worshippers or else attracts others to himself. The follower should not precede or synchronize with the leader in his actions, but should be a little after him; he should not bend for the Bowing until the leader has come to the end of the Bowing, and he should not bend for the Prostration so long as the leader's forehead has not touched the earth.

Friday

Friday is the festival of the believers. It is an excellent day, ordained specially for this community by God (may He be magnified and glorified). In the course of it there is a period, the exact time of which is unknown; and if any Muslim, making request to God most high for what he needs, chances to do so in this period, God grants his request. Prepare then for it (*sc.* the Friday) on the Thursday by cleansing of the clothes, by many acts of praise and by asking forgiveness on Thursday evening, for that is an hour equal in merit to the (*sc.* unknown) hour of the Friday. Make the intention of fasting on Friday, but do so on Saturday or Thursday as well, since there is a prohibition on fasting on Friday alone.

When the morning breaks, wash, since Friday washing is obligatory on every adult, that is, it is 'established' and 'confirmed.' Then array yourself in white clothes, for these are the most pleasing to God. Use the best perfume you have. Cleanse your body thoroughly by shaving, cutting your hair and nails, using the tooth-stick, and practising other forms of cleanliness, as well as by employing fragrant perfumes. Then go early to the mosque, walking quietly and calmly. Muhammad (God bless and preserve him) has said: 'Whoever goes at the first hour, it is as if he offered a camel; whoever goes at the second hour, it is as if he offered a cow; whoever goes at the third hour, it is as if he offered a ram; whoever goes at the fourth hour, it is as if he offered a chicken; whoever goes at the fifth hour, it is as if he offered an egg.' He said likewise: 'And when the leader comes out, the leaves are rolled up, the pens are raised, and the angels gather together at the pulpit listening to the invocation of God.' It is said that, in respect of nearness to the beholding of the face of God, people come in the order of their earliness for the Friday Observance.

When you have entered the mosque, make for the first (*sc.* nearest) row. If the congregation has assembled, do not step between their necks and do not pass in front of them while they are praying. Place yourself near a wall or pillar so that people do not pass in front of you. Before sitting say the prayer of 'greeting.' Best of all, however, is to perform four *rak'ahs*, in each of which you recite the Surah of Purity (112). There is a Tradition to the effect that whoever does that will not die until he has seen, or, in a variant reading, has been shown, his place in Paradise. Do not omit the prayer of 'greeting' even if the leader is giving the address. It is a usage to recite in four *rak'ahs* the Surahs of the Cattle, the Cave, TH and YS (6, 8, 20, 36); but, if you cannot manage these, then take the Surahs of YS, the Smoke, ALM the Worship, and the Angel (36, 44, 32, 67). Do not omit the recitation of the last Surah on Friday evening, for in it is great merit. Whoever cannot do that well, should recite the Surah of Purity (112) many times, and frequently repeat the Blessing on the Messenger of God (God bless and preserve him), especially on this day.

When the leader has come out to commence the Worship, break off your private Worship and conversation, and occupy yourself with responding to the muezzin, and then by listening to the address and taking it to heart. Do not speak at all during the address. It is related in a Tradition that 'whoever says "Hush!" to his neighbour while the leader is giving the address, has spoken idly, and whoever speaks idly has no Friday Observance (*sc.* credited to him)'; the point is that in saying 'Hush' he was speaking, whereas he ought to have checked the other man by a sign, not by a word.

Then follow the leader in the Worship as explained above. When you have finished and said the Salutation, before speaking recite the Fātiḥah, the Surah of

Purity, and the two Surahs of Seeking Refuge, each seven times. That keeps you safe from one Friday to the next, and is a protection for you against Satan.

After that say: 'O God, Who art rich and praiseworthy, Who createst and restorest to life, Who art merciful and loving, make me to abound in what is lawful in Thy sight, in obedience to Thee and in grace from Thee, so that I turn from what is unlawful, from disobedience and from all other than Thou.'

After the Friday Observance perform two *rak'ahs*, or else four or six in pairs. All this is traditionally related of the Messenger of God (God bless and preserve him) in various circumstances. Then remain in the mosque until the Sunset Worship or at least until the Late-afternoon Worship. Watch carefully for the 'excellent hour,' for it may occur in any part of the day, and perhaps you will light upon it while making humble supplication to God. In the mosque do not go to the circles of people nor the circles of story-tellers, but to the circle of profitable knowledge, that is, the knowledge which increases your fear of God most high and decreases your desire for this world; ignorance is better for you than all knowledge which does not draw you away from this world towards the next. Take refuge with God from unprofitable knowledge. Pray much at the rising, declining and setting of the sun, at the Institution of the Worship, at the preacher's ascending of the pulpit, and at the rising of the congregation for the Worship; the likelihood is that the 'excellent hour' will be at one of these times. Endeavour on this day to give such alms as you can manage, even if it is little. Divide your time between the Worship, fasting, alms-giving, reciting the Qur'an, recollection of God, solitary devotions and 'waiting for prayer.' Let this one day of the week be specially devoted to what pertains to the future life, and perhaps it will be an atonement for the rest of the week.

12.4 A Modern Muslim Woman's Perspective

Laleh Bakhtiar is a contemporary American Muslim educational psychologist. Her article "Moral Healing Through Fasting" is from her edited volume *Ramadan: Motivating Believers to Action—An Interfaith Perspective*. The book contains a number of interesting views on the Ramadan fast, including discussions by Muslim physicians of its medical effects and benefits.

12.4a Fasting to Control Passions

The self (*khudi*) in the traditional perspective is described as a circle of unity. The center from which the circle emerges is known as the heart. From this center—the heart—emerges a threefold division. The uppermost segment is known as cognition, intellect or reason, the *nafs lawwamah* (the soul which blames, reproaches self

From Laleh Bakhtiar, "Moral Healing Through Fasting" in Laleh Bakhtiar, ed., *Ramadan: Motivating Believers to Action—An Interfaith Perspective* (Chicago: The Institute for Traditional Psychoethics and Guidance, 1995), pp. 141–145.

for wrongdoing). It symbolizes that aspect of self which God blew into the human form. By doing so, God created Adam in His image. This upper segment is the human angelic quality.

The bottom two segments, known collectively as the animal soul (*nafs ammarah*), are referred to as avoidance of harm/pain and attraction to pleasure. These two segments and aspects of self make up what are called the passions. Attraction to pleasure is the center of lust or desires while avoidance of pain is the center of anger. These two are the human animal qualities.

The purpose of creation in this view is for the human self to struggle (*jihad*) to attain the highest human perfection possible. This struggle is known as the greater struggle (*jihad al-akbar*). It is a struggle between reason and the passions for the attention of the heart. If reason succeeds in attracting the heart to itself, the self is turned towards the spiritual and external world. If the passions succeed, the self is turned towards the material and impermanent world. This struggle is a significant one for the goal-setting believer's strategies because it reinforces those values which the model human being—Muhammad (ﷺ)—manifested. That is, when reason succeeds in attracting the heart towards itself, the self gains control and mastery over the passions—lust and anger. Gaining mastery, the self can then process values to which it has been guided by revelation and turn away from the disvalues which guidance through revelation has discredited.

This struggle—a continuous kind of tension—is a more difficult one requiring one's constant attention to remember and recall the purpose of life. Forgetfulness and heedlessness, seen as aspects of satanic-ego temptations, are as strong a natural force which when in control of self, allow for the responses of lust and anger to take over the self. It is then that the animal qualities within rule over the angelic or, in other words, the passions rule over reason.

Traditional prescribed fasting, which is always accompanied by prescribed prayer and supplication, serves to cut off the energies to the passions, weakening their response. This, in turn, strengthens the powers of reason. There are three kinds of fasts for the believer: prescribed, recommended and disapproved. One of the recommended fasts is that practiced by Zachariah and the Virgin Mary. It is a fast of silence. As regards the recommended fast of the Virgin Mary, God says to her once Jesus has been conceived, *"So eat and drink and be glad and if you see any human being, say, 'Verily I have vowed a fast to the Compassionate so I shall not speak to any human being this day.'"*

The Traditions relating to this verse all reinforce the idea that once one makes a vow or promise to follow a command of God, one should keep one's promise. One Tradition says, "The Messenger said, 'The best amongst you people are those living in my generation, then those coming after them, and then those coming after the second generation.' I do not know whether the Messenger mentioned two or three generations after his, but he then added, 'There will be some people after you who will be dishonest and will not be trustworthy and will bear witness without being asked to bear witness and will vow but not fulfill their vows and obesity will appear among them.'"

The Sufi Sayf al-Din, describes the role of the prescribed fast in subduing the ego.

The prescribed fast during the month of Ramadan further enhances the possibility of reason to win the struggle with the passions because of its duration. As the passions are weakened and the heart is attracted towards reason and the spiritual, the heart begins to see the mysteries of the universe. These mysteries are veiled from the heart during normal times by satanic whisperings or human ego desires which are symbolized by shadows covering the heart. Holding to the vow to the prescribed fast once made helps to remove the shadows over the heart. This is confirmed for the believer by the Tradition, 'If the satans did not swarm around the hearts of the children of Adam, they would look at the dominion of the heavens.' The instruments used by the satanic forces in leading the self astray and misguiding it are the passions—anger and lust.

> Could Adam have been brought down
>   from the Garden
> had the peacock and serpent
>   not guided Iblis?
> Your anger and lust
>   are peacock and serpent—
> The first helps satanic forces
> The second the animal soul.

Further elucidating this analogy, Sayf al-Din says, 'Through hunger the substance of anger and lust is weakened.' Thereby satan becomes thin since, 'The satan of the person of faith is emaciated.' When satan has no instrument or weapon left, it cannot whisper. The Seal of the Prophets—the Merciful's blessings be upon him—explained this meaning as follows, 'Satan runs in the child of Adam like blood. So constrict his running places through hunger and thirst.' Hence Jesus—God's blessings be upon him—counseled his disciples by saying, 'Keep your bellies hungry, your bodies naked, and your livers thirsty so that perhaps your hearts may see God.'

> The cause of anger and lust
>   is a bite of bread,
> the blight of mind and wisdom
>   is a bite of bread.

However, excessive hunger also causes harm. It carries the danger of madness, corruption of the brain and other illnesses. In short, a middle course is desirable in all things. The seeker must always keep 'the best of affairs is their middlemost' before their eyes. 'Both sides of moderation in affairs are blameworthy.' This alerts you to a universal law. And from God, aid is sought.[1]

Mastering, controlling the passions is traditionally known as moral healing. Anything that reinforces and strengthens the power of reason to attract the heart, the center of self, towards the Real, the Truth, serves to morally heal and balance the self. Prescribed fasting is one of the best disciplines to reinforce values about what is right or wrong for the believer.

For the believer, remembrance of the afterlife and the eternal possibility of self gives life meaning and connection to the unseen world. It is this 'eternal possibility of self' which, for the believer, needs to control 'the preservation of the species' or

---

[1] As quoted from William C. Chittick: *Faith and Practice of Islam: Three Thirteenth Century Sufi Texts* (Albany: State University of New York Press, 1992), pp. 142–143.

lust and 'the preservation of the individual' or anger. If a person does not believe what he or she is doing is the right thing to do, is a reinforcement of the eternal possibility of self, there will be inner conflict. This inner conflict will cause two effects: either a weakening of will power which will, in turn, undermine the believer's ability to attain the goal he or she set forth to perform the prescribed fast in the month of Ramadan or secondly, the believer may fast, but it will be an even greater struggle than it has to be. Once the values of the believer are clarified, resulting in a relaxing of the tension between attachment to this world vs. attachment to the eternal world, the struggle within the self becomes more manageable and with greater chance of success. The prescribed fast then becomes a means for the believer to express gratitude for the blessings one has received. This is brought out in a Tradition related by Ayisha, the Messenger's wife. While the Messenger was in a state free of negative traits, yet his prescribed prayers, fasting and supplications were intense. One day she said, "Oh Messenger of God, God has forgiven your sins, but you still invite this discipline upon yourself." He immediately replied, "Should I not be grateful?"

12.5 The Divine Name in Muslim Worship

The formal Pillars of Islam are only the major categories of Muslim devotional life. There are many details concerning each pillar that one comes to know only through their observance and living a Muslim life with fellow believers. Following is a description and discussion of an important area of Muslim piety: the use of the Divine Name in devotional life. The author of the following extract is Constance Padwick, a twentieth-century English Christian who lived for many years in Muslim lands, where she enjoyed learning about the many forms and dimensions of Muslim worship—individual and communal as well as official, popular, and esoteric. She published the results of her researches in her book *Muslim Devotions: A Study of Prayer-Manuals in Common Use.*

12.5A The Name in Worship

Basmala, al-Asmā'u 'l-Ḥusnā

The central part of the section of the prayer-rite known as *al-qirā'a,* "the recital," is a brief Qur'ān recitation. This must be introduced, however, by the *basmala,* the saying of the opening phrase attached to every *sūra* of the Qur'ān, much as the *Gloria* is attached in Christian worship to the end of every Psalm.

This phrase, *Bismi 'llāhi 'r-raḥmāni 'r-raḥīm,* usually translated into English by "In the Name of God the Merciful the Compassionate," is for ever on Muslim lips and pens. While the Jewish people honoured the Name by refusal to pronounce it, Muslims choose to honour it by constant use. All the events of life and the little fears of the heart are to be tamed, as it were, and made innocuous and set at rest by coming under the control of the Name.

This constant naming of the Name may be an act of simple confidence, or a light superstitious nothing; a conjuration charged with magical power; or, in saintly lives, a bringing of all things into relation with God, a signing of all life with his Name. Like the use of the sign of the Cross, the *basmala* may mean everything or nothing.

Popular Use of the Basmala

The late Mr A. T. Theobald of Algeria kindly communicated the following observations of popular usage there which might be duplicated or added to from many another land:

> You must say the *basmala* on entering a room or a house, or on opening a book. Never tread on a piece of paper, the Name of God may be written upon it.
>
> Often in market places, when we are selling portions of the Bible, the books are brought back to us by purchasers because on the title page the *basmala* does not appear. Our bookseller points out that the name of Allāh occurs in the first verse of Genesis, but is told, "No, we are forbidden to read anything which does not begin *bismi 'llāhi 'r-raḥmāni 'r raḥīm.*"
>
> Always put your hand before your mouth when you yawn, lest the devil enter in. Should you forget to do this, repeat the *basmala* and then spit three times.
>
> If you do not utter the Name of God before you drink, the demons get the first drink. If you do not repeat the Name before you eat, the demons get the first mouthful.
>
> Should you forget to say the *basmala* before entering your bed, the evil ones will be there before you, and you will pass a restless night.
>
> Once upon a time two malicious spirits met together; one was extremely stout and well-favoured and the other miserably thin and weak. The stout one addressed his friend and said, "How is it, brother, you are so thin?" "Ah, I live in a very holy place: they all repeat the Name of God so faithfully that I can find but little to eat and drink, neither can I rest day nor night." The well-favoured one said, "I am glad that I live in a wicked town where no one remembers the Name of God. I have all I need because of their forgetfulness."

The popular saying about eating without the *basmala* is supported by a tradition quoted in our manuals:

> (From Umayya ibn Makhshī.) The Apostle of God was sitting with a man who was eating and did not name the Name of God Most High till he reached the last mouthful of his food. Then as he raised that to his mouth he said, "In the Name of God, the first of it and the last of it." And the Prophet laughed and said, "A *shaiṭān* had been eating with him all the while, and when he made mention of the name of God the food in that *shaytān's* belly turned to poison." *al-Kalimu 't-ṭayyib*, p. 78 (Aḥmad I, 208).

A similar idea in pre-Islamic times of the necessity of "saining" food is found among the fathers of the Egyptian desert.

> Because the blessed fathers knew the wiles of Satan, and that they would certainly bring upon them that which would do them harm by means of such things as are

employed as food, they signed what they ate with the holy sign of the great Cross, so that they might slay all the craftiness of the Calumniator.

> *Questions and Answers on the Ascetic*
> *Rule* in *The Paradise of the Fathers*,
> translated from Syriac by Wallis
> Budge, II, 269.

The story of the happy and the unhappy devil, a cliché in popular preaching, and coming in this instance from Algeria, is much older than Islam in the Near East and also had its counterpart in the third and fourth century life of the Egyptian desert:

> Abba Pachomius heard one of them (the devils) saying, "I have (strife) with a man who constantly (defieth) me, for whensoever I approach to sow thoughts in his mind, immediately he turneth to prayer, and I depart from him consumed with fire." And another devil said, "I have (strife) with a man who is easy to persuade and he doeth whatsoever I counsel him to do and I love him dearly." It is right, then O my brethren that we should keep ourselves awake always, and that, making ourselves mighty men in the Name of the Lord, we should strive against the devils, and then they will never be able to overcome us. (Wallis Budge, *op. cit.*, I, 359.)

Traditions support the use of the *basmala* on all kinds of occasions, on entering the market or the house, on paying the *zakāt*, or on putting the right foot over the threshold of the mosque.

The formula in writing should stand at the beginning of every book, and though sometimes omitted from modern works in the European style, it does generally so stand, not only in religious books but even in pornographic books and grubby little crime stories. *Shī'a* books sometimes use the form *bismi 'llāhi 'l-mu'izzi 'l-muta'āl*. The *basmala* has of course its part to play in the writing of charms; it stands at the beginning of each *ḥizb* or *wird* in our prayer-manuals, and often over the entrance to houses or shops. It is the preface to the ablution before the prayers, some holding that the validity of the rite depends on it.

> He has made no ablution who has not invoked the Name of God upon it. *Adhkār*, an-Nawawī p. 34.

Another ritual use is on slaying the victim at the Feast of Sacrifice.

> It is not approved that a man shall say, "I do so and so over the Name of God," for his Name, glory be to Him, is over everything. The Qāḍī 'Iyāḍ and others say that this statement is an error. For sound traditions have confirmed that at the Feast of Sacrifice the Prophet said to his companions, "Sacrifice over the Name of God, which means saying, 'In the Name of God.'" Ibid., p. 169.

"Saining"

What is the feeling behind all this popular usage? Sometimes an essentially irreligious one. Here in the *basmala* is something with *baraka* in it. A tiny coin of supernatural value that may be spent for one's own profit. Often from the sense that weak and sin-stained man in a jinn-haunted dangerous world needs at every turn the protection of something strong and pure and holy. The closest usage to this in Christendom is represented by the old word "sained," and the use of the sign of the Cross to control or purify what is suspect of evil influence, and to bless and sanctify the common acts of life. In the Near East the Christian peasant puts the sign of the Cross over his house door, and the Muslim peasant says his *basmala* as he enters his. Both practices, by their very simplicity, may easily become mechanical and meaningless. No one can claim that they are not often so. Yet both have been and may be acts of conquering faith in the Holy Strong One.

The *basmala* is much used in the morning to "sain," to place in safety, the acts of the forthcoming day. Thus our manuals order repetitions of it after the dawn prayer-rite. Or the form:

> The Name of God over my religious practice, over myself and my child and my family and my property. (*Majinūʿu ʾl-ʾawrādi ʾl-kabīr*, M. ʿUthmān al-Mirghanī, and frequently in the manuals.)

is included in morning devotions, and is also expanded after the fashion of these prayers into

> I say over myself and over my religious practice and over my kinsfolk and over my children and over my property and over my friends and over their religious practices and over their property a thousand thousand basmalas. *Ḥizbu ʾn-Nawawī* in *Dalāʾilu ʾl-khairāt maʿa ʾl-awrād*, p. 220.

or still more generously:

> The name of God on my religious practice and on myself and my children.
> The Name of God on my property and my kinsfolk.
> The Name of God on all things that my Lord has bestowed on me.
> With the Name of God, Lord of the seven heavens and the seven earths and of the Great Throne.
> With the Name of God, with whose Name nothing in earth or heaven is harmful.
> With the Name of God, best of all names in earth and heaven.
> With the Name of God I begin and with that Name I conclude. Allāh! Allāh! Allāh! Allāh! Ibid., p. 227. (Such sainings can be matched in many devotions.)

Similarly the *basmala* may be used as a committal prayer on going to bed, a saining against the dangers of the night, a kind of holy insurance:

> And say when going to sleep, "In the Name of God the Merciful the Compassionate," twenty-one times, for it is a safeguard against theft and fire and flood. *al-ʿAṭiyyatu ʾl-haniyya*, ʿAlī ibn Ḥasan al-ʿAṭṭās, p. 116.

The first two of the morning forms given above are also employed for bedtime. Another evening form of self-committal and one claiming Prophetic usage is:

In thy Name I die and live (Sleep being a little death). *Wirdu 'l-ghurūb*, Muṣṭafa 'l-Bakrī.

(From Abū Huraira.) The Prophet said, "If one of you gets up from his bed at night, then returns to it, let him dust it three times with the fringe of his head-cloth, for he cannot tell what may have taken his place on the bed when he left it. And when he lies down let him say, 'In thy Name my Lord I lay me down and in Thee I raise me up.'" *al-Kalimu 'ṭ-ṭayyib*, p. 18 (agreed tradition).

A Word of Power

It is clear that the *basmala* formula is above all things a word of power. We have here the Semitic belief in the power and mystery of a name, reminding us of the Hebrew *Ba'al Shem*. And we have in some prayers the tendency to pass from simple confidence in Him who is named, to confidence in the power of the formula, which is sometimes wielded like a weapon against foes, or handed up to God, as a coin of proved value.

O God, by the excellence of "In the Name of God the Merciful the Compassionate" let us enter into thy inviolate fortress. O God, by the excellence of "In the Name of God the Merciful the Compassionate" cause us to dwell in Thy inviolate fortress. (*Basmala* for driving away fatigue and for wandering over the earth. *Ḥizbu 'l-baḥr*, ash-Shādhilī.)

> "In the Name of God" upon my heart that its thirst may be quenched.
> "In the Name of God" upon my knees that they may be strengthened.
> "In the Name of God" upon the earth that it may be traversed.
> *al-Fuyūḍātu 'r-rabbāniyya*, 'Abd al-Qādir al Jīlānī, p. 196.

(Against foes or the evils of mankind.) I set forth as a barrier before me and before them "In the Name of God the Merciful the Compassionate" and likewise on my right and their right and likewise on my left and their left and likewise in front of me and in front of them, and likewise above me and above them and likewise below me and below them, and likewise enclosing me and enclosing them. *Ḥizbu 'n-Nawawī*, also in *Ḥīzbu 'n-naṣr* of 'Abd al-Qādir al-Jīlānī and in a *Ḥizb* attributed to the Imām al-Ghazālī in *Majmū'atu 'l-Aḥzāb* of Aḥmad Ḍiyā'u 'd-Dīn.

Al-Nawawī's whole *Ḥizb* is in reality an enlargement and application of the *basmala*. Later, passing from the thought of foes to friends, he again applies his safeguard in all directions:

Then breathe out without spitting, three times on your right and three times on your left, three times in front of you and three times behind. Then say, "I have hidden myself and them in the treasures of 'In the Name of God the Merciful the Compassionate.'" *Ḥizbu 'n-Nawawī* in *Majmū'u 'l-awrād li-Muṣṭafā al-Bakrī*.

The Letters of the Basmala

There is clearly for these worshippers a mysterious power in the very formula itself.

> I beseech Thee by virtue of every mystery which Thou has set in "In the Name of God the Merciful, the Compassionate." *Duʿāʾu Yā Sīn, Majmūʿatu ʾl-aḥzāb*, Aḥmad Ḍiyāʾu ʾd-Dīn, p. 395.

Many worshippers feel that the mystery is latent in the very letters of which the formula is composed. For Arab minds have seen "signs" of God not only in the verses (*āyāt*) of the Qurʾān but in the very Arabic letters in which the revelation was embodied. Some have held them to have been created before the worlds.

There is a science of letters (*ʿilmu ʾl-ḥurūf*) and of their inner meaning and philosophical value (*ʿilmu ʾl-jafr*), connected with their numerical values, and not confined to mystical circles. Goldziher gives reasons for thinking that the legends underlying this passed from rabbinical circles to Islam, though there was probably also a return current flowing from Islam to Jewish *haggada*. This science of letters partly lies behind the cabbalistic use of them in charms, but it also has a nobler and more truly religious life of its own. In the devotions based on the *basmala* it often comes to the fore, for here, the writers feel, we are near the heart of all mysteries. The very letters become numinous.

PART V
ETHICS

CHAPTER 13
IN JUDAISM

13.1 THE NATURE OF THE MORAL STRUGGLE

The twelfth-century Spanish-Egyptian halakhist and philosopher Moses Maimonides is most famous in European tradition for his philosophical treatise *The
Guide of the Perplexed.* In Jewish tradition, however, he is more usually known as
the author of a magnificent halakhic code, the *Mishneh Torah,* and for his commentary on the Mishnah. It is through these latter works that Maimonides' ethical
thought had its impact on a wide Jewish audience. The following passage is taken
from the introduction to his commentary on the Mishnah's collection of ethical
maxims, Tractate Avot ("Founders"). Maimonides' main concern here—to show
that the appetites and pleasures of the body are valuable, but must be subordi-
nated to the mind's search for knowledge of God—reveals the Aristotelian foundations of his ethical thought.

13.1A *EIGHT CHAPTERS*

Man needs to subordinate all his soul's powers to thought . . . and to set his sight
on a single goal: the perception of God (may He be glorified and magnified), I
mean, knowledge of Him, in so far as that lies within man's power. He should direct all his actions . . . and all his conversation toward this goal so that none of his

actions is in any way frivolous, I mean, an action not leading to this goal. For example, he should make his aim only the health of his body when he eats, drinks, sleeps, has sexual intercourse, is awake, and is in motion or at rest. The purpose of his body's health is that the soul find its instruments healthy and sound in order that it can be directed toward the sciences and toward acquiring the moral and rational virtues, so that he might arrive at that goal. . . .

If a man sets this notion [i.e., knowledge of God] as his goal, he will discontinue many of his actions and greatly diminish his conversation. For someone who adheres to this goal will not be moved to decorate walls with gold or to put a gold border on his garment—unless he intends thereby to give delight to his soul for the sake of its health and to drive sickness from it, so that it will be clear and pure to receive the sciences. Thus, they said: "An attractive dwelling, an attractive wife, attractive utensils, and a bed prepared for the disciples of the wise give delight to the mind of a man" (Talmud, Berakhot 57b). For the soul becomes weary and the mind dull by continuous reflection upon difficult matters, just as the body becomes exhausted from undertaking toilsome occupations until it relaxes and rests and then returns to equilibrium. In a similar manner, the soul needs to rest and to do what relaxes the senses, such as looking at beautiful decorations and objects, so that weariness be removed from it. . . . Now it is doubtful that when done for this purpose, these are bad or futile, I mean, decorating and adorning buildings, vessels, and garments.

In the talmudic literature and, especially, in the medieval literature inspired by the Zohar, one commonly finds an association between ascetic denial of the body, study of Torah, and a comprehensive life of repentance for sins. These associations were brought to acute expressions of ascetic, mystical piety in the sixteenth-century kabbalistic movements associated with Rabbi Isaac Luria and Rabbi Moses Cordevero. What follows is a selection from a popular handbook of kabbalistic ethics *The Beginning of Wisdom*, published in 1579 by a disciple of Cordevero, Rabbi Elijah de Vidas.

13.1B *The Beginning of Wisdom*

One must accustom himself to rising every night at midnight and studying Torah until dawn. How many marvelous things occur by virtue of rising at midnight for the purpose of studying Torah? Among these is the subjugation of the evil shells [i.e., *kelipot*, the material condensations of divine light remaining from the creation process], a topic which is treated in the Zohar [I, 242a–b].

We have already mentioned above that the confusion of mind which a person may experience while engaged in praying or studying Torah is on account of

From Rabbi Elijah de Vidas, *The Beginning of Wisdom*, in Lawrence Fine, translator, *Safed Spirituality: Rules of Mystical Poetry, The Beginning of Wisdom*. Copyright © 1984 by The Missionary Society of Saint Paul the Apostle in the State of New York. Reprinted with the permission of Paulist Press.

his sins, insofar as he renders himself unqualified for unifying God. Sin functions as an evil accuser which comes between a person and God; but when an individual accustoms himself to rise in the middle of the night in order to study Torah, he throws off the Evil One and atones for his sins. Through such means he purifies his thoughts, and his efforts to unify God are not hampered. The reason for this is that night normally nourishes the [sefirotic] forces of strict judgment. The night is transformed from darkness into light, from the quality of judgment to the quality of compassion, however, by virtue of the study of Torah. And since the night becomes "sweetened," so too are all those who are bound up with it. . . .

Therefore, every penitent must deny himself sleep at night by means of study of the Torah and prayer so as to destroy the strength of the evil shells. To be sure, this will serve as an important aid to him in accomplishing repentance. Refer to what is written concerning this in the *Tiqqunim* [86b] where you will see that the Holy One, blessed be He, was restored to His proper place because King David remained awake at night. From the example of King David each and every person ought to learn that when an individual's sinfulness causes the Holy One, blessed be He and His *Shekhinah* to be exiled from their proper place, it is only fitting that he repent and deny himself sleep in order to restore them to the place where they belong.

In de Vidas's ethical thought, a person's actions must all be motivated by a complex balance of fear (awe) of God and love. This is expressed in the scrupulous avoidance of sin, which cuts the sinner off from God. Fear of sin, then, is fear of being alienated from the God whom one loves with all one's heart (Fine, pp. 92–93).

A person who desires to achieve perfect repentance must begin by acquiring knowledge of the fear and love of God, of which there are two aspects. First, when an individual recognizes that the Creator, may He be blessed, is the Master who created all humankind, he will learn to appreciate God's greatness. He will realize that everything which the Holy One, blessed be He, created was for the sake of His glory only, and that all living things are subject to His will. No person may go beyond the parameters within which the Creator of all things has placed him, as exemplified in the case of the sea, concerning which it is said, "Thus far shalt thou come, but no further" [Job 38:11]. And thus, if a person strays beyond the boundaries of the Torah, it is proper for him to return to the place to which he belongs as the Creator has enjoined him, and not disobey His word.

The second aspect concerns the blemish which extends throughout all the upper regions [i.e., the world of the supernal Sefirot], whether it be injury incurred by one's body, vital-soul, spirit, or super-soul. This is the most important reason that a person should practice repentance and be completely remorseful; that is, when he clearly realizes the harm caused by his deeds, in addition to considering the punishment which he will receive in this world as well as in the next. Sin causes the body to be cut off from this world and the soul from the world to come.

Hence, it is proper for an individual to protect himself, for even animals flee from fire when they realize that they are in a life-threatening situation. How can a person fail to protect himself inasmuch as the Creator, blessed be He, endowed him with intelligence superior to that of all other animals? How much more is this true in the case of Israel, His chosen people, which is distinguished from the idolatrous nations on account of the Torah? It protects itself when it sees that it might fall into a deep pit, into a place from which it may be unable to climb out. Surely, Israel's very existence and eminence is due to the Torah, as well as to the Sages in whom there dwelled the Holy Spirit. It is they who instructed us concerning the rewards of Paradise and the punishment of *Gehinnom*.

13.2 GUIDES TO MORAL EXCELLENCE

In the sixteenth-century kabbalistic milieu, it was common for important teachers to draw up "rules for living" that might be emulated by disciples. Such "rules" were not akin to halakhic norms, but rather constituted recommended attitudes and practices that might inculcate fear and love of God, the proper posture from which to engage halakhic norms. Following is a list of rules (Fine, pp. 55–57) supplied by Rabbi Joseph Karo, famous in Jewish tradition as the author the halakhic code, the *Shulkhan Arukh,* which serves until today as the primary halakhic source for Orthodox Judaism. Karo did not claim authorship of these rules. Rather he regarded them as revealed to him by a "Maggid," a supernal visitor who, in the form of the Mishnah, spoke the words through Karo's mouth in a trance.

13.2A RABBI JOSEPH KARO, *MAGGID MESHARIM*

1. To begin with, take care never to think about anything, at any time whatsoever, other than the Mishnah, the Torah, and the commandments. And should some other thought occupy you, thrust it away.
2. Be careful to avoid thinking about anything at the hour of prayer besides the words of the prayer themselves. This even includes avoiding thoughts of Torah and the commandments.
3. Be careful never to indulge in idle conversation whatsoever, neither during the day nor at night.
4. Take care to avoid engaging in any kind of talk which may lead to frivolity. And if you should overhear conversation of this sort, do not indulge in laughter whatsoever. This extends to the complete avoidance of mockery.
5. Never become angry about anything at all having to do with material things.
6. Do not consume much meat; even on the Sabbath take care to eat meat sparingly.
7. Do not drink wine except for one drink only at the conclusion of the meal.
8. Be gentle in speech to all people.

9. Never act pridefully whatsoever; rather, be exceedingly humble.

10. Conduct yourself modestly, even in relationship to your wife.

11. Be careful to avoid taking pleasure while eating meat and drinking, or while partaking of any other kind of enjoyment. Act as if a demon were forcing you to eat this food or indulge in enjoyable activity. You should very much prefer it were it possible to exist without food and drink altogether, or were it possible to fulfill the obligation of procreation without enjoyment.

12. Always have your transgressions in mind and preoccupy yourself with them.

13. Never eat dessert more than one measure, and not more than twenty of melon, grapes and raisins. Do not eat more than a single kind of fruit at a meal, except on Sabbaths or Festivals. At the beginning of the meal cut three measures of bread and refrain from eating more than this at that meal. And when you drink water, avoid fully satisfying your thirst.

14. Acquire the habit of always keeping your eyes cast downward so that you do not chance to gaze upon a woman who is forbidden to you.

15. Occupy your mind with thought of the Mishnah during a meal; when you have finished eating, study a chapter of the Mishnah prior to the recitation of the Grace after meals.

16. Do not cease thinking about Me [i.e., the Mishnah], even for the slightest moment, and limit your enjoyment. When you are eating and you desire to eat or drink still more, refrain from doing so. If you behave in this manner at every meal it will be tantamount to offering a sacrifice. Your table will serve as an actual altar upon which you slaughter the evil inclination.

17. Do not drink wine at a meal all at once and be careful when it comes to measuring it. Have no fear that this will diminish your eyesight. On the contrary, your eyesight will be strengthened as will your power.

18. Limit the pleasure which you receive from eating and drinking. And if you experience enjoyment while eating some particular food, refrain from eating it on a regular basis. Learn to eat something else from which you do not derive as much pleasure.

In the moral struggle, sexuality is a fundamental field of battle, for it brings the most basic instinctual needs up against the constraints of cultural norms. Halakhic tradition imposes upon all men the obligation to procreate within the setting of marriage. With sexual celibacy not available as a way of conquering sexual desire, it became necessary to channel sexual expression in such a way that the pleasure derived could be devoted to a divinely sanctioned end. Many medieval ethicists reflected deeply on this problem with conceptual tools provided by Kabbalah. The following selection is from a book about sexual life ascribed, probably erroneously, to the great thirteenth-century talmudist, Moses ben Nahman (Nahmanides).

13.2B THE HOLY LETTER

Intercourse is holy and clean when done when it is proper and the time is right and the intention right. Anyone who says that there is a taint and ugliness in inter-

Translated by Rachel Biale, *Women and Jewish Law* (New York: Schocken Books, 1984), p. 140.

course, God forbid such a view! For intercourse is called [in biblical Hebrew] knowing . . . and this is its hidden meaning. For a drop of seed, when it is brought out in holiness and purity brings down with it knowledge and wisdom from the brain. And it is well known that if it were not an act of great holiness intercourse would not have been called knowing. . . .

And it is clear that just like the hands, when they write a Torah scroll they are dignified and excellent and elevated but if they do an act of wickedness they are despicable and ugly. So also were the tools [organs] of intercourse to Adam and Eve before they sinned.

And this is the secret of knowledge which we are telling you about. Man is contained in the secret of wisdom, reason and knowledge. The man is wisdom, the woman is the secret of reason and pure intercourse is the secret of knowledge, therefore intercourse is an elevated and great thing when it is proper. . . . But when a man's intention is not pure, that same seed which he brings forth is only a smelly drop in which God has no part. . . .

The heritage of rabbinic and kabbalistic reflection upon the moral struggle reached rich expression on the nineteenth-century movements of Hasidism and Musar. In the first passage, the founder of the Habad-Lubavitch dynasty of Hasidism, Rabbi Shneur Zalman of Liady, reflects upon the conflict in the soul of anyone who strives to be what Rabbi Shneur Zalman terms an "intermediate man" (*benoni*), that is, a person who is neither wholly righteous nor wholly evil. The passage is from his classic work in hasidic ethics, *Tanya* ("We Have Learned"), first published in 1796.

13.2c TANYA, THE BOOK FOR THE INTERMEDIATES

The "intermediate man" (*benoni*) is he in whom evil never attains enough power to capture the "small city" (the heart), so as to clothe itself in the body and make it sin. That is to say, the three "garments" of the animal soul, namely, thought, speech and act, originating in the *kelipah* (the sefirotic source of evil), do not prevail within him over the divine soul to the extent of clothing themselves in the body—in the brain, in the mouth and in the other 248 organs—thereby causing them to sin and defiling them, God forbid. . . .

However, the essence and being of the divine soul, which are its ten faculties (corresponding to the Sefirot), do not constantly hold undisputed sovereignty and sway over the "small city," except at appropriate times, such as during the recital of the Shma or the Amidah, which is a time when the Supernal Intellect is in a sublime state; and likewise below, this is a propitious time for every man, when he binds his HaBaD faculties (i.e., the attributes of Wisdom, Understanding and Knowledge) to God, to meditate deeply on the greatness of the blessed Infinite, and to arouse the burning love in right part of his heart, to cleave to Him by virtue of the fulfillment of the Torah and its commandments out of love. . . . At such time

From Nissan Mindel, tr., *Likutei Amarim-Tanya: Bi-Lingual Edition* (Brooklyn, NY: Soncino Press, 1973), pp. 47–49.

the evil that is in the left part of the heart is subjected to, and nullified in, the goodness that is diffused in the right part, from the Wisdom, Understanding and Knowledge in the brain, which are bound to the greatness of the Infinite.

However, after prayer, when the state of sublimity of the Intellect of the blessed Infinite departs, the evil in the left part reawakens, and he begins to feel a desire for the lusts of the world and its delights. Yet, because the evil has not the sole authority and dominion over the "city," it is unable to carry out this desire from the potential into the actual. . . . because the brain rules over the heart . . . by virtue of its innately created nature. For this is how man is created from birth, that each person may, with the will-power in his brain, restrain himself and control the drive of lust that is in his heart, preventing his heart's desires from expressing themselves in action, word, or thought, and divert his attention altogether from the craving of his heart toward the completely opposite direction, particularly in the direction of holiness.

In contrast to Rabbi Shneur Zalman's confidence in the power of the will and intellect to conquer desire, the Musar movement, spawned by Rabbi Israel Salanter in the mid-nineteenth century, viewed the conscious will as a tool of powerful unconscious forces. These had to be mastered before the intellect could exert its power. Rabbi Salanter's introduction to his famous "Musar Letter" (*Iggerat HaMusar*) of 1858 captures this perspective.

13.2D MUSAR LETTER

Man is free in imagination, but fettered in intellect. His imagination leads him wildly by the heart of his desire, dauntless in the face of the certain future, the time when he will be chastised by severe judgments, no other will be taken captive on his account, he alone will bear the fruit of his iniquity, he is one who commits the crime and who is penalized for it. How bitter, man cannot say this is my sickness and I will endure it.

The earthly afflictions are lesser, vastly so, over against sin's punishments; the soul of man will loathe in full measure, a day will be reckoned as a year. Woe to the imagination, this evil enemy, it is of our own hands, it is in our power to make him remote.

Upon our lending an attentive ear to the intellect, to seek truthful, rational insight, to evaluate a sin's gain as against its loss; but what are we to do, the imagination is a flooding stream, and intellect will drown, unless we guide it in a ship, namely, the stirring of the soul and the rousing of the spirit.

This and following selection from Rabbi Israel Salanter, *Iggerat HaMusar* and *The Tree Bearing Fruit,* from H. Goldberg, translator, *Israel Salanter: Text, Structure, Idea.* Copyright © 1982. Reprinted with the permission of Ktav Publishing House, Inc.

The struggle of the moral person to identify the inner, concealed sources of even the most noble desires and actions is clearly framed by Rabbi Salanter in this passage from *The Tree Bearing Fruit,* a collection of writings published in 1881.

13.2E THE TREE BEARING FRUIT

Let us now explain the words of the Talmud, Tractate Sukkah 52a: "The Evil Urge appears to the righteous like a huge mountain, while to the wicked it appears like the thread of a hair. . . . The righteous weep, saying: How can we conquer such a huge mountain? And the wicked weep, saying: How is it possible that we cannot conquer such a thread of hair?"

Now to understand the Sages' words we must first consider what we find there: "Whoever is greater than his colleague, has a more powerful Evil Urge." It would appear, at first glance, to the contrary: that a righteous person who fears God has the desire to further improve himself. If so (contrary to the Sages) wouldn't the Evil Urge have been diminished within him? Nevertheless—we shall see that matters are otherwise.

Consider a person who does not fear (his inner, unconscious motives). The Evil Urge will first attach itself to external (i.e., conscious) motives in order to corrupt them, but it will pay little attention to inner motives. This is already written in the midrash: "The wicked are full of regrets. The reason for their regret is that external motives do not accumulate to take possession of a person. (Their desire to sin exists) only at the moment an object of desire is before them—as they said: "The eye sees and the heart desires." And therefore when the object of desire is gone and his external motives have calmed, at that moment are aroused the inner motives which have not been perverted, and they bring him to such profound regret that he wants to forsake the acts motivated by the external motives.

But in the case of a person who fears (his inner, unconscious, motives), the external motives appear impeccable. For this reason, the Evil Urge attempts first to effect its influence on the inner motives. And the more a man is righteous, the Urge will penetrate that much more deeply into his inwardness, and the person will not be aware of this or of the evil influences upon him.

But the person who fears (his inner motives) with a total wholeness will labor and prove himself through his laudatory external motives, most essentially through the gift of the Torah, in order to transform at its very root the Evil Urge which inhabits the inner motives, and to repair these inner motives, no matter how difficult this weighs upon one.

Now this is the point of stating that, to the wicked, the Evil Urge appears like a thread of hair, because (the purity of) his inner motives was never so perverted. Therefore, only a bit of stock-taking and study of Torah and Musar will enable him to awaken and strengthen the inner motives which will overcome the external motives and transform even them to good. But the righteous, whose inner motives have been perverted by the Evil Urge—he truly has his work cut out for him to use his laudable external motives alone in order to overpower the inner motives and to repair them. That is why they seem like an enormous mountain to him.

13.3 Moral Struggle Beyond the Halakhic Framework

There have been few more influential Jewish voices in modern religious thought than that of Martin Buber, the German Israeli social philosopher. Although Buber never succeeded in creating a Jewish community reflective of his own beliefs about the role of revelation in human experience, he continues to speak for many Jews who see traditional halakhic norms as incommensurate with an engaged religious existence. He articulated some of these views in a famous exchange of letters with his close friend and fellow theologian Franz Rosenzweig between 1922 and 1924. The reference to *The Builders* in the letters is to Rosenzweig's book on the role of halakhic tradition in modern Jewish religious renewal.

13.3A Buber to Rosenzweig, June 24, 1924

Dear Friend:

I hear that at first you had agreed to have *The Builders* published but then had reconsidered. I would like to recommend to you that you have it printed, no matter how it had originally been announced. I would prefer to have that epistle published by itself. . . . I agree with everything that follows from the letter's premises, but not to those premises themselves. It is my faith that prevents me from doing this. You know, my dear, that I do not use this word lightly, and yet here it is quite appropriate. I do not believe that *revelation* is ever a formulation of law. It is only through man in his self-contradiction that revelation becomes legislation. This is the fact of man. I cannot admit the law transformed by man into the realm of my will, if I am to hold myself ready as well for the unmediated word of God directed to a specific hour of my life.

It is part of my being that I cannot accept both [the Law and the word of God] together and I cannot imagine that his position will ever change for me. . . . I cannot approach the fact of the Law, nor even its concept except from the point of view of my faith. . . .

13.3B Buber to Rosenzweig, July 13, 1924

. . . I told you that for me, though man is a law-receiver, God is not a law-giver, and therefore the Law has no universal validity for me, but only a personal one. I accept, therefore, only what I think is being spoken to me (e.g., the older I become, and the more I realize the restlessness of my soul, the more I accept for myself the Day of Rest [Sabbath]). *The Builders* want to make me accept the Law as something universal, the way I accept the Teaching [Torah] as something to be learned in its totality. The analogy you suggest does not exist. You will realize indirectly that this is so when you consider that we can atone for what we have done, but not for what one has experienced. This indicates that the deed differs not only quantitatively

From Nahum Norbert Glatzer, tr., *Franz Rosenzweig: On Jewish Learning,* pp. 111, 115.

from experience, but qualitatively. You will realize this *directly* as well when you consider how different the two are in relation to the fact which concerns us here, the fact of the imperative, not the philosophical, but the divine and human one, for I am responsible for what I do or leave undone in a different way than for what I learn or leave unlearned. Therefore, the division between revelation and teaching (human teaching) is for me neither a thorn nor a trial, but that between revelation and law (human law) is both. . . .

In the twentieth century, Reform (or Liberal) Judaism has been the most vigorous proponent of an individualist ethic in defining Jews' obligations to the inherited halakhic tradition and a universalist ethic in defining the relation of Jews to the larger world. The contemporary theologian Eugene Borowitz has been the most articulate and widely read spokesman for these principles in the American Reform community.

13.3c LIBERAL JUDAISM

If, then, caring Reform Jews inquire about their religious responsibilities or . . . if they ask whether "they must do all the commandments and traditions," the answer is simple but indirect. As honest people, they must do whatever follows from their Jewish religious beliefs. Thus, their obligations in matter of prayer and ritual will directly flow from whatever modern understanding of God they accept. As Jews, they do not serve God in lonely solitude but as a member of the Jewish people. Now their belief in the people of Israel's relation to God comes into play. What mix of ethnicity and religion do they think best expresses its character? What, if any, uniqueness do they ascribe to its ancient alliance with God? And to all such questions must be added their view of Torah, in the broad sense. Does God "speak" to us as God did to the prophets or did they or do we have qualitatively superior levels of insight? And what weight do we assign to Jewish tradition in our religious life—almost compelling, highly instructive, significant, or merely advisory? . . .

Of course you should live as a self-determining person. Your freedom to choose what you will do is the precious premise of your humanhood, and your modernity consists mainly in acknowledging and acting upon it. As moderns who are Jews, we are called upon to use our freedom in terms of "the claims of Jewish tradition" upon us, for we are part of our people's millennial relationship with God. . . . Not everyone will read the Jewish tradition the same way and thus "hear" the same call being made to them. We are too individualistic for that and it is too complex for such uniformity. We should then approach it and decide out of the depth of "knowledge" which befits a significant decision. We should also do so in terms of our deepest "commitment" for, when we ask about religious duties, we are speaking of the service of God. Then whatever we choose from the past or create for the present should rest upon us with the full force of commandment. For only by being false to ourselves and to what we believe will we be able to ignore or transgress it. . . .

By the 1980's the almost total identification of Jewish ethics with the agenda of liberal politics had ended. Two major shifts in attitude had produced differing views about Jewish social responsibility.

The first of these arose out of disenchantment with government as a moral leader. . . . The ills perpetrated by government programs, from creating dependency in the needy to building immobile bureaucracies, have not infrequently offset or overbalanced their successes.

The second change in Jewish attitudes came with the rise of an urgent sense of self-interest: If the Jewish community did not give primary attention to its own problems, its survival might be in doubt. One major reason for this new particularism was the perilous situation of the State of Israel. Without sustained, heavy American Jewish support, the Israelis would find it most difficult to maintain a viable country. Practically speaking, energies summoned in this commanding ethnic cause would not be available for universal social programs. . . .

The internal aspect of this new self-concern was the community's anxiety about its own future. The symptoms of its failing health were immediately evident: a high rate of intermarriage, a low rate of reproduction, static or declining institutional involvement, and widespread ignorance, apathy, and indifference. Externally, American culture no longer offered anything like salvation, and the increase in anti-semitic incidents and intergroup distance impelled Jews to search for their roots. A sizable minority of Jews began giving Judaism increased priority in their lives. Some particularists now demanded . . . that Jewish energies be exclusively devoted to Jewish causes. Others counseled a pragmatic strategy: participating in universal causes only as required to maintain our political alliances and keep us from bad repute. On the whole, now new community consensus has emerged. . . .

This ambivalent situation is unlikely soon to disappear. Contemporary liberal Judaism affirms both the universal God and the particular people Covenanted to God. We remain devotedly liberal because we personally are living testimony to the human benefits that come from actualizing universal ethics. As supreme beneficiaries of democracy, we have a special responsibility to be involved in the solution of its problems. We are also devoted Jews. The survival of our people must be one of our highest priorities. Whatever we can do for humankind must begin with our efforts to see that our own people flourishes. Yet our people's vision has always transcended its own well-being. Most Jewish generations could do little directly to contribute to this greater goal. Jews in democratic lands have an unparalleled Jewish opportunity to make our idealism felt in our nations and among humankind as a whole. We cannot say simply how Jews ought to face those social choices which seem to pit their loyalty to their people against that to humankind. Yet we know that we will not be true to the special situation in which God has placed us if we do not make the human issues of our age a major part of our Jewish duty.

ETHICS

CHAPTER 14
IN CHRISTIANITY

14.1 FAITH, WORKS, AND THE WORLD IN EARLY CHRISTIAN HISTORY

Whereas the Gospels approach ethical questions with broad brush strokes, Paul's letters are filled with specific and even minute details. Paul, the former Pharisee, used letters to teach, inspire, admonish, answer questions, and quell disputes among the Christian communities he had helped to establish throughout the eastern Mediterranean. Various aspects of Christian behavior are directly addressed by Paul in these passages. Whether or not his advice was followed within these communities is immaterial, for his opinions became timeless and universally binding as soon as his letters became holy writ for the Christian churches.

14.1A PAUL'S LETTERS, ROMANS 12–13

Exhortation

Spiritual Worship

Think of God's mercy, my brothers, and worship him, I beg you, in a way that is worthy of thinking beings, by offering your living bodies as a holy sacrifice, truly pleasing to God. Do not model yourselves on the behavior of the world around you, but let your behavior change, modeled by your new mind. This is the only way to discover the will of God and know what is good, what it is that God wants, what is the perfect thing to do.

Humility and Charity

In the light of the grace I have received I want to urge each one among you not to exaggerate his real importance. Each of you must judge himself soberly by the standard of the faith God has given him. Just as each of our bodies has several parts and each part has a separate function, so all of us, in union with Christ, form one body, and as parts of it we belong to each other. Our gifts differ according to the grace given us. If your gift is prophecy, then use it as your faith suggests; if administration, then use it for administration; if teaching, then use it for teaching. Let the preachers deliver sermons, the almsgivers give freely, the officials be diligent, and those who do works of mercy do them cheerfully.

Do not let your love be a pretense, but sincerely prefer good to evil. Love each other as much as brothers should, and have a profound respect for each other. Work for the Lord with untiring effort and with great earnestness of spirit. If you have hope, this will make you cheerful. Do not give up if trials come; and keep on praying. If any of the saints are in need you must share with them; and you should make hospitality your special care.

Charity to Everyone, Including Enemies

Bless those who persecute you: never curse them, bless them. Rejoice with those who rejoice and be sad with those in sorrow. Treat everyone with equal kindness; never be condescending but make real friends with the poor. Do not allow yourself to become self-satisfied. Never repay evil with evil but let everyone see that you are interested only in the highest ideals. Do all you can to live at peace with everyone. Never try to get revenge; leave that, my friends, to God's anger. As scripture says: *Vengeance is mine—I will pay them back,* the Lord promises. But there is more: *If your enemy is hungry, you should give him food, and if he is thirsty, let him drink. Thus you heap red-hot coals on his head.* Resist evil and conquer it with good.

Submission to Civil Authority

You must all obey the governing authorities. Since all government comes from God, the civil authorities were appointed by God, and so anyone who resists authority is rebelling against God's decision, and such an act is bound to be punished. Good behavior is not afraid of magistrates; only criminals have anything to fear. If you want to live without being afraid of authority, you must live honestly and authority may even honor you. The state is there to serve God for your benefit. If you break the law, however, you may well have fear: the bearing of the sword has its significance. The authorities are there to serve God: they carry out God's revenge by punishing wrongdoers. You must obey, therefore, not only because you are afraid of being punished, but also for conscience' sake. This is also the reason why you must pay taxes, since all government officials are God's officers. They serve God by collecting taxes. Pay every government official what he has a right to ask—whether it be direct tax or indirect, fear or honor.

Love and Law

Avoid getting into debt, except the debt of mutual love. If you love your fellow men you have carried out your obligations. All the commandments: *You shall not commit adultery, you shall not kill, you shall not steal, you shall not covet,* and so on, are summed up in this single command: *You must love your neighbor as yourself.* Love is the one thing that cannot hurt your neighbor; that is why it is the answer to every one of the commandments.

Children of the Light

Besides, you know "the time" has come: you must wake up now: our salvation is even nearer than it was when we were converted. The night is almost over, it will be daylight soon—let us give up all the things we prefer to do under cover of the dark; let us arm ourselves and appear in the light. Let us live decently as people do in the daytime: no drunken orgies, no promiscuity or licentiousness, and no wrangling or jealousy. Let your armor be the Lord Jesus Christ; forget about satisfying your bodies with all their cravings. . . .

14.1B I CORINTHIANS 5:9–5:13; 6:9–6:20; 7:1–7:16; 7:25–7:30; 13:1–13:13

When I wrote in my letter to you not to associate with people living immoral lives, I was not meaning to include all the people in the world who are sexually immoral, any more than I meant to include all usurers and swindlers or idol worshipers. To do that, you would have to withdraw from the world altogether. What I wrote was that you should not associate with a brother Christian who is leading an immoral life, or is a usurer, or idolatrous, or a slanderer, or a drunkard, or is dishonest; you should not even eat a meal with people like that. It is not my business to pass judgment on those outside. Of those who are inside, you can surely be the judges. But of those who are outside, God is the judge.
You must drive out this evildoer from among you. . . .
You know perfectly well that people who do wrong will not inherit the kingdom of God: people of immoral lives, idolaters, adulterers, catamites, sodomites, thieves, usurers, drunkards, slanderers and swindlers will never inherit the kingdom of God. These are the sort of people some of you were once, but now you have been washed clean, and sanctified, and justified through the name of the Lord Jesus Christ and through the Spirit of our God.
"For me there are no forbidden things"; maybe, but not everything does good. I agree there are no forbidden things for me, but I am not going to let anything dominate me. Food is only meant for the stomach, and the stomach for food:

yes, and God is going to do away with both of them. But the body—this is not meant for fornication; it is for the Lord, and the Lord for the body. God, who raised the Lord from the dead, will by his power raise us up too.

You know, surely, that your bodies are members making up the body of Christ; do you think I can take parts of Christ's body and join them to the body of a prostitute? Never! As you know, a man who goes with a prostitute is one body with her, since *the two,* as it is said, *become one flesh.* But anyone who is joined to the Lord is one spirit with him.

Keep away from fornication. All the other sins are committed outside the body; but to fornicate is to sin against your own body. Your body, you know, is the temple of the Holy Spirit, who is in you since you received him from God. You are not your own property; You have been bought and paid for. That is why you should use your body for the glory of God.

Now for the questions about which you wrote. Yes, it is a good thing for a man not to touch a woman; but since sex is always a danger, let each man have his own wife and each woman her own husband. The husband must give his wife what she has the right to expect, and so too the wife to the husband. The wife has no rights over her own body; it is the husband who has them. In the same way, the husband has no rights over his body; the wife has them. Do not refuse each other except by mutual consent, and then only for an agreed time, to leave yourselves free for prayer; then come together again in case Satan should take advantage of your weakness to tempt you. This is a suggestion, not a rule: I should like everyone to be like me, but everybody has his own particular gifts from God, one with a gift for one thing and another with a gift for the opposite.

There is something I want to add for the sake of widows and those who are not married: it is a good thing for them to stay as they are, like me, but if they cannot control the sexual urges, they should get married, since it is better to be married than to be tortured.

For the married I have something to say, and this is not from me but from the Lord: a wife must not leave her husband—or if she does leave him, she must either remain unmarried or else make it up with her husband—nor must a husband send his wife away.

The rest is from me and not from the Lord. If a brother has a wife who is an unbeliever, and she is content to live with him, he must not send her away; and if a woman has an unbeliever for her husband, and he is content to live with her, she must not leave him. This is because the unbelieving husband is made one with the saints through his wife, and the unbelieving wife is made one with the saints through her husband. If this were not so, your children would be unclean, whereas in fact they are holy. However, if the unbelieving partner does not consent, they may separate; in these circumstances, the brother or sister is not tied: God has called you to a life of peace. If you are a wife, it may be your part to save your husband, for all you know; if a husband, for all you know, it may be your part to save your wife. . . .

About remaining celibate, I have no directions from the Lord but give my own opinion as one who, by the Lord's mercy, has stayed faithful. Well then, I believe that in these present times of stress this is right: that it is good for a man to stay as he is. If you are tied to a wife, do not look for freedom; if you are free of a wife, then do not look for one. But if you marry, it is no sin, and it is not a sin for a young girl to get married. They will have their troubles, though, in their married life, and I should like to spare you that.

Brothers, this is what I mean: our time is growing short. Those who have wives should live as though they had none, and those who mourn should live as though they had nothing to mourn for; those who are enjoying life should live as though there were nothing to laugh about; those whose life is buying things should live as though they had nothing of their own; and those who have to deal with the world should not become engrossed in it. I say this because the world as we know it is passing away. . . .

If I have all the eloquence of men or of angels, but speak without love, I am simply a gong booming or a cymbal clashing. If I have the gift of prophecy, understanding all the mysteries there are, and knowing everything, and if I have faith in all its fullness, to move mountains, but without love, then I am nothing at all. If I give away all that I possess, piece by piece, and if I even let them take my body to burn it, but am without love, it will do me no good whatever.

Love is always patient and kind: it is never jealous; love is never boastful or conceited; it is never rude or selfish; it does not take offense, and is not resentful. Love takes no pleasure in other people's sins but delights in the truth; it is always ready to excuse, to trust, to hope, and to endure whatever comes.

Love does not come to an end. But if there are gifts of prophecy, the time will come when they must fail; or the gift of languages, it will not continue for ever; and knowledge—for this, too, the time will come when it must fail. For our knowledge is imperfect and our prophesying is imperfect; but once perfection comes, all imperfect things will disappear. When I was a child, I used to talk like a child, and think like a child, and argue like a child, but now I am a man, all childish ways are put behind me. Now we are seeing a dim reflection in a mirror; but then we shall be seeing face to face. The knowledge that I have now is imperfect; but then I shall know as fully as I am known.

In short, there are three things that last: faith, hope and love; and the greatest of these is love.

14.1C EPHESIANS 4:1–4:6; 4:17–5:20; 6:10–6:20

A Call to Unity

I, the prisoner in the Lord, implore you therefore to lead a life worthy of your vocation. Bear with one another charitably, in complete selflessness, gentleness and patience. Do all you can to preserve the unity of the Spirit by the peace that binds you together. There is one Body, one Spirit, just as you were all called into one and the same hope when you were called. There is one Lord, one faith, one baptism, and one God who is Father of all, over all, through all and within all. . . .

The New Life in Christ

In particular, I want to urge you in the name of the Lord, not to go on living the aimless kind of life that pagans live. Intellectually they are in the dark, and they are estranged from the life of God, without knowledge because they have shut their hearts to it. Their sense of right and wrong once dulled, they have abandoned themselves to sexuality and eagerly pursue a career of indecency of every kind. Now that is hardly the way you have learned from Christ, unless you failed to hear him properly when you were taught what the truth is in Jesus. You must give up your old way of life; you must put aside your old self, which gets corrupted by following illusory desires. Your mind must be renewed by a spiritual revolution so that you can put on the new self that has been created in God's way, in the goodness and holiness of the truth.

So from now on, there must be no more lies: *You must speak the truth to one another*, since we are all parts of one another. *Even if you are angry, you must not sin;* never let the sun set on your anger or else you will give the devil a foothold. Anyone who was a thief must stop stealing; he should try to find some useful manual work instead, and be able to do some good by helping others that are in need. Guard against foul talk; let your words be for the improvement of others, as occasion offers, and do good to your listeners, otherwise you will only be grieving the Holy Spirit of God who has marked you with his seal for you to be set free when the day comes. Never have grudges against others, or lose your temper, or raise your voice to anybody, or call each other names, or allow any sort of spitefulness. Be friends with one another, and kind, forgiving each other as readily as God forgave you in Christ.

Try, then, to imitate God, as children of his that he loves, and follow Christ by loving as he loved you, giving himself up in our place *as a fragrant offering and a sacrifice to God*. Among you there must be not even a mention of fornication or impurity in any of its forms, or promiscuity; this would hardly become the saints! There must be no coarseness or salacious talk and jokes—all this is wrong for you; raise your voices in thanksgiving instead. For you can be quite certain that nobody who actually indulges in fornication or impurity or promiscuity—which is worshiping a false god—can inherit anything of the kingdom of God. Do not let anyone deceive you with empty arguments: it is for this loose living that God's anger comes down on those who rebel against him. Make sure that you are not included with them. You were darkness once, but now you are light in the Lord; be like children of light, for the effects of the light are seen in complete goodness and right living and truth. Try to discover what the Lord wants of you, having nothing to do with the futile works of darkness but exposing them by contrast. The things which are done in secret are things that people are ashamed even to speak of; but anything exposed by the light will be illuminated and anything illuminated turns into light. That is why it is said:

> Wake up from your sleep,
> rise from the dead,
> and Christ will shine on you.

So be very careful about the sort of lives you lead, like intelligent and not like senseless people. This may be a wicked age, but your lives should redeem it. And do not be thoughtless but recognize what is the will of the Lord. Do not drug yourselves with wine; this is simply dissipation: be filled with the Spirit. Sing the words and tunes of the psalms and hymns when you are together, and go on singing and chanting to the Lord in your hearts, so that always and everywhere you are giving thanks to God who is our Father in the name of our Lord Jesus Christ. . . .

The Spiritual War

Finally, grow strong in the Lord, with the strength of his power. Put God's armor on so as to be able to resist the devil's tactics. For it is not against human enemies that we have to struggle, but against the Sovereignties and the Powers who originate the darkness in this world, the spiritual army of evil in the heavens. That is why you must rely on God's armor, or you will not be able to put up any resistance when the worst happens, or have enough resources to hold your ground. . . .

Pray all the time, asking for what you need, praying in the Spirit on every possible occasion. Never get tired of staying awake to pray for all the saints; and pray for me to be given an opportunity to open my mouth and speak without fear and give out the mystery of the gospel of which I am an ambassador in chains; pray that in proclaiming it I may speak as boldly as I ought to.

Traditionally attributed to the apostle James, who was related to Jesus, this letter appears to have been written for a Jewish Christian community in the late fifties CE. The bulk of this epistle is dedicated to moral exhortation, with a heavy emphasis on the virtuous loving behavior demanded of Christians. Whereas Paul had emphasized a dichotomy between Law and Gospel, works and faith, James here stresses their interrelatedness. Martin Luther, who preferred to interpret the whole Bible through Paul, dismissed *James* as an "epistle of straw" because of its accent on the good works demanded of Christians.

14.1D THE LETTER OF JAMES 1:1–1:4; 1:13–2:4; 2:14–2:25; 5:1–5:10

Address and Greetings

From James, servant of God and of the Lord Jesus Christ. Greetings to the twelve tribes of the Dispersion.

Trials a Privilege

My brothers, you will always have your trials but, when they come, try to treat them as a happy privilege; you understand that your faith is only put to the test to make you patient, but patience too is to have its practical results so that you will become fully developed, complete, with nothing missing. . . .

Never, when you have been tempted, say, "God sent the temptation"; God cannot be tempted to do anything wrong, and he does not tempt anybody. Everyone who is tempted is attracted and seduced by his own wrong desire. Then the desire conceives and gives birth to sin, and when sin is fully grown, it too has a child, and the child is death.

Make no mistake about this, my dear brothers: it is all that is good, everything that is perfect, which is given us from above; it comes down from the Father of all light; with him there is no such thing as alteration, no shadow of a change. By his own choice he made us his children by the message of the truth so that we should be a sort of first fruits of all that he had created.

True Religion

Remember this, my dear brothers: be *quick to listen* but *slow* to speak and slow to rouse your temper; God's righteousness is never served by man's anger; so do away with all the impurities and bad habits that are still left in you—accept and submit to the word which has been planted in you and can save your souls. But you must do what the word tells you, and not just listen to it and deceive yourselves. To listen to the word and not obey is like looking at your own features in a mirror and then, after a quick look, going off and immediately forgetting what you looked like. But the man who looks steadily at the perfect law of freedom and makes that his habit—not listening and then forgetting, but actively putting it into practice—will be happy in all that he does.

Nobody must imagine that he is religious while he still goes on deceiving himself and not keeping control over his tongue; anyone who does this has the wrong idea of religion. Pure, unspoiled religion, in the eyes of God our Father is this: coming to the help of orphans and widows when they need it, and keeping oneself uncontaminated by the world.

Respect for the Poor

My brothers, do not try to combine faith in Jesus Christ, our glorified Lord, with the making of distinctions between classes of people. Now suppose a man comes into your synagogue, beautifully dressed and with a gold ring on, and at the same time a poor man comes in, in shabby clothes, and you take notice of the well-dressed man, and say, "Come this way to the best seats"; then you tell the poor man, "Stand over there" or "You can sit on the floor by my footrest." Can't you see that you have used two different standards in your mind, and turned yourselves into judges, and corrupt judges at that? . . .

Talk and behave like people who are going to be judged by the law of freedom, because there will be judgment without mercy for those who have not been merciful themselves; but the merciful need have no fear of judgment.

Faith and Good Works

Take the case, my brothers, of someone who has never done a single good act but claims that he has faith. Will that faith save him? If one of the brothers or one of the sisters is in need of clothes and has not enough food to live on, and one of you says to them, "I wish you well; keep yourself warm and eat plenty," without giving them these bare necessities of life, then what good is that? Faith is like that: if good works do not go with it, it is quite dead.

This is the way to talk to people of that kind: "You say you have faith and I have good deeds; I will prove to you that I have faith by showing you my good deeds—now you prove to me that you have faith without any good deeds to show. You believe in the one God—that is creditable enough, but the demons have the same belief, and they tremble with fear. Do realize, you senseless man, that faith without good deeds is useless. You surely know that Abraham our father was justified by his deed, because he *offered his son Isaac on the altar?* There you see it: faith and deeds were working together; his faith became perfect by what he did. This is what scripture really means when it says: *Abraham put his faith in God, and this was counted as making him justified;* and that is why he was called "the friend of God."

You see now that it is by doing something good, and not only by believing, that a man is justified. . . .

Now an answer for the rich. Start crying, weep for the miseries that are coming to you. Your wealth is all rotting, your clothes are all eaten up by moths. All your gold and your silver are corroding away, and the same corrosion will be your own sentence, and eat into your body. It was a burning fire that you stored up as your treasure for the last days. Laborers mowed your fields, and you cheated them—listen to the wages that you kept back, calling out: realize that the cries of the reapers have reached the ears of the Lord of hosts. On earth you have had a life of comfort and luxury; in the time of slaughter you went on eating to your heart's content. It was you who condemned the innocent and killed them; they offered you no resistance.

A Final Exhortation

Now be patient, brothers, until the Lord's coming. Think of a farmer: how patiently he waits for the precious fruit of the ground until it has had the autumn rains and the spring rains! You too have to be patient; do not lose heart, because the Lord's coming will be soon. Do not make complaints against one another, brothers, so as not to be brought to judgment yourselves; the Judge is already to be seen waiting at the gates.

14.2 Christians Versus "The World"

During the first three centuries of their existence, Christians embraced an ethic of martyrdom by necessity. Suffering and dying for one's faith became a multidimensional act, heavily laden with symbolic sacrificial meaning; and it also became the ultimate imitation of Christ. Early Christians embraced martyrdom as the most conclusive proof of salvation and as the surest road to heaven. Ignatius, bishop of Antioch, wrote this impassioned discourse on his own impending martyrdom around 107 CE. Here we can see clearly—and more vividly than in most other documents—how a dualistic understanding of the relation between "this world" and God's could lead Christians to long for a horrific death.

14.2A IGNATIUS OF ANTIOCH, LETTER TO THE ROMANS

I shall coax them [the beasts] on to eat me up at once and not to hold off, as sometimes happens, through fear. And if they are reluctant, I shall force them to it. Forgive me—I know what is good for me. Now is the moment I am beginning to be a disciple. May nothing seen or unseen begrudge me making my way to Jesus Christ. Come fire, cross, battling with wild beasts, wrenching of bones, mangling of limbs, crushing of my whole body, cruel tortures of the devil—only let me get to Jesus Christ! Not the wide bounds of earth nor the kingdoms of this world will avail me anything. "I would rather die" and get to Jesus Christ, than reign over the ends of the earth. That is whom I am looking for—the One who died for us. That is whom I want—the One who rose for us. I am going through the pangs of being born. Sympathize with me, my brothers! Do not stand in the way of my coming to life—do not wish death on me. Do not give back to the world one who wants to be God's; do not trick him with material things. Let me get into the clear light and manhood will be mine. Let me imitate the Passion of my God. If anyone has Him in him, let him appreciate what I am longing for, and sympathize with me, realizing what I am going through.

The prince of this world wants to kidnap me and pervert my godly purpose. None of you, then, who will be there, must abet him. Rather be on my side—that is, on God's. Do not talk Jesus Christ and set your heart on the world. Harbor no envy. If, when I arrive, I make a different plea, pay no attention to me. Rather heed what I am now writing to you. For though alive, it is with a passion for death that I am writing to you. My Desire has been crucified and there burns in me no passion for material things. There is living water in me, which speaks and says inside me, "Come to the Father." I take no delight in corruptible food or in the dainties of this life. What I want is God's bread, which is the flesh of Christ, who came from David's line; and for drink I want his blood: an immortal love feast indeed!

I do not want to live any more on a human plane. And so it shall be, if you want it to. Want it to, so that you will be wanted! . . . It is not that I want merely to be called a Christian, but actually to *be* one. Yes, if I prove to be one, then I can have the name. Then, too, I shall be a convincing Christian only when the world sees me no more. Nothing you can see has real value. Our God Jesus Christ, indeed, has

From Ignatius of Antioch, Letter to the Romans, from Cyril Richardson, *Early Christian Fathers.* Reprinted with the permission of Westminster John Knox Press.

revealed himself more clearly by returning to the Father. The greatness of Christianity lies in its being hated by the world, not in its being convincing to it.

I am corresponding with all the churches and bidding them all realize that I am voluntarily dying for God—if, that is, you do not interfere. I plead with you, do not do me an unseasonable kindness. Let me be fodder for wild beasts—that is how I can get to God. I am God's wheat and I am being ground by the teeth of wild beasts to make a pure loaf for Christ. I would rather that you fawn on the beasts so that they may be my tomb and no scrap of my body be left. Thus, when I have fallen asleep, I shall be a burden to no one. Then I shall be I real disciple of Jesus Christ when the world sees my body no more. Pray Christ for me that by these means I may become God's sacrifice. I do not give you orders like Peter and Paul. They were apostles: I am a convict. They were at liberty: I am still a slave. But if I suffer, I shall be emancipated by Jesus Christ; and united to him, I shall rise to freedom.

Even now as a prisoner, I am learning to forgo my own wishes. All the way from Syria to Rome I am fighting with wild beasts, by land and sea, night and day, chained as I am to ten leopards (I mean to a detachment of soldiers), who only get worse the better you treat them. But by their injustices I am becoming a better disciple, "though not for that reason am I acquitted." What a thrill I shall have from the wild beasts that are ready for me! I hope they will make short work of me.

14.3 Christians Versus Popular Culture

Separation from "the world" was not an abstract concept for Christians, especially when they were outlawed and persecuted by the state. All sorts of practical questions came to the fore: Should Christians wear wigs or use cosmetics? Should Christians attend the spectacles of the Roman circus or the theater? One Christian community, the Montanists, held the extreme view that Christians should not mingle with the rest of world at all. Convinced as they were that the apocalypse was near, Montanists refused to compromise more intensely than orthodox Christians. In this selection by Tertullian (ca. 160–225), who became a Montanist, we can see this particular strain of Christian ethical reasoning at work. It should be noted that Tertullian's rigorous views on this particular issue were not all that different from those of orthodox Christian leaders.

14.3a Tertullian, *On Pagan Shows*

In how many other ways shall we yet further show that nothing which is peculiar to the shows has God's approval, or without that approval is becoming in God's servants? If we have succeeded in making it plain that they were instituted entirely for the devil's sake, and have been got up entirely with the devil's things (for

From Tertullian, *On Pagan Shows,* in George W. Forell, ed., *Christian Social Teachings* (New York: Doubleday, 1966). Copyright © 1966 by George W. Forell.

all that is not God's, or is not pleasing in His eyes, belongs to His wicked rival), this simply means that in them you have that pomp of the devil which in the "seal" of our faith we abjure. But we should have no connection with the things which we abjure, whether in deed or word, whether by looking on them or looking forward to them. But do we not abjure and rescind that baptismal pledge, when we cease to bear its testimony? Does it then remain for us to apply to the heathens themselves? Let them tell us, then, whether it is right in Christians to frequent the show. Why, the rejection of these amusements is the chief sign to them that a man has adopted the Christian faith. If any one, then, puts away the faith's distinctive badge, he is plainly guilty of denying it. What hope can you possibly retain in regard to a man who does that? When you go over to the enemy's camp, you throw down your arms, desert the standards and the oath of allegiance to your chief: you cast in your lot for life or death with your new friends.

Seated where there is nothing of God, will one be thinking of his Maker? Will there be peace in his soul when there is eager strife there for a charioteer? Wrought up into a frenzied excitement, will he learn to be modest? Nay, in the whole thing he will meet with no greater temptation than that gay attiring of the men and women. The very intermingling of emotions, the very agreements and disagreements with each other in the bestowment of their favours, where you have such close communion, blow up the sparks of passion. And then there is scarce any other object in going to the show, but to see and to be seen. When a tragic actor is declaiming, will one be giving thought to prophetic appeals? Amid the measures of the effeminate player, will he call up to himself a psalm? And when the athletes are hard at struggle, will he be ready to proclaim that there must be no striking again? And with his eye fixed on the bites of bears, and the sponge-nets of the net-fighters, can he be moved by compassion? May God avert from His people any such passionate eagerness after a cruel enjoyment! For how monstrous it is to go from God's church to the devil's—from the sky to the stye, as they say; to raise your hands to God, and then to weary them in the applause of an actor; out of the mouth, from which you uttered Amen over the Holy Thing, to give witness in a gladiator's favour; to cry "for ever" to any one else but God and Christ!

Why may not those who go into the temptations of the show become accessible also to evil spirits? We have the case of the woman—the Lord Himself is witness—who went to the theatre, and came back possessed. In the out-casting, accordingly, when the unclean creature was upbraided with having dared to attack a believer, he firmly replied, "And in truth I did it most righteously, for I found her in my domain." Another case, too, is well known in which a woman had been hearing a tragedian, and on the very night she saw in her sleep a linen cloth—the actor's name being mentioned at the same time with strong disapproval—and five days after that woman was no more. How many other undoubted proofs we have had in the case of persons who, by keeping company with the devil in the shows, have fallen from the Lord! For no one can serve two masters. What fellowship has light with darkness, life with death?

We ought to detest these heathen meetings and assemblies, if on no other account than that there God's name is blasphemed—that there the cry "To the lions!"

is daily raised against us—that from thence persecuting decrees are wont to emanate, and temptations are sent forth. What will you do if you are caught in that
heaving tide of impious judgments? Not that there any harm is likely to come
to you from men: nobody knows that you are a Christian; but think how it fares
with you in heaven. For at the very time the devil is working havoc in the church,
do you doubt that the angels are looking down from above, and marking every
man, who speaks and who listens to the blaspheming word, who lends his tongue
and who lends his ears to the service of Satan against God? Shall you not then shun
those tiers where the enemies of Christ assemble, that seat of all that is pestilential,
and the very superincumbent atmosphere all impure with wicked cries? . . .

We cannot sit down in fellowship with them, as neither can they with us.
Things in this matter go by their turns. Now they have gladness and we are troubled. "The World," says Jesus, "shall rejoice; ye shall be sorrowful." Let us mourn,
then, while the heathen are merry, that in the day of their sorrow we may rejoice;
lest, sharing now in their gladness, we share then also in their grief.

14.4 Salvation by Faith Alone

An Augustinian monk, Martin Luther eventually rejected monasticism itself and
much of medieval Christian ethical thinking. Influenced by Augustine in his interpretation of Paul's *Romans* and *Galatians,* Luther became convinced that no human
being could ever become truly holy in the sight of God, much less do any works
that would *merit* salvation. The central theological insight of Luther's Reformation
was that one was saved by faith alone, not by good works. In other words, Luther
taught that God accepted no one to salvation because they had *cooperated* with his
gift of grace and become virtuous; on the contrary, even the most seemingly holy
Christians were always stained by sin and truly worthy of damnation in the eyes
of God. Salvation meant being accepted by God in spite of the fact that one was always a vile sinner. How to turn this insight into practical ethical advice was one of
Luther's greatest challenges. In this letter to one of his former students who suffered from a deep depression and its accompanying feelings of guilt and worth-
lessness, Luther lays bare the paradoxical nature of salvation by faith alone and is
willing to go out on a pastoral limb.

14.4a Martin Luther, *Letter to Jerome Weller*

Grace and peace in Christ.

My dear Jerome:

You must believe that this temptation of yours is of the devil, who vexes you
so because you believe in Christ. You see how contented and happy he permits the

From Martin Luther, *Letter to Jerome Weller*, in *Letters of Spiritual Counsel.* Reprinted with the permission
of Westminster John Knox Press.

worst enemies of the gospel to be. Just think of Eck,[1] Zwingli,[2] and others. It is necessary for all of us who are Christians to have the devil as an adversary and enemy; as Saint Peter says, "Your adversary, the devil, walketh about."[3]

Excellent Jerome, you ought to rejoice in this temptation of the devil because it is a certain sign that God is propitious and merciful to you. You say that the temptation is heavier than you can bear, and that you fear that it will so break and beat you down as to drive you to despair and blasphemy. I know this wile of the devil. If he cannot break a person with his first attack, he tries by persevering to wear him out and weaken him until the person falls and confesses himself beaten. Whenever this temptation comes to you, avoid entering upon a disputation with the devil and do not allow yourself to dwell on those deadly thoughts, for to do so is nothing short of yielding to the devil and letting him have his way. Try as hard as you can to despise those thoughts which are induced by the devil. In this sort of temptation and struggle, contempt is the best and easiest method of winning over the devil. Laugh your adversary to scorn and ask who it is with whom you are talking. By all means flee solitude, for the devil watches and lies in wait for you most of all when you are alone. This devil is conquered by mocking and despising him, not by resisting and arguing with him. Therefore, Jerome, joke and play games with my wife and others. In this way you will drive out your diabolical thoughts and take courage.

This temptation is more necessary to you than food and drink. Let me remind you what happened to me when I was about your age. When I first entered the monastery it came to pass that I was sad and downcast, nor could I lay aside my melancholy. On this account I made confession to and took counsel with Dr. Staupitz (a man I gladly remember)[4] and opened to him what horrible and terrible thoughts I had. Then said he: "Don't you know, Martin, that this temptation is useful and necessary to you? God does not exercise you thus without reason. You will see that he intends to use you as his servant to accomplish great things." And so it turned out. I was made a great doctor (for I may with propriety say this of myself) although at the time when I suffered this temptation I never would have believed it possible. I have no doubt that this will happen to you too. You will become a great man. Just see to it that you are of good courage in the meantime, and be persuaded that such utterances, especially those which fall from the lips of learned and great men, are not without prophetic quality.

I remember that a certain man whom I once comforted on the loss of his son said to me, "Wait and see, Martin, you will become a great man." I have often thought of these words, for, as I have said, such utterances have something of a prophetic quality. Be of good courage, therefore, and cast these dreadful thoughts out of your mind. Whenever the devil pesters you with these thoughts, at once

---

[1] John Eck (1486–1543), a leading Catholic opponent of Luther.

[2] The Swiss Reformer, Huldreich Zwingli (1484–1531), had been locking horns with Luther over the interpretation of Holy Communion.

[3] I Peter 5:8.

[4] Luther frequently referred with commendation to the help he received in the monastery from the Augustinian vicar-general John von Staupitz (d. 1524).

seek out the company of men, drink more, joke and jest, or engage in some other form of merriment. Sometimes it is necessary to drink a little more, play, jest, or even commit some sin in defiance and contempt of the devil in order not to give him an opportunity to make us scrupulous about trifles. We shall be overcome if we worry too much about falling into some sin.

Accordingly if the devil should say, "Do not drink," you should reply to him, "On this very account, because you forbid it, I shall drink, and what is more, I shall drink a generous amount." Thus one must always do the opposite of that which Satan prohibits. What do you think is my reason for drinking wine undiluted, talking freely, and eating more often if it is not to torment and vex the devil who made up his mind to torment and vex me? Would that I could commit some token sin simply for the sake of mocking the devil, so that he might understand that I acknowledge no sin and am conscious of no sin. When the devil attacks and torments us, we must completely set aside the whole Decalogue. When the devil throws our sins up to us and declares that we deserve death and hell, we ought to speak thus: "I admit that I deserve death and hell. What of it? Does this mean that I shall be sentenced to eternal damnation? By no means. For I know One who suffered and made satisfaction in my behalf. His name is Jesus Christ, the Son of God. Where he is, there I shall be also."

Yours,
Martin Luther.

14.5 SOCIAL JUSTICE AND CHRISTIAN ETHICS

Liberation theology emerged in Latin America in the late 1960s in response to long-term inequities in Latin American societies. Led by Roman Catholic clergy, liberation theology called upon the church to resist injustice and oppression and to lead the cause of liberation from the old order. From its beginnings as a theology based upon certain views of economic and political wrongs, liberation theology grew to encompass the concerns of Christian feminists, African Americans, and other groups searching for religious standpoints from which to resist exploitation. Gustavo Gutiérrez emerged as a leader of the movement in Latin America—and eventually influential elsewhere as well—as his writings were translated into other languages. In this excerpt from "Liberation Praxis and Christian Faith" (1974), he outlined the notion of liberation as a spiritual as well as sociopolitical enterprise.

14.5A LIBERATION PRAXIS AND CHRISTIAN FAITH

The option for the poor, for the oppressed strata of society, and for the struggles of the proletariat of Latin America, comports a whole new political outlook and calls for a concrete praxis of liberation. This outlook and this praxis place us in a different universe. All these things lead to a new spiritual experience, at the very heart of this praxis. That experience is the matrix of a new understanding of the word of God, of God's free gift bursting into human existence and transforming it.

God and the Poor

Liberating involvement is the locus of a spiritual experience in which we encounter once more that great prophetic theme of the Old Testament and of Jesus' preaching alike: God and the poor person. To know God is to do justice, is to be in solidarity with the poor person. And it is to be in solidarity with that poor person as he or she actually exists today—as someone who is oppressed, as a member of an exploited class, or ethnic group or culture, or nation.

At the same time, a relationship with the God who has loved me—loved me first and loved me freely—despoils me, strips me. It universalizes my love for others and makes it gratuitous too. Each of the two movements demands the other, dialectically. Hence, for the Bible, there is no authentic worship of God without solidarity with the poor.

Living According to the Spirit

All this entails entering into a different world. A new Christian experience takes shape, an experience filled with possibilities and promises—but with detours and blind alleys, too. There is no easy, triumphal road for the life of faith. There are those who, when they become absorbed by the political demands of the liberation commitment and begin to live the tensions of solidarity with the exploited, then find themselves belonging to a church many of whose members are staunch advocates of the prevailing social order. They then lose their dynamic faith, and suffer the anguish of a dichotomy between being a Christian and being committed to political action.

More cruel still is the case of those who suffer the loss of the love of God in favor of the very thing that love arouses and sustains—love for their fellow human beings. A love like that, unable to maintain itself in the oneness demanded by the gospel, never comes to know the fullness it has locked up inside itself.

Such cases exist. The most elementary honesty forces this admission upon us. When you are out on the frontier of the Christian community where the revolutionary commitment is most intense, you are not in tranquil waters. A lucid, refined analysis is called for here, for many factors are at work. Christians involved in the liberation process are subject to many pressures. They are vulnerable to romanticism, emotional tensions, and even ambiguous doctrinal stances, which can lead them to attitudes of exasperation—or a facile breach with Christianity. But the responsibility of Christians who take refuge in their comfortable "orthodoxy," safe, secure, self-satisfied, and assiduously absent from any focal point where anything "new" is going on, content merely to point an accusing finger from time to time, is scarcely something to be congratulated either.

The difficulties, then, are real. But the paths to a solution can begin only from within the heart of the problem itself. Keeping oneself protected cloaks the reality and postpones a fruitful response. And it betokens a forgetfulness of the urgency and gravity of the reasons impelling us to involve ourselves with those exploited by a cruel, impersonal system. Ultimately, keeping aloof and "not wanting to get involved" is a failure to believe in the power of the gospel and the faith. The gospel proclamation may appear to sink away into the pure concrete historical *here*; but *here* is where theological reflection should spring up, together with the spirituality of a new preaching of the Christian message, in the here and now, incarnate, undiluted.

To evangelize, Chenu has written, is to enflesh, to incarnate, the gospel in time. This time of ours, today, is a confused and darksome one only for those who lack in hope, and hence do not know, or hesitate to believe, that the Lord is present within them.

And indeed for many Christians the liberation commitment is an authentic spiritual experience—in the original, biblical sense of the word: living in the Spirit, who leads us to see ourselves as free and creative children of the Father and sisters and brothers of all men and women. "God has sent the Spirit of his Son into our hearts; the Spirit that cries, 'Abba, Father'" (Gal. 4:6). It is only through concrete deeds of love and solidarity that our encounter with the poor person, with the exploited human being, will be effective—and in that person our encounter with Christ (for "you did it to me"—Matt. 25:40) will be valid as well. Our denial of love and solidarity will be a rejection of Christ ("You neglected to do it to me"—Matt. 25:45).

The poor person, the other, becomes the revealer of the Utterly Other. Life in this involvement is a life in the presence of the Lord at the heart of political activity, with all its conflict and with all its demand for scientific reasoning. It is the life of—to paraphrase a well-known expression—contemplatives in political action.

This is a notion to which we are little accustomed. A spiritual experience, we like to think, should be something out beyond the frontiers of human realities as profane and tainted as politics. And yet this is what we strive for here, this is our aim and goal: an encounter with the Lord, not in the poor person who is "isolated and good," but in the oppressed person, the member of a social class that burns with struggle for its most elemental rights and for the construction of a society in which persons can live as human beings.

History, concrete history, is the place where God reveals the mystery of God's personhood. God's word comes to us in proportion to our involvement in historical becoming. But this history is a conflictual one, a history of conflicts of interest, of struggles for greater justice, a history of the marginalization and exploitation of human beings, of aspirations for liberation. To make an option for the poor, for the exploited classes, to identify with their lot and share their fate, is to seek to make this history that of an authentic community of brothers and sisters. There is no other way to receive the free gift of filiation, of the status of children of God. It is an option for Christ's cross, in the hope of his resurrection. This is what we celebrate in the Eucharist: we express our wish and intent to make our own the meaning Jesus Christ gave to his life, and to receive the Spirit, the gift of loving as he loved.

It is in these concrete conditions that the process of evangelical conversion takes place, that central element of all spirituality. Conversion is an abandonment of oneself and an opening up to God and others. It implies breach, but most of all it implies new departure. And this is precisely why it is not a purely "interior," private attitude, but a process occurring in the socioeconomic, political, and cultural milieu in which we live, and which we ought to transform.

Encounter with Christ in the poor person constitutes an authentic spiritual experience. It is a life in the Spirit, the bond of love between Father and Son, between God and human being, and between human being and human being. It is in this profound communion that Christians involved in a concrete historical liberation praxis strive to live—in a love for Christ in solidarity with the poor, in faith in our status as children of the Father as we forge a society of sisters and brothers, and in the hope of Christ's salvation in a commitment to the liberation of the oppressed.

This is the life and attitude of a growing number of Latin American Christians—laity, bishops, priests, and religious. It is a unifying experience, one that frequently has difficulty expressing itself adequately, perhaps owing to the manipulated condition of theologies that tend to separate the two elements of this experience, and even to oppose them to each other, or perhaps owing to a defensive attitude on the part of Christians who see the liberation commitment as a threat to their privileges in the prevailing social order. This Christian experience is not exempt from the risk of oversimplified identifications and distortive reductions. But it is one that is striving, with daring and depth, to live in Christ by taking on the concrete experience of suffering and injustice of the poor of Latin America. This experiment has already partially succeeded in expressing itself authentically, succeeded in freeing itself from an indirect, mediated language, and to this extent its contribution has already begun to bear fruit for the whole ecclesial community.

The spirituality of liberation is admirably expressed in the Magnificat. The Magnificat is a song of thanksgiving for the gifts of the Lord, in the humble joy of being loved by him: "And my spirit exults in God my savior; because he has looked upon his lowly handmaid, . . . for the Almighty has done great things for me" (Luke 1:47–49).

But at the same time it is one of the most liberating and political passages in the New Testament. This thanksgiving and this joy are intimately bound up with the liberating activity of God in favor of the oppressed and his bringing low the mighty: "He has pulled down princes from their thrones and exalted the lowly. The hungry he has filled with good things, the rich sent empty away" (Luke 1:52–53).

The future of history lies with the poor and the exploited. Authentic liberation will be the deed of the oppressed themselves: in them, the Lord will save history. The spirituality of liberation will have its point of departure in the spirituality of the *anawim.*

Poverty and Solidarity

The praxis of liberation is coming of age. It is beginning to ask questions. Henceforth it will be the framework of politics, in the sense in which we have defined it above, where Christians committed to the poor and to the liberation of the exploited classes will live and think their faith. Christians will spontaneously orientate themselves toward poverty, a fundamental demand of the gospel. Identification with Christ, who came into the world to proclaim the gospel to the poor and to liberate the oppressed, demands poverty. Those who undertake this identification will be surprised at what they discover.

Poverty in the Catholic Church, in theory as well as in practice, has been a prisoner of the "religious life." It has been limited to a particular way of living the *vow* of poverty. Viewed in itself, apart from the purity and nobility of the intentions of its practitioners, it was viewed as something private—and as the private property of a particular type of Christians, who sometimes gave the impression of being rather wealthy in their poverty. Most Christians, it was said, are not called to poverty. In little doses, under the form of certain sobriety of life, it was to be "counseled," but it was not a "precept," not anything that pertained to the essence of Christian life.

Basically it was not a bad division of labor, from the standpoint of the Christians who lived the vow of poverty. They were considered to be living in a "state of perfection," for they had renounced the goods and pleasures of this world. Those who continued to enjoy these goods and pleasures were not evil as such, but they paid a price for living in a lower state of the Christian life. Of course, by the very fact that they lived in the world they could gain something by supporting the practitioners of poverty with their alms. Thus almost everyone gained something. The gospel, however, gained nothing.

And the poor and exploited of this world gained nothing. For there was a graver—and more subtle—evil afoot here. Poverty was proclaimed as a Christian ideal. And its character as an ideal was maintained in a rather generalized way, so that the door was open to all sorts of abuses. In the Bible, material poverty is a subhuman situation, the fruit of injustice and sin. This poverty should not be a Christian ideal. This would mean aspiring to something considered demeaning for a human being. Further, it would place the gospel demands at cross-purposes with humanity's great desire and striving—to break free of subjection to nature, to eliminate human exploitation, and to create better conditions of life for everyone. It would likewise—and no less gravely—mean the justification, however unintentional, of the situation of injustice and exploitation that is the basic cause of poverty—real poverty, which the great majority suffer in Latin America. And yet, all this is exactly what became accepted, in theory and in practice.

But the witness of poverty, and theological reflection on it, has begun to undergo a change in recent years. The first cries for reform came from religious communities whose spirituality was centered on a life of poverty and contemplation. (The combination was no accident, and the natural link between poverty and contemplation continues to be verified today, however new the context.) Then the demand began to spread to other types of religious communities in the church. The vow of poverty began to reclaim its roots and grow richer in meaning. Finally the movement overflowed the confines of the religious life itself, and broad sectors of Christian laity began to make their own the demand for a more real and more radical witness to poverty. For they saw in poverty an essential trait of life in conformity with the gospel. Now poverty was calling the whole church to account, and any counter-testimony in its regard met with critical and strong resistance.

But what we are dealing with here is not a simple extension of the demand for a poor life. Still less is it a mechanical transfer of "religious poverty" to new segments of Christian society. It is the manner of living and understanding poverty that has changed and is changing. Solidarity with the poor, involvement with the liberation of the exploited classes, and entry into the world of the political, has led a good many Christians to do a rereading of the gospel. For only a critique from within a liberation praxis enables one to denounce the ideological function performed by the various ways of misunderstanding poverty; this then leads to a reinterpretation of the gospel. Medellín, bolstered by the new experiences of numerous Christian groups, took its stand along the lines of this rereading.

Now evangelical poverty began to be lived as an act of love and liberation toward the poor of this world. It began to be lived as solidarity with them and protest against the poverty they live in, as identification with the interests of the oppressed classes, and as indictment of the exploitation of which they are the victims.

The ultimate cause of exploitation and alienation is selfishness. The deep reason for voluntary poverty is love of neighbor. Poverty—the fruit of social injustice, whose deepest roots are sin—is taken up not in order to erect it into an ideal of life, but in order to bear testimony to the evil it represents. Our sinful condition, and its consequences, were not assumed by Christ in order to idealize them, surely, but in order to redeem us from sinfulness, to battle human selfishness, to abolish all injustice and division among human beings, to suppress what divides us into rich and poor, exploiters and exploited.

The witness of poverty, lived as an authentic imitation of Christ, instead of alienating us from the world, places us at the very heart of a situation of spoliation and oppression. From there it proclaims liberation and full communion with the Lord. From there it proclaims, and lives, spiritual poverty: total availability to God.

ETHICS

CHAPTER 15
IN ISLAM

15.1 INTRODUCTION

Islam, like Judaism and Christianity, is a major example of ethical monotheism. The Qur'an is profoundly attuned to the moral nature of God and its implications for the divine-human encounter. Although philosophical ethics has an honored place in the history of Muslim thought, it is in the area of Islamic law that ethics has its natural home for Muslims. The following essay is by Fazlur Rahman (1919–1988), one of the twentieth century's most brilliant and independent Muslim thinkers. Educated in both Islamic studies and philosophy in his native India as well as at Oxford, Fazlur Rahman held important academic posts in England, Canada, Pakistan, and the United States. During the last twenty years as professor in the University of Chicago's Department of Near Eastern Languages and Civilizations and its Divinity School, Fazlur Rahman attracted both Muslim and non-Muslim students from around the world to that institution's doctoral programs in Islamic studies. The following essay was written for the Ninth Giorgio Levi Della Vida Biennial Conference convened in Fazlur Rahman's honor at the University of California at Los Angeles in 1983. The prestigious Levi Della Vida Medal was awarded to the author for work that has "significantly and lastingly advanced the study of Islamic civilization."

15.1A FAZLUR RAHMAN, LAW AND ETHICS IN ISLAM

The Qur'ān regards the conduct of man, individually and collectively, in private and in public, as being under divine command: "Those who do not judge (or decide) in accordance with what God has sent down, these are the disbelievers" (5.44; see also 5.45, 5.47, etc.). Indeed, in 2.213 God's primary purpose in sending revealed books is to decide matters under dispute among people. The Qur'ān, therefore, attributes the commands to prayer or to fast to God, and it is exactly the same with rules concerning financial transactions. Hence Islamic law, from the beginning, was conceived as an indivisible totality in the sense that it was derived from God's Word and thus possessed the same and uniform divine sanction. Some scholars of Islam, both Muslim and non-Muslim, maintain that this characteristic of Islamic law derives from the historical reality. Since there was no government or political ruler in Arabia, as there was, for example, at the birth of Christianity, Muhammad had to assume the roles of ruler, commander, and lawgiver in addition to dispensing a "religious" teaching. This argument has been developed further by Muslim secularists to show that the combination of a dual authority, religious and political, in Muḥammad was therefore accidental and that with changed conditions, the duality should be separated. But in the Qur'ān, rules concerning political, legal, social, and other matters are not referred to Muḥammad but to God; strictly speaking, the lawgiver *(shāri')* is not Muḥammad, but God.

God's right or function, then, is to command *(shar', amr)*, while man must accept and obey *(dīn, ṭā'a)*. It is clear that this approach, which brings all human conduct under the concept of duty or obedience to God, cannot formally distinguish between justiciable and nonjusticiable actions. For example, it is man's duty to God not to tell a lie, and it is also his duty to God—this time through man—not to steal, even though the latter is justiciable in a court of law while the former may be justiciable only at the "bar of conscience" before God. Therefore, in the overall value-structure of human conduct the primary valuation is religiomoral and, although of course humanly administered justice plays a basic role in ordering society, it is definitely secondary to the real value-order, which is the moral order. This point on the character of Islamic law has been made often,[1] but the exact implications of the relationship between law and ethics have not been fully treated. This is the central question I wish to explore.

It is well to recall that in Islam there exists a sharp distinction, even a cleavage, between law and ethics, among the users of the law if not among its producers or dispensers. The existence of *ḥiyal* literature, whose avowed purpose is to teach people how to evade law, points to a certain dislocation between morality

---

[1]For an excellent and concise statement on this point see H. A. R. Gibb, *Mohammedanism* (Oxford: Oxford University Press, 1952), Chapter 6.

and law. Al-Ghazālī regarded *fiqh* as "a mere science of this world" if it was not practiced with a religious attitude. He relates the following incident in the *Iḥyā'*: Someone reported to Abū Ḥanīfa that his disciple, Abū Yūsuf, was resorting to the morally questionable practice of evading payment of zakat by transferring his property to his wife before it had been in his possession a whole year, as required by the law of zakat, and that his wife did the same with her property. Upon hearing this, Abū Ḥanīfa remarked, "Abū Yūsuf is *faqīh* [as opposed to a man of religion] and, as such, he is perfectly within his rights in doing so." Al-Ghazālī condoned Abū Ḥanīfa's alleged response by insisting that law is a science of this world and therefore has nothing to do with the real science of faith, which is '*ilm al-ākhira* (science of the hereafter).[2]

With al-Ghazālī, however, we are dealing with a mystic who is concerned with the purely spiritual aspect of human behavior. In the *Kitāb Mīzān al-'Amal*, for example, he observes that prayer, like dancing, contains certain physical movements and postures. If these are performed without an understanding of the true spiritual import of prayer, they are no better—and no worse—than the movements of a dancer. In the case of a dancer, at least, the movements are understandable.[3] And when al-Ghazālī and others complain about the "lawyers or *qāḍīs* of our times," it is not difficult to see what they mean. But how can one explain the allegation that Abū Ḥanīfa not only condoned but indeed was doing what a faqīh can do? Abū Ḥanīfa, we are told, was a person who refused the caliph's offer of an appointment as chief qāḍī because he was fearful of the responsibility the position entailed. Fiqh, if not the center of dīn, as al-Ghazālī would say, is certainly the bedrock of Islam. But then why should fiqh, under certain conditions, and according to al-Ghazālī probably even under normal conditions, turn out to be antagonistic to dīn?

Similarly, Ibn Taimīya, some two centuries later, while discussing the execution of al-Ḥallāj, talks of fiqh or legal *ijtihād* and its relationship with the sharī'a as well as the relationship of the Sufi inspiration of *kashf* to the sharī'a. Ibn Taimīya complains that people often equate sharī'a not only with law but also with the actual decisions of judges. He then states that when Sufi intuition and the ulama's ijtihād differ, then neither can claim validity but both must compete with each other for sharī'a proofs of their respective legitimacy.[4] He does not actually define sharī'a, but from his discussion it appears that by sharī'a he means those norms or values or ideals that have been laid down by God, explicitly or implicitly, which are to be applied, through fiqh, to human conduct, which then must be judged against them. It is quite clear that shāri' (lawgiver) in this sense is God alone, and not the Prophet.

---

[2]*Iḥyā' 'Ulūm al-Dīn*, vol. 1 (Cairo: al-Maktaba al-Tijārīya al-Kubrā, n.d.), *Kitāb al-'Ilm*, pp. 18 ff. (see also the following reference). Later, on p. 24, ll. 10 ff., al-Ghazālī, somewhat inconsistently, says that his criticism of the *fuqahā'* has reference only to the later pseudo-fuqahā' and does not apply to the very early ones.

[3]See F. Rahman, "Theology and Law in Islam," in G. E. von Grunebaum, ed., *Theology and Law in Islam* (Wiesbaden: Otto Harassowitz, 1971), p. 93; see also al-Ghazālī's text referred to therein.

[4]F. Rahman, *Islam* (2d ed.; Chicago: University of Chicago Press, 1979), p. 113, top, quotation from Ibn Taimīya.

Thus there is a distinction between legal rules and an Ideal Law, and it is the latter which, strictly speaking, is the law or the Will of God. In the Qur'ān, verbal derivatives from the term "fiqh" are frequently used but they mean "understanding" of central issues preached by the Prophet and are usually equivalent to *'ilm* (knowledge), which also always implies understanding. In only one place is fiqh used specifically for religion, in Sura 9.122, which advises Muslims that they should not all participate in wars, but that "from every segment a group should devote themselves to acquiring a deeper understanding of the Faith *(liyafafaqqahū fī'l-dīn)* and should teach their people when they return so that these too shall receive admonition." Here "fiqh fī'l-dīn" means "deeper understanding of the Faith," which may include rules of conduct but is certainly much more general and comprehensive. Another most important and interesting point in verse 9.122 concerns the function of the fuqahā' or ulama. That function is not to rule, as Khomeini contends in *Vilāyet-i Faqīh* in opposition to the Qur'ān, but to teach the community at large in order to minimize the differences between an *'ālim* and a non-*'ālim*, for the Qur'ān undoubtedly requires a community whose members are enlightened enough about Islamic teaching to be able to carry on *shūrā* (decision-making) through mutual discussion and consultation.

Despite the distinction between legal rules and the Ideal Law, a distinction supported by the Qur'ān and the later tradition—I have already mentioned al-Ghazālī and Ibn Taimīya—both fiqh and sharī'a became generally equated with specific rules, and it is obedience to these rules that constituted the fulfillment of God's Will. Yet, as noted earlier, in Islam the paramount valuation of human conduct was moral, not legal, and decisions by judges in the courts, and even the opinions of *muftīs* or jurisconsults, did not constitute the primary manifestation of the divine will, although they were very important and were perceived, in some sense, as flowing from that will. The problem, then, is: What happened to the Ideal Law or Will of God, where was it to be located, and in what actual relationship, if any, did it stand to the fiqh law?

In order to be in a position to give anything like a satisfactory answer to these questions, we should look at certain telling examples from the Qur'ān. These examples will, I think, show that whenever there are specific Qur'ānic commands and prohibitions, lawyers take them very seriously, but whenever the lawyers are faced with general Qur'ānic requirements with an ethical import, they do not know how to deal with them, and in many cases do not even try. Sura 4.2, for example, severely criticizes certain guardians of orphans for abusing the latter's property—a theme that goes back well into the Meccan period—and 4.127 states that these guardians, rather than return their property to orphan girls when they come of age, would prefer to marry them (and enjoy their property). Further, in 4.3, the Qur'ān states that if these guardians cannot do justice to the orphan girls' properties, then they may marry up to four from among the latter, provided they do justice among co-wives; but if they cannot do justice to each, they must marry only one. In 4.129, again, the Qur'ān categorically denies the possibility of justice among a plurality of wives. Now the lawyers understood 4.3 to grant a specific legal permission for marrying up to four wives; as for the justice clause, they understood it not as a specific rule but only as a general command to do justice and a recommendation to the husband's conscience. In recent times, the legislation concerning multiple marriages has been reversed in some countries; Tunisian family law, for instance, assumes that polygamy was permitted only temporarily and under certain conditions, and that the Qur'ānic command to do justice, coupled with a denial of the possibility of such justice, necessitates the prohibition of polygamy.

In 23.44, the Qur'ān gives Muslims a general command to execute freedom-purchasing contracts with their slaves, if the latter so desire, and to give such of them as are destitute a part of their own wealth. Most early fuqahā' maintained that this is only a recommendation, not a command, and Mālik (d. 179/795) states unequivocally that he never met an 'ālim who believed otherwise.[5] Again, in 42.32, the Qur'ān enumerates the moral characteristics of those who have faith and states that men of faith must decide their affairs by shūrā (mutual consultation), a democratic pre-Islamic Arab institution which the Qur'ān upholds. Shūrā was not developed into any institutionalized form until Muslim Modernists insisted upon a constitutional form of government in the nineteenth and twentieth centuries. It is true that the fuqahā' had little political power to either implement, or to cause the implementation of, shūrā, but they could at least have attempted to formulate its necessary elements, structure, and the like, something they never did.

The Qur'ān, from its very beginning, has been very emphatic regarding the amelioration of conditions for the poor and the deprived and has strongly advocated socioeconomic justice. In fact, these are cornerstones of the entire Qur'ānic teaching. The Qur'ān also prescribes the levying of zakat. Further, Sura 59.7, concerning the distribution of booty, defines the categories in which booty is to be divided and adds: "This is so that wealth should not circulate only among the rich ones of the society." To implement this general economic requirement it was necessary to have political power, which the fuqahā' lacked. They did, however, have the necessary intellectual power and the opportunity, to explain what was meant by "circulation of wealth in the society as a whole" and to show how this could be brought about. Yet the fuqahā' did little to reinterpret zakat, which in any event had become a fixed law. On the question of general economic justice, we have only the disturbing opinion of the Zāhiri Ibn Ḥazm (d. 450/1058), who believed that it is an Islamic duty for the poor to revolt against the rich and against political authority if their plight is such that they are threatened with starvation. This passage of Ibn Ḥazm's[6] has been played up in recent Muslim socialist literature, but it is an isolated example and is not explicitly related to the Qur'ānic teaching on economic justice.

It is striking, indeed, how the fuqahā' felt either helpless before these general Qur'ānic directives or did not feel their importance strongly enough to try to explicate their legal imperatives. The fuqahā' did draw a distinction between *fatwā* and *taqwā*, that is, between legal imperatives and deeper moral obligations. For ex-

---

[5]Ibid., "Epilogue," p. 298, ll. 5 ff.

[6]See F. Rahman, "Sources and Meaning of Islamic Socialism," in Donald E. Smith, ed., *Religion and Political Modernization* (New Haven: Yale University Press, 1974), p. 256, ll. 5 ff.

ample, the majority of the fuqahā᾽ prohibited any excess charge on a sum loaned, for that would constitute *ribā*, which the Qur᾽ān bans; this is fatwā, or a legal norm. But many fuqahā᾽ also stated that it is unlawful, or rather, immoral for a creditor to exploit in any way the situation of the debtor vis-à-vis himself. Thus it would be reprehensible for a creditor to as much as ride on his debtor's riding beast or to take shelter from the sun in the shade of his debtor's house; this is taqwā, or a moral demand, which of course cannot be enforced through a court of law. Yet even in this example, it is both interesting and significant that instead of formulating a general principle to the effect that a creditor must not take any advantage, big or small, of anyone indebted to him, fiqh literature prefers to cite concrete examples, such as a creditor riding the debtor's beast or seeking shelter in the shade of his house.

It would be tempting to argue, as several Western writers have done, that the Arab mind is more concrete than abstract, that it works by imagination rather than by reason, and therefore can deal with particulars and minutiae better than with universals. Such theories were common in nineteenth-century Europe. I too hold that the Arab mind possesses a strong imagination and loves the concrete, but the second part of the proposition, namely, the "atomicity" of the Arab mind, to use Hamilton A. R. Gibb's phrase,[7] does not necessarily follow. In any case, not all jurists were Arab, particularly in Iraq; Abū Ḥanīfa himself was an Iranian. I think the answer must be sought in the nature of the culture, rather than in any romanticizing of ethnicity.

The Arab-Islamic culture values a living sense of moral rectitude in human conduct above everything else. Intellectualism for the sake of intellectualism—the hallmark of Greek culture and of much of modern Western culture—is perceived as a sin against human nature, if not a crime as well, for it deliberately distorts the human perspective. The nearest antecedent to Arab-Islamic culture is Syriac Christianity, which according to many Western scholars is also causally connected with it. Among the three main streams of classical Christianity, it is the Syriac which kept the Semitic moral Weltanschauung most alive. This has been adduced to explain the curious fact that the Qur᾽ān, in the Meccan period, hardly mentions the New Testament but refers to the Book of Moses six times as its great forerunner, despite the fact that at the time there were more Christians than Jews in and around the Arabian Peninsula. The explanation is that in Syriac Christianity, the Old Testament was given more prominence than the New Testament.

The Qur᾽ān is not a book of abstract ethics, but neither is it the legal document that Muslim lawyers have made it out to be. It is a work of moral admonition through and through. A large part, which deals with human relations (and which also includes many of the stories), is full of statements on the necessity of justice, fair play, goodness, kindness, forgiveness, guarding against moral peril (*ʿadl, qisṭ, iḥsān, taqwā*, and their equivalents), and so on. It is clear that these are general directives, not specific rules. But they are not abstract moral propositions either; they

---

[7]See H. A. R. Gibb, *Modern Trends in Islam* (Chicago: University of Chicago Press, 1946), Chapter 1, p. 6; but the entire chapter should be read.

have a driving power, a compelling force, which abstract propositions cannot yield. This fact was acknowledged also by the Mu'tazila Rationalists, who, while insisting that "good" and "bad" (i.e., moral truth) were knowable by natural reason without the aid of Revelation, nevertheless believed that Revelation was not superfluous but helped motivate people to pursue goodness.[8]

Of course, besides certain general pronouncements made in the Qur'ān, of which we have already cited some examples and which the jurists do not appear to have taken seriously in their legislation, all the specific injunctions of the Qur'ān contain general principles as well. The jurists, at least theoretically, acknowledge that the specific injunctions of the Qur'ān are meant to satisfy these general requirements or principles. They also maintain that these requirements or principles constitute the *rationes legis* (*'ilal 'l-aḥkām*) of the Qur'ānic injunctions. Their whole theory of *qiyās* (analogical reasoning) is based upon this premise. Thus they seek to deduce law by extricating the *ratio legis* of a certain legal text that is analagous to the case under consideration and then applying it to the given case, allowing for differences. This *ratio legis* is nothing more than a general principle which is presented as the essence of the law. In other words, it is the moral value that the law seeks to embody and realize. If values and principles were to be derived from the entire Qur'ān, it would be possible to build an ethical system that would be genuinely Qur'ānic.

If such a task had been attempted, jurists would not have been compelled to resort to principles like *istiḥsān* and *maṣlaḥa mursala*, which are specific formulations of the principle of equity and justice in general. The trouble with these principles is the difficulty of applying them well and avoiding arbitrariness. Also, these principles, as they were formulated and applied, seemed to secularize Islamic law. We are told that the function of maṣlaḥa mursala is to locate and formulate a value wherein a certain legitimate interest of the community lies but which is not connected with any sharī'a value (aṣl shar'ī). In other words, it is in some sense definitely secular in terms of the basic nature of Islamic legislation. The case with istiḥsān (equity) is not much better. It is sometimes defined as a deviation from qiyās. This second formulation seems highly meaningful because it implies an appeal to a higher principle or value than the one upon which strict qiyās was supposed to be based. This would call for some systematization of values in terms of priorities. But this is precisely what was never done, and the two bases of legislation appeared so arbitrary that al-Shāfi'ī felt compelled to say regarding istiḥsān that whoever resorts to it claims to lay down a new sharī'a.[9]

These three free-floating principles—maṣlaḥa, istiḥsān, and ḍarūra (necessity)—in medieval times gave the administrative authorities an instrument of great flexibility for applying sharī'a, and afforded later rulers, particularly the Ottomans, the opportunity to systematically introduce a new state-made law that

---

[8]On Mu'tazila ethics and theology see the masterly treatment by George Hourani, *Islamic Rationalism* (New York: Oxford University Press, 1971).

[9]See n. 3; see also F. Rahman, introduction to *Islam and Modernity: Transformation of an Intellectual Tradition* (Chicago: University of Chicago Press, 1984).

claimed to be sanctioned by sharī'a law. The Ottoman experience, in turn, paved the way for the introduction of secular law in Turkey. Modern legal systems in Egypt and Iraq, drafted by the late Sanhūrī Pāshā, are also based on systematic appeals to the same principles of community interest and necessity without any attempt to relate them to relevant shar'ī values. Yet the same and indeed far better results could have been achieved by the juridic procedure of extracting the *rationes legis* of Qur'ānic injunctions, formulating them into general principles or values, systematizing these principles or values, and deriving law from them. One case will illustrate the point. The Qur'ān (2.178; see also 2.92) enunciates the *lex talionis* and also confirms the system of settling a murder through blood-money *(diya)*, which was practiced in pre-Islamic Arabia. This, of course, makes of murder a private crime and upon this premise rests the classical fiqh law of murder. Elsewhere, however, the Qur'ān refers to the murder of Abel by Cain and states: "For this reason, we laid it down upon the Children of Israel that whoever kills one human without his having the right to it or without there being a state of war, it is as though he has killed all mankind, and whoever gives life to one human, it is as though he has given life to all humanity . . ." (5.32), which explicitly makes the crime of murder a crime against humanity. Now a legal solution could have been derived from this general statement, but this was never done.

I am not suggesting that if the development of Qur'ānic ethics had taken place and law had been deduced from it, differences of legal opinion would have been eliminated—that would be neither possible nor desirable. But differences of opinion would have been grounded more soundly and would have been better controlled or rationalized and chaos would have been minimized. Moreover, the evolution of law could have proceeded more smoothly, the so-called "closure of the gate of ijtihād" would not have occurred and, in fact, would have become inconceivable. Resort to principles like maṣlaḥa, which were never well formulated, whose operations were uncontrolled and often arbitrary, and which were, indeed, amorphous, would have been related to sharī'a principles. It is true that because of the lack of cohesiveness an astonishingly rich wealth of opinion on virtually all important issues has been generated along the entire legal spectrum. Abū Ḥanīfa and Mālik, for example, prohibit sharecropping and absentee landlordism; from Abū Yūsuf onward, however, most jurists allow it. In retrospect, it can be seen that between Mālik and Abū Yūsuf the differences in milieu made the crucial difference. Still, the reasoning of all three—Abū Ḥanīfa, Mālik, and Abū Yūsuf—is abstract and there is no appeal to any common principle; the differences in reasoning can be attributed to different interpretations of ḥadīth. The question of birth control may serve as another example. Opinions range from outright prohibition to strong recommendation, the reasoning on both sides having no common basis; those who prohibit birth control use the necessity of strengthening the community as their main argument; others, like al-Ghazālī, say that a couple must avoid having children if they are too poor to feed them and fear that economic hardship might compel them to obtain money by unlawful means. Both sides of the issue have assumed large proportions in today's Muslim world and the division of opinion among Muslims can have grave consequences.

Perhaps the most interesting case of grave neglect of propounding theories based on sharī'a principles is in the political field. From Morocco to Indonesia we see a continuous spectacle of personal rule (even discounting central Asia and Afghanistan, which are under Russian occupation): monarchs, military dictators, religious autocrats, all offering themselves as the best alternative and the best form of rule for the Muslim community. The Qur'ān, as has been pointed out, gives the principle of shūrā (mutual consultation and discussion) to the Muslim community as a decision-making process, but shūrā was never developed into an institution. Instead, the caliphal form of government became, in the course of time, for Muslims and Muslim political theorists, the only valid form of rule, even though there is no word about it either in the Qur'ān or in the Prophet's sunna, except for an obviously spurious ḥadīth according to which the Prophet said, "Obey me and my rightly guided successors (al-khulafā' al-rāshidūn)." Since the mid-nineteenth century, practically all Modernist Muslim thinkers have contended that the only valid Muslim rule is through shūrā, which in the world of today means a representative form of government. In conformity with this ideology parliaments were instituted in several Muslim countries. But the current deluge of secular and fundamentalist dictatorships has, at least for the time being, submerged that entire democratic orientation. The curious thing is that in the Islamic dictatorships of Khomeini and Ziaul Haq, no actual reference is made either to the Qur'ān or to its shūrā principle. In fact, both men have tried to undermine that principle by insisting that the common Muslim has no sense of right and wrong, and that consequently guidance must come to him from above. Now if this argument is correct, and if the Qur'ān puts the responsibility for shūrā on the community and not on Khomeini or Ziaul Haq, then it must be concluded that the Muslim community is not in existence. Perhaps most interesting of all is the fact that while Muslim Modernists, including Shī'a thinkers like Amīr 'Alī, have insisted that Islam cannot be a theocracy since it has no priestly class, Khomeini and his colleagues are saying precisely that there is a priestly class in Islam and that it must rule; this is essentially true of Ziaul Haq's stance as well.

What lies at the bottom of this dilemma and how, if at all, can it be resolved? If I have been able to give a satisfactory answer to this question and to suggest a way towards a solution to its underlying problem, then a way will have been opened for Muslims to attain their goal, namely, a proper rediscovery of Islam—if we Muslims really wish to do so. The answer, in brief, is that the Qur'ān's message must be understood as a unity and not as so many isolated commands and injunctions. But in order to bring out the Qur'ān's message as a unity, one must start with the theology and ethics of the Qur'ān and only then approach the realm of law. The Islamic developments in history started with the law, and Muslims subsequently developed a theology that in its genesis and historical development had no connection with the law. The theology later claimed for itself the status of "crown of the sharī'a sciences" and the function of protector of the law. As Ibn Taimīya has stated, a theology which rejects the freedom and efficacy of the human will ill accords with a law that assumes human freedom and responsibility.[10] The formula-

---

[10]Rahman, *Islam,* p. 113.

tion of a proper Qur'ānic theology is necessary particularly in order to define the God-man relationship. A Qur'ānic ethics was never worked out by Muslims. In the present volume, the participants at the Ninth Levi Della Vida Conference discuss the different ethical traditions that developed in Islam, some that are nearer to the Qur'ān than others, but almost none that have grown out of the Qur'ān proper. The reason, I believe, is that such an ethics presupposes a satisfactory theology. After ethics comes law, and that law must satisfy the demands of the Qur'ān as a unitary teaching.

The rise and development of Islamic law, as they actually occurred, kept the Muslims' attention focused on details, at the expense, I think, of the general requirements of the Qur'ān. It is true that the fabric of daily life is made up of details and minutiae; these can, however, be managed and properly directed, but only by recourse to ultimate principles. Whether a particular sales transaction is lawful and valid, or whether and to what extent a tailor is liable for the loss of material he had in his possession, are examples of the problems men face throughout their lives. Unless there is a mechanism for defining the nature of human responsibility and for applying the concepts of justice, fair play, kindness, and mercy to *all* the data of actual life—concepts which the Qur'ān emphasizes so untiringly—the law cannot really provide the necessary foundation for "the good life" envisaged by the great jurists. Eventually law must run the risk of a critique such as that of al-Ghazālī, quoted earlier.

In the absence of a living link with ultimate principles, it became necessary, through the second century in particular, to invoke the infallible authority of the Prophet—*Prophetus ex machina,* as it were—and attribute to him all the trivia of daily life. The minutiae of law were spun out as isolated items of legislation, with the Ḥanafīs invoking "considered opinion *(ra'y)*" or "analogical reasoning (qiyās)," and the Mālikis relying on "the practice of Madina" *('amal ahl al-Madīna).* In the absence of any substantive unifying principles that could bind these isolated items into a system, the need for an infallible authority is understandable.

What was needed was the development of ijtihād and ijmā' in constant interaction with each other. Ijtihād was needed not only for a horizontal deduction of law as it was actually used, but also for a vertical development of arching and overarching general principles in order to progressively subsume the multiplicity of principles under them. Later jurists like al-Shāṭibī (d. 1388 C.E.) and Ibn Rushd (d. 1198 C.E.) worked on the general principles of the sharī'a from different points of view, but this was a somewhat different exercise. Al-Shāṭibī and 'Izz al-Dīn ibn 'Abd al-Salām al-Sulamī (d. 1182 C.E.) aimed at extracting the purpose of the laws *(aghrād al-sharī'a or al-maṣāliḥ).* Ibn Rushd tried to clarify the basis and methodology of different schools of law and to explain their divergence, particularly between the Ḥanafīs and the Mālikis, a task to which he brought a cogency and a lucidity which only philosophical training could have given him. Al-Shāṭibī is fully aware that isolated sharī'a proofs, like individual verses of the Qur'ān or ḥadīths (even if the latter are *mutawātir,* i.e., handed down by an overwhelming number of transmitters), cannot constitute sharī'a proofs properly speaking and cannot reach the point of certainty, unless such proofs, of different provenance, converge upon one specific point *(taḍāfur al–adilla).*[11] Although al-Shāṭibī, so far as I can read him, is talking about individual points to be proved, for example, the obligation of prayers, his argument definitely has the potentiality of being applicable to Islam as a whole, or to the message of the Qur'ān as a whole. This would necessarily entail not only a horizontal movement but a vertical movement as well. The famous maxim quoted by many lawyers and numerous commentators on the Qur'ān, which states that "parts of the Qur'ān are mutually explanatory *(al-Qur'ān yufassiru ba'ḍuhū ba'ḍan),*" also implies that the Qur'ān is a unity and not a jumble of isolated or mutually contradictory ideas.

Ethics may be defined as a theory of moral right and wrong. This is exactly what the Qur'ān claims to do; for this is what guidance (hudā) means. In this definition, the terms "theory" and "moral right and wrong" are basic. Some might argue that the two concepts are incompatible because moral right and wrong are practical and, as such, have to be intuited rather than theorized, and that the more one theorizes about right and wrong, the more one recedes from a real sense of what they are. I suspect that this type of consideration was, perhaps unconsciously, working among Muslims. In fact, I suspect that it was at work in the Semitic culture alluded to earlier, which manifests a sort of instinctive abhorrence of general abstract propositions, particularly in the moral field, which in that culture constitutes the primary field of human endeavor. Morality is not expressed in terms of propositions but rather in terms of divine dictates and actions. On this view, right and wrong, which are primarily qualities of actions, cannot be determined by an appeal to general propositions but only with reference to the state of mind called taqwā or the living sense of God's presence. There is, no doubt, a point here and one can even say that the more ethical theorization there has been in modern times, the less concern there has been about actual right and wrong. This was the crux of the difference between the Mu'tazila and their opponents, the Ash'arites, who believed that right and wrong originate in the divine imperative rather than in rational propositions, and that "good" and "bad" are known through Revelation rather than through Reason (although, as I pointed out earlier, the Mu'tazila did admit that Revelation has a motive power which Reason does not possess, at least not sufficiently).

This is why I stress the need for a system of ethics that grows out of the Qur'ān. I do not say that Greek ethics or Persian ethics or, indeed, modern ethical theories are necessarily antagonistic to the Qur'ān, but for Muslims there are multiple reasons why a Qur'ānic ethics must be worked out. First of all, Muslims believe that the Qur'ān is the Word of God. Second, they believe that the Qur'ān contains, actually or potentially, the answers to all the questions of everyday life. Since the questions are infinite, the Qur'ān must contain the answers potentially. To get actual answers requires the exercise of mind and spirit: There is a profound statement on this subject attributed by the Shī'a tradition to 'Alī: "The Qur'ān

[11]Rahman, *Islam and Modernity*, pp. 21–22.

speaks (only) if you ask it to speak," that is, you ask sincerely;[12] this is ijtihād. But if one uses ijtihād to elicit trivial details from the Qur'ān, one will feel the need for some validating authority, and this is why, as I have stated, at a certain stage of the development of fiqh, the need for Prophetic authority was felt and then satisfied by the fabrication of ḥadīth. The early Ḥanafīs were able to a large extent to avoid this drastic solution by their stated position—which remained effective even after al-Shāfiʿī's wholesale introduction of ḥadīth into law—that in the presence of a definite principle derived from the Qur'ān *(aṣl qaṭʿī)*, they would reject a ḥadīth if it was in conflict with either. What is this aṣl qaṭʿī, or definite principle derived from Revelation? It is none other than what I previously described as the *ratio legis,* or generalized statement. This is the beginning of the vertical movement or discovery of the more general principle. Such a principle needs no authentication of its details by a ḥadīth report because it is more reliable than most ḥadīths, and certainly the *akhbār al-āḥād* (i.e., ḥadīths transmitted in a single chain), which, in fact, constitute the majority of ḥadīths in the sphere of law.

If the argument thus far is correct, then the term uṣūl al-fiqh is better applied to the general precepts and principles that are either explicitly formulated in the Qur'ān or are explicable from its *rationes legis,* than to the celebrated "four roots of law," namely, the Qur'ān, the sunna, ijtihād, and ijmāʿ or consensus. For, on the view that we have tried to expound, uṣūl al-fiqh, or principles of law, is that body of ethical teaching which will have emerged as a result of a systematic formulation of the *rationes legis* or objectives of the Qur'ānic legislation and injunctions. The Qur'ān and the authentic sunna of the Prophet are the *material sources of law,* while ijtihād and ijmāʿ are the *methodology of Islamic theology, ethics, and law.* Through this methodology, what is to be worked out in the first instance is the theology, and then the value-structure or higher objectives and goals of the Qur'ān: What kind of man does the Qur'ān desire to mold and, granted such individuals, what kind of sociopolitical order does it want to establish on earth?

In classical Islamic law, because ultimate values were not distinguished from instrumental ones, a good deal of confusion arose regarding the nature of laws of different provenance. It is certain, for example, that the Qur'ān views the establishment of a Muslim community as essential for its task and will not be content with good individuals only; further, this community is charged with the task of establishing a sociopolitical order. The community is thus the necessary instrument for this purpose. Later, not only was the community declared inerrant, most probably through considerations of the infallibility of ijmāʿ, but, in law it came to be regarded as something ultimate. A person's decision to abjure the community or the Islamic faith, for example, was made a capital crime. The Qur'ān states: "Those who believed, then disbelieved, again believed and once again disbelieved and then became entrenched in disbelief, God will not pardon them nor show them a right way" (4.137; cf. 3.90). In 2.256 the Qur'ān clearly formulates the principle of

---

[12]See *K. al-Kāfī,* vol. 1 (Tehran: al-Ṣadūq Press, 1381/1961), p. 61, 1. 7; for the saying attributed to Jaʿfar al-Ṣādiq, see also p. 59, ll. 7 ff.

freedom of faith: "There can be no coercion in matters of faith—truth has become clear from falsehood." This is a good illustration of the conflict between the values and principles laid down by the Qur'ān and those deduced by the jurists on the basis of the logic of the Islamic Imperium, which emerged by swift conquests shortly after the Prophet's death. Before the conquests, however, immediately on hearing the news of the Prophet's death, many Arab tribes rebelled against the political authority of Medina and reverted to their old tribal sovereignty. They did not abjure Islam—although Muslim historians and lawyers have called the reaction by the misnomer "apostasy movement"—but insisted that they would pay taxes not to the central authority at Medina but to their own tribal organizations. Otherwise they would carry out all the duties devolving upon a Muslim, like prayer, fasting, pilgrimage, and so on. This shows clearly that theirs was a political rebellion. The rebellion was put down by force of arms, but by a mistaken argument Muslim lawyers deduced from this that a person who leaves the faith of Islam deserves capital punishment. The clearly stated Qur'ānic verse 4.137, quoted above, was ignored. Hence the source of the Islamic law on apostasy is not the Qur'ān but the logic of the Islamic Imperium. The science of Qur'ānic ethics will have to decide the relative place of both in the structure of Islam.

15.2 A PRACTICAL GUIDE TO WHAT IS LAWFUL AND WHAT IS PROHIBITED IN ISLAM

The previous selection is a scholarly discussion of important theoretical aspects of Islamic law and ethics in their interrelations. The following one is a practical introduction to the principles of the lawful and prohibited in Islam, drawn from a tremendously influential and detailed contemporary handbook *The Lawful and the Prohibited in Islam* by the Egyptian specialist in Islamic law, Yusuf al-Qaradawi. Originally published in Arabic in 1960, the book is also available in Indonesian and English translations.

15.2A THE LAWFUL AND THE PROHIBITED IN ISLAM

Definitions

Al-Halal (the lawful):	That which is permitted, with respect to which no restriction exists, and the doing of which the Law-Giver, Allah, has allowed.
Al-Haram (the prohibited or unlawful):	That which the Law-Giver has absolutely prohibited; anyone who engages in it is liable to incur the punish-

From Yusuf al-Qaradawi, *The Lawful and the Prohibited in Islam,* translated by Kamal El-Helbawy, M. Moinuddin Siddique, and Syed Shukry (Indianapolis: American Trust Publications, n.d.). Copyright © 1960. Reprinted with the permission of American Trust Publications.

	ment of Allah in the Hereafter as well as a legal punishment in this world.
Al-Makruh (the detested):	That which is disapproved by the Law-Giver but not very strongly. The *makruh* is less in degree than the *haram,* and the punishment for *makruh* acts is less than for those that are *haram,* except when done to excess and in a manner which leads an individual toward what is *haram.*

Chapter One

The Islamic Principles Pertaining to Halal and Haram

- The basic *asl*[1] is the permissibility of things.
- To make lawful and to prohibit is the right of Allah alone.
- Prohibiting the *halal* and permitting the *haram* is similar to committing *shirk.*[2]
- The prohibition of things is due to their impurity and harmfulness.
- What is *halal* is sufficient, while what is *haram* is superfluous.
- Whatever is conducive to the *haram* is itself *haram.*
- Falsely representing the *haram* as *halal* is prohibited.
- Good intentions do not make the *haram* acceptable.
- Doubtful things are to be avoided.
- The *haram* is prohibited to everyone alike.
- Necessity dictates exceptions.

The question of what ought to be *halal* (lawful) and *haram* (prohibited) was one of the matters concerning which, prior to the advent of Islam, the peoples of the world had gone very far astray and were utterly confused, permitting many impure and harmful things and prohibiting many things that were good and pure.

They erred grievously, going either far to the right or far to the left. On the extreme right was the ascetic Brahmanism of India and the self-denying monasticism of Christianity. In addition to these two, there were other religions which were based on the principles of the mortification of the flesh, abstention from good food, and avoidance of other enjoyments of life which Allah has provided for human beings. Christian monasticism attained its peak during the Middle Ages when the avoidance of good and pure things among the monks, thousands in number, reached the point at which washing one's feet was considered a sin and entering a bath was something to regret and repent. On the extreme left, the Mazdak philosophy emerged in Persia, advocating absolute freedom and allowing people to take whatever they wanted and do whatever they pleased, even exhorting them to violate what is naturally held inviolable by human beings.

---

[1] *Asl,* plural *usul,* denotes origin, source, foundation, basis, fundamental or principle. (Trans.)
[2] Ascribing partners, or associating others, with Allah. (Trans.)

The Arabs of the pre-Islamic era provide a noteworthy example of utter confusion regarding the criteria for making lawful or prohibiting things and actions. They permitted the drinking of alcohol, the taking of usury at exorbitant rates, the torturing and secluding of women, and many similar practices. Those who had diabolical minds made alluring to many of them the killing of their own children, until, suppressing their natural paternal feelings, they obeyed them. As Allah Subhanahu wa Ta'ala says:

> Thus have their partners made alluring to many of the idolaters the killing of their children, in order to destroy them and to confuse for them their religion. (6:137)

These "partners" from among the guardians of the idols had devised many impressive arguments to persuade fathers to kill their children; among them were the fear of actual or anticipated poverty, the impending shame in case of a daughter, and the closeness to the gods to be attained by the sacrifice of a son.

It is strange that these same people who permitted the killing of their children by cutting their throats or burying them alive had prohibited to themselves the eating of certain agricultural produce and the flesh of cattle. Stranger still is that they considered such prohibitions as part of their religion, attributing them to Allah's command.[3] But Allah rejected their false claim:

> And they say, 'These cattle and crops are sacred; none shall eat of them except those whom we wish',—so they assert—'and cattle whose backs are prohibited (to burden), as well as cattle on which (at slaughter) the name of Allah is not mentioned' a forgery against Him. He will assuredly recompense them for what they have forged. (6:138)

Moreover, the Qur'an exposed the error of those who made *halal* what should have been prohibited and made *haram* what should have been permitted:

> Lost are those who kill their children in folly, without knowledge and prohibited what Allah has provided them, forging (lies) against Allah. They have indeed gone astray and are without guidance. (6:140)

When Islam came, the errors, confusions, and deviations with respect to the question of *halal* and *haram* were very widespread. One of Islam's initial accomplishments was, therefore, to establish certain legal principles and measures for rectifying this important matter; these principles were then made the determining criteria on which the questions of what is *halal* and what is *haram* were to be based. Thus this vital aspect was determined according to the correct perspective, and rules related to matters of *halal* and *haram* were established on the basis of principles of justice. The *ummah* (nation) of Islam thus became an *ummah* occupying a position between the extremist deviations to the right and left, which Allah Ta'ala

---

[3]It should be noted that while worshipping and ascribing powers to numerous male and female deities, the pagan Arabs of the pre-Islamic era possessed the concept of a supreme Deity, Allah, ascribing to Him many false attributes and laws. (Trans.)

describes as a "middle *ummah,* the best *ummah* that has ever been brought forth for mankind." (3:110)

1. THE BASIC ASL[4] REFERS TO THE PERMISSIBILITY OF THINGS. The first *asl,* or principle, established by Islam is that the things which Allah has created and the benefits derived from them are essentially for man's use, and hence are permissible. Nothing is *haram* except what is prohibited by a sound and explicit *nas*[5] from the Law-Giver, Allah Subhanahu wa Ta'ala. If the *nas* is not sound, as for example in the case of a weak *hadith,* or if it is not explicit in stating the prohibition, the original principle of permissibility applies.

The scholars of Islam have derived this principle of the natural usability and permissibility of things from the clear verses of the Qur'an. For example, Allah says:

> It is He who created all that is in the earth for you. . . . (2:29)
> He has subjected to you, from Himself, all that is in the heavens and all that is on the earth. . . . (45:13)
> Do you not see that Allah has subjected to you whatever is in the heavens and what is on earth, and has showered upon you His favors, both apparent and unseen? (31:20)

It cannot be that Allah, may He be glorified, would create all these things, give man control over them, count them as His favors upon him, and subsequently inform him that their use is prohibited; how could this be when He created all this for man's use and benefit? Indeed, He has prohibited only a few things for specific reasons, the wisdom of which will be discussed later.

In Islam the sphere of prohibited things is very small, while that of permissible things is extremely vast. There is only a small number of sound and explicit texts concerning prohibitions, while whatever is not mentioned in a *nas* as being lawful or prohibited falls under the general principle of the permissibility of things and within the domain of Allah's favor. In this regard the Prophet (peace be on him) said:

> What Allah has made lawful in His Book is *halal* and what He has forbidden is *haram,* and that concerning which He is silent is allowed as His favor. So accept from Allah His favor, for Allah is not forgetful of anything. He then recited, "And thy Lord is not forgetful." (19:64)[6]

Salman al-Farsi reported that when the Messenger of Allah (peace be on him) was asked about animal fat, cheese, and fur, he replied,

---

[4]*Asl,* plural *usul,* denotes origin, source, foundation, basis, fundamental or principle. (Trans.)
[5]*Nas* denotes either a verse of the Qur'an or a clear, authentic, and explicit *sunnah* (practice or saying) of Prophet Muhammad. These are the two main sources of Islamic law, i.e., its *Shari'ah.* (Trans.)
[6]This *hadith* was reported by al-Hakim, classified as *sahih* (sound), and quoted by al-Bazzar.

The *halal* is that which Allah has made lawful in His Book and the *haram* is that which He has forbidden, and that concerning which He is silent He has permitted as a favor to you.[7]

Thus, rather than giving specific answers to what the questioner had asked, the Prophet (peace be on him) referred to the general criterion for determining the *halal* and the *haram*. Accordingly, it is sufficient for us to know what Allah has made *haram*, since what is not included in it is pure and permissible. The Prophet (peace be on him) also said:

Allah has prescribed certain obligations for you, so do not neglect them; He has defined certain limits, so do not transgress them; He has prohibited certain things, so do not do them; and He has kept silent concerning other things out of mercy for you and not because of forgetfulness, so do not ask questions concerning them.[8]

I would like to emphasize here that the principle of natural permissibility is not only limited to things and objects but also includes all human actions and behavior not related to acts of worship, which may be termed living habits or day-to-day affairs. Here again, the principle is that these are allowed without restriction, with the exception of a small number of things which are definitely prohibited by the Law-Giver, Allah Subhanahu wa Ta'ala, Who says:

. . . He (Allah) has explained to you what He has made *haram* for you. . . . (6:119)

including both objects and actions.

The case is different, however, in relation to acts of worship. These are purely religious acts which can be taken only from what Allah Himself reveals. Concerning this we have a sound *hadith*:

"Any innovation in our matter (worship) which is not a part of it must be rejected."[9]

Anyone who invents or originates a form of worship on his own has gone astray and must be repudiated, for only the Law-Giver Himself has the right to originate acts of worship through which human beings may seek nearness to Him. Living habits and day-to-day matters, however, did not originate with the Law-Giver; they were originated and acted upon by human beings themselves. Thus the Law-Giver intervenes only to rectify, to moderate, or to refine them, and occasionally to identify some practices which are harmful or which may lead to strife.

The great Islamic scholar Ibn Taymiyyah states,

Peoples' sayings and actions are of two kinds: acts of worship by which their religion is established, and customary practices which are required for day-to-day living. From the principles of the *Shari'ah*, we know that acts of worship are those acts which

---

[7]Reported by al-Tirmidhi and Ibn Majah.
[8]Reported by al-Darqutni and classified as *hasan* (good) by al-Nawawi.
[9]This *hadith* is classified as *muttafaq 'alayh* ("agreed upon" by the two great scholars al-Bukhari and Muslim).

have been prescribed by Allah or approved by Him; nothing is to be affirmed here except through the *Shariʿah*. However, as far as the worldly activities of people are concerned, they are necessary for everyday life. Here the principle is freedom of action; nothing may be restricted in this regard except what Allah Subhanahu wa Taʿala has restricted. This is the case because commanding and prohibiting are both in Allah's hands. As far as worship is concerned, there has to be a command from Him concerning it. Thus, when it requires a command (from Allah) to establish something, how can we say that something is restricted without His command?

This is why Ahmad (bin Hanbal) and other jurists, who base their judgements on *ahadith*,[10] say: In relation to acts of worship, the principle is limitation *(tawqeef)*; that is to say, nothing can be legislated in this regard except what Allah Himself has legislated. To do otherwise is to incur the risk of being included in the meaning of the *ayah*: 'Do they have partners (with Allah) who have prescribed for them in religion that concerning which Allah has given no permission?' (42:21) But as far as living habits are concerned, the principle is freedom because nothing can be restricted in this regard except what Allah Himself has prohibited. Here, to do otherwise, is to be included in the meaning of His saying: 'Say: Do you see what Allah has sent down to you for sustenance? Yet you have made some part of it *halal* and some part *haram.'* (10:59)

This is a great and beneficent principle, on the basis of which we can say that buying, selling, leasing, giving gifts, and other such matters are necessary activities for people, as are eating, drinking, and the wearing of clothes. If the *Shariʿah* says something concerning these mundane matters, it is in order to teach good behavior. Accordingly, it has prohibited whatever leads to strife, has made obligatory that which is essential, has disapproved that which is frivolous, and has approved that which is beneficial. All this has been done with due consideration for the kinds of activities involved, their magnitudes, and properties.

Since this is the stand of the *Shariʿah*, people are free to buy, sell, and lease as they wish, just as they are free to eat and to drink what they like as long as it is not *haram*. Although some of these things may be disapproved, they are free in this regard, since the *Shariʿah* does not go to the extent of prohibiting them, and thus the original principle (of permissibility) remains.[11]

This principle is also supported by what is reported in a sound *hadith* by the Prophet's Companion, Jabir bin ʿAbdullah. He said, "We used to practice *ʿazl* (*coitus interruptus*, or withdrawal before ejaculation during intercourse) during the period when the Qurʾan was being revealed. If the practice were to have been prohibited, the Qurʾan would have prohibited it." He therefore concluded that if the divine revelation was silent about something, it was permissible and people were free to practice it. Assuredly the Prophet's Companions (may Allah be pleased with them) had a perfect understanding of the *Shariʿah*. Accordingly, this great principle—that no worship can be legislated except by the command of Allah, and no practice can be prohibited except by His prohibition—is firmly established.

---

[10]Plural of *hadith*. (Trans.)

[11]*Al-Qawaʿid al-Nuraniyah al-Fiqhiyah* by Ibn Taymiyyah, pp. 112–113. In accordance with this principle, Ibn Taymiyyah, his pupil, Ibn al-Qayyim, and the Hanbali jurists in general hold that contracts and the conditions laid down in them are essentially permissible, as any contract not involving any matter which is textually established as *haram* is valid.

PART VI
RELIGION AND
POLITICAL ORDER

CHAPTER 16
IN JUDAISM

16.1 JEWISH ETHNIC AUTONOMY IN LATE ANTIQUITY

The origins of the Palestinian Patriarchate are difficult to isolate. But from the mid-second century CE to the first quarter of the fifth, a single family—that of Gamaliel—seems to have controlled the institution. The earliest non-Jewish reference to the Patriarch (he is called here the "Ethnarch") comes from the mid-third century Palestinian Christian theologian Origen, in his *Letter to Africanus.* Clearly, the unidentified Patriarch mentioned here is perceived to wield independent authority comparable to a head of state.

16.1A ORIGEN, *LETTER TO AFRICANUS*

Now that the Romans rule and the Jews pay the two drachmas [a tax] to them, we who have had experience of it, know how much power the ethnarch has among them and that he differs little from a king of the nation. Trials are held according to the law, and some are condemned to death. And though there is not full permission for this, still it is not done without the knowledge of the ruler, as we learned and were convinced of when we spent much time in the country of that people.

From Origen, *Letter to Africanus,* in Martin Goodman, "The Roman State and the Jewish Patriarchy in the Third Century" in L. Levine, ed., *The Galilee in Late Antiquity* (New York: Jewish Theological Seminary of America/Harvard University Press, 1992), page 128.

In rabbinic tradition, Rabbi Judah the Patriarch is held to be the model of the ideal Patriarch—wise, urbane, wealthy, and well connected to sources of Roman power. Stories told about other Patriarchs, however, suggest that there was at least in principle a certain amount of tension between the Patriarch and the rabbinic scholars whom he trained and placed in positions of judicial and administrative authority. Instructive is the following narrative set in the patriarchate of Rabban Shimon ben Gamaliel, Rabbi Judah's father. The passage, from the Babylonian Talmud's tractate on judicial error (*Horayot* 13b), cites a traditional description of protocol in the Sanhedrin, the rabbinic legislative and judicial hub, and explains the tradition as the result of patriarchal suppression of a "palace revolt" among disgruntled sages.

16.1B HORAYOT, 13B

Our Rabbis transmitted an oral tradition:

> When the Patriarch enters the Sanhedrin all the people rise, and they do not sit until he says: Be seated. When the Chief Justice enters, they rise and form a row on one side of him and a row on the other side until he takes his place. When the Sage enters, each one rises and sits in sequence as he passes, until he takes his place. The sons of Sages and disciples of Sages—when they are needed by the assembly, they stride over the heads of the seated people without the latter extending any ceremony.

[This passage continues at length with other items of protocol and is subject to some clarification. Then the Talmud continues as follows:]

Said Rabbi Yohanan: This tradition was transmitted in the days of Rabban Shimon ben Gamaliel, who served as Patriarch in the Academy of Yavneh. Rabban Shimon was the Patriarch, Rabbi Meir the Sage and Rabbi Nathan of Babylonia the Chief Justice. Now, when Rabban Shimon ben Gamaliel was there all would rise before him. When Rabbi Meir and Rabbi Nathan would enter, all would rise before them. Said Rabban Shimon ben Gamaliel: Shouldn't there be some distinction between my office and theirs? He then established this tradition as binding.

That day Rabbi Meir and Rabbi Nathan were not there. The next day, when they came and saw that the scholars did not rise before them they said: What's this? The scholars said: This is what Rabban Shimon ben Gamaliel has established! Said Rabbi Meir to Rabbi Nathan: I am the Sage and you are the Chief Justice—let us improve matters for ourselves! What shall we do to him? We'll say to him: "interpret for us the details of the laws of uncleanness transmitted to vegetables from their stems"—for he hasn't mastered [this notoriously difficult material]! And when he cannot explain it we'll say to him: "'Who can recount the mighty acts of Adonai? The one who sounds forth all His praises!' (Ps. 106:2)—Who is entitled to recount the mighty act of Adonai before the scholars? One who is able to sound forth all His praises!" And then we shall depose him. I will be Chief Justice and you will be Patriarch!

Rabbi Jacob b. Qorshai heard them and said: Perhaps, Heaven forbid, this thing will lead to disgrace? He went and sat behind Rabban Shimon ben Gamaliel's study, explaining the law, studying it aloud and repeating it. He learned and re-peated. Said Rabban Shimon ben Gamaliel: What's up? Perhaps, Heaven forbid, something's going on in the house of study? He applied all his intelligence and studied the topic.

The next day, they said to him: Let the Master come and teach Vegetable-Stem-Uncleanness! He began his discourse and spoke. After he concluded, he said to them: Had I not studied it, you would have disgraced us! He gave an order and they were removed from the house of study. Thereafter, Rabbi Meir and Rabbi Nathan would write notes on legal difficulties and throw them into the house of study. Those which Rabban Shimon ben Gamaliel could resolve, he resolved. As to those which the scholars could not resolve, Rabbi Meir and Rabbi Nathan would write solutions and throw them back into the house of study. Said Rabbi Yose: Torah is outside and we are within! Rabban Shimon ben Gamaliel said to them: Let us bring them back in. However, we will punish them in that legal traditions will not be transmitted in their names.

Therefore, they transmitted Rabbi Meir's traditions with the phrase, "others say," and Rabbi Nathan's with the phrase, "some say."

Rabbi Meir and Rabbi Nathan were told in dreams to go and apologize to Rabban Shimon ben Gamaliel. Rabbi Nathan went, but Rabbi Meir said: Dream-instructions don't amount to anything. When Rabbi Nathan went, Rabban Shimon ben Gamaliel said to him: Just because your father's influence [in Babylonia] helped you become Chief Justice, shall we also set you up as Patriarch?

Rabban Shimon ben Gamaliel's dismissive reference to Rabbi Nathan's influential father in Babylonia leads us to the question of Jewish communal autonomy in Sasanian Mesopotamia. The Exilarch, like his Palestinian counterpart, was a royal appointee charged with administering Jewish affairs. Like the Patriarch, he also used rabbinic sages in his administration and, it appears, could be both revered and envied by them. One late-third-early-fourth—century sage, Rav Nahman bar Jacob, was particularly close to the Exilarch, serving as his principal administrative assistant. The following story is interesting for two reasons. First, it assumes that the Exilarch might apply Persian as well as rabbinic law; second, it claims that Rav Nahman bar Jacob had the authority to revise the Exilarch's rulings in line with rabbinic preferences, thus portraying him as the "power behind the throne."

16.1c Bava Kamma, 58b

A certain person cut down a date tree belonging to a neighbor. When he appeared before the Exilarch, the latter said to him, "I myself saw the place. Three date-trees

From the Babylonian Talmud (*Bava Kamma* 58b), adapted from Jacob Neusner, *Israel's Politics in Sassanian Iran* (Lanham, Maryland: University Press of America, 1980), page 68.

stood close together, and they were worth one hundred zuz. Go therefore and pay the other thirty-three and a third." The defendant said, "What have I to do with an Exilarch who judges in accordance with Persian law?" He therefore came to Rav Nahman, who said that the valuation should be made in conjunction with sixty [times as much].

Many talmudic narratives stress that, despite his political power and his influence in rabbinic circles, the exilarch's knowledge of rabbinic law was often wanting. In the following story, set in the late third or early fourth century, the sage Rav Sheshet is portrayed as being unwilling even to eat in the exilarch's house for fear that the rabbinic dietary restrictions are routinely violated.

16.1D GITTIN, 67B

The Exilarch said to Rav Sheshet, "Why does the Master not eat with us?" He said, "Because your servants are not reliable, for they are suspected of [not observing the prohibition of eating] a limb from a living animal." He said, "Do you say so?" Rav Sheshet said, "Now I shall show you." He told his servant, "Go and steal for me a leg from an animal and bring it to me." When he brought it to Rav Sheshet, he said to them, "Place the pieces of the animal before me." They did so. He said to them, "Did this animal have only three legs?" They then cut off the leg of an animal and brought it to him. He then said to his servant, "Now bring forth yours." Rav Sheshet said to them, "Did this animal have five legs?" The Exilarch said to him, "In that case, let them prepare the food in your presence and you may eat." "Fine," he said. They brought a table and placed meat before him, and set in front of him the "portion which chokes the mother-in-law [i.e., a huge piece]." Rav Sheshet felt it [he was blind], and took it and wrapped it in his scarf. When he had eaten, they said to him, "A silver cup has been stolen from us" [so as to search him]. While they were looking they came and found what he had wrapped in his scarf. They said to the Exilarch, "See how he has not wanted to eat, but only to trouble." He said to him, "I did eat, but I found in it the taste of a boil [which makes the meat unfit to eat according to rabbinic tradition]." They said to him, "No animal with a boil was prepared for us today." He said, "Examine the place." They examined and found that it was so.

From the Babylonian Talmud (*Gittin* 67b) adapted from Jacob Neusner, *Israel's Politics in Sassanian Iran* (Lanham, Maryland: University Press of America, 1980), page 84–85.

Seder Olam Zuta, a rabbinic work of the early Gaonic period, records a remarkable—and otherwise unattested—story about the rebellion of a late-fifth- early-sixth-century exilarch, Mar Zutra, against the Persians, leading to the creation of a Jewish state. Although most recent historians doubt that such a state existed, the story is important for its assumptions that the exilarch could mobilize Jewish military power against a world empire. Note also that a divine sign—a pillar of fire—is instrumental to the rise and fall of Mar Zutra's state.

16.1E SEDER OLAM ZUTA

And Mar Zutra was Exhilarch twenty years. . . . In his days Mar Rav Yitzhak head of the school was killed. On that day a great one went forth from the hand of a greater one—may the memory of our prince be for the life of the world to come! A pillar of flame appeared to Mar Zutra, and with him four hundred men went forth. They did battle with the Persians and founded a kingdom. He collected taxes for seven years.

In the end of the seven years the rebels who were with him sinned, for it was found that they had drunk wine used for pagan libations and had eaten in the palace of the kings of gentiles. The pillar of fire which had moved before him disappeared.

The Persians took and killed him and crucified the Exilarch, Mar Zutra and the head of the school on the bridge in Mahoza. Then the king commanded that they return him to the place of the Exilarch. On the day on which Mar Zutra was killed . . . a son was born to him, and they called him Mar Zutra according to the name of his father.

16.2 JEWISH AUTONOMY UNDER CHRISTENDOM AND ISLAM

As the Roman Empire became a Christian Empire from the fourth to the sixth centuries, imperial law modified the rights of Jewish citizens in light of the requirements of Christian theological views of Judaism. For the most part, as in the fifth-century *Theodosian Code,* Jewish life, property, and rights of religious practice were protected by law. Nevertheless, the state was free to introduce its own standards into Jewish religious life. The occasion for the following law, issued by the Emperor Justinian in 553, appears to be an intra-Jewish dispute about the propriety of reading the Torah in Greek in the synagogue. Justinian permits the Greek text in the version preferred by Christian tradition, hoping it will help the Jews see the errors of their ways. Furthermore, he bans the study of rabbinic tradition, regarded as human convention unfounded in revelation.

From the *Seder Olam Zuta,* in Jacob Neusner, *Israel's Politics in Sassanian Iran* (Lanham, Maryland: University Press of America, 1980), pages 167–168.

16.2A *NOVELLAE,* no. 146

It was right and proper that the Hebrews, when listening to the Holy Books, should not adhere to the literal writings but look for the prophecies contained in them, through which they announce the Great God and Saviour of the human race, Jesus Christ. However, although they have erred from the right doctrine till today, given as they are to senseless interpretations, when we learnt that they dispute among themselves, we could not bear to leave them with an unresolved controversy . . .

We decree, therefore, that it shall be permitted to those Hebrews who want it to read the Holy Books in their synagogues . . . in the Greek language before those assembled and comprehending, or possibly in our ancestral language (we speak of the Italian language), or simply in all other languages, changing language and reading according to the different places; and that through this reading the matters read shall become clear to all those assembled and comprehending, and that they shall live and act according to them. . . . Furthermore, those who read in Greek shall use the Septuagint tradition, which is more accurate than all the others, and is preferable to the others. . . . Apart from these, who will not be amazed by this thing about these men, who lived a long time before the saving revelation of the great God and our Saviour Jesus Christ yet carried out the translation of the Holy Books as if they saw that this revelation was to happen in future, and as if illuminated by a prophetic grace? . . .

What they call Mishnah, on the other hand, we prohibit entirely, for it is not included among the Holy Books, nor was it handed down from above by the prophets, but it is an invention of men in their chatter, exclusively of earthly origin and having in it nothing of the divine. Let them read the holy words themselves, therefore, . . . without hiding what is said in them, on the one hand, and without accepting extraneous and unwritten nonsense they themselves had contrived to the perdition of the more simple minded, on the other.

In consequence of this permission granted by us, those who adopt the Greek language and the other languages shall not be subjected to any penalty at all, neither shall they be hindered by any person, nor shall those who are called among them Archipherekitae [head teachers?], or possibly Presbyters [priests] or Didascolai [rabbis], have the license to hinder them from this by any deceits or excommunations, unless they would wish to be chastened for these deeds by corporal punishment as well as by loss of property, and obey us—who desire and command deeds better and more pleasing to God—against their will.

In the various medieval Christian territories, the legal rights of Jews varied upon local circumstances. Some terms were rather restrictive, others much more gener-

From A. Linder, translator, *The Jews in Roman Imperial Legislation* (Detroit: Wayne State University Press, 1987), pp. 408–409. Copyright © 1987 by The Israel Academy of Sciences and Humanities. Reprinted with the permission of The Israel Academy of Sciences and Humanities.

ous. An example of the former is the Seven Part Code (*Las Siete Partidas*), promulgated by the Spanish Christian monarch Alfonso X in 1265. It imposes rather explicit restrictions on Jewish civil and religious freedom in relation to Christians and raises an early version of the suspicion that Jews engage in ritualized murder of Christians. In contrast, compare the rather broad protections offered in 1244 by the charter granted by the Duchy of Austria under Frederick the Belligerent, who encouraged the flow of Jewish liquid assets into his realm.

16.2B *LA SIETE PARTIDAS*, PARTS II, IV

Jews should pass their lives among Christians quietly and without disorder, practicing their own religious rites, and not speaking ill of the faith of Our Lord Jesus Christ, which Christians acknowledge. Moreover a Jew should be very careful to avoid preaching to, or converting any Christian, to the end that he may become a Jew, by exalting his own belief and disparaging ours. Whoever violates this law shall be put to death and lose all his property. And because we have heard it said that in some places Jews celebrated, and still celebrate Good Friday, which commemorates the Passion of Our Lord Jesus Christ, by way of contempt: stealing children and fastening them to crosses, and making images of wax and crucifying them, when they cannot obtain children; we order that, hereafter, if in any part of our dominions anything like this is done, and can be proved, all persons who were present when the act was committed shall be seized, arrested and brought before the king; and after the king ascertains that they are guilty, he shall cause them to be put to death in a disgraceful manner, no matter how many there may be. . . .

A synagogue is a place where the Jews pray, and a new building of this kind cannot be erected in any part of our dominions, except by our order. Where, however, those which formerly existed there are torn down, they can be built in the same spot where they originally stood; but they cannot be made any larger or raised to any greater height, or painted. . . . And for the reason that a synagogue is a place where the name of God is praised, we forbid any Christian to deface it, or remove anything from it, or take anything out of it by force; except where some malefactor takes refuge there; for they have a right to remove him by force in order to bring him before the judge. . . .

16.2C *CHARTER OF THE JEWS OF THE DUCHY OF AUSTRIA*

1. We decree, therefore, first, that in cases involving money, or immovable property, or a criminal complain touching the person or property of a Jew, no Christian shall be admitted as a witness against a Jew unless there is a Jewish witness together with the Christian. . . .

3. Likewise, if a Christian has deposited a pledge with a Jew, stating that he had left it with the Jew for a smaller sum than the Jew admits, the Jew shall then take an oath upon the pledge pawned with him, and the Christian must not refuse to pay the amount that the Jew has proved through his oath. . . .

9. Likewise, if a Christian should inflict any sort of wound upon a Jew, the accused shall pay to the Duke twelve marks of gold which are to be turned in to the treasury. . . .

12. Likewise, wherever a Jew shall pass through our territory no one shall offer any hindrance to him or molest or trouble him. [The Jew is to pay no road-fees in all Austrian lands.] If, however, he should be carrying any goods or other things for which he must pay duty at all custom offices, he shall pay only the prescribed duty which a citizen of that town . . . pays. . . .

22. Likewise, the [Christian] judge of the Jews shall bring no case that has arisen among the Jews before his court, unless he be invited due to a complaint. [Civil suits between Jews were settled by the Jews themselves.] . . .

From the twelfth century, Jewish communities in Western Europe were periodically subjected to expulsion orders. These were usually motivated by mixtures of theological enmity and considerations of financial gain. The expulsion of French Jewry in 1182 by King Philip is described in a Latin biography of the king, written shortly thereafter by a monk named Rigord. According to him, Philip's motive for the expulsion was to rid the kingdom of Jewish ritual murderers. The narrative, however, shows that confiscation of Jewish wealth was also a principal motive.

16.2D *Gesta Philippi Augusti*

The most Christian King Philip heard of these things, and compassion was stirred within him. He took counsel with a certain hermit, Bernard by name, a holy and religious man, who at that time dwelt in the forest of Vincennes, and asked him what he should do. By his advice the King released all Christians of his kingdom from their debts to the Jews, and kept a fifth part of the whole amount for himself. . . .

In the year of our Lord's Incarnation 1182, in the month of April, which is called by the Jews Nisan, an edict went forth from the most serene king, Philip Augustus, that all the Jews of his kingdom should be prepared to go forth by the coming feast of St. John the Baptist [June 24]. And then the King gave them leave to sell each his movable goods before the time fixed. . . . But their real estate, that is, houses, fields, vineyards, barns, winepresses, and such like, he reserved for himself and his successors, the kings of the French. . . .

The infidel Jews, perceiving that the great of the land, through whom they had been accustomed easily to bend the King's predecessors to their will, had suf-

From Jacob R. Marcus, *The Jew in the Medieval World*. Copyright 1938 by the Union of American Hebrew Congregations. Reprinted with the permission of The Jewish Publication Society of America.

fered repulse, and astonished and stupefied by the strength of mind of Philip the King and his constancy in the Lord, exclaimed with a certain admiration: "Shma Israel!". . . and prepared to sell all their household goods. The time was now at hand when the King had ordered them to leave France altogether, and it could not be in any way prolonged. Then did the Jews sell all their movable possessions in great haste, while their landed property reverted to the crown. Thus the Jews, having sold their goods and taken the price for the expenses of their journey, departed with their wives and children and all their households in the aforesaid year of the Lord 1182.

The terms of Jewish autonomy in Ashkenazic lands were quite favorable to the development of a sophisticated tradition of rabbinic legal scholarship. Local rabbis frequently handled a variety of ritual and civil cases without interference from Christian authorities. Accordingly there developed, as in Islamic lands, a rich literature of *responsa,* responses to specific legal problems. Rabbi Meir of Rothenburg (1220–1293) left an influential legacy of responsa. The following example deals with a case of personal injury between Jews that one party had first brought to a Christian court.

16.2E *RESPONSUM,* #177

I will respond briefly. As to the claim which is commonly heard that one who acts in the heat of anger is not liable, I reply in general that if he handed him over to the secular courts and caused him to lose money, then even though it was in the heat of anger, the defendant is responsible for the loss. This is because the obligation is not less binding than when two men injure one another where they each have to pay complete damages. Even though Rueben injured Simon at the outset, Simon retaliated and caused an even greater injury to Reuben, and therefore Simon must pay. He is not free to say that it was in the heat of anger and that no man is responsible for what he does in anger. I frankly do not know where that line of reasoning comes from. . . .

If it seems that the amount of damages for his injury is equivalent to the damages he caused the victim to lose by turning him over to the government, then we may relieve him of all further liability. If the amount for the injury is less than what he caused the other party to lose by informing on him, then we deduct the amount of the injury and he must pay the rest even though it was in the heat of anger. . . .

Finally, if in fact it is the case, as Simon claims, that he never handed Reuben over to the secular court and did not make him lose any money or that Reuben forgave him, then we do not need to be concerned with the remedies in this response,

From Rabbi Meir of Rothenberg (1220–1293) in Elliott N. Dorff and Arthur Rosett, *A Living Tree: Roots and Growth of Jewish Law.* Copyright © 1988 by State University of New York. Reprinted with the permission of the authors and State University of New York Press.

provided Simon will swear to Reuben in court that he did not cause Reuben to lose any money or will swear that Reuben forgave him.

Unlike the situation of Ashkenazi Jewry, Jews of Islamic lands lived in empires in which both Jews and Christians were minorities under a third religious power. Both religious communities were guaranteed protection by the Islamic government and granted substantial self-rule under their own religious leaders. In return for such autonomy, protected communities (*ahl al-dhimma*) were required to pay a substantial tax (*jizya*). The following prescriptions for the collection of this tax comes from the early Abbasid period (750–800).

16.2F *KITAB AL-KHARAJ*

The *jizya* is required of all the *ahl al-dhimma* in the Sawad . . . Hira, and the rest of the conquered lands, namely, the Jews, the Christians, the Zoroastrians, Sabaeans, and Samaritans. . . . The *jizya* is incumbent upon all adult males, but not upon women and children. For the wealthy the tax is forty-eight dirhams, for those of medium income twenty-four, and for the poor, the agricultural workers and manual laborers, twelve dirhams. It is to be collected from them each year. It may be paid in kind, for example, beasts of burden, goods, and other such things. These are to be accepted in accordance with their value.

No one of the *ahl al-dhimma* should be beaten in order to exact payment of the *jizya*, nor made to stand in the hot sun, nor should hateful things be inflicted upon their bodies, or anything of that sort. Rather, they should be treated with leniency. They should be imprisoned until they pay what they owe. They are not to be let out of custody until the *jizya* is collected from them in full. No governor may release any Christian, Jew, Zoroastrian, Sabaean, or Samaritan unless the *jizya* is collected from him. . . .

In the following passage, the medieval Muslim historian al-Tabari records measures taken by the ninth-century Abbasid Caliph al-Mutawakkil to restrict the social freedoms of Jewish and Christian subjects.

16.2G *TA'RIKH AL-RUSUL WA'L-MULUK*

In that year (850), al-Mutawakkil ordered that the Christians and the rest of the *ahl al-dhimma* be made to wear honey-colored hoods and the *zunnar* belts. [The text continues to describe other distinguishing forms of dress. . . .] He gave orders that any of their houses of worship built after the advent of Islam were to be destroyed

The selections from *Kitab al-Kharaj* and *Ta'rikh al-Rusul* are from N. Stillman, translator, *The Jews of Arab Lands: A History and Sourcebook.* Copyright © 1979 by The Jewish Publication Society of America. Reprinted with the permission of the publishers.

and that one-tenth of their homes be confiscated. If the place was spacious enough, it was to be converted into a mosque. If it was not suitable for a mosque, it was to be made an open space. He commanded that wooden images of devils be nailed to the doors of their homes to distinguish them from the homes of Muslims.

He forbade their being employed in the government offices or in any official business whereby they might have authority over Muslims. He prohibited their children studying in Muslim schools. Nor was any Muslim permitted to teach them. He forbade them to display crosses on their Palm Sunday, and he prohibited any Jewish chanting in the streets. He gave orders that their graves should be made level with the ground so as not to resemble the graves of Muslims. And he wrote to all his governors regarding this.

The Exilarchate and the Gaonate were the primary official organs of Jewish self-government throughout the Abbasid dynasty's duration. The appointment of the Exilarchate, in which the two Geonim of the Sura and the Pumbeditha academies played a role, was a matter of great religious and political moment. The Exilarchate's inauguration to office, accordingly, was a regal affair, much like the installation of royalty. *Seder Olam Zuta* preserves a report by one Rabbi Nathan HaKohen of Babylonia, describing the ceremony of the exilarch's installation.

16.2H *SEDER OLAM ZUTA*

When there was a communal consensus on the appointment, the two Heads of the Academies, together with their students, all the leaders of the congregation and the elders, would gather in some prominent individual's house in Baghdad. He would be one of the greatest of that generation, such as Netira or the like. . . .

The community would gather in the main synagogue on Thursday. The Exilarch would be installed by the laying on of hands. The shofar was sounded to let all the people know from the youngest to the eldest. And when everyone heard it, each of them would send him a gift . . . All the leaders of the congregation and the wealthy would send him fine clothes, jewelry, and gold and silver vessels—each as he saw fit. The Exilarch, for his part, would take great pains in preparing a feast for Thursday and Friday which included all kinds of food and drink, and all sorts of confections, such as various sweets.

[The main ceremony of installation occurred during the Sabbath morning service. During the first part of the ceremony, the new Exilarch and the Gaonim were hidden from the congregation. After the public recitation of the Amidah, the following occurred.] When everyone was seated, the Exilarch would emerge from the place where he was hidden, and when the people saw him, they would all rise to their feet and remain standing until he was seated alone on the dais that had been set up for him. Next, the Head of the Sura Academy would come out and take a seat on the dais after bowing to the Exilarch, who would return the bow. After

From N. Stillman, translator, *The Jews of Arab Lands: A History and Sourcebook.* Copyright © 1979 by The Jewish Publication Society of America. Reprinted with the permission of the publishers.

him the Head of the Pumbeditha Academy emerges, bows, and sits to the Exilarch's left. Throughout all this, the people remain standing until all three have taken their seats—the Exilarch in the center, the Sura Gaon on his right, and the Pumbedithan Gaon on his left. An empty space remained between each of the Geonim and the Exilarch. Over his head was spread a canopy of precious fabric which was suspended by a cord of fine linen and purple.

[After a blessing by the prayer leader, it is time for the sermon.] The Exilarch now begins the sermon, expounding on the Torah portion for that Sabbath. Or, he might give permission to the Sura Gaon to open the sermon, and the Sura Gaon, in turn, would grant permission to the Pumbeditha Gaon. In this way they show their deference to one another, until finally, the Head of the Sura Academy begins. An interpreter who is standing near him passes his words on to the people. He would deliver the sermon in an awe-inspiring manner with his eyes closed. He would envelop himself in his prayershawl which he pulled over his head and down to the brow. No one in the congregation would open his mouth, twitter, or say a word while he was speaking. Should he feel, however, that someone was talking, he would open his eyes, and fear and trembling would descend over the congregation. . . .

[The Exilarch is then given the honor of reading from the Torah, as the Sura Gaon translates it into Arabic for the congregation. At the conclusion of the service, a procession begins.] As the Exilarch departs, all the people accompany him to his house in a procession, going before and after him. The Exilarch does not permit any of the scholars who have accompanied him to his house to leave until they have enjoyed at least seven days' hospitality. From that time on, he does not leave his house. People gather and pray with him there, be it on secular days, sabbaths, or holidays. If he does have to go out on some business, he rides in the litter of an official similar to that of the Caliph's ministers. He would be beautifully attired. Behind him would walk a train of as many as fifteen men. His servant would run after him. Should he happen to pass any Israelites, they would run up to him, touch his hands, and greet him. . . . He would never go out without his entourage, just like any of the Caliph's ministers.

Under the Abbasid government, as in earlier Sasanian Babylonia, the jurisdiction of rabbinic law was confined to matters deemed beyond the interest of the state. Consequently, rabbinic jurisdiction did not include, among other things, the right to impose fines for civil damages, this being deemed a state prerogative. The talmudic sages accepted this limitation of jurisdiction under the Talmudic principle, "the law of the state is the law." Bound to this principle by tradition and political realities, it fell to the later geonic jurists to devise ways of using their authority to enforce compliance of Jews in areas in which their jurisdiction was questionable. Among these was the threat of excommunication, that is, publishing a notice that forbade all Jews from having religious, social, and economic relations with a particular individual. The following responsum, from the late-tenth-century Gaon of Sura, Rav Tzemakh Tzedek, addresses this question.

14.21 *Otzar Hageonim, Bava Kamma, #182*

In regard to what you asked, i.e., can we collect fines so that the sinner is not rewarded [for his sin through our powerlessness to fine him, I answer this:] The Rabbis announced this rule, that fines are not collected in Babylonia, for Rav Nahman sent a responsum to Rav Hisda saying: "Hisda, do you collect fines in Babylonia?" Therefore it is a widespread law that we do not collect fines except in Jerusalem through a small court of 23, and moreover we rule according to Rava, who said, "Payment for damage done to chattel by animals or for damage done to chattel by man can be collected even in Babylonia, whereas payment for injuries done to a man by another man or for injuries done to a man by animals cannot be collected in Babylonia." But so that a sinner will not be rewarded, and so that the Children of Israel will not be dissolute in causing injuries (for since they know that we do not impose fines in Babylonia, they may strike one another), the latest authorities have become accustomed to excommunicate the culprit until he satisfies the injured party through money or until many of his friends come to him and pacify him with words.

And there is a precedent in regard to someone who knocked out someone else's tooth, and the culprit came before Rav Tzadok Gaon of Sura, may his memory be blessed, who said to him: "I am not decreeing a specific amount that you must pay him, but go and satisfy him with either money or words." And now that all of the laws of fines are null and void, the custom which our master, Rav Tzadok Gaon, established . . . is what we do too.

16.3 The Jews and the Modern State

The French Revolution of 1789 sparked a debate that lasted throughout the nineteenth century about the relations of the Jews to the European state. Proponents of Jewish Emancipation—both Jews and Christians—argued that the state had no interest in legislating religion for its citizenry and that the Jews were a religious community. Accordingly, their religion should be no barrier to full participation in the life of the state. The terms of the debate are clearly enunciated by the Count of Clermont-Tonnerre, in this selection from his speech to the French National Assembly of 1789. The second passage reproduces the actual resolution of the French National Assembly, September 28, 1791, granting full rights to the Jews.

16.3A Count of Clermont-Tonnerre, Speech to the French National Assembly, 1789

Every religion must prove one thing—that it is moral. If there is a religion that commands theft and arson, it is necessary not only to refuse eligibility to those who profess it, but further to outlaw it. This consideration cannot be applied to the Jews. The reproaches that one makes of them are many. The gravest are unjust, the others are merely wrong. Usury, one says, is permitted them. This assertion is founded on nothing but a false interpretation of a principle of charity and brotherhood which forbids them to lend at interest among themselves. . . . Men who possess nothing but money cannot live but by making that money valuable, and you have always prevented them from possessing anything else. . . .

The Jews should be denied everything as a nation, but granted everything as individuals. They must be citizens. It is claimed that they do not want to be citizens, that they say this and that they are [thus] excluded; there cannot be one nation within another nation. . . . It is intolerable that the Jews should become a separate political formation or class in the country. Every one of them must individually become a citizen; if they do not want this, they must inform us and we shall then be compelled to expel them. The existence of a nation within a nation is unacceptable to our country . . .

The Jews must be assumed to be citizens as long as it is not proven that they are not citizens. By their petition they demand to be considered as such; the law must recognize a right that prejudice alone refuses. But, one says, the law does not rule over prejudice. That was true when the law was the work of only one man [i.e., the king]; when it is the work of all [i.e., the citizens], that is false.

16.3B RESOLUTION OF THE FRENCH NATIONAL ASSEMBLY, 1791

The National Assembly, considering that the conditions requisite to be a French citizen, and to become an active citizen, are fixed by the constitution, and that every man who, being duly qualified, takes the civic oath, and engages to fulfill all the duties prescribed by the constitution, has a right to all the advantages it insures.

Annuls all adjournments, restrictions, and exceptions, contained in the preceding decrees, affecting individuals of the Jewish persuasion, who shall take the civic oath, which shall be considered as a renunciation of all privileges in their favor.

As emancipation proceeded in its jagged course during the nineteenth century, Jews were frequently called upon to explain the nature of their Jewish loyalties and how these permitted loyalty to non-Jewish political communities. The first official Jewish pronouncement on such matters was made in France in 1806. The Emperor Napolean convened an Assembly of Jewish Notables to answer a number of pointed questions about Jewish loyalties. The substance of their reply was formulated in a document published in 1807 by a Jewish communal institution, the Grand Sanhedrin, created by Napolean to serve as an authoritative voice of official French Jewry.

This, preceding, and next two selections from Paul Mendes-Flohr and Judah Reinharz, eds., *The Jew in the Modern World* (New York: Oxford University Press, 1995), pp. 114, 118, 135–136, 333–334.

16.3C PROCLAMATION OF THE GRAND SANHEDRIN

Blessed for ever be the name of the Lord, God of Israel, who has placed upon the thrones of France and of the Kingdom of Italy a prince after His heart. God has seen the humiliation of the descendants of Jacob of old, and He has chosen Napolean the Great as the instrument of His compassion. . . . Under the shadow of his name security has come into our hearts and our dwellings and from this time on we are permitted to build, to sow, to reap, to cultivate all human knowledge, to be one with the great family of the State, to serve him and be glorified in his lofty destiny. . . . Gathered this day under his mighty protection, in the good city of Paris, we, learned men and leaders of Israel, to the number of seventy one, constitute ourselves the Grand Sanhedrin to the end that we may find the means and the strength to promulgate religious decrees which shall conform to the principles of our sacred laws and which shall serve as a standard to all Israelites. These decrees shall teach the nations that our dogmas are in keeping with the civil laws under which we live, and that we are in no wise separated from the society of men.

We therefore declare that the divine Law, the precious heritage of our ancestors, contains within itself dispositions which are political and dispositions which are religious; that the religious dispositions are, by their nature, absolute and independent of circumstances and of the age; that this does not hold true of the political dispositions, that is to say, of the dispositions which were taken for the government of the people of Israel in Palestine when it possessed its own kings, pontiffs, and magistrates; that these political dispositions are no longer applicable, since Israel no longer forms a nation; that in consecrating a distinction which has already been established by tradition, the Grand Sanhedrin lays down an incontestable truth . . . : that, if the Sanhedrin of old did not establish this distinction, it is because the political situation did not at that time call for it, and that, since the dispersion of Israel, no Sanhedrin has ever been assembled until the present one.

. . . Thus, by virtue of the right vested in us by our ancient usage and by our sacred laws, which have determined that the assembly of the learned of the age shall possess the inalienable right to legislate according to the needs of the situation, and which impose upon Israel the observance of these laws . . . we hereby religiously enjoin on all obedience to the State in all matters civil and political.

Vigorous objections to Jewish political and civil rights were voiced in a variety of quarters from the first decades of the nineteenth century. Only after 1870, however, did these sentiments find expression in single-issue political parties devoted to purging European states of Jewish political and cultural influence. These parties called themselves anti-Semitic parties, drawing upon racial theories of the day to assert that the Aryan races of northern Europe were being threatened by a foreign, Semitic race (the Jews) bent upon world conquest. An important anti-Semitic politician was Karl Eugen Duehring, whose book, *The Jewish Question as a Racial, Moral and Cultural Question* (1881), is cited here. Such sentiments were successfully exploited and amplified a half century later by the German Nazi Party under Adolf Hitler.

16.3D KARL EUGEN DUEHRING, *THE JEWISH QUESTION AS A RACIAL, MORAL AND CULTURAL QUESTION*

A Jewish question would still exist, even if every Jew were to turn his back on his religion and join one of our major churches. . . . It is precisely the baptized Jews who infiltrate furthest, unhindered in all sectors of society and political life. It is as though they have provided themselves with an unrestricted passport, advancing their stock to those places where members of the Jewish religion are unable to follow. . . . Through these portals the racial Jew, who has forsaken his religion, can enter unhindered. A situation similar to the one involving baptized Jews results as soon as all civic rights and opportunities become available to members of the Jewish religion. Thereupon they force themselves into all aspects of social and political life, just like those who have converted to Christianity. . . .

I return therefore to the hypothesis that the Jews are to be defined solely on the basis of race, and not on the basis of religion. I dismiss all conclusions hitherto upheld. . . . The Mosaic attempt to locate within the base of our people a Jewish component only makes the Jewish question a more burning issue. . . . The sprinkling of racial Jewry in the cracks and crevices of our national abode must inevitably lead to a reaction. It is impossible that close contact [between Germans and Jews] will take effect without the concomitant realization that this infusion of Jewish qualities is incompatible with our best impulses.

One of Jewry's most cogent and successful responses to anti-Semitic ideologies was the Zionist ideology of Jewish nationalism. Zionists proposed diverse analyses of the causes of anti-Semitism and equally diverse visions of what the re-creation of a Jewish State in Palestine could mean for the Jewish political, cultural, and spiritual future. Following are statements of three representative figures. The first is Theodore Herzl's analysis of anti-Semitism in his book *The Jewish State* (1896). Following is a 1920 essay by the visionary ideologist of "Jewish Labor," A. D. Gordon, an account of an apolitical goal of Jewish national regeneration through agricultural work ("Our Tasks Ahead"). Finally comes a statement from David ben Gurion, an influential Socialist-Zionist activist who became the first prime minister of the State of Israel. It is part of a speech—"The Imperatives of the Jewish Revolution"—given in 1944 to a Zionist youth group as the magnitude of the destruction of European Jewry was becoming clear.

16.3E *THE JEWISH STATE*

Modern anti-Semitism is not to be confused with the persecution of the Jews in former times, though it does still have a religious aspect in some countries. The

From Theodor Herzl, *The Jewish State*, translated from the German by Sylvie D'Avigdor, from Ludwig Lewisjohn, ed., *Theodor Herzl: A Portrait for this Age* (Cleveland: World Publishing Company, 1955), as found in Arthur Hertzberg, *The Zionist Idea: A Historical Analysis and Reader* (New York: Atheneum Publishers, 1977), pp. 218–220.

main current of Jew-hatred is today a different one. In the principal centers of anti-Semitism, it is an outgrowth of the emancipation of the Jews. When civilized nations awoke to the inhumanity of discriminatory legislation and enfranchised us, our enfranchisement came too late. Legislation alone no longer sufficed to emancipate us in our old homes. For in the ghetto we had remarkably developed into a bourgeois people and we emerged from the ghetto a prodigious rival to the middle class. Thus we found ourselves thrust, upon emancipation, into this bourgeois circle, where we have a double pressure to sustain, from within and without. The Christian bourgeoisie would indeed not be loath to cast us as a peace offering to socialism, little though that would avail them.

At the same time, the equal rights of Jews before the law cannot be rescinded where they have been once granted. Not only because their recision would be contrary to the spirit of our age, but also because it would immediately drive all Jews, rich and poor alike, into the ranks of the revolutionary parties. No serious harm can really be done us. In olden days our jewels were taken from us. How is our movable property to be seized now? . . . The very impossibility of getting at the Jews nourishes and deepens hatred of them. Anti-Semitism increases day by day and hour by hour among the nations; indeed, it is bound to increase, because the causes of its growth continue to exist and are ineradicable. Its remote cause is the loss of our assmilibility during the Middle Ages; its immediate cause is our excessive production of mediocre intellectuals, who have no outlet downward or upward—or rather, no wholesome outlet in either direction. When we sink, we become a revolutionary proletariat, the corporals of every revolutionary party; and when we rise, there rises also our terrifying financial power.

. . . We are one people—our enemies have made us one whether we will or not, as has repeatedly happened in history. Affliction binds us together, and thus united, we suddenly discover our strength. Yes, we are strong enough to form a State, and, indeed, a model State. We possess all the requisite human and material resources.

16.3F OUR TASKS AHEAD

. . . There is a primal force within every one of us, which is fighting for its own life, which seeks its own realization. This is our ethnic self, the cosmic element of which we spoke, which combined with the historical element, forms one of the basic ingredients of the personality of each and every one of us. The ethnic self may be described as a peculiar national pattern of mental and physical forces, which affects the personality of every individual member of the ethnic group. . . .

Jewish life in the Diaspora lacks this cosmic element of national identity. . . . What we have come to find in Palestine is the cosmic element. In the countries of the Exile we are compelled to lead an inanimate existence, lacking in national creativity.... There our ethnic self is forced into a ruinously constricted and shrunken form; having no living source of spontaneous vitality, it must perforce draw on our past and become ever more desiccated, or it must tap alien sources and become blurred, dissolving in the spirit of its environment.

It is life we want, no more and no less than that, our own life feeding on our own vital sources, in the fields and under the skies of our Homeland, a life based on our own mental and physical labors; we want vital energy and spiritual richness from this living source. We come to our Homeland in order to be planted in our natural soil from which we have been uprooted, to strike our roots deep into its life-giving substances, and to stretch out our branches in the sustaining and creating air and sunlight of the Homeland.... We, who have been torn away from nature, who have lost the savor of natural living—if we desire life, we must establish a new relationship with nature; we must open a new account with it....

We are engaged in a creative endeavor the like of which is not to be found in the whole history of mankind: the rebirth and rehabilitation of a people that has been uprooted and scattered to the winds. It is a people half dead, and the effort to recreate it demands the exclusive concentration of the creator on his work. The center of our national work, the heart of our people, is here, in Palestine, even though we are but a small community in this country, for here is the mainspring of our life.... Here something is beginning to flower which has greater human significance and far wider ramifications than our history-makers envisage.... Here in Palestine is the force attracting all the scattered cells of the people to unite into one living national organism....

We must draw our inspiration from our land, from life on our own soil, from the labor we are engaged in, and must be on guard against allowing too many influences from outside to affect us. What we seek to establish in Palestine is a new, recreated Jewish people, not a mere colony of Diaspora Jewry, not a continuation of Diaspora life in a new form. It is our aim to make Jewish Palestine the mother country of world Jewry, with Jewish communities of the Diaspora as its colonies— and not the reverse. We seek the rebirth of our national self, the manifestation of our loftiest spirit, and for that we must give our all.

16.3G DAVID BEN GURION "THE IMPERATIVES OF THE JEWISH REVOLUTION"

The absorption of immigration will be a more difficult task than ever before and will require of us new and unprecedented efforts. The new immigrants will be coming to us from misery and poverty and will need prolonged care and intensive help from the pioneer vanguard. Where can we get such pioneering leadership, now that the great reserves in Poland, Lithuania, Galicia, and Czechoslovakia have been done to death? The youth of the homeland must now assume these pioneering tasks. It is impossible to fill the terrible void left by the destruction of European Jewry. This dreadful loss is irreplaceable—and a greater obligation is therefore placed on Israeli youth. . . .

. . . The ingathering of the exiles into a socialist Jewish state is in fact only a precondition for the fulfillment of the real mission of our people. We must first break the constricting chains of national and class oppression and become free men, enjoying complete individual and national independence on the soil of the redeemed homeland. After that we can address ourselves to the great mission of man on this earth—to master the forces of nature and to develop his unique creative genius to the highest degree.

. . . Let us all remain faithful without any reservation, faithful in thought and deed, in emotion and will, to the demands and the mission of the Jewish revolution; let us preserve our inner dignity and unity and our continuing solidarity with both the Jewish people as a whole and the international labor movement; and let us transform the beaten and downtrodden into the pioneers of a work of immigration and resettlement equal to the grave crisis and the redemptive vision of our people. If such be our program, there is hope that many of us will live to see the consummation of the Jewish revolution—the concentration of the majority of our people in a homeland transformed into a socialist Jewish state.

16.4 THE HOLOCAUST, ISRAEL, AND CONTEMPORARY JEWRY

The close historical coincidence of the destruction of European Jewry and the creation of the State of Israel has had a powerful symbolic resonance among contemporary Jews. The following statement, written as a kind of "generational statement" by the historian of Judaism Jacob Neusner, vividly captures the emotional force of the Holocaust and Israel as symbolic realities for those American Jews born after 1930.

16.4A *STRANGER AT HOME*

Once upon a time, when I was a young man, I felt helpless before the world. I was a Jew, when being Jewish was a bad thing. As a child, I saw my old Jewish parents, speaking a foreign language and alien in countless ways, isolated from America. And I saw America, dimly perceived, to be sure, exciting and promising, but hostile to me as a Jew. I could not get into a good college. I could not aspire to medical school. I could not become an architect or an engineer. I could not even work for an electric utility. . . . Above all, I saw myself as weak and pitiful. I could not do anything about being a Jew nor could I do much to improve my lot as a Jew.

Then came Hitler and I saw that what was my private lot was the dismal fate of every Jew. Everywhere Jew hatred was raised from the gutter to the heights. Not from Germany alone, but from people I might meet at work or in the streets I learned that being Jewish was a metaphysical evil. . . . As I approached maturity, a still more frightening fact confronted me. People guilty of no crime but Jewish birth were forced to flee their homeland, and no one would accept them. Ships filled with ordinary men, women and children searched the oceans for a safe harbor. And I and they had nothing in common but one fact, and that fact made all else inconsequential. Had I been there, I should have been among them. I, too, should not have been saved at sea.

Then came the war and, in its aftermath, the revelation of the shame and horror of holocaust, the decay and corrosive hopelessness of the Displaced Persons camps, the contempt of the nations, who would neither accept nor help the saved remnants of hell.

At the darkest hour came the dawn. The State of Israel saved the remnant and gave meaning and significance to the inferno. After the dawn, the great light: Jews no longer helpless, weak, unable to decide their own fate, but strong, confident, decisive. And then came the corrupting doubt; if I were there, I should have died in hell. But now has come redemption and I am here, not there.

How much security in knowing that if it should happen again I shall not be lost. But how great a debt paid in guilt for being where I am and who I am!

North American Jewry is composed of various subcommunities divided by deep ideological differences regarding what it means to be a Jew. Thus, many Jewish secularists reject notions that Jewish identity must include religious beliefs, whereas religiously oriented Jews are themselves divided into Orthodox, Reform, Conservative, and Reconstructionist forms of belief and practice. Nevertheless, this same American Jewish community supports many national organizations that pursue charitable or political goals in the name of the Jewish community as a whole. These organizations attempt to remind Jews of values and experiences that all may share. Public advertising of these organizations, therefore, offers valuable insight into common aspects of Jewish identification. The following ad was created for the American Jewish Committee. It is one of a series run during the High Holiday season of 1993, in which a number of well-known American Jews shared their feelings about "What Being Jewish Means to Me." The author is Ann Roiphe, a widely read journalist and novelist of Jewish ethnic background who has recently "returned to Judaism." What seem to be the most salient aspects of shared Jewishness assumed in this brief essay?

16.4B ANN ROIPHE, "WHAT BEING JEWISH MEANS TO ME"

This Rosh Ha-Shanah, the year 5754 when everything begins again, the sound of the shofar cracks open my heart. Hopeful rumors are rustling in the thicket: Peace?

I was ankle-deep in middle age, wading down the waters of assimilation when I discovered that being Jewish was more than I have ever dreamed. How lucky for me. Now I mark the calendar with the Jewish cycle of celebrations, my table turns with Seder plate, Challah bread, and honey for the New Year. I've learned the whole story. I learned where Chelm, the town of fools, lies on the map. I can tell you wild tales about Jewish gangsters in Chicago and Jewish soldiers in the Czar's army. I expanded my family. Freud and Einstein are cousins of mine, so are Rashi and Maimonides. Once I knew only about Jewish catastrophe, now I can tell a Jewish joke . . . and I have seen Torah pointers, cups for Elijah and menorahs made of clay.

I am the same old feminist I always was. I am still a left-of-center, First Amendment, anti-war sort of person. I am the same former field-hockey player chasing the ball, socks falling down. But now I have pictures in my mind of the destruction of the Temple, of the exile from Spain, of transport trains. I know the stories of Gluckel of Hameln and Rabbi Nachman of Bratslav. I have seen tomatoes growing in the Negev and can imagine the Baal Shem Tov dancing in the forest. I am no longer the child who asks what has this to do with me. I was proud at Entebbe [when Israeli soldiers slipped into Uganda to rescue Jews from terrorists], my heart skipped beats when the [Iraqi] Scuds flew over Tel Aviv [during the Gulf War]. When Russian Jews and Ethiopian Jews arrive at Ben-Gurion airport, I feel like a child at her birthday party. The survival of Israel, its difficult, quarrelsome, glorious bark, soothes me.

Today I frequently argue with a God whose existence I question, but I think that the Jewish people has a purpose, a destiny, a reason for being, perhaps only in the wonder of our plot, the continuing efforts to make us shape up, behave decently, look at ourselves with a moral eye. I am no longer a mere particle of genetic material spinning out a single life span. I have a past, present, and future among my people. Am I ever surprised!

Among Israeli Jews, the symbols of European Holocaust and redemption in Israel are thoroughly intertwined with the daily reality of generations of Jewish-Arab violence. In such an environment, great pressure is routinely placed on Jewish religious tradition to support a variety of ideological positions regarding the nature of the problem. In not a few versions, the Arab resistance to Israel is viewed as a continuation of the genocidal European assault against the Jews. What follows are some probing reflections by Charles Liebman, an American immigrant to Israel, a Jew with abiding commitments to Jewish religion, and an influential sociologist. His remarks were made in a 1983 speech at the University of Capetown, South Africa.

From Ann Roiphe, "What Being Jewish Means to Me" (The American Jewish Committee ad, High Holiday season 1993). Reprinted with the permission of The American Jewish Committee.

16.4c Charles Liebman, "Attitudes Toward Jewish-Gentile Relations in the Jewish Tradition and Contemporary Israel"

I have said that present Israeli conceptions of the *Goy* (Gentile) or of Jewish-Gentile relations are a return to a major motif of the tradition. But there is one important difference. Jews in Israel now possess political and military power to act out certain conceptions which, within the rabbinic tradition were pure hyperbole or hypothetical constructions. These constructions served as ideological weapons to comfort and console an otherwise defenceless people. Today, however, they may serve to encourage and legitimate violence and terror. . . . Dare we lightly dismiss an essay by the former campus rabbi of Bar Ilan University titled "Genocide Is a Commandment from the Torah"—an essay looking forward to the day that all Amelikites will be exterminated; or an editor's column in a student newspaper which invokes a rabbinic homily that the only way to treat the non-Jewish residents of the Holy Land is to murder them? Do these statements make you squirm? Then think how I who live among these people feel when I hear them. But I am even more upset when I hear justifications of the outrages committed by some Israeli troops, or by some of the Jewish settlers on the West Bank, in the name of rabbinic tradition. . . .

What I want to urge is a conception of Jewish-Gentile relations which unravels both the Zionist and the traditional rabbinic package. As I said, I deny that we must choose between one package with its conceptions of Jewish normalcy and rejection of the tradition and denial of any meaning to the Holocaust, and the other package which affirms the tradition, preaches Jewish-Gentile hostility and interprets the Holocaust as the inevitable outcome of Jewish defencelessness and the absence of a Jewish State. . . .

There is more to the Holocaust than lessons and morals. But let us confine ourselves now to their elucidation. I deny that the Holocaust teaches us that if Jews are not strong enough or do not have a state the *Goyim* will destroy us. This is a foolish lesson. Of course the Jews and Israel must be strong. If my Arab neighbors were capable of destroying me then unfortunately there is no question they would do so. I do not need the Holocaust or the rabbinic tradition to teach me that. But to generalize from the Holocaust that *Goyim* will kill Jews if Jews are not strong enough is foolish because all Jews would long since have been dead. . . .

The primary lesson of the Holocaust, for me, is that . . . if I choose to be Jewish I am making a momentous choice, fraught with consequence. I had better be absolutely sure I know what I'm choosing. Surely "Jewish survival" is not enough. . . . At no point, at no place in the tradition are Jews instructed to survive. This is not our mandate. This is God's problem. We must only obey Him. And if all I want is personal survival I can do a lot better than join my lot to the Jewish people in general and the State of Israel in particular. . . .

From Charles Liebman, "Attitudes Toward Jewish-Gentile Relations in the Jewish Tradition and Contemporary Israel" (excerpts), 1983 speech at the University of Capetown, Kaplan Center for Jewish Studies and Research. Reprinted with the permission of the author.

The second lesson I learn from the Holocaust is the special responsibility that my experience as a Jew imposes upon me. This also reinforces my understanding of the Jewish tradition, but you must remember that I am primarily a product of the west, not of eastern European Jewry from which I am two generations removed. So the tradition is filtered to me through the more liberal and universalist perspectives of the rabbis of the west. If the events of the Holocaust affect me in some special way; if I, as a Jew, experience the Holocaust however vicariously, in a way non-Jews did not and cannot experience it, then I understand in a way they do not understand the consequence of indifference to evil and suffering. Therefore I cannot remain indifferent to evil and suffering even when they seem not to affect me as a Jew—as in South Africa.

RELIGION AND POLITICAL ORDER

CHAPTER 17
IN CHRISTIANITY

17.1 THE TWO REALMS

When Jesus commissions his twelve hand-picked apostles in the Gospel of Matthew, he knowingly sends them out into a hostile world. Christian thinking on the relation between the church and the "world"—or more precisely, between church and state—has always been framed in terms of the dichotomies highlighted by Jesus in these passages.

17.1A MATTHEW 10:1, 5, 7–10, 17–39

The Mission of the Twelve

He summoned his twelve disciples, and gave them authority over unclean spirits with power to cast them out and to cure all kinds of diseases and sickness.

These twelve Jesus sent out, instructing them as follows: "as you go, proclaim that the kingdom of heaven is close at hand. Cure the sick, raise the dead, cleanse the lepers, cast out devils. You received without charge, give without charge. Provide yourselves with no gold or silver, not even with a few coppers for your purses, with no haversack for the journey or spare tunic or footwear or a staff, for the workman deserves his keep. . . .

The Missionaries Will Be Persecuted

"Beware of men: they will hand you over to Sanhedrins and scourge you in their synagogues. You will be dragged before governors and kings for my sake, to bear witness before them and the pagans. But when they hand you over, do not worry about how to speak or what to say; what you are to say will be given to you when the time comes; because it is not you who will be speaking; the Spirit of your Father will be speaking in you.

"Brother will betray brother to death, and the father his child; children will rise against their parents and have them put to death. You will be hated by all men on account of my name: but the man who stands firm to the end will be saved. If they persecute you in one town, take refuge in the next; and if they persecute you in that, take refuge in another. I tell you solemnly, you will not have gone the round of the towns of Israel before the Son of Man comes.

"The disciple is not superior to his teacher, nor the slave to his master. It is enough for the disciple that he should grow to be like his teacher, and the slave like his master. If they have called the master of the house Beelzebul, what will they not say of his household?

Open and Fearless Speech

"Do not be afraid of them therefore. For everything that is now covered will be uncovered, and everything now hidden will be made clear. What I say to you in the dark, tell in the daylight; what you hear in whispers, proclaim from the housetops.

"Do not be afraid of those who kill the body but cannot kill the soul; fear him rather who can destroy both body and soul in hell. Can you not buy two sparrows for a penny? And yet not one falls to the ground without your Father knowing. Why, every hair on your head has been counted. So there is no need to be afraid; you are worth more than hundreds of sparrows.

"So if anyone declares himself for me in the presence of men, I will declare myself for him in the presence of my Father in heaven. But the one who disowns me in the presence of men, I will disown in the presence of my Father in heaven.

Jesus, the Cause of Dissension

"Do not suppose that I have come to bring peace to the earth: it is not peace I have come to bring, but a sword. For I have come to set *a man against his father, a daughter against her mother, a daughter-in-law against her mother-in-law. A man's enemies will be those of his own household.*

Renouncing Self to Follow Jesus

"Anyone who prefers father or mother to me is not worthy of me. Anyone who prefers son or daughter to me is not worthy of me. Anyone who does not take his cross and follow in my footsteps is not worthy of me. Anyone who finds his life will lose it; anyone who loses his life for my sake will find it."

No other text in the Bible can rival *Luke* for its impact on Christian political thinking. For two millennia, the deceptively simple distinction made here by Jesus between the realms of Caesar and God has dominated Christian discourse and Christian political life as well. However, distinguishing between those aspects of social life that are under the government's authority and those that pertain to the church has never been easy. More often than not, those who run church and state have disagreed on the interpretation of this passage.

17.1B THE GOSPEL OF LUKE 20:20–20:26

But for their fear of the people, the scribes and the chief priests would have liked to lay hands on him. . . .

So they waited their opportunity and sent agents to pose as men devoted to the Law, and to fasten on something he might say and so enable them to hand him over to the jurisdiction and authority of the governor. They put to him this question, "Master, we know that you say and teach what is right; you favor no one, but teach the way of God in all honesty. Is it permissible for us to pay taxes to Caesar or not?" But he was aware of their cunning and said, "Show me a denarius. Whose head and name are on it?" "Caesar's," they said. "Well then," he said to them, "give back to Caesar what belongs to Caesar—and to God what belongs to God."

As a result, they were unable to find fault with anything he had to say in public; his answer took them by surprise and they were silenced.

The political drama of Jesus' trial and execution by the Roman authorities figures prominently in John's Gospel. This narrative portrays Jesus as unwilling to meddle in worldly politics even when his life is at stake. Jesus' declaration "Mine is not a kingdom of this world" has been variously employed to delimit or expand the role of the church in the world. The same could be said of Jesus' retort to Pilate: "You would have no power over me if it had not been given you from above." The frustration felt by Pilate in this Gospel narrative seems adequately prophetic, for all secular rulers who have tangled with church authorities have been placed in a similarly uncomfortable situation.

17.1C GOSPEL OF SAINT JOHN 18:28–19:22

Jesus Before Pilate

They then led Jesus from the house of Caiaphas to the Praetorium. It was now morning. They did not go into the Praetorium themselves or they would be defiled and unable to eat the passover. So Pilate came outside to them and said, "What charge do you bring against this man?" They replied, "If he were not a criminal, we should not be handing him over to you." Pilate said, "Take him yourselves, and try him by your own Law." The Jews answered, "We are not allowed to put a man to death." This was to fulfill the words Jesus had spoken indicating the way he was going to die.

So Pilate went back into the Praetorium and called Jesus to him, "Are you the king of the Jews?" he asked. Jesus replied, "Do you ask this of your own accord, or have others spoken to you about me?" Pilate answered, "Am I a Jew? It is your own people and the chief priests who have handed you over to me: what have you done?" Jesus replied, "Mine is not a kingdom of this world; if my kingdom were of this world, my men would have fought to prevent my being surrendered to the Jews. But my kingdom is not of this kind." "So you are king then?" said Pilate. "It is you who say it," answered Jesus. "Yes, I am a king. I was born for this, I came into the world for this: to bear witness to the truth; and all who are on the side of truth listen to my voice." "Truth?" said Pilate. "What is that?"; and with that he went out again to the Jews and said, "I find no case against him. But according to a custom of yours I should release one prisoner at the Passover; would you like me, then, to release the king of the Jews?" At this they shouted: "Not this man," they said, "but Barabbas." Barabbas was a brigand.

Pilate then had Jesus taken away and scourged; and after this, the soldiers twisted some thorns into a crown and put it on his head, and dressed him in a purple robe. They kept coming up to him and saying, "Hail, king of the Jews!"; and they slapped him in the face.

Pilate came outside again and said to them, "Look, I am going to bring him out to you to let you see that I find no case." Jesus then came out wearing the crown of thorns and the purple robe. Pilate said, "Here is the man." When they saw him the chief priests and the guards shouted, "Crucify him! Crucify him!" Pilate said, "Take him yourselves and crucify him: I can find no case against him." "We have a Law," the Jews replied, "and according to that Law he ought to die."

When Pilate heard them say this his fears increased. Re-entering the Praetorium, he said to Jesus, "Where do you come from?" But Jesus made no answer. Pilate then said to him, "Are you refusing to speak to me? Surely you know I have power to release you and I have power to crucify you?" "You would have no power over me," replied Jesus, "if it had not been given you from above; that is why the one who handed me over to you has the greater guilt.". . .

From that moment Pilate was anxious to set him free, but the Jews shouted, "If you set him free you are no friend of Caesar's; anyone who makes himself king is defying Caesar." Hearing these words, Pilate had Jesus brought out, and seated himself on the chair of judgment at a place called the Pavement, in Hebrew Gabbatha. It was Passover Preparation Day, about the sixth hour. "Here is your king," said Pilate to the Jews. "Take him away, take him away!" they said. "Crucify him!" "Do you want me to crucify your king?" said Pilate. The chief priests answered, "We have no king except Caesar." So in the end Pilate handed him over to them to be crucified. . . .

They then took charge of Jesus, and carrying his own cross he went out of the city to the place of the skull or, as it was called in Hebrew, Golgotha, where they crucified him with two others, one on either side with Jesus in the middle. Pilate wrote out a notice and had it fixed to the cross; it ran: "Jesus the Nazarene, King of the Jews." The notice was read by many of the Jews, because the place where Jesus was crucified was not far from the city, and the writing was in Hebrew, Latin and Greek. So the Jewish chief priests said to Pilate, "You should not write 'King of the Jews,' but 'This man said: I am King of the Jews.'" Pilate answered, "What I have written, I have written."

This portion of *Romans* is the foundation of much of Christian political thought, alongside Jesus' gospel admonition to distinguish between Caesar and God. The message here is not ambiguous at all: Paul argues that God rules human society through the established authorities—even those that are obviously evil—and asks all Christians to be good citizens. Needless to say, this text has long been a favorite of secular rulers, for it assigns a sacred dimension to their rulership.

17.1D PAUL'S LETTER TO THE ROMANS 12:14–13:7

Bless those who persecute you: never curse them, bless them. Rejoice with those who rejoice and be sad with those in sorrow. Treat everyone with equal kindness; never be condescending but make real friends with the poor. Do not allow yourself to become self-satisfied. Never repay evil with evil but let everyone see that you are interested only in the highest ideals. Do all you can to live at peace with everyone. Never try to get revenge; leave that, my friends, to God's anger. As scripture says: *Vengeance is mine—I will pay them back*, the Lord promises. But there is more: *If your enemy is hungry, you should give him food, and if he is thirsty, let him drink. Thus you heap red-hot coals on his head.* Resist evil and conquer it with good.

Submission to Civil Authority

You must all obey the governing authorities. Since all government comes from God, the civil authorities were appointed by God, and so anyone who resists authority is rebelling against God's decision, and such an act is bound to be punished. Good behavior is not afraid of magistrates; only criminals have anything to fear. If you want to live without being afraid of authority, you must live honestly and authority may even honor you. The state is there to serve God for your benefit. If you break the law, however, you may well have fear: the bearing of the sword has its significance. The authorities are there to serve God: they carry out God's revenge by punishing wrongdoers. You must obey, therefore, not only because you are afraid of being punished, but also for conscience' sake. This is also the reason why you must pay taxes, since all government officials are God's officers. They serve God by collecting taxes. Pay every government official what he has a right to ask—whether it be direct tax or indirect, fear or honor.

Augustine dominates the history of Western Christian political thought. In the early fifth century, as the Roman Empire was collapsing, Augustine formulated a political theology based upon the dichotomy between the spiritual and earthly realms. Augustine understood human society to be composed of two groups of people: those who loved themselves and those who loved God. It was the latter, of course, who were predestined to redemption. In his *City of God*, Augustine juxtaposed the two societies—or cities—that of God ruled by true love against that of this world ruled by self-love. For Augustine, civil government was a necessary evil, a by-product of fallen human nature, rather than an essential and natural human drive. This negative assessment of human political life served to elevate the status of the church in the minds of many who read him. Augustine was too complex a thinker to identify the City of God as the church, however: in truth, he said, the two cities would be commingled until the end of time. Other thinkers and ecclesiasts were less subtle. As could be expected, Augustine's pessimism about human political life was often used to promote the superiority of the church over the state. In these passages from *The City of God*, we see him laying the foundation for much of medieval thought.

17.1E AUGUSTINE OF HIPPO, THE TWO CITIES

Origins of Coercive Government

Fallen Nature and the Two Cities

God, desiring not only that the human race might be able by their similarity of nature to associate with one another, but also that they might be bound together in harmony and peace by the ties of relationship, was pleased to derive all men from one individual. And He created men with such a nature that the members of the race should not have died, had not the first two (of whom one was created out of nothing, and the other out of him) merited this with their disobedience; for by them so great a sin was committed, that by it the human nature was altered for the worse, and was transmitted also to their posterity.

That the whole human race has been condemned in its first origin, this life itself, if life it is to be called, bears witness by the host of cruel ills with which it is filled. Is not this proved by the profound and dreadful ignorance which produces all the errors that enfold the children of Adam, and from which no man can be delivered without toil, pain, and fear? Is it not proved by his love of so many vain and hurtful things, which produces gnawing cares, disquiet, griefs, fears, wild joys, quarrels, law-suits, wars, treasons, angers, hatreds, deceit, flattery, fraud, theft, robbery, perfidy, pride, ambition, envy, murders, parricides, cruelty, ferocity, wickedness,

From Augustine of Hippo, "The Two Cities," in Henry Paolucci, ed., *The Political Writings of St. Augustine*. Reprinted with the permission of Regnery Publishing, Inc., Washington, DC.

luxury, insolence, impudence, shamelessness, fornications, adulteries, incests, and the numberless uncleannesses and unnatural acts of both sexes, which it is shameful so much as to mention; sacrileges, heresies, blasphemies, perjuries, oppression of the innocent, calumnies, plots, falsehoods, false witnessings, unrighteous judgments, violent deeds, plunderings, and innumerable other crimes that do not easily come to mind, but that never absent themselves from the actuality of human existence? These are indeed the crimes of wicked men, yet they spring from that root of error and misplaced love which is born with every son of Adam. For who is there that has not observed with what profound ignorance, manifesting itself even in infancy, and with what superfluity of foolish desires, beginning to appear in boyhood, man comes into this life, so that, were he left to live as he pleased, and to do whatever he pleased, he would plunge into all, or certainly into many of those crimes and iniquities which I mentioned, and could not mention?

But because God does not wholly desert those whom He condemns, nor shuts up in His anger His tender mercies, the human race is restrained by law and education, which keep guard against the ignorance that besets us, and oppose the assaults of vice, but are themselves full of labour and sorrow. For what mean those multifarious threats which are used to restrain the folly of children? What mean pedagogues, masters, the birch, the strap, the cane, the schooling which Scripture says must be given a child, "beating him on the sides lest he wax stubborn," and it be hardly possible or not possible at all to subdue him? Why all these punishments, save to overcome ignorance and bridle evil desires—these evils with which we come into the world? . . . Does not this show what vitiated nature inclines and tends to by its own weight, and what succour it needs if it is to be delivered? . . .

But, besides the punishments of childhood, without which there would be no learning of what the parents wish—and the parents rarely wish anything useful to be taught—who can describe, who can conceive the number and severity of the punishments which afflict the human race—pains which are not only the accompaniment of the wickedness of godless men, but are a part of the human condition and the common misery—what fear and what grief are caused by bereavement and mourning, by losses and condemnations, by fraud and falsehood, by false suspicions, and all the crimes and wicked deeds of other men? For at their hands we suffer robbery, captivity, chains, imprisonment, exile, torture, mutilation, loss of sight, the violation of chastity to satisfy the lust of the oppressor, and many other dreadful evils. What numberless casualties threaten our bodies from without—extremes of heat and cold, storms, floods, inundation, lightning, thunder, hail, earthquakes, houses falling; or from the stumbling, or shying, or vice of horses; from countless poisons in fruits, water, air, animals; from the painful or even deadly bites of wild animals; from the madness which a mad dog communicates, so that even the animal which of all others is most gentle and friendly to its own master, becomes an object of intenser fear than a lion or dragon, and the man whom it has by chance infected with this pestilential contagion becomes so rabid, that his parents, wife, children, dread him more than any wild beast! What disasters are suffered by those who travel by land or sea! What man can go out of his own house without being exposed on all hands to unforeseen accidents? . . .

As to bodily diseases, they are so numerous that they cannot all be contained even in medical books. And in very many, or almost all of them, the cures and remedies are themselves tortures, so that men are delivered from a pain that destroys by a cure that pains. Has not the madness of thirst driven men to drink human urine, and even their own? Has not hunger driven men to eat human flesh, and that the flesh not of bodies found dead, but of bodies slain for the purpose? Have not the fierce pangs of famine driven mothers to eat their own children, incredibly savage as it seems? In fine, sleep itself, which is justly called repose, how little of repose there sometimes is in it when disturbed with dreams and visions; and with what terror is the wretched mind overwhelmed by the appearances of things which are so presented, and which, as it were, so stand out before the senses, that we cannot distinguish them from realities! . . .

From this hell upon earth, the deserved penalty of sin would have hurled all headlong even into the second death, of which there is no end, had not the undeserved grace of God saved some therefrom. And thus it has come to pass, that though there are very many and great nations all over the earth, whose rites and customs, speech, arms, and dress, are distinguished by marked differences, yet there are no more than two kinds of human society, which we may justly call two cities, according to the language of our Scriptures. The one consists of those who wish to live after the flesh, the other of those who wish to live after the spirit.

In enunciating this proposition of ours, then, that because some live according to the flesh and others according to the spirit there have arisen two diverse and conflicting cities, we might equally well have said, "because some live according to man, others according to God.". . .

He who resolves to love God, and to love his neighbor as himself, not according to man but according to God, is on account of this love said to be of a good will; and this is in Scripture more commonly called charity, but it is also, even in the same books, called love. . . . The right will is, therefore, well-directed love, and the wrong will is ill-directed love. . . .

Two cities have been formed, therefore, by two loves: the earthly by love of self, even to contempt of God; the heavenly by love of God, even to contempt of self. The former glories in itself, the latter in the Lord. For the one seeks glory from men; but the greatest glory of the other is God, the witness of conscience. The one lifts up its head in its own glory; the other says to its God, "Thou art my glory, and the lifter up of mine head." In the one, the princes and the nations it subdues are ruled by the love of ruling; in the other, the princes and the subjects serve one another in love, the latter obeying, while the former take thought for all. The one delights in its own strength, represented in the persons of its rulers; the other says to its God, "I will love Thee, O Lord, my strength." And therefore the wise men of the one city, living according to man, have sought for profit to their own bodies or souls, or both. . . .

But in the other city there is no human wisdom, but only godliness, which offers due worship to the true God, and looks for its reward in the society of the saints, of holy angels as well as holy men, "that God may be all in all." And when these two cities severally achieve what they wish, they live in peace, each after its kind.

Now peace is a good so great, that even in this earthly and mortal life there is no word we hear with such pleasure, nothing we more strongly desire, or enjoy more thoroughly when it comes. So that if we dwell for a little longer on this subject, we shall not, in my opinion, be wearisome to our readers who will bear with us both for the sake of understanding what is the end of this city of which we speak, and for the sake of the sweetness of peace which is dear to all.

Everyone who has observed the conduct of men's affairs and common human nature will agree with me in this: that just as there is no man who does not long for joy, so there is no man who does not long for peace. Even those who want war, want it really only for victory's sake: that is, they want to attain a glorious peace by fighting. For what is victory if not the subjugation of those who resist us? And when this is done, peace follows.

It is therefore with the desire for peace that wars are waged, even by those who take pleasure in exercising their warlike nature in command and battle. And hence it is obvious that peace is the end sought for by war. For every man seeks peace by waging war, but no man seeks war by making peace. For even they who intentionally interrupt the peace in which they are living have no hatred of peace, but only wish it changed into a peace that suits them better. They do not, therefore, wish to have no peace, but only one more to their mind. And in the case of sedition, when men have separated themselves from the community, they yet do not effect what they wish, unless they maintain some kind of peace with their fellow-conspirators. And therefore even robbers take care to maintain peace with their comrades, that they may with greater effect and greater safety invade the peace of other men. . . . And thus all men desire to have peace with their own circle whom they wish to govern as suits themselves. For even those whom they make war against they wish to make their own, and impose on them the laws of their own peace. . . .

But to make war on your neighbours, and thence to proceed to others, and through mere lust of dominion to crush and subdue people who do you no harm, what else is this to be called than great robbery?

Indeed, without justice, what are kingdoms but great robberies? For what are robberies themselves, but little kingdoms? The band itself is made up of men; it is ruled by the authority of a prince, it is knit together by the pact of the confederacy; the booty is divided by the law agreed on. If, by the admittance of abandoned men, this evil increases to such a degree that it holds places, fixes abodes, takes possession of cities, and subdues peoples, it assumes the more plainly the name of a kingdom, because the reality is now manifestly conferred on it, not by the removal of covetousness, but by the addition of impunity. Indeed, that was an apt and true reply which was given to Alexander the Great by a pirate who had been seized. For when that king had asked the man what he meant by keeping hostile possession of the sea, he answered with bold pride, "What thou meanest by seizing the whole earth; but because I do it with a petty ship, I am called a robber, whilst thou who dost it with a great fleet art styled emperor." . . .

17.2 God and Caesar in the Reformation

How does a religious leader defend the authority of the state when he has himself been declared an outlaw by the highest authority in the land? This was Luther's delicate task in 1522. At the urging of his local supporter Duke John of Saxony, Luther published this treatise in which he defends the separation of church and state and argues that "neither one is sufficient in the world without the other." Luther's political thought is deeply Augustinian on many points, but especially so in its affirmation of the "two kingdoms" in which all Christians simultaneously dwell: that of Christ and that of "the world." Luther owed his survival to those German princes who decided to disobey the Holy Roman Emperor Charles V, and he was keenly aware of this. His political thought, therefore, was no academic abstraction, but rather a practical guide for reform and survival in a troubled era.

17.2A Martin Luther, "Temporal Authority: To What Extent It Should Be Obeyed"

First, we must provide a sound basis for the civil law and sword so no one will doubt that it is in the world by God's will and ordinance. The passages which do this are the following: Romans 13, "Let every soul be subject to the governing authority, for there is no authority except from God; the authority which everywhere exists has been ordained by God. He then who resists the governing authority resists the ordinance of God, and he who resists God's ordinance will incur judgment." Again, in I Peter 2 [:13–14], "Be subject to every kind of human ordinance, whether it be to the king as supreme, or to governors, as those who have been sent by him to punish the wicked and to praise the righteous."

The law of this temporal sword has existed from the beginning of the world. For when Cain slew his brother Abel, he was in such great terror of being killed in turn that God even placed a special prohibition on it and suspended the sword for his sake, so that no one was to slay him [Gen. 4:14–15]. He would not have had this fear if he had not seen and heard from Adam that murderers are to be slain. Moreover, after the Flood, God reestablished and confirmed this in unmistakable terms when he said in Genesis 9 [:6], "Whoever sheds the blood of man, by man shall his blood be shed." This cannot be understood as a plague or punishment of God upon murderers, for many murderers who are punished in other ways or pardoned altogether continue to live, and eventually die by means other than the sword. Rather, it is said of the law of the sword, that a murderer is guilty of death and in justice is to be slain by the sword. . . .

From Martin Luther, "Temporal Authority: To What Extent It Should be Obeyed" (excerpts), translated by J. J. Schindel, revised by Walther I. Brandt, ed., *Luther's Works, Vol. 45.* Copyright © 1962 by Muhlenberg Press. Reprinted with the permission of Augsburg Fortress.

Afterward it was also confirmed by the law of Moses, Exodus 21 [:14], "If a man wilfully kills another, you shall take him from my altar, that he may die." And again, in the same chapter, "A life for a life, an eye for an eye, a tooth for a tooth, a foot for a foot, a hand for a hand, a wound for a wound, a stripe for a stripe." In addition, Christ also confirms it when he says to Peter in the garden, "He that takes the sword will perish by the sword" [Matt. 26:52], which is to be interpreted exactly like the Genesis 9 [:6] passage, "Whoever sheds the blood of man," etc. Christ is undoubtedly referring in these words to that very passage which he thereby wishes to cite and to confirm. John the Baptist also teaches the same thing. When the soldiers asked him what they should do, he answered, "Do neither violence nor injustice to any one, and be content with your wages" [Luke 3:14]. If the sword were not a godly estate, he should have directed them to get out of it, since he was supposed to make the people perfect and instruct them in a proper Christian way. Hence, it is certain and clear enough that it is God's will that the temporal sword and law be used for the punishment of the wicked and the protection of the upright.

Second. There appear to be powerful arguments to the contrary. Christ says in Matthew 5 [:38–41], "You have heard that it was said to them of old: An eye for an eye, a tooth for a tooth. But I say to you, Do not resist evil; but if anyone strikes you on the right cheek, turn to him the other also. And if anyone would sue you and take your coat, let him have your cloak as well. And if anyone forces you to go one mile, go with him two miles," etc. Likewise Paul in Romans 12 [:19], "Beloved, defend not yourselves, but leave it to the wrath of God; for it is written, 'Vengeance is mine; I will repay, says the Lord.'" And in Matthew 5 [:44], "Love your enemies, do good to them that hate you." And again, in I Peter 2 [3:9], "Do not return evil for evil, or reviling for reviling," etc. These and similar passages would certainly make it appear as though in the New Testament Christians were to have no temporal sword.

Hence, the sophists also say that Christ has thereby abolished the law of Moses. Of such commandments they make "counsels" for the perfect. They divide Christian teaching and Christians into two classes. One part they call the perfect, and assign to it such counsels. The other they call the imperfect, and assign to it the commandments. This they do out of sheer wantonness and caprice, without any scriptural basis. They fail to see that in the same passage Christ lays such stress on his teaching that he is unwilling to have the least word of it set aside, and condemns to hell those who do not love their enemies. Therefore, we must interpret these passages differently, so that Christ's words may apply to everyone alike, be he perfect or imperfect. For perfection and imperfection do not consist in works, and do not establish any distinct external order among Christians. They exist in the heart, in faith and love, so that those who believe and love the most are the perfect ones, whether they be outwardly male or female, prince or peasant, monk or layman. For love and faith produce no sects or outward differences.

Third. Here we must divide the children of Adam and all mankind into two classes, the first belonging to the kingdom of God, the second to the kingdom of the world. Those who belong to the kingdom of God are all the true believers who are in Christ and under Christ, for Christ is King and Lord in the kingdom of God, as Psalm 2 [:6] and all of Scripture says. For this reason he came into the world, that he might begin God's kingdom and establish it in the world. Therefore, he says before Pilate, "My kingdom is not of the world, but every one who is of the truth hears my voice" [John 18:36–37]. . . .

Now observe, these people need no temporal law or sword. If all the world were composed of real Christians, that is, true believers, there would be no need for or benefits from prince, king, lord, sword, or law. They would serve no purpose, since Christians have in their heart the Holy Spirit, who both teaches and makes them to do injustice to no one, to love everyone, and to suffer injustice and even death willingly and cheerfully at the hands of anyone. Where there is nothing but the unadulterated doing of right and bearing of wrong, there is no need for any suit, litigation, court, judge, penalty, law, or sword. For this reason it is impossible that the temporal sword and law should find any work to do among Christians, since they do of their own accord much more than all laws and teachings can demand, just as Paul says in I Timothy 1 [:9], "The law is not laid down for the just but for the lawless."

Why is this? It is because the righteous man of his own accord does all and more than the law demands. But the unrighteous do nothing that the law demands; therefore, they need the law to instruct, constrain, and compel them to do good. A good tree needs no instruction or law to bear good fruit; its nature causes it to bear according to its kind without any law or instruction. I would take to be quite a fool any man who would make a book full of laws and statutes for an apple tree telling it how to bear apples and not thorns, when the tree is able by its own nature to do this better than the man with all his books can describe and demand. Just so, by the Spirit and by faith all Christians are so thoroughly disposed and conditioned in their very nature that they do right and keep the law better than one can teach them with all manner of statutes; so far as they themselves are concerned, no statutes or laws are needed.

You ask: Why, then, did God give so many commandments to all mankind, and why does Christ prescribe in the gospel so many things for us to do? Of this I have written at length in the Postils and elsewhere. To put it here as briefly as possible, Paul says that the law has been laid down for the sake of the lawless [I Tim. 1:9], that is, so that those who are not Christians may through the law be restrained outwardly from evil deeds, as we shall hear later. Now since no one is by nature Christian or righteous, but altogether sinful and wicked, God through the law puts them all under restraint so they dare not wilfully implement their wickedness in actual deeds. . . .

Fourth. All who are not Christians belong to the kingdom of the world and are under the law. There are few true believers, and still fewer who live a Christian life, who do not resist evil and indeed themselves do no evil. For this reason God has provided for them a different government beyond the Christian estate and kingdom of God. He has subjected them to the sword so that, even though they would like to, they are unable to practice their wickedness, and if they do practice it they cannot do so without fear or with success and impunity. In the same way a savage wild beast is bound with chains and ropes so that it cannot bite and tear as it would normally do, even though it would like to; whereas a tame and gentle animal needs no restraint, but is harmless despite the lack of chains and ropes.

If this were not so, men would devour one another, seeing that the whole world is evil and that among thousands there is scarcely a single true Christian. No one could support wife and child, feed himself, and serve God. The world would be reduced to chaos. For this reason God has ordained two governments: the spiritual, by which the Holy Spirit produces Christians and righteous people under Christ; and the temporal, which restrains the un-Christian and wicked so that—no thanks to them—they are obliged to keep still and to maintain an outward peace. Thus does St. Paul interpret the temporal sword in Romans 13 [:3], when he says it is not a terror to good conduct but to bad. And Peter says it is for the punishment of the wicked [I Pet. 2:14].

If anyone attempted to rule the world by the gospel and to abolish all temporal law and sword on the plea that all are baptized and Christian, and that, according to the gospel, there shall be among them no law or sword—or need for either—pray tell me, friend, what would he be doing? He would be loosing the ropes and chains of the savage wild beasts and letting them bite and mangle everyone, meanwhile insisting that they were harmless, tame, and gentle creatures; but I would have the proof in my wounds. Just so would the wicked under the name of Christian abuse evangelical freedom, carry on their rascality, and insist that they were Christians subject neither to law nor sword, as some are already raving and ranting.

To such a one we must say: Certainly it is true that Christians, so far as they themselves are concerned, are subject neither to law nor sword, and have need of neither. But take heed and first fill the world with real Christians before you attempt to rule it in a Christian and evangelical manner. This you will never accomplish; for the world and the masses are and always will be un-Christian, even if they are all baptized and Christian in name. Christians are few and far between (as the saying is). Therefore, it is out of the question that there should be a common Christian government over the whole world, or indeed over a single country or any considerable body of people, for the wicked always outnumber the good. Hence, a man who would venture to govern an entire country or the world with the gospel would be like a shepherd who should put together in one fold wolves, lions, eagles, and sheep, and let them mingle freely with one another, saying, "Help yourselves, and be good and peaceful toward one another. The fold is open, there is plenty of food. You need have no fear of dogs and clubs." The sheep would doubtless keep the peace and allow themselves to be fed and governed peacefully, but they would not live long, nor would one beast survive another.

For this reason one must carefully distinguish between these two governments. Both must be permitted to remain; the one to produce righteousness, the other to bring about external peace and prevent evil deeds. Neither one is sufficient in the world without the other. . . .

You ask whether a Christian too may bear the temporal sword and punish the wicked, since Christ's words, "Do not resist evil," are so clear and definite that the sophists have had to make of them a "counsel." Answer: You have now heard two propositions. One is that the sword can have no place among Christians;

therefore, you cannot bear it among Christians or hold it over them, for they do not need it. The question, therefore, must be referred to the other group, the non-Christians, whether you may bear it there in a Christian manner. Here the other proposition applies, that you are under obligation to serve and assist the sword by whatever means you can, with body, goods, honor, and soul. For it is something which you do not need, but which is very beneficial and essential for the whole world and for your neighbor. Therefore, if you see that there is a lack of hangmen, constables, judges, lords, or princes, and you find that you are qualified, you should offer your services and seek the position, that the essential governmental authority may not be despised and become enfeebled or perish. The world cannot and dare not dispense with it. . . .

Thus the word of Christ is now reconciled, I believe, with the passages which establish the sword, and the meaning is this: No Christian shall wield or invoke the sword for himself and his cause. In behalf of another, however, he may and should wield it and invoke it to restrain wickedness and to defend godliness.

Here you inquire further, whether constables, hangmen, jurists, lawyers, and others of similar function can also be Christians and in a state of salvation. Answer: If the governing authority and its sword are a divine service, as was proved above, then everything that is essential for the authority's bearing of the sword must also be divine service. There must be those who arrest, prosecute, execute, and destroy the wicked, and who protect, acquit, defend, and save the good. Therefore, when they perform their duties, not with the intention of seeking their own ends but only of helping the law and the governing authority function to coerce the wicked, there is no peril in that; they may use their office like anybody else would use his trade, as a means of livelihood. For, as has been said, love of neighbor is not concerned about its own; it considers not how great or humble, but how profitable and needful the works are for neighbor or community. . . .

Part Two: How Far Temporal Authority Extends

We come now to the main part of this treatise. Having learned that there must be temporal authority on earth, and how it is to be exercised in a Christian and salutary manner, we must now learn how far its arm extends and how widely its hand stretches, lest it extend too far and encroach upon God's kingdom and government. . . .

It is to be noted first that the two classes of Adam's children—the one in God's kingdom under Christ and the other in the kingdom of the world under the governing authority, as was said above—have two kinds of law. For every kingdom must have its own laws and statutes; without law no kingdom or government can survive, as everyday experience amply shows. The temporal government has laws which extend no further than to life and property and external affairs on earth, for God cannot and will not permit anyone but himself to rule over the soul. Therefore, where the temporal authority presumes to prescribe laws for the soul, it encroaches upon God's government and only misleads souls and destroys them. We want to make this so clear that everyone will grasp it, and that our fine gentlemen, the princes and bishops, will see what fools they are when they seek to coerce the people with their laws and commandments into believing this or that. . . .

If your prince or temporal ruler commands you to side with the pope, to believe thus and so, or to get rid of certain books, you should say, "It is not fitting that Lucifer should sit at the side of God. Gracious sir, I owe you obedience in body and property; command me within the limits of your authority on earth, and I will obey. But if you command me to believe or to get rid of certain books, I will not obey; for then you are a tyrant and overreach yourself, commanding where you have neither the right nor the authority," etc. Should he seize your property on account of this and punish such disobedience, then blessed are you; thank God that you are worthy to suffer for the sake of the divine word. Let him rage, fool that he is; he will meet his judge. For I tell you, if you fail to withstand him, if you give in to him and let him take away your faith and your books, you have truly denied God.

You must know that since the beginning of the world a wise prince is a mighty rare bird, and an upright prince even rarer. They are generally the biggest fools or the worst scoundrels on earth; therefore, one must constantly expect the worst from them and look for little good, especially in divine matters which concern the salvation of souls. They are God's executioners and hangmen; his divine wrath uses them to punish the wicked and to maintain outward peace. Our God is a great lord and ruler; this is why he must also have such noble, highborn, and rich hangmen and constables. He desires that everyone shall copiously accord them riches, honor, and fear in abundance. It pleases his divine will that we call his hangmen gracious lords, fall at their feet, and be subject to them in all humility, so long as they do not ply their trade too far and try to become shepherds instead of hangmen. If a prince should happen to be wise, upright, or a Christian, that is one of the great miracles, the most precious token of divine grace upon that land. . . .

Here you will ask: "Is a prince then not to go to war, and are his subjects not to follow him into battle?" Answer: This is a far-reaching question, but let me answer it very briefly. To act here as a Christian, I say, a prince should not go to war against his overlord—king, emperor, or other liege lord—but let him who takes, take. For the governing authority must not be resisted by force, but only by confession of the truth. If it is influenced by this, well and good; if not, you are excused, you suffer wrong for God's sake. If, however, the antagonist is your equal, your inferior, or of a foreign government, you should first offer him justice and peace, as Moses taught the children of Israel. If he refuses, then—mindful of what is best for you—defend yourself against force by force, as Moses so well describes it in Deuteronomy 20 [:10–12]. But in doing this you must not consider your personal interests and how you may remain lord, but those of your subjects to whom you owe help and protection, that such action may proceed in love. Since your entire land is in peril you must make the venture, so that with God's help all may not be lost. If you cannot prevent some from becoming widows and orphans as a consequence, you must at least see that not everything goes to ruin until there is nothing left except widows and orphans.

In this matter subjects are in duty bound to follow, and to devote their life and property, for in such a case one must risk his goods and himself for the sake of others. In a war of this sort it is both Christian and an act of love to kill the enemy without hesitation, to plunder and burn and injure him by every method of warfare until he is conquered (except that one must beware of sin, and not violate wives and virgins). And when victory has been achieved, one should offer mercy and peace to those who surrender and humble themselves. . . .

What if a prince is in the wrong? Are his people bound to follow him then too? Answer: No, for it is no one's duty to do wrong; we must obey God (who desires the right) rather than men [Acts 5:29]. What if the subjects do not know whether their prince is in the right or not? Answer: So long as they do not know, and cannot with all possible diligence find out, they may obey him without peril to their souls.

17.3 THE CHRISTIAN MILLENNIAL KINGDOM

Many nations, across a broad chronological spectrum, have conceived their destiny in religious terms. Frequently, those visions have taken the form of expectation of a millennial kingdom, a utopian society in which religion is thoroughly harmonized with the operations of the state. In the late eighteenth century, the U.S. theologian Samuel Hopkins (1721–1803) described the features of that millennial kingdom in *A Treatise on the Millennium* (1793). Hopkins translated themes and images present in *The Revelation to John* into a richly detailed picture of life in the fully realized Christian future. The following excerpt is taken from the heading, "The Millennial State, Particularly Described." It foresees in strikingly optimistic terms the emotional satisfactions, intellectual achievements, religious perfections, and physical comforts of the thousand-year Christian state.

17.3A SAMUEL HOPKINS, "THE MILLENNIAL STATE, PARTICULARLY DESCRIBED"

The following things will take place in the Millennium in an eminent degree, as they never did before; which may be mentioned as generals, including many particulars, some of which will be afterwards suggested.

I. That will be a time of eminent holiness, when it shall be acted out by all, in a high degree, in all the branches of it, so as to appear in its true beauty, and the

From Samuel Hopkins, *A Treatise on the Millennium* (New York, 1971), pp. 57–82. Originally published 1793.

happy effects of it. This will be the peculiar glory, and the source of the happiness of the Millennium. The Prophet Zechariah, speaking of that day, says, "In that day, shall there be upon the bells of the horses, HOLINESS UNTO THE LORD; and the pots of the Lord's house shall be like the bowls before the altar. Yea, every pot in Jerusalem and in Judah, shall be holiness unto the Lord of hosts." In these metaphorical expressions, is declared the eminent degree of holiness of that day, which will consecrate everything, even all the utensils and the common business and enjoyments of life, unto the Lord.

Holiness consists in love to God, and to man, with every affection and exercise implied in this, which being expressed and acted out, appears in the exercise of piety towards God, in every branch of it; and of righteousness and goodness, or disinterested benevolence towards man, including ourselves. This, so far as it shall take place, will banish all the evils which have existed and prevailed in the world; and becoming universal, and rising to a high and eminent degree, will introduce a state of enjoyment and happiness, which never was known before on earth; and render it a resemblance of heaven in a high degree. . . .

II. There will be a great increase of light and knowledge to a degree vastly beyond what has been before. This is indeed implied in the great degree of holiness, which has been mentioned. For knowledge, mental light, and holiness, are inseparably connected; and are, in some respects, the same. Holiness is true light and discerning, so far as it depends upon a right taste, and consists in it; and it is a thirst after every kind and degree of useful knowledge; and this desire and thirst for knowledge, will be great and strong, in proportion to the degree of holiness exercised. And forms the mind to constant attention, and to make swift advances in understanding and knowledge; and becomes a strong guard against mistakes, error and delusion. Therefore, a time of eminent holiness, must be a time of proportionably great light and knowledge. This is the representation which the scripture gives of that time. The end of binding satan, and casting him into the bottomless pit, is said to be, "That he should deceive the nations no more, till the thousand years should be fulfilled." This will put an end to the darkness, and multiplicity of strong delusions, which do prevail, and will prevail, till that time, by which satan supports and promotes his interest and kingdom among men.—Then "The face of the covering cast over all people, and the vail spread over all nations, shall be taken away and destroyed": "And the eyes of them that see, shall not be dim; and the ears of them that hear, shall hearken. The heart also of the wrath, shall be ready to speak plainly." The superior light and knowledge of that day, is metaphorically represented in the following words: "Moreover, the light of the moon shall be as the light of the sun, and the light of the sun shall be seven fold, as the light of seven days, in the day that the Lord bindeth up the breach of his people, and healeth the stroke of their wound." In that day, "The earth shall be full of the knowledge of the Lord, as the waters cover the sea."

The holy scriptures will then be attended to by all, and studied with care, meekness, humility and uprightness of heart, earnestly desiring to understand them, and know the truth; and the truths they contain will be received with a high relish and delight: And the Bible will be much better understood, than ever before. Many things expressed or implied in the scripture, which are now overlooked and disregarded, will then be discovered, and appear important and excellent; and those things which now appear intricate and unintelligible, will then appear plain and easy.

III. It will be a time of universal peace, love and general and cordial friendship. War and all strife and contention shall then cease, and be succeeded by mutual love, friendship and beneficence. Those lusts of men, which originate in self love, or selfishness, which produce all the wars and strifes among men, shall be subdued and mortified, and yield to that disinterested benevolence, that heavenly wisdom, which is peaceable, gentle and easy to be entreated. This will effectually put an end to war, as the scripture teaches. "And he shall judge among the nations, and shall rebuke many people: And they shall beat their swords into plowshares, and their spears into pruning hooks: Nation shall not lift up sword against nation, neither shall they learn war any more. And my people shall dwell in a peaceable habitation, and in sure dwellings, and in quiet resting places." The whole world of mankind will be united as one family, wisely seeking the good of each other, in the exercise of the most sweet love and friendship, founded upon the best and everlasting principles. "The meek shall inherit the earth, and shall delight themselves in the abundance of peace." This change, which shall then take place, in which men, who were in ages before, like savage beasts, injurious, cruel, revengeful and destructive to each other, shall lay aside all this, and become harmless, humble and benevolent, is set in a striking, beautiful light in prophecies, representing it by the most fierce and cruel beasts of prey, changing their nature, and living quietly with those creatures which they used to destroy; and so tame and pliable that a little child might lead them; and by the most venomous creatures and insects becoming harmless, so that a child might play with them without any danger of being hurt.

IV. In that day, men will not only be united in peace and love, as brethren; but will agree in sentiments, respecting the doctrines and truth contained in the Bible, and the religious institutions and practice, which are there prescribed.

Professing Christians have been from the beginning of Christianity to this day, greatly divided, and have opposed each other in their religious sentiments and practices; and are now divided into various parties, sects and denominations, while all appeal to divine revelation, and profess to take their sentiments and practices from that.

V. The Millennium will be a time of great enjoyment, happiness and universal joy.

This is often mentioned in prophecy, as what will take place in that day, in a peculiar manner and high degree. "For ye shall go out with joy, and be led forth with peace: The mountains and the hills shall break forth before you into singing, and all the trees of the field shall clap their hands. Be you glad, and rejoice forever in that which I create; for I create Jerusalem a rejoicing, and her people a joy." The enjoyments of that day are represented by a rich and plentiful feast for all people, consisting in provision of the most agreeable and delicious kind. "And in this mountain shall the Lord of hosts make unto all people a feast of fat things, a feast of wines on the lees, a feast of fat things full of marrow, of wines on the lees well refined." The enjoyments and happiness of the Millennium, are compared to a marriage supper. "Let us rejoice and give honour to him: For the marriage of Lamb is come, and his wife hath made herself ready. Blessed are they who are called unto the marriage supper of the Lamb." And there will be a great increase of happiness and joy in heaven, at the introduction of that day, and during the continuance of it." "There shall be joy in heaven, and there is joy in the presence of the angels of God, over one sinner that repenteth."

There are many other things and circumstances which will take place in that day, which are implied in what has now been observed, or may be inferred from it, and from the scripture, by which the advantages, happiness and glory of the Millennium will be promoted; some of which will be mentioned in the following particulars:

1. All outward worldly circumstances will then be agreeable and prosperous, and there will be for all, sufficiency and fullness of every thing needed for the body, and for the comfort and convenience of every one.

The intemperance, excess, extravagance and waste, in food and raiment, and the use of the things of life, which were before practiced, will be discarded and cease, in that day. By these, a great part of the productions of the earth, which are for the comfort and convenience of man, are now wasted and worse than lost, as they are, in innumerable instances, the cause of debility of body, sickness and death. But every thing of this kind will be used with great prudence and economy; and in that way, measure and degree, which will best answer the ends of food, drink and clothing, and all other furniture, so as to be most comfortable, decent and convenient, and in the best manner furnish persons for their proper business and duty. Nothing will be sought or used to gratify pride inordinate, sensual appetite or lust: So that there will be no waste of the things of life: Nothing will be lost.

2. In that day, mankind will greatly multiply and increase in number, till the earth shall be filled with them.

When God first made mankind, he said to them, "Be fruitful, and multiply, and replenish, (or fill) the earth, and subdue it." And he renewed this command to Noah and his sons, after the flood, and in them to mankind in general. "And God blessed Noah and his sons, and said unto them, Be fruitful, and multiply, and replenish the earth." This command has never yet been obeyed by mankind; they have yet done but little, compared with what they ought to have done, in subduing and filling the earth. Instead of this, they have spent a great part of their time and strength in subduing and destroying each other; and in that impiety, intemperance, folly and wickedness, which have brought the divine judgments upon them; and they have been reduced and destroyed in all ages by famine, pestilence and poverty, and innumerable calamities and evil occurrents; so that by far the greatest part of the earth remains yet unsubdued, and lies waste without inhabitants. And where it has been most subdued and cultivated and populous, it has been, and still is, far from being filled with inhabitants, so that it could support no more, except in a very few instances, if in any. An exact calculation cannot be made; but it is presumed that every man, who considers the things which have been mentioned above, will be sensible that this earth may be made capable of sustaining thousands to one of mankind who now inhabit it; so that if each one were multiplied to many thousands, the earth would not be more than filled, and all might have ample provision for their sustenance, convenience and comfort. This will not take place, so long as the world of mankind continue to exercise so much selfishness, unrighteousness and impiety as they do now, and always have done.

3. In the Millennium, all will probably speak *one language:* So that one language shall be known and understood all over the world, when it shall be filled with inhabitants innumerable.

The whole earth was once, and originally of one language, and of one speech. And the folly and rebellion of men was the occasion of their being confounded in speaking and understanding this one language, and the introduction of a variety of languages. This was considered as in itself a great calamity, and was ordered as such: And it can be considered in no other light. Had men been disposed to improve the advantages of all speaking and understanding one language, to wise and good purposes, this diversity never would have taken place. And when men shall become universally pious, virtuous and benevolent, and be disposed to use such an advantage and blessing as having one speech and language will be, for the glory of God and the general good, it will doubtless be restored to them again. This may easily and soon be done, without a miracle, when mankind and the state of the world shall be ripe for it.

17.4 CIVIL DISOBEDIENCE

Religious calls to resist the state have taken a variety of forms in Christianity, ranging from the organized and violent use of force in public to the private actions of individual citizens. The Reverend Martin Luther King Jr. (1929–1968), who was influenced by the ideas and example of Mahatma Gandhi, preached nonviolent civil disobedience to injustices enforced by the state. He grounded that message in a certain understanding of Christian love and suffering. In "Love, Law, and Civil Disobedience," an address delivered in 1961, King spoke of the capability of Christian faith and struggle to overcome injustice embedded in the state and social institutions.

17.4A Martin Luther King, Jr., "Love, Law, and Civil Disobedience"

Members of the Fellowship of the Concerned, of the Southern Regional Council, I need not pause to say how very delighted I am to be here today, and to have the opportunity of being a little part of this very significant gathering. I certainly want to express my personal appreciation to Mrs. Tilly and the members of the Committee, for giving me this opportunity. I would also like to express just a personal word of thanks and appreciation for your vital witness in this period of transition which we are facing in our Southland, and in the nation, and I am sure that as a result of this genuine concern, and your significant work in communities all across the South, we have a better South today and I am sure will have a better South tomorrow with your continued endeavor and I do want to express my personal gratitude and appreciation to you of the Fellowship of the Concerned for your significant work and for your forthright witness.

Now, I have been asked to talk about the philosophy behind the student movement. There can be no gainsaying of the fact that we confront a crisis in race relations in the United States. This crisis has been precipitated on the one hand by the determined resistance of reactionary forces in the South to the Supreme Court's decision in 1954 outlawing segregation in the public schools. And we know that at times this resistance has risen to ominous proportions. At times we find the legislative halls of the South ringing loud with such words as interposition and nullification. And all of these forces have developed into massive resistance. But we must also say that the crisis has been precipitated on the other hand by the determination of hundreds and thousands and millions of Negro people to achieve freedom and human dignity. If the Negro stayed in his place and accepted discrimination and segregation, there would be no crisis. But the Negro has a new sense of dignity, a new self-respect and new determination. He has reevaluated his own intrinsic worth. Now this new sense of dignity on the part of the Negro grows out of the same longing for freedom and human dignity on the part of the oppressed people all over the world; for we see it in Africa, we see it in Asia, and we see it all over the world. Now we must say that this struggle for freedom will not come to an automatic halt, for history reveals to us that once oppressed people rise up against that oppression, there is no stopping point short of full freedom. On the other hand, history reveals to us that those who oppose the movement for freedom are those who are in privileged positions who very seldom give up their privileges without strong resistance. And they very seldom do it voluntarily. So the sense of struggle will continue. The question is how will the struggle be waged.

Now there are three ways that oppressed people have generally dealt with their oppression. One way is the method of acquiescence, the method of surrender;

that is, the individuals will somehow adjust themselves to oppression, they adjust themselves to discrimination or to segregation or colonialism or what have you. The other method that has been used in history is that of rising up against the oppressor with corroding hatred and physical violence. Now of course we know about this method in Western civilization because in a sense it has been the hallmark of its grandeur, and the inseparable twin of western materialism. But there is a weakness in this method because it ends up creating many more social problems than it solves. And I am convinced that if the Negro succumbs to the temptation of using violence in his struggle for freedom and justice, unborn generations will be the recipients of a long and desolate night of bitterness. And our chief legacy to the future will be an endless reign of meaningless chaos.

But there is another way, namely the way of nonviolent resistance. This method was popularized in our generation by a little man from India, whose name was Mohandas K. Gandhi. He used this method in a magnificent way to free his people from the economic exploitation and the political domination inflicted upon them by a foreign power.

This has been the method used by the student movement in the South and all over the United States. And naturally whenever I talk about the student movement I cannot be totally objective. I have to be somewhat subjective because of my great admiration for what the students have done. For in a real sense they have taken our deep groans and passionate yearnings for freedom, and filtered them in their own tender souls, and fashioned them into a creative protest which is an epic known all over our nation. As a result of their disciplined, nonviolent, yet courageous struggle, they have been able to do wonders in the South, and in our nation. But this movement does have an underlying philosophy, it has certain ideas that are attached to it, it has certain philosophical precepts. These are the things that I would like to discuss for the few moments left.

I would say that the first point or the first principle in the movement is the idea that means must be as pure as the end. This movement is based on the philosophy that ends and means must cohere. Now this has been one of the long struggles in history, the whole idea of means and ends. Great philosophers have grappled with it, and sometimes they have emerged with the idea, from Machiavelli on down, that the end justifies the means. There is a great system of thought in our world today, known as communism. And I think that with all of the weakness and tragedies of communism, we find its greatest tragedy right here, that it goes under the philosophy that the end justifies the means that are used in the process. So we can read or we can hear the Lenins say that lying, deceit, or violence, that many of these things justify the ends of the classless society.

This is where the student movement and the nonviolent movement that is taking place in our nation would break with communism and any other system that would argue that the end justifies the means. For in the long run, we must see that the end represents the means in process and the ideal in the making. In other words, we cannot believe, or we cannot go with the idea that the end justifies the means because the end is preexistent in the means. So the idea of nonviolent resistance, the philosophy of nonviolent resistance, is the philosophy which says that the means must be as pure as the end, that in the long run of history, immoral destructive means cannot bring about moral and constructive ends.

There is another thing about this philosophy, this method of nonviolence which is followed by the student movement. It says that those who adhere to or follow this philosophy must follow a consistent principle of non-injury. They must consistently refuse to inflict injury upon another. Sometimes you will read the literature of the student movement and see that, as they are getting ready for the sit-in or stand-in, they will read something like this, "If you are hit do not hit back, if you are cursed do not curse back." This is the whole idea, that the individual who is engaged in a nonviolent struggle must never inflict injury upon another. Now this has an external aspect and it has an internal one. From the external point of view it means that the individuals involved must avoid external physical violence. So they don't have guns, they don't retaliate with physical violence. If they are hit in the process, they avoid external physical violence at every point. But it also means that they avoid internal violence of spirit. This is why the love ethic stands so high in the student movement. We have a great deal of talk about love and nonviolence in this whole thrust.

Now when the students talk about love, certainly they are not talking about emotional bosh, they are not talking about merely a sentimental outpouring; they're talking something much deeper, and I always have to stop and try to define the meaning of love in this context. The Greek language comes to our aid in trying to deal with this. There are three words in the Greek language for love; one is the word *eros*. This is a beautiful type of love, it is an aesthetic love. Plato talks about it a great deal in his Dialogue, the yearning of the soul for the realm of the divine. It has come to us to be a sort of romantic love, and so in a sense we have read about it and experienced it. We've read about it in all the beauties of literature. I guess in a sense Edgar Allan Poe was talking about *eros* when he talked about his beautiful Annabelle Lee, with the love surrounded by the halo of eternity. In a sense Shakespeare was talking about *eros* when he said "Love is not love which alters when it alteration finds, or bends with the remover to remove; O'no! It is an ever fixed mark that looks on tempests and is never shaken, it is the star to every wandering bark." (You know, I remember that because I used to quote it to this little lady when we were courting; that's *eros*.) The Greek language talks about *philia* which was another level of love. It is an intimate affection between personal friends, it is a reciprocal love. On this level you love because you are loved. It is friendship.

Then the Greek language comes out with another word which is called the *agape*. *Agape* is more than romantic love, *agape* is more than friendship. *Agape* is understanding, creative, redemptive, good will to all men. It is an overflowing love which seeks nothing in return. Theologians would say that it is the love of God operating in the human heart. So that when one rises to love on this level, he loves men not because he likes them, not because their ways appeal to him, but he loves every man because God loves him. And he rises to the point of loving the person who does an evil deed while hating the deed that the person does. I think this is what Jesus meant when he said "love your enemies." I'm very happy that he didn't say like your enemies, because it is pretty difficult to like some people. Like is sentimental, and it is pretty difficult to like someone bombing your home; it is pretty difficult to like somebody threatening your children; it is difficult to like congressmen who spend all of their time trying to defeat civil rights. But Jesus says love them, and love is greater than like. Love is understanding, redemptive, creative, good will for all men. And it is this idea, it is this whole ethic of love which is the idea standing at the basis of the student movement.

There is something else: that one seeks to defeat the unjust system, rather than individuals who are caught in that system. And that one goes on believing that somehow this is the important thing, to get rid of the evil system and not the individual who happens to be misguided, who happens to be misled, who was taught wrong. The thing to do is to get rid of the system and thereby create a moral balance within society.

Another thing that stands at the center of this movement is another idea: that suffering can be a most creative and powerful social force. Suffering has certain moral attributes involved, but it can be a powerful and creative social force. Now, it is very interesting at this point to notice that both violence and nonviolence agree that suffering can be a very powerful social force. But there is this difference: violence says that suffering can be a powerful social force by inflicting the suffering on somebody else: so this is what we do in war, this is what we do in the whole violent thrust of the violent movement. It believes that you achieve some end by inflicting suffering on another. The nonviolent say that suffering becomes a powerful social force when you willingly accept that violence on yourself, so that self-suffering stands at the center of the nonviolent movement and the individuals involved are able to suffer in a creative manner, feeling that unearned suffering is redemptive, and that suffering may serve to transform the social situation.

Another thing in this movement is the idea that there is within human nature an amazing potential for goodness. There is within human nature something that can respond to goodness. I know somebody's liable to say that this is an unrealistic movement if it goes on believing that all people are good. Well, I didn't say that. I think the students are realistic enough to believe that there is a strange dichotomy of disturbing dualism within human nature. Many of the great philosophers and thinkers through the ages have seen this. It caused Ovid the Latin poet to say, "I see and approve the better things of life, but the evil things I do." It caused even Saint Augustine to say "Lord, make me pure, but not yet." So that is in human nature. Plato, centuries ago said that the human personality is like a charioteer with two headstrong horses, each wanting to go in different directions, so that within our own individual lives we see this conflict and certainly when we come to the collective life of man, we see a strange badness. But in spite of this there is something in human nature that can respond to goodness. So that man is neither innately good nor is he innately bad; he has potentialities for both. So in this sense, Carlyle was right when he said that, "there are depths in man which go down to the lowest hell, and heights which reach the highest heaven, for are not both heaven and hell made out of him, ever-lasting miracle and mystery that he is?" Man has the capacity to be good, man has the capacity to be evil.

And so the nonviolent resister never lets this idea go, that there is something within human nature than can respond to goodness. So that a Jesus of Nazareth or a Mohandas Gandhi, can appeal to human beings and appeal to that element of goodness within them, and a Hitler can appeal to the element of evil within them. But we must never forget that there is something within human nature that can respond to goodness, that man is not totally depraved; to put it in theological terms, the image of God is never totally gone. And so the individuals who believe in this movement and who believe in nonviolence and our struggle in the South, somehow believe that even the worst segregationist can become an integrationist. Now sometimes it is hard to believe that this is what this movement says, and it believes it firmly, that there is something within human nature that can be changed, and this stands at the top of the whole philosophy of the student movement and the philosophy of nonviolence.

It says something else. It says that it is as much a moral obligation to refuse to cooperate with evil as it is to cooperate with good. Noncooperation with evil is as much a moral obligation as the cooperation with good. So that the student movement is willing to stand up courageously on the idea of civil disobedience. Now I think this is the part of the student movement that is probably misunderstood more than anything else. And it is a difficult aspect, because on the one hand the students would say, and I would say, and all the people who believe in civil rights would say, obey the Supreme Court's decision of 1954 and at the same time, we would disobey certain laws that exist on the statutes of the South today.

This brings in the whole question of how can you be logically consistent when you advocate obeying some laws and disobeying other laws. Well, I think one would have to see the whole meaning of this movement at this point by seeing that the students recognize that there are two types of laws. There are just laws and there are unjust laws. And they would be the first to say obey the just laws, they would be the first to say that men and women have a moral obligation to obey just and right laws. And they would go on to say that we must see that there are unjust laws. Now the question comes into being, what is the difference, and who determines the difference, what is the difference between a just and an unjust law?

Well, a just law is a law that squares with a moral law. It is a law that squares with that which is right, so that any law that uplifts human personality is a just law. Whereas that law which is out of harmony with the moral is a law which does not square with the moral law of the universe. It does not square with the law of God, so for that reason it is unjust and any law that degrades the human personality is an unjust law.

Well, somebody says that that does not mean anything to me; first, I don't believe in these abstract things called moral laws and I'm not too religious, so I don't believe in the law of God; you have to get a little more concrete, and more practical. What do you mean when you say that a law is unjust, and a law is just? Well, I would go on to say in more concrete terms that an unjust law is a code that the majority inflicts on the minority that is not binding on itself. So that this becomes difference made legal. Another thing that we can say is that an unjust law is a code which the majority inflicts upon the minority, which that minority had no part in enacting or creating, because that minority had no right to vote in many instances, so that the legislative bodies that made these laws were not democratically elected. Who could ever say that the legislative body of Mississippi was democratically elected, or the legislative body of Alabama was democratically elected, or the legislative body even of Georgia has been democratically elected, when there are people in Terrell County and in other counties because of the color of their skin who cannot vote? They confront reprisals and threats and all of that; so that an unjust law is a law that individuals did not have a part in creating or enacting because they were denied the right to vote.

Now the same token of just law would be just the opposite. A just law becomes saneness made legal. It is a code that the majority, who happen to believe in that code, compel the minority, who don't believe in it, to follow, because they are willing to follow it themselves, so it is saneness made legal. Therefore the individuals who stand up on the basis of civil disobedience realize that they are following something that says that there are just laws and there are unjust laws. Now, they are not anarchists. They believe that there are laws which must be followed; they do not seek to defy the law, they do not seek to evade the law. For many individuals who would call themselves segregationists and who would hold on to segregation at any cost seek to defy the law, they seek to evade the law, and their process can lead on into anarchy. They seek in the final analysis to follow a way of uncivil disobedience, not civil disobedience. And I submit that the individual who disobeys the law, whose conscience tells him it is unjust and who is willing to accept the penalty by staying in jail until that law is altered, is expressing at the moment the very highest respect for law.

This is what the students have followed in their movement. Of course there is nothing new about this; they feel that they are in good company and rightly so. We go back and read the Apology and the Crito, and you see Socrates practicing civil disobedience. And to a degree academic freedom is a reality today because Socrates practiced civil disobedience. The early Christians practiced civil disobedience in a superb manner, to a point where they were willing to be thrown to the lions. They were willing to face all kinds of suffering in order to stand up for what they knew was right even though they knew it was against the laws of the Roman Empire.

We could come up to our own day and we see it in many instances. We must never forget that everything that Hitler did in Germany was "legal." It was illegal to aid and comfort a Jew, in the days of Hitler's Germany. But I believe that if I had the same attitude then as I have now I would publicly aid and comfort my Jewish brothers in Germany if Hitler were alive today calling this an illegal process. If I lived in South Africa today in the midst of the white supremacy law in South Africa, I would join Chief Luthuli and others in saying break these unjust laws. And even let us come up to America. Our nation in a sense came into being through a massive act of civil disobedience for the Boston Tea Party was nothing but a massive act of civil disobedience. Those who stood up against the slave laws, the abolitionists, by and large practiced civil disobedience. So I think these students are in good company, and they feel that by practicing civil disobedience they are in line with men and women through the ages who have stood up for something that is morally right.

Now there are one or two other things that I want to say about this student movement, moving out of the philosophy of nonviolence, something about what it is a revolt against. On the one hand it is a revolt against the negative peace that has encompassed the South for many years. I remember when I was in Montgomery, Alabama, one of the white citizens came to me one day and said—and I think he was very sincere about this—that in Montgomery for all of these years we have been such a peaceful community, we have had so much harmony in race relations and then you people have started this movement and boycott, and it has done so much to disturb race relations, and we just don't love the Negro like we used to love them, because you have destroyed the harmony and the peace that we once had in race relations. And I said to him, in the best way I could say and I tried to say it in nonviolent terms, we have never had peace in Montgomery, Alabama, we have never had peace in the South. We have had a negative peace, which is merely the absence of tension; we've had a negative peace in which the Negro patiently accepted his situation and his plight, but we've never had true peace, we've never had positive peace, and what we're seeking now is to develop this positive peace. For we must come to see that peace is not merely the absence of some negative force, it is the presence of a positive force. True peace is not merely the absence of tension, but it is the presence of justice and brotherhood. I think this is what Jesus meant when he said, "I come not to bring peace but a sword." Now Jesus didn't mean he came to start war, to bring a physical sword, and he didn't mean, I come not to bring positive peace. But I think what Jesus was saying in substance was this, that I come not to bring an old negative peace, which makes for stagnant passivity and deadening complacency, I come to bring something different, and whenever I come, a conflict is precipitated, between the old and the new, whenever I come a struggle takes place between justice and injustice, between the forces of light and the forces of darkness. I come not to bring a negative peace, but a positive peace, which is brotherhood, which is justice, which is the Kingdom of God.

And I think this is what we are seeking to do today, and this movement is a revolt against a negative peace and a struggle to bring into being a positive peace, which makes for true brotherhood, true integration, true person-to-person relationships. This movement is also revolt against what is often called tokenism. Here again many people do not understand this, they feel that in this struggle the Negro will be satisfied with tokens of integration, just a few students and a few schools here and there and a few doors open here and there. But this isn't the meaning of the movement and I think that honesty impels me to admit it everywhere I have an opportunity, that the Negro's aim is to bring about complete integration in American life. And he has come to see that token integration is little more than token democracy, which ends up with many new evasive schemes and it ends up with new discrimination, covered up with such niceties of complexity. It is very interesting to discover that the movement has thrived in many communities that had token integration. So this reveals that the movement is based on a principle that integration must become real and complete, not just token integration.

It is also a revolt against what I often call the myth of time. We hear this quite often, that only time can solve this problem. That if we will only be patient, and only pray—which we must do, we must be patient and we must pray—but there are those who say just do these things and wait for time, and time will solve the problem. Well the people who argue this do not themselves realize that time is neutral, that it can be used constructively or destructively. At points the people of ill will, the segregationists, have used time much more effectively than the people of good will. So individuals in the struggle must come to realize that it is necessary to aid time, that without this kind of aid, time itself will become an ally of the insurgent and primitive forces of social stagnation. Therefore, this movement is a revolt against the myth of time.

There is a final thing that I would like to say to you, this movement is a movement based on faith in the future. It is a movement based on a philosophy, the possibility of the future bringing into being something real and meaningful. It is a movement based on hope. I think this is very important. The students have developed a theme song for their movement, maybe you've heard it. It goes something like this, "We shall overcome, deep in my heart, I do believe, we shall overcome," and then they go on to say another verse, "We are not afraid, we are not afraid today, deep in my heart I do believe, we shall overcome." So it is out of this deep faith in the future that they are able to move out and adjourn the councils of despair, and to bring new light in the dark chambers of pessimism. I can remember the times that we've been together, I remember that night in Montgomery, Alabama, when we had stayed up all night discussing the Freedom Rides, and that morning came to see that it was necessary to go on with the Freedom Rides, that we would not in all good conscience call an end to the Freedom Rides at that point. And I remember the first group got ready to leave, to take a bus for Jackson, Mississippi, we all joined hands and started singing together. "We shall overcome, we shall overcome." And something within me said, now how is it that these students can sing this, they are going down to Mississippi, they are going to face hostile and jeering mobs, and yet they could sing, "We shall overcome." They may even face physical death, and yet they could sing, "We shall overcome." Most of them realized that they would be thrown into jail, and yet they could sing, "We shall overcome, we are not afraid." Then something caused me to see at that moment the real meaning of the movement. That students had faith in the future. That the movement was based on hope, that this movement had something within it that says somehow even though the arc of the moral universe is long, it bends toward justice. And I think this should be a challenge to all others who are struggling to transform the dangling discords of our Southland into a beautiful symphony of brotherhood. There is something in this student movement which says to us, that we shall overcome. Before the victory is won some may have to get scarred up, but we shall overcome. Before the victory of brotherhood is achieved, some will maybe face physical death, but we shall overcome. Before the victory is won, some will lose jobs, some will be called communists, and reds, merely because they believe in brotherhood, some will be dismissed as dangerous rabblerousers and agitators merely because they're standing up for what is right, but we shall overcome.

That is the basis of this movement, and as I like to say, there is something in this universe that justifies Carlyle in saying no lie can live forever. We shall overcome because there is something in this universe which justifies William Cullen Bryant in saying truth crushed to earth shall rise again. We shall overcome because there is something in this universe that justifies James Russell Lowell in saying, truth forever on the scaffold, wrong forever on the throne. Yet that scaffold sways the future, and behind the dim unknown standeth God within the shadows keeping watch above His own. With this faith in the future, with this determined struggle, we will be able to emerge from the bleak and desolate midnight of man's inhumanity to man, into the bright and glittering daybreak of freedom and justice. Thank you.

RELIGION AND POLITICAL ORDER

CHAPTER 18
IN ISLAM

18.1 SAYYID QUTB AND "JAHILIYYAH"

The great Islamic revival of the present has various sources, but the principle of reform and revival is historically a hallmark of Islam. Al-Ghazālī was widely believed to have been the "renewer" (*mujaddid*) of Islam in his time, and many others have been similarly perceived over the centuries. One of the principal influences in the most recent processes of reform and revitalization is the Egyptian Sayyid Qutb (d. 1966). The following passage is the Introduction to his famous book *Milestones*, which laid out the principle of *jāhiliyyah* (ignorance, barbarism) as referring both to pre-Islamic Arabian paganism and to the present world system as it stands in contrast to Islam. Qutb's writings, which include a commentary of the Qur'an, have been influential among Muslims worldwide in a variety of revivalist and, especially, fundamentalist forms of Islam.

18.1A SAYYID QUTB, "INTRODUCTION"

Mankind today is on the brink of a precipice, not because of the danger of complete annihilation which is hanging over its head—this being just a symptom and not the real disease—but because humanity is devoid of those vital values for its healthy development and real progress. Even Western scholars realize that their

From Sayyid Qutb, *Milestones, Revised Translation.* Reprinted with the permission of American Trust Publications.

civilization is unable to present healthy values for the guidance of mankind and does not possess anything to satisfy its own conscience or justify its existence.

Democracy in the West has become sterile to such an extent that its intellectuals borrow from the systems of the Eastern bloc, especially in the economic sphere, under the name of socialism. It is the same with the Eastern bloc. Foremost among its social theories is Marxism, which in the beginning attracted a large number of people not only from the East but also from the West as a way of life based on a creed. But now Marxism stands intellectually defeated and it is not an exaggeration to say that in practice not a single nation in the world is truly Marxist.

Marxist theory conflicts with man's nature and its needs; it prospers only in a degenerate society or in a society which is tyrannized over a period and becomes docile and cowed as a result of it. But now, even under these extreme circumstances, its materialistic economic system is failing, although this was the only foundation on which its structure was based. The Soviet Union which has been the leader of the Communist countries in Europe and the Americas, is itself suffering from shortages of food. During the times of the Tsars, Russia used to produce surplus food, but now it has to import food from abroad and has to sell its reserves of gold for this purpose. The main reason for this is the failure of the system of collective farming, or, one can say more basically, the failure of an entire system that is against human nature.

It is essential for mankind to have new leadership! The leadership of mankind by the West is now on the decline, not because Western culture has become poor materially or because its economic and military power has become weak. The era of the Western system has come to an end primarily because it has lost those life-giving values that enabled it to be the leader of mankind.

It is necessary for the new leadership to preserve and develop the material fruits of the creative genius of Europe, and also to provide mankind with the high ideals and values previously unknown in the West, that can restore harmony with human nature, in a positive, constructive, and practical way of life.

Islam is the only system that possesses these values and this way of life.

The era dominated by the resurgence of science has also come to an end. This period, which began with the Renaissance in the sixteenth century A.C. and reached its zenith in the eighteenth and nineteenth centuries, does not possess a spirit capable of reviving a dynamic civilization.

All the nationalistic and chauvinistic ideologies that have appeared in modern times, and all the movements and theories derived from them, have also lost their vitality. In short, all man-made theories, both individualistic and collectivist, have proved to be failures.

At this crucial and bewildering juncture, the time for Islam and the Muslim community has arrived because it has the needed values. Islam does not stand in the way of material progress or prohibit material inventions. Rather, it considers material prosperity and creativity to be an obligation given to man at the very beginning of time, when Allah granted him the vicegerency on earth. Islam regards initiative in multiplying the bounties of Allah on earth with the proper intent as worship of Allah and one of the purposes of man's creation.

And remember the time when your Sustainer said to the angels, "I will create a vicegerent on earth." I have only created jinns and men that they may serve Me.

Thus the turn of the Muslim community has come to fulfill its divinely appointed task for mankind.

> You are the best community raised for mankind, enjoining what is right and forbidding what is wrong, and you believe in Allah. (Q. 3:110)

> And thus have We made of you a community justly balanced, that you may be witnesses over the nations, and the Messenger a witness over yourselves. (Q. 2:143)

Islam cannot fulfill its role except by taking a concrete form in a society, or more precisely, in a nation. Men do not listen, especially in this age, to an abstract theory which is not seen materialized in a living society. From this point of view, we can say that the Muslim community has been extinct for a few centuries, for this Muslim community does not denote the name of a land in which Islam resides, nor is it a people whose forefathers lived under the Islamic system at some earlier time. It is the name of a group of people whose manners, ideas and concepts, rules and regulations, values and criteria, are all derived from the Islamic source, so that the Muslims' way of life is an example to all mankind, just as the Messenger is an example to them: "And thus have We made of you a community justly balanced that you may be witnesses over the nations, and the Messenger a witness over yourselves."

Islam cannot fulfill its role except by providing the leadership for all of mankind, for which the Muslim community must be restored to its original form. That Muslim community is now buried under the debris of the man-made traditions of several generations and is crushed under the weight of those false laws and customs that are not even remotely related to the Islamic teachings. In spite of all this the modern Muslim world calls itself the "world of Islam." I am aware that between the attempt at "revival" and the attainment of "leadership" there is a great distance, as the Muslim community has long ago vanished from existence and the leadership of mankind has long since passed to other ideologies and other nations, other concepts and other systems. This was the era during which Europe's genius created its marvelous works in science, culture, law, and material production, due to which mankind has progressed to great heights of creativity and material comfort. It is not easy to find fault with the inventors of such marvelous things, especially since what we call the "world of Islam" is completely devoid of all this beauty.

But the growing bankruptcy of Western civilization makes it necessary to revive Islam. The distance between the revival of Islam and the attainment of world leadership may be vast, and there may be great difficulties on the way; but the first step must be taken towards this revival.

If we are to perform our task with insight and wisdom, we must first clearly know the nature of the qualities on the basis of which the Muslim community can fulfill its obligation as the leader of the world. This is essential so that we may not commit any blunders at the very first stage of its reconstruction and revival.

The Muslim community today is neither capable of nor is required to present before mankind great genius in material inventions, such as would make the world bow its head before its supremacy and thus re-establish once more its world leadership. Europe's creative mind is far ahead in this area, and for a few centuries to come we cannot expect to compete with Europe and attain supremacy over it in these fields.

Hence we must have some other quality, a quality that modern civilization does not possess.

But this does not mean that we should neglect material progress. We should also give our full attention and effort in this direction, not because at this stage it is an essential requirement for attaining the leadership of mankind, but because it is an essential condition for our very existence. Islam elevates man to the position of vicegerent of Allah on earth, and, under certain conditions, considers the responsibilities of this vicegerency as worship of Allah and the purpose of man's creation. The responsibility of this vicegerency includes the material progress that comes from multiplying the bounties of Allah.

To attain the leadership of mankind, we must have something to offer besides material progress, and this other quality can only be a faith and a way of life that both promotes the benefits of modern science and technology and fulfills basic human needs. The same effort that has produced material comfort and leisure should be exerted to design and apply technology in meeting the minimum needs of the poor. And then this faith and way of life must take concrete form in a human society—in other words, in a Muslim society.

If we look at the sources and foundations of modern modes of living, it becomes clear that the whole world is steeped in *jahiliyyah,* and all the marvelous material comforts and advanced inventions do not diminish its ignorance. This *jahiliyyah* is based on rebellion against the sovereignty of Allah on earth. It attempts to transfer to man one of the greatest attributes of Allah, namely sovereignty, by making some men lords over others. It does so not in the simple and primitive ways of the ancient *jahiliyyah,* but in the more subtle form of claiming that the right to create values, to legislate rules of collective behavior, and to choose a way of life rests with men, without regard to what Allah has prescribed. The result of this rebellion against the authority of Allah is the oppression of His creatures. Thus the humiliation of the common man under the communist systems and the exploitation of individuals and nations due to the greed for wealth and imperialism under capitalist systems are but a corollary of the rebellion against the authority of Allah and the denial of the dignity of man bestowed upon him by Allah.

In this respect, Islam's way of life is unique, for in systems other than Islam, people worship others in one form or another. Only in the Islamic way of life do all men become free from the servitude of some men to others and devote themselves to the worship of Allah alone, deriving guidance from Him alone, and bowing before Him alone.

This dignity of man in submission to Allah is where the roads separate, and this is the new concept that we possess and can present to mankind. This concept and the way of life covering all the practical aspects of man's life is the vital message that mankind lacks. We call it the Islamic *din* [religous system]. It is not a product of Western invention nor of European genius, whether of "socialism" or "capitalism."

Without doubt, we are able to offer this *din* which is perfect to the highest degree, and which most of mankind still knows only dimly and is not capable of "producing." But as we have stated before, the beauty of this new system cannot be appreciated unless it takes a concrete form. It is essential that a community arrange its affairs according to it and show it to the world. In order to bring this about, we need to initiate the movement of Islamic revival in some Muslim country. Only such a revivalist movement will eventually—sooner or later—attain world leadership.

How to initiate the revival of Islam? A vanguard must set out with this determination and then keep going, marching through the vast ocean of *jahiliyyah* which encompasses the entire world. During its course, this vanguard, while distancing itself somewhat aloof from this all-encompassing *jahiliyyah* should also retain contacts with it.

The Muslims in this vanguard must know the landmarks and the milestones on the road to this goal so that they would know the starting point as well as the nature, the responsibilities, and the ultimate purpose of this long journey. Not only this, but they ought to be aware of their position vis-à-vis this *jahiliyyah,* which has struck its stakes throughout the earth. They must know when to cooperate with others and when to separate from them; what characteristics and qualities they should cultivate; and with what characteristics and qualities the *jahiliyyah,* immediately surrounding them, is armed; how to address the people of *jahiliyyah* in the language of Islam; what topics and problems to discuss with them; and where and how to obtain guidance in all these matters.

The milestones will necessarily be determined in the light of the first source of this faith—the Noble Qur'an—and from its basic teachings. The milestones will reflect the concept that the Qur'an created in the minds of the first generation of Muslims, those whom Allah raised to fulfill His will, those who did change the course of human history in the direction ordained by Allah.

I have written Milestones for this vanguard, which I consider to be a waiting reality about to be materialized.

18.2 THE SHARĪʿA AND TODAY'S WORLD

The Sharīʿa is the supreme authority for Islamic faith and order because it is based upon God's Word as revealed in the Qur'an and upon the teaching and example of the Prophet Muhammad, as preserved in his Sunna. In the modern period, most Muslim peoples have adopted non-Muslim legal codes and practices, partly as a result of colonialism but also because of modernizing tendencies and the emergence of nation states. In recent decades, however, there has been a return to the Sharīʿa, at least as an ideal that Muslims should strive to follow. The Islamic Republic of Iran, since its establishment in 1979, has followed a version of the Sharīʿa as understood by the Shi'ite rulers there. Saudi Arabia is ruled by Sharī'a law, as is Sudan. Other Muslim countries provide for the rule of Sharī'a in greater or lesser degree (e.g. in marriage, divorce, and inheritance), even if they are not Islamic states; an example is Indonesia. But with increasing numbers of Muslims living in the West, the question of whether and to what extent the Sharī'a can be invoked is a major debate. Further, is it possible to adapt the Sharī'a to Western attitudes and practices? The following essay, "The Sharī'ah and Changing Historical Conditions," addresses these issues. Seyyed Hossein Nasr is one of the world's most distinguished scholars of Islam and religious studies. A native of Iran and trained in the history and philosophy of science, he is now professor of Islamic Studies at George Washington University in Washington, D.C.

18.2A SEYYED HOSSEIN NASR, "THE SHARĪ'AH AND CHANGING HISTORICAL CONDITIONS"

I

In the tension between tradition and modernism, one of the most acute problems faced by the contemporary Muslim is the relationship between the *Sharī'ah*, and especially the parts belonging to the domain of personal law, and modern theories and legal practices. However, being neither a jurisprudent or *faqīh* in the traditional sense, nor an advocate in the modern one, but rather a student of Islam and Islamic civilisation in its intellectual and spiritual aspects, we feel it our duty to confine ourselves to the analysis and clarification of the general principles which underlie the very issue implied by the subject of this essay. The discussion of their detailed application we leave to those more competent in matters of jurisprudence.

It must be made clear that in discussing Muslim personal law, we are dealing with the *Sharī'ah* and not simply man-made laws. Thus, the emphasis is more on religion than on law, as these two terms are used in European languages today. Every discussion of Islamic Law involves the most basic religious beliefs and attitudes of Muslims. This is because in Islam the Divine Will manifests itself concretely as specific law, and not abstractly as more or less general moral injunctions. Christianity teaches that God asks man to be charitable or humble as the teachings of Christ clearly indicate. However, one is not told how in a concrete sense one should apply these virtues, so that the general religious teaching remains on an ab-

---

This essay is the development of a paper which was delivered originally in India some years ago on the occasion of a colloquium on Muslim personal law. It is, therefore, concerned as much with a particular 'climate' and situation as with general principles. Also certain arguments have been repeated as a result of the particular circumstances in which this paper was delivered and the conditions which resulted from the cogency of the subject matter for the millions of Muslims of India whose personal lives depended upon the conclusions reached in the colloquium.

stract level unaffected by changes in the concrete laws which govern human society. That is why Europeans, as well as modernised Muslims who are more at home in Western culture than in their own, cannot understand the insistence of traditional Muslims on preserving the letter of the Divine Law.

It could be said quite justifiably that the modern West is not the product of Christianity. Yet even those who oppose Christianity in the modern world cannot eradicate *ad hoc* two thousand years of a heritage which they carry in their souls in spite of themselves. This heritage manifests itself clearly when such a question as Muslim personal law is approached. Here, the attitude of secularists and Christians, and also many modernised Muslims, is the same. All is based on the general attitude taken towards law in Western civilisation derived mostly from the particular nature of Christianity as a 'way of love' without a Divine Law.

What must be taken into account is the profound difference between the Semitic and more particularly Islamic conception of law on the one hand and the modern one on the other. The Semitic conception, shared by Judaism and Islam, sees law as the embodiment of the Divine Will, as a transcendent reality which is eternal and immutable, as a model by which the perfections and shortcomings of human society and the conduct of the individual are judged, as the guide through which man gains salvation and, by rejecting it, courts damnation and destruction. It is like the Law of Manu of Hinduism and the *dharma* which each human being must follow in order to gain felicity. To discuss law in Islam is therefore as essential to the Islamic religion as the discussion of theology is to Christianity. To discuss, much less change, Islamic Law cannot be done by anyone except those competent in the *Sharīʿah*, no more than Christian theology could be discussed and doctrines of the Christian church altered by any other than those vested with authority in such matters. It would be as unthinkable from the Islamic point of view to change Muslim personal law through any simply elected legislative body as it would be to change doctrines of the Christian church through a similar body of laymen. It is only because the similarity of the role of theology in Christianity to the Divine Law in Islam is not understood that the validity of such an analogy is not accepted by so many people today.

Let us now examine how the *Sharīʿah* is related to the world in which we live. To many people, reality is exhausted by the physico-psychological world which surrounds us and what does not conform to this world is considered to be unreal. Islamic doctrine, like all other traditional metaphysics, is based on the belief that reality is comprised of multiple states of existence *marātib al-wujūd*) of which the physical world is the lowest and furthest removed from the Divine Origin of all reality. Therefore the *Sharīʿah*, being an eternal truth belonging to a higher order of existence, is by no means abrogated if it does not conform to the particular conditions of a certain point in space or moment in time. Rather, it is the world which must conform to the Divine Law. The Law loses nothing if it is not followed by men. Conversely man and his world lose everything by not conforming to the Divine Will of which the *Sharīʿah* is the concrete embodiment.

These days we are often told that we must keep up with the times. Rarely does one ask what have the 'times' to keep up with. For men who have lost the vision of a reality which transcends time, who are caught completely in the mesh of time and space and who have been affected by the historicism prevalent in modern European philosophy, it is difficult to imagine the validity of a truth that does not conform to their immediate external environment. Islam, however, is based on the principle that truth transcends history and time. Divine Law is an objective transcendent reality, by which man and his actions are judged, not vice versa. What are called the 'times' today are to a large extent a set of problems and difficulties created by man's ignorance of his own real nature and his stubborn determination to 'live by bread alone.' To attempt to shape the Divine Law to the 'times' is therefore no less than spiritual suicide because it removes the very criteria by which the real value of human life and action can be objectively judged and thus surrenders man to the most infernal impulses of his lower nature. To say the least, the very manner of approaching the problem of Islamic Law and religion in general by trying to make them conform to the 'times' is to misunderstand the whole perspective and spirit of Islam.

Islam has always considered the positive aspect of the intellect (*ʿaql*) and man's ability to reach the cardinal doctrine of Islam, that is to say the doctrine of Unity (*tawḥīd*), through his *ʿaql*. In fact, the Quran often describes those who have gone astray from religion as those who cannot 'intellect' (*lā yaʿqilūn*). But this is no licence for rationalism and an *ad hoc* treatment of the *Sharīʿah* as judged by human reason, because man can reach *tawḥīd* through his own *ʿaql* only under the condition that this *ʿaql* is in a wholesome state (*salīm*). And it is precisely the *Sharīʿah* whose practice removes the obstacles in the soul which prevent the correct functioning of the intellect and obscure its vision. It is the *Sharīʿah* that guarantees the wholesomeness of the intellect so that to change the *Sharīʿah* through the judgement of human reason with the excuse that the Quran has ordered man to use his intellectual faculties, is no more than sheer sophistry and a chimerical manner of leading simple souls astray.

II

We may ask why the question of changing Muslim personal law has been posed at all in so many parts of the Islamic world. Having briefly outlined the nature of Islamic law, we must now turn to two elements which deserve to be analysed: one the question of change and the other personal law. In traditional Muslim sources, there is no term to denote personal law, because theoretically the *Sharīʿah* covers all human life, both personal and social. If such a term has come into recent usage and has even found its way into contemporary Islamic law (the adjective *shakhṣiyyah* being usually used for personal), it is because even during the Umayyad period the *Sharīʿah* was in practice not applied fully in certain realms such as that of general taxation. Also, many political dealings of Muslim rulers remained outside its injunctions. That is why the so-called reforms carried out by many Muslim states in their attempt to introduce certain European codes, such as the *Tanzīmāt* of the Ottomans, did not profoundly affect the structure of Islamic society. What has remained intact through the ages has been that aspect of the *Sharīʿah* which concerns directly the human person, such as marriage, divorce and inheritance. These are thus labelled as personal law. This domain has been the refuge and stronghold that has enabled Islamic society to remain Islamic in spite of the various forms of political institution that have ruled over it in past centuries. Therefore what is under discussion is the last refuge of the legal aspect of the *Sharīʿah* in Islamic society as a whole.

As for the question of change involved in the subject matter of this essay, it lies in that complex set of factors which characterise modernism in general, in the West as well as in the East. First of all, through the spread of belief in that false idol of eighteenth- and nineteenth-century European philosophy, namely progress, many in the East unconsciously equate change with progress. And, since they have surrendered their intelligence to the dictum of historicism, they evaluate all things in the light of change and becoming rather than with regard to their immutable aspect. They thus equate the immutability of the Truth with solidification and petrifaction. Secondly, the structure of Western civilisation, even before modern times, was such as to view law only in its mutable aspect. This trait has been inherited by modernism, which is naturally a product of Western civilisation. Christianity was by nature an esotericism (*ṭarīqah*) externalised. It was devoid of a *Sharīʿah* so that it had to integrate Roman law into its structure in order to become the religion of a whole civilisation. Therefore, even if Roman law had a Divine aspect from the point of view of Roman religion, it was not an integral part of the Christian revelation, so that the Christians never regarded their law in the same manner as did the Jews and Muslims, or the Hindus for that matter. That is the basic reason why Westerners cannot usually understand the meaning of the *Sharīʿah* and Westernised Muslims approach the problems of Islamic Law in the modern world from the point of view so prevalent today.

To this misunderstanding must be added the psychological factors which are the result of centuries of pressure imposed by the West on all Oriental civilisations. In the minds of many Muslims, there is a sense of inferiority *vis-à-vis* the West, which forces them to be its blind followers and to regard their own tradition either with disdain or at best with an attitude of apologetic acceptance. In that state of mind, they usually try to change those aspects of their religion and law which do not conform to today's fashions and which, to cover one's intellectual and spiritual weakness, is called 'keeping up with the times.'

For example, let us take the question of polygamy, which is far from limited to Islam (we remember that Charlemagne had many wives). Many modernised Muslims feel embarrassed by this feature of the *Sharīʿah* for no other reason than that Christianity eventually banned it and that in the West today it is forbidden. The arguments against it are not so much logical as sentimental and carry mainly the weight and prestige of the modern West with them. All the arguments given, based on the fact that polygamy is the only way of preventing many social ills of today, have no effect on those for whom the fashion of the day has replaced the *Sunnah* of the Holy Prophet. One can speculate that, if modernism had originated in the Himalayan states rather than in Europe, the modern Muslim apologists would not have tried to interpret the teachings of the *Sharīʿah* as permitting polyandry, as today they interpret its teaching only in the monogamous sense which is current Western practice.

Of course we do not propose that Muslims should remain oblivious of the world around them. This is neither desirable nor possible. No Islamic state can avoid owning trains and planes, but Muslims can avoid hanging surrealistic paintings on their walls. By this is meant that there are certain conditions in twentieth-century life which the Muslim world cannot alter and with which it must live while others can be avoided. The whole difference lies in the attitude towards the modern world. One can regard a situation as one in which it is difficult to practise the *Sharī'ah* fully, not because the *Sharī'ah* itself is imperfect, but because the conditions in which we live have fallen short of those immutable principles which of necessity ultimately govern all things. One can still follow and practise Islamic Law in such conditions by following the teachings of Islam itself, for the Prophet even allowed prayers to be said on horseback in time of war.

Or one can, as is so common today, take the world as the sole reality and judge the validity of the *Sharī'ah* according to its degree of conformity to this world. This attitude is totally un-Islamic and is like putting the cart before the horse. Such an attitude makes the world and man's imperfect judgements informing it take the place of God. Such an attitude commits the sin which theologically is the gravest of all in Islam, namely *shirk* or 'polytheism.'

Islam is a way of peace based on the establishment of equilibrium between all human tendencies and needs, which must of necessity serve as a basis for all man's spiritual strivings. The *Sharī'ah* is the maker and preserver of this equilibrium and the personal laws play a particularly significant role in keeping this human order and equilibrium. Were this equilibrium to be destroyed, both inner and outward peace, which everyone seeks today but rarely finds, would disappear. All 'reforms' and changes—especially in matters of personal law—proposed today should aim to preserve and build rather than destroy this equilibrium whose chief symbol in Islam is the square Ka'bah. The question of changing Islamic personal law should be approached with the spirit of belief in the *Sharī'ah*, thereby attempting to apply and preserve it to the extent possible in the modern world, and to build the life of Muslim society according to it. It should not be approached with a firm belief in all 'values' and norms prevalent in the West today according to which one should seek to change Islamic Law. These practices and 'values' which seem permanent today are as impermanent as the most impermanent aspect of human nature upon which they are based.

If the question of changes in Islamic Law is approached by the Muslim intelligentsia in the spirit thus proposed, it will be seen in a completely different light. The rift between the Western-educated classes and the rest of the Muslim community will pass and everyone will realise the real significance of the *Sharī'ah* as the basis of stability in human life. They will also learn that, although to concern oneself with matters pertaining to Islam is the duty of every Muslim, applying the *Sharī'ah* in detail to newly created situations is a question of *fiqh* that should be dealt with by the *fuqahā'*. If one understands the real nature of the *Sharī'ah*, one would think no more of passing on a sick person to someone who is not a physician than to turn over matters concerning Muslim personal laws to one who is not a specialist in the *Sharī'ah,* that is to say a *faqīh* or *'ālim* who specialises in *fiqh.* Otherwise, in both cases, the patient, whether he be an individual or a society, faces the danger of a graver malady and even death.

III

In conclusion, it may be added that the blind following of Western ideas in matters concerned with law, as in so many other domains, will never solve any basic problem of Islamic society. It is a form of *taqlīd* or blind following much more dangerous than the traditional type of *taqlīd* which has always been decried by Muslim sages over the ages. Only by accepting the validity of the *Sharī'ah* and especially of the personal laws promulgated by it and by relying upon these laws can Islamic society face the problems of the modern world. And only through the *Sharī'ah* can meaningful change be brought about. In fact the value of any change can only be gauged *vis-à-vis* a permanent truth. If we were to lose the *Sharī'ah,* we would lose that very thing for whose subsistence we are trying to 'reform' our present society. In such a case, our reformations would only become deformations. Thus we would only let loose forces which would disrupt the very basis of our society and open doors which would enable individual whims and fancies to exert themselves over the Divine Norm which alone gives meaning to human life.

18.3 MUSLIM WOMEN'S STRUGGLE FOR INDEPENDENCE

One of the problems that Westerners have in thinking about women in the Islamic world is assuming that their condition is the same everywhere. Nothing could be further from the truth. In fact, Muslim societies vary considerably, and women (as well as men) in them experience many of the same problems and strains as people in Western societies: two wage earners needed to support a family, increased urbanization and the loss of traditional supportive communities, a desire for education and independence from male domination, the glass ceiling in employment, and so forth. One issue that is specific to Muslim women is whether or not to wear a veil (*hijāb*), which can be a simple covering of the hair or a veiling of the face, as well. The veil is a symbol of the contemporary Islamic revival in many places, and it has manifold meanings: for example, compliance with strict Islamic principles, reserving one's physical beauty for one's husband and immediate family, marking one as a member of a preferred group, repentance and genuine devotion to Islam, fashion, and concealing one's identity so as to move freely in public. The following selection is from Bouthaina Shaaban's candid and revealing nonfiction book *Both Right and Lefthanded: Arab Women Talk about Their Lives.* Ms. Shaaban is a professor of English literature at Damascus University in Syria.

18.3A Bouthaina Shaaban, "A Syrian Muslim Woman Speaks Her Mind"

Syria is today one of the major powers in the Middle East. Like Lebanon, it was mandated to France after the First World War (while Palestine and Jordan went to the British), and independence did not follow until 1945. Between 1958 and 1961 it was part of a United Arab Republic with Nasser's Egypt. Since then it has been almost continuously governed by the Baath Socialist Party, which has over the years introduced a comprehensive programme of social reform: a mixed economy, with centralised co-operative and state-owned sectors; national education programmes, for girls as well as boys; and 'guaranteed' rights for all citizens regardless of sex, colour or religion. As in Algeria, mass organisations of workers, women and students are expected to play a role in the national political life.

Thus there is no doubt that women have benefited immeasurably from Baathist progressive social policies. But social attitudes change more slowly than official policies, as the following interviews show very clearly. Syrian women remain subject to a body of religious family law which places their daily lives under the control of fathers and husbands.

Guaranteed Rights for All, Except at Home

As our plane probed the glittering sky above Damascus at about 1 A.M. in late August, I could almost feel the cool, gentle breeze which normally accompanies these moonlit nights. I came to appreciate Damascus August nights which are cool, serene and poetic in contrast to the brilliant sunshine of the unbearably hot days. I looked out from the window and saw the shadow of the plane flying over Ghota with its endless green fruit trees. Back in our small village near Homs, August used to be the month of night festivities and parties. Come August, the night is no longer claimed by sleeping, but by walking, meeting people and jubilation. Jubilation over what it is hard to tell; perhaps over nature at its best, at its most pleasant. Along the Roman canal which ran through my village boys and girls would spend the best part of the night walking in groups of three or four, sometimes washing salad in the crystal-clear water, laughing and chattering about school, village and discreet love affairs.

Between 7 and 8 in the evening a lively hum would start in the village, gradually getting louder and louder until the sounds of talking, singing and traditional dancing could be distinguished. Almost everyone would go out for a walk, while mothers of very young babies and elderly men and women would take chairs out and sit in front of their homes chatting about their daily concerns.

After listening to the stories of my favourite people I would hurry to join my friends, who would sometimes leave the village for the hills and valleys nearby.

Nothing disturbed the tranquillity of the village except the sound of small portable radios. There was no traffic, of course, except the one minibus which left the surrounding villages to go to town at six o'clock in the morning and came back with much welcomed travellers at about four o'clock in the afternoon.

For me and for my ex-school mates this world now lives only in memory: the Roman canal has dried up and the August moonlight has been overpowered by the electric street lighting. I wonder whether young people any longer go out in spontaneous gatherings.

Two hours before my appointment with Abla was due I decided to go to the hairdresser, for whenever a Syrian woman steps out of her home she has to look as if she is going to the opera at Covent Garden. The atmosphere in the hairdresser was that of *Harem,* where it is permissible for women to do whatever they like so long as they are at a safe distance from male intruders. Women who wore *Al Hijab* in the streets and looked quite conservative were in see-through dresses, revealing blouses, and their hairstyles and make-up were *à la mode*. One woman with long hair attracted my attention. Three women were bending over her, pulling, plaiting and curling her hair—one felt that the woman's head had metamorphosed into a wig which was being chemically and mercilessly treated by these professional hairdressers. When they eventually finished, her hair was as decorated as a Christmas cake. Yet before leaving the shop she stood in front of the mirror and covered her head completely with a huge scarf, making her long, pale face look even longer and paler. What is the point, I wondered, of spending all that time and money on having a hairstyle which she is going to cover up? When I expressed surprise at what I saw I was told she was to attend a women's party that evening. Then I recalled that women in my country go to a great deal of trouble to be as elegant and presentable as they can be, even when no men are going to attend their parties— in fact, especially when no men are allowed to attend. The women enjoy each other's elegance and beauty and seem to give expression to their love and even sexual feelings amongst each other.

In the back of the shop where I went to the lavatory, there was a sink, a small cooker, food shelves and an old bunk bed. On that bed there were two women in their petticoats, embracing and kissing each other. One of them held the other's head in her hands, looked straight into her eyes and said to her, 'Oh, you are beautiful.' I must have been looking askance, trying to understand an unusual scene in the most unexpected of places when I was struck by another, equally puzzling episode. As the woman with the hairstyle was leaving the shop, another veiled woman who wore *Al Hijab* was coming in speaking loudly and addressing herself to no one in particular, just like a rich man at an Arabic wedding who starts throwing money up into the sky without looking into anyone's eyes, knowing full well that people around him are both grateful and admiring. '*Salem, Salem,*' she was almost shouting as she entered the shop and before she could lay her eyes on the owner she added hastily: 'Do you have a girl whom you would like to marry off to a rich Saudi?' Her eyes roved over the shop and she added in an even louder voice, 'What do you think, girls? Hey! Would any of you like to get married to a Saudi?'

The shop owner's eyes glittered at hearing the phrase and she gave me the impression that had she been a little bit younger (she was over 60) she wouldn't have minded taking up the offer. Indeed, she was as excited and as anxious as a fisherman who has netted a golden fish.

'Can't we see him?' asked one of the girls, laughing.

'Well,' the woman answered wryly. 'First you must know that he is not young but he is rich and is prepared to pay. Think about it, anyway,' the woman gave a last call before leaving the shop as briskly as she had entered it. Detecting my embarrassment and disgust the shop owner pulled her chair nearer to me and started whispering in my ear: 'Look, my dear girl. My own daughter is married to a rich Saudi who is 30 years her senior, yet she is very happy with him. The important thing for the woman, I believe, is to secure her rights before getting married; she should make the man buy her a flat and put a large sum of money into her bank account and let him go to hell afterwards. Look at this woman,' she said, pointing to a young, lovely-looking woman sitting next to her. 'She is married to a Syrian who has been working in Saudi Arabia for the last ten years during which time she has had four children.'

'How did you manage to have these four children, then?' I asked the woman jokingly.

'Oh, he visits us sometimes,' she replied. 'In fact, every summer he comes to spend a month with us. During this month I realise how much nicer it is to live without a man; I can't wait to see the back of him. He is, of course, our only source of income, but other than that his absence is better than his presence. During this one month which he spends with us I feel like an ill-used slave. I go round the clock cleaning, washing, cooking and serving tea and coffee to his uninterrupted stream of guests.'

Are these women lesbians, I wondered to myself. What I saw a few minutes ago in the back of the shop seemed to suggest that and what I was hearing now seemed to confirm this. Do they just express their feelings to one another as their only outlet in a sexually oppressive society where woman's sexuality never seems to matter or even exist? One thing seems certain, however, and that is that these women don't seem to see any relation between marriage and love, or even between marriage and making love. They seem to get married to old, rich Saudis to secure a comfortable and socially desirable material life and then to go about satisfying their sexual desires the way they see fit. Not bad logic, perhaps.

Both the posh, quiet avenue and the building's entrance told of upper-middle-class inhabitants. Children were playing in the gardens or in the hall built especially for them on the ground floor. It was a five-storey building of what seemed to be an elegant block of flats.

I was invited into a huge room. The floor was almost completely covered with colourful, fine Persian carpets, and a mahogany cabinet and china closet added the final, elegant touch to the place.

'You've changed a lot,' Abla started. 'You are wearing your hair short; it suits you better than long hair. You also look terribly well for a pregnant woman in this heat.'

'Oh, yes,' I said. 'I never feel as good as when I am pregnant. Pregnancy seems to improve me physically and to provide me with some extra energy.'

'Where have you left your little daughter?' Abla continued to interview me before granting me the chance to do the same to her.

'With her father, of course,' I answered, fully aware of the tinge of surprise which my tone betrayed.

'Oh, good.' Her rising tone intimated that that was the exception rather than the rule. 'None of my brothers-in-law,' she added, 'baby-sits for their wives. They just don't want to know about their children. But, of course, you are married to an Iraqi; Iraqi men are much better with their women than Syrian men. My aunt is married to an Iraqi. He does everything at home. He is a better cook and better housekeeper than she is. Generally speaking, Iraqi men take women more as equals than do Syrian men.'

While it took some time to catch up on mutual news for the last ten years, eventually Abla and I began the informal interview which ran as follows.

'I was born in 1928 and was the eldest of eight children in a happy family headed by quite an enlightened father. It was the norm in those days that girls, especially the eldest, be kept at home to help with the housework and eventually be married off between the ages of 12 and 14. Aware of his humble financial position and of what was then considered to be the duty of the father to secure a good future for his children by leaving them money or land, my father decided to provide us with good education instead. Thus he sent us all, boys and girls, to school, which was quite unusual. I did very well at school and loved all subjects, particularly history. Unusually privileged by my father's constant backing, I was glad to invest my hard work and energy in acquiring the formal education provided at that time. From elementary school I moved to the secondary school which was the only one for girls in the whole of Damascus and maybe in Syria. My academic career culminated happily in 1947 with my joining the history department at the University of Damascus.

'So I was one of the very few privileged girls of those days to have both opportunities and choices and to face absolutely no social or family problems in acquiring an education—generally thought to be an exclusively male domain. Most girls had to suffer the boredom of spending their time in total isolation at home waiting for eligible husbands to knock on their doors. Some of the better off girls could study for a few years if only to escape illiteracy, and others who managed to continue their studies had to put the Islamic veil on whenever they left the house. I knew such girls as friends and colleagues at the university. Clearly they put on the veil as a result of social pressures rather than from conviction—they used to take it off whenever they were at the university or out of risk areas.'

'How were you received by your male colleagues at the university?'

'Our male colleagues' attitudes towards women's new ventures were ambivalent. Generally, we were received calmly and Platonic relationships were soon established. Yet a suspicious question was evidently forming in their heads: "Since men are the bread winners what the hell are these women doing here?" We had to be reticent, decently dressed and socialised circumspectly. Furthermore, we had to take part, wittingly or otherwise, in a bizarre race against the social pretence of male superiority. Indeed, we had to prove our intellectual merits all the time; needless to say we had great energy and were able to provide everybody, both in and out of the university, with the proof that we were equal to, if not better than, men. I remember once when, against the advice and apprehension of many of my friends, I stood the challenge of a public lecture with a male colleague and fared better than he did. Many women would not have dared to do such a thing. When I graduated from the university I gave another blow to the pretence of male superiority as I came out first in my class.

'Immediately after university I started looking for a job, and here again my advance proceeded unhindered. I got a teaching job almost straight away after my graduation. I had no difficulty in going to work and, indeed, faced no trouble at all as a teacher. Somehow, it came to be socially accepted that teaching was an apt profession for women. Even today, teaching is still considered a traditional province for women.

'However, being a woman, my progress was bound to be doomed eventually by the social constraints of the 1950s. The first setback I had to suffer and accede to as a woman was the termination of any chance to study abroad for a higher degree. I was actually offered a grant to do a PhD in Egypt. If I had been a man my father wouldn't have hesitated to send me. I still resent not having gone; it is my greatest regret in life. My father trusted me but, taking the advice of other men, including my teachers at the university, he decided that I should not go abroad alone to face all the social problems which that would inevitably bring, even though there was clear evidence that I was an independent, strong and successful woman. The second setback came shortly after this when I had the chance to move to a much better job. I was offered a job at the Museum of Ancient History which was in line with my training, and this was the very thing I would have loved to have done. Here again my father asked me to turn the offer down in order, as he put it, to prevent any possible gossip which might erupt about me or my family. It is such a shame when I think of it now. I could have been in a completely different place, now, and I would have done something worth doing with my life. What makes me more angry is that I lost these two precious chances solely because I was a woman.

'My family always gave me the impression that I was allowed to have emotional relationships, but as I never tried to I am not sure how far I could have gone. My male colleagues considered me as their sister. On the whole, we, as women, were far more mature and rational than they were. To us they were only boys, immature boys, so none of us ever thought of any of our colleagues as a prospective husband. I didn't get married then because whenever anyone came to ask for my hand my father would ask me, "What do you think?" "What can I think?" I would answer. "I don't know the man."

'It is true I was able to see the man once or twice before making up my mind, but that was not enough. Two men with PhDs proposed to me. I found them so immature; I admired neither of them. I so desperately wanted a man whom I could admire and respect. I have still to meet that man. I found the men whom I happened to meet through work or social meetings very shallow and almost silly; perhaps if I had loved someone I would have married him, regardless, and there would have been no problem. But I was never in love. In our family we have complete freedom to choose the partner we want, but I found this total freedom the wrong kind of freedom. One should at least have some hints from one's parents, but my father never interfered and I was not mature enough, in this sense perhaps, to make the right decision. On the other hand, my family's circumstances weren't helpful. Being the eldest of my brothers and sisters, I felt deeply responsible for them when my father died, leaving them all of school age. I used to think: How can I leave my brothers and sisters with no one to support or look after them? I couldn't. And I didn't meet the man who was worth the sacrifice. I never thought, of course, that I wouldn't get married at all and that I would find myself one day as an elderly, single woman. Still, I have no regrets.'

In saying this she no longer could restrain the tears which had been on the point of streaming over her face for quite a while. On the one hand I felt glad that she liked me enough to be able to cry in front of me and on the other I felt so sorry that she had to put up with so much for the sake of others.

I was totally absorbed with my thoughts when I suddenly realised that Abla had stopped crying. Her eyes were fixed on my face waiting for me to look at her. When I did so she asked me what I was thinking about. 'Nothing much,' I replied. 'Perhaps about the different problems of other women. But do you live here on your own?' I hastened to ask. 'What do you think of the problem of Arab women who say that if we have the freedom to live on our own we won't accept living with our husbands or with our families?' Abla smiled gently and replied:

'I shall tell you a story about this. I saved enough money in a building society to buy myself a flat, and eventually I bought one. I said to my uncle, "Come, I want to show you my new flat."

'He looked aghast and asked me why I should want to buy a flat. "For whom?" "For myself," I replied. "Do you think I would live with any of my married brothers or sisters?"

'My uncle gave me a very strange look and said, "Is that possible? Can you possibly think of living on your own?"

'"Of course, I can," I answered.

'Our society does not accept the idea of women living on their own; what we need is a few brave, strong women who challenge this notion and break it once and for all. We need to make people realise there is no reason why women shouldn't live on their own since they are just as qualified to have their own independent homes as men are. I want to tell you another little story, too. Many years ago, after my father's death, I wanted to go to Beirut. Such an endeavour, in the past, required official permission for women intending to travel on their own. I applied for the exit permit. The man in charge there asked me for the permission of my guardian. "I haven't got one," I said. "My father is dead and all my brothers are younger than me. I have a young brother," I added, "who doesn't dare leave the house without asking me. You want *him* to give me *his* permission to travel?"

'He hesitated and said, "But this is the law!"

'"What law?" I almost screamed in his face. "How am I to invent a guardian for myself when I am the head of the whole family?" Finally, I managed to get the okay, but with great difficulty. As women, we have to fight such degrading and outdated laws. The purpose of this law was to prevent women travelling without their husbands' consent. I always believed that women should be free to travel wherever they liked whenever they liked, and, indeed, women nowadays are free to travel. Although this law still exists no one dares mention it or ask a travelling woman if she has such permission because things have changed so much over the last two decades.'

'As someone who has lived women's problems from the 1950s until now, what do you think of the changes which have occurred regarding women's position in Syria?'

'In reality, women's position here has improved beyond recognition, particularly in the last two decades. Take as an example the entrance of women to the university in huge numbers and to all faculties of their choice. The proportion of women at universities now is at least 50 per cent. Even religious, uneducated and poor men work day and night to pay for their daughters' higher education. Teaching jobs at primary and secondary schools are mostly occupied by women. We hardly have any male teachers at primary school level. In a few years' time we expect primary school teaching to be undertaken exclusively by women. The present educational policy of the government is to turn all schools into mixed ones. This target has almost been achieved at primary school level. Even in secondary schools you find women teachers working at exclusively boys' schools. On the whole working women constitute at least 50 per cent of the working population in Syria. Just wait in the centre of town at 2.30 P.M. when employees leave work and you will see that most of them are women, and a good many of these are veiled women too. Women make up half the students in medical and engineering colleges and probably 70 per cent in pharmacy colleges. As for other professions, most workers in the factories are women. Part of the reason for this is that a huge number of men enrol in the army, so the country is in need of women workers. Essentially, however, the reason is that women started to fight for a better life and for their independence. Women want to be economically independent; they no longer want to rely on fathers, brothers or husbands for their living. The woman teacher who has four children is having a rough time; she is exhausted but she wants to raise her standard of living; she wants to work to be somebody of much value to herself, even if this has to be at the expense of her leisure or health.'

'Do you think the Syrian woman of today is more of an equal to the Syrian man now that she is educated and has a job?'

'The economically independent woman is not totally free in her private life. Of course she is in a better position now. She can keep herself, afford to buy things for her children and has more confidence in herself. But some men still try to control their wives by administering their salaries. She goes out to work all day to come back home exhausted and then has to do all the housework. As usual, she has to cook, clean the house, wash, do the washing up and look after the children. So she has to work a double day. What is more, she has to iron better, cook better and clean better—because she is educated. In this sense, the opportunities for formal education and work have only achieved moral equality for women, not a real equality. The real achievement has meant exhaustion and extra work besides the traditional housework. To have a job, run a house, look after a family and bring up children certainly needs a superwoman. We have nurseries and kindergartens for babies and children but they are not enough. The government is trying to open nurseries at all job centres which have more than five women working in them. The Women's Union also runs its own nurseries. Even so, the increase in the number of women going out to work every year by far exceeds the number of nurseries which are opened and are supposed to cater for the children of these women. The ministry of education has started opening nurseries at schools, the ministry of electricity, the research centre and quite a few factories now have their own nurseries. The women there are very happy with the conditions. Mothers are very pleased to be able to come to work with their babies, to have a look at them during lunch breaks and to go back home with them after work. It is expected that all other ministries and job centres will provide such nurseries very soon. For mothers need to go to work feeling sure that their babies are in safe hands and well looked after rather than be torn apart by worry and anxiety. It is not an easy task, of course, but what can safely be said is that the country and government recognise the importance of cheap and efficient nurseries and are encouraging all institutions to try to provide these for working women.'

'Do you think that women's achievements in most fields will be quite different if they have equal opportunities and real equality with men?'

'Certainly. They will indeed be more original and more inventive than men. Women have more patience, more ambition, more dreams and more imagination than men. All that men have is physical power. But a woman, given equal opportunities, will definitely do better. It is true that the Koran said, concerning inheritance, that a man's share should be twice as much as a woman's, but that was because the man used to be the sole bread winner in the family. As a woman's income is nowadays equal to a man's, I can't see the justification for such legislation.'

'Do you think it would be possible to update our Islamic laws to suit women's emancipation?'

'Islamic law can be understood and interpreted in a way which serves women and helps them achieve their equality with men, but men don't want this: rather, they strongly resist it. Also, women are not working hard enough to bring such change about. Women have to fight and be persistent in their determination in such matters. The equality they have achieved has become a burden to them because of the many new responsibilities it has brought with it. Our men are selfish and they want to be in constant control of our lives. They might like their wives, but they love themselves and their leisure better. There are some men who help at home but most men don't. Women are not going to stand this for ever. They will soon reach a point where they can't take any more and then they are going to fight for a change.'

'What do you think is best for women: to fight personal battles or to fight through their own organisations?'

'I believe that personal struggle is crucial as well as struggle through women's organisations. Women should fight for their rights and our women's organisations should be more serious about women's struggle for liberation and equality. There are women in the Women's Union who are very serious about all this but they are still a minority. The first obligation of the Women's Union is to attract young, intelligent and enthusiastic women who are keen to fight for women's rights. I used to be a member of the union but I left because I could not do anything worthwhile. What we need is a gradual invasion of the organisation by young, ideologically mature and feminist women who are willing to work persistently, because personal struggle is not really enough.'

'How do you compare the position of the Syrian woman with that of the European woman?'

'I believe the European woman is not quite happy, either; she must also be exhausted for similar reasons as outlined above. But she has got more social rights than we have. Personally, I would like to see the Syrian woman treading her own path rather than following in the European woman's footsteps. I would like to keep the positive aspects of our family relationships; it is very nice to have an intimate family and I think it must be painful to lose this security which the European family has mostly lost. It must be hard for the individual to survive without the support and backing of a family. There are good things in our culture which we should try hard to keep. We are capable of finding our own way without imitating the European woman in everything and I believe we have already started doing that, and quite successfully, too.

'Women should be able to reach complete independence; they should reach the job and the station they want without being thwarted because of their sex.'